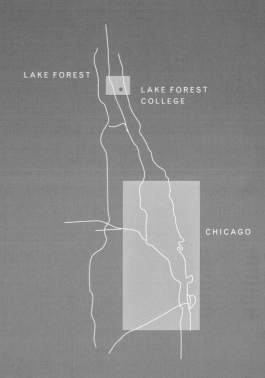

LAKE FOREST

LAKE FOREST
COLLEGE

CHICAGO

# 30 Miles North

Franz Schulze, Rosemary Cowler,
and Arthur H. Miller

Lake Forest College
Lake Forest, Illinois

Distributed by the
University of Chicago Press

A History of
Lake Forest College,
Its Town, and
Its City of Chicago

# Contents

MIDDLE CAMPUS, CA. 1899.

MIDDLE CAMPUS, 1999.

Copyright © 2000
Lake Forest College
Lake Forest, Illinois

Produced by Kim
Coventry, Chicago

Design by studio blue,
Chicago

5,000 copies printed by
R.R. Donnelley & Sons
Company in Roanoke,
Virginia.

Library of Congress
Cataloging-in-
Publication Data

Schulze, Franz, 1927–
30 miles north : a history
of Lake Forest College, its
town, and its city of
Chicago / Franz Schulze,
Rosemary Cowler, and
Arthur H. Miller.
p. cm.
Includes bibliographical
references and index.
ISBN 0-9638189-6-1
1. Lake Forest College –
History. I. Title: Thirty
miles north. II. Cowler,
Rosemary, 1925– III.
Miller, Arthur H. IV.
Title.

LD2918.S38 2000
378.773'11 – dc21
99-088321

**Front cover.** A detail of
the entrance to Henry C.
Durand Art Institute.

**Frontispiece.** Entrance
of Durand Art Institute,
Henry Ives Cobb,
architect.

**Opposite.** Students
outside Hansen's Ivy
Inn, 1957.

**Back cover.** The
academic proces-
sion at the 1908
Commencement.

Following a proposal made by President David Spadafora of Lake Forest College in 1997 that a history of the school be prepared for publication, archival research was not long in revealing the outlines of a substantially more provocative story than anyone, even those close to the project, had anticipated. While it was local common knowledge that the origins of the College and the town of Lake Forest were connected, the relationship proved to be surprisingly intricate, unexpectedly engaging, and more than a little related to a third community, the city of Chicago, without which neither College nor town could have been conceived. The College's history has proven impossible to write without treating it as part of a tightly interwoven fabric meshing these strands.

Names as famous in the history of Chicago and the Middle West as McCormick, Swift, Bross, Dick, and Donnelley belonged to citizens who, for better or worse, acted upon the destiny of the College with as much authority as they exercised in shaping the village and in conducting their business affairs in Chicago. Further research has disclosed the richness of this multiplicity of roles and its elaborate effect upon town and campus. Only lately, for example, have scholars begun to reflect on the striking disparity between the genuinely innovative street plan on which Lake Forest was laid out and the deeply conservative nature of the townsmen who commissioned it. A comparable discrepancy, in many ways paradoxical, may be discerned between the sternly traditional outlook of the College's Presbyterian founders and the academic adventuresomeness of its early presidents. Contrasts sometimes bred compromise, sometimes conflict, both conditions leading after the turn of the century to a major change in the school's identity, from a multipart institution with secondary as well as professional schools that rightly called itself Lake Forest University to a single entity both reduced and distilled: Lake Forest College, an undergraduate operation devoted fundamentally, down to the present day, to the liberal arts.

In the course of the century and a half of its existence, the school has experienced, one might say survived, a range of vicissitudes that finds it at the millennium in an academic state proud enough to warrant the study President Spadafora requested. The result is an exceptional collegiate history tied to a celebrated residential community and in turn to one of the world's foremost cities.

### Editorial note

In the early stages of this study the authors, representing different disciplines and perspectives, met together frequently to discuss, debate, and finally agree upon the form and content. Arthur Miller, the College's Archivist and Librarian for Special Collections, was responsible for much of the preparation of the fundamental story line, most of the research on which it is based, and its documentation. Rosemary Cowler, Hotchkiss Presidential Professor of English, Emerita, and Director of the College's Graduate Program in Liberal Studies, the book's editor, was also central to the conceptualization of the narrative and carried out much of the research covering academic questions as distinct from more general historical issues. The principal text was written by Franz Schulze, Hollender Professor of Art, Emeritus. Illustrations were selected by Mr. Miller under the guidance of Kim Coventry, the book's producer. Mr. Miller also contributed the captions and shared in writing the sidebars with Ms. Cowler.

The documentation was assembled from three types of research material. In the early chapters the sources were mostly external, with later sections depending chiefly on data taken from the College's own archives. In the chapters dealing with recent periods accessible to living memory, oral recollection provided additional background information.

# Preface

# The Presbyterian Vision of President Patterson

1857—1878

A measure of the historically unique relationship between Lake Forest College, the village of Lake Forest, and the city of Chicago is suggested by the singular nature of a decision that was reached on an afternoon in 1855.

Late in the spring of that year five men – one imagines them in the business suits and stovepipe hats of the period[1] – mounted a train in Chicago and headed north on the newly laid tracks of the Chicago & Milwaukee Railroad.[2] At an isolated point, thirty miles north of Chicago and some ten miles short of the end of the line in Waukegan,[3] they persuaded the conductor to stop and let them off.[4] They then proceeded east on foot. Although a mile of trees and tangled underbrush separated them from the shore of Lake Michigan, each of them was alert to every natural feature encountered. They were on a mission, not out for a country stroll, and once they had clambered over and through

1842

**The Reverend Patterson arrives in Chicago to found the Second Presbyterian Church.**

**The shore at Lake Forest as published in *Picturesque America*, 1874. In 1876, Robert W. Patterson, the first president of the University, would write of Lake Forest, "Its sylvan features, system of ravines, and lakefront, give it natural beauty."**

several deep ravines to the splendid ninety-foot bluff overlooking the lake, they agreed that they had found what they were searching for. It seemed fitting even then and there to give the place a name. With the vast expanse of water before them and the mile of woods behind them, they called it Lake Forest.[5]

It must have been an odd, slightly surreal scene, five gentlemen no doubt well attired and conversing earnestly while standing silhouetted against the Midwestern sky in a lonely, untended, rural setting. On the other hand, they themselves must have found the moment exhilarating. They had been charged with the responsibility of touring the Chicago area and determining a locale where an institution of higher learning and a supportive community might be built that would be expressive of the values of their Presbyterian faith.[6] They or their deputies – these five consisted of four clergymen and a layman – had already made several trips throughout the southern and western suburbs, but now, at last, virtually everything about this newly found site on the lake's shore seemed favorable: It was close enough to a city absorbed in the business and speculation that drove the material ambitions of their fellow believers, yet sufficiently distant from its ruder aspects to ensure privacy for the residential and institutional pursuit of a culture of godliness.[7] Besides, the picturesque landscape of ravines culminating in a handsome headland bore less resemblance to the flatness of northern Illinois and more to places in the East and Southeast where many of their group had been born and reared.[8] Even the train ride that took two and one-half hours at the speed of twelve miles per hour[9] – impressively fast for the time – soon became more comfortable and shorter still as the railroad grew and spread throughout America, an unsurpassed symbol of the nation's collective destiny and Chicago's unrivaled growth.

The five urban explorers[10] were the Reverend Robert W. Patterson[11] of the Second Presbyterian Church of Chicago, the Reverend Harvey Curtis[12] of First Presbyterian, the Reverend Ira M. Weed[13] of Waukegan and the Presbyterian Home Missionary Society, the Reverend J. J. Slocum,[14] a visitor from Cincinnati experienced in establishing schools, and

Devillo Holt,[15] a pioneer settler of Chicago who had become one of its most prominent businessmen. The assembly they represented were people of substance, fated to take their place in a complicated relationship that unfolded over a century and a half between Lake Forest, in its own right devoted to gentility and desirous of its pronounced and separate identity, and the bumptious young metropolitan giant, Chicago, on which it was no less dependent. It is a history, in fact, exceptional in its dualities, bordering on paradox, many of them echoed in the relationship between Lake Forest the town and Lake Forest the educational institution, whose anticipated twin birth prompted the railroad expedition in the first place.

If this group of Chicago Presbyterians cherished their ties to the New England and Scottish traditions of their church,[16] they could also commit themselves consciously and firmly to a more provisional day-to-day life in the West. In a sense the pastors on the bluff were evangelists, seeking to pass on their values, especially to their young, yet they were just as surely a pragmatic, enterprising lot eager to promote and preserve the sources of their parishioners' worldly well-being. No single figure illustrated this double role more memorably than the Reverend Patterson, who was destined, not incidentally, to become the College's first president. As a youth in the late 1830s he had been a favorite student of Lyman Beecher[17] when that Connecticut-born Calvinist cleric, the "leading exponent of the New England way of life in the Midwest,"[18] was president of Lane Theological

**Above.** This portrait of the Reverend Ira M. Weed (1804–71) was a gift to the College in 1925 from his daughter. "He was one of the best helpers I had in inaugurating the enterprise of the Lake Forest University," wrote the Reverend Patterson in a memorial tribute to him.

**Below right.** The Reverend Robert W. Patterson (1814–94) of the Second Presbyterian Church, who—with his two colleagues pictured here—chose the site for the town of Lake Forest and its projected university. In 1876, as the first president of the newly re-opened Lake Forest University, he wrote, "This is a fair beginning. It is the hope and purpose of the trustees to make the University at Lake Forest an educational center for the Northwest."

**Below left.** Devillo R. Holt (1823–99), a pioneer Chicago lumber baron, depicted in 1878, eighteen years after building a formidable home in Lake Forest at the corner of College and Sheridan roads. Actively involved in the founding of the University, he sent his daughter Anna, Class of 1882, there and saw his son, Alfred Lincoln Holt (1862–90), marry Lily Reid (1865–95), Class of 1884, for whom the Lily Reid Holt Chapel is named.

Seminary in Cincinnati, a Presbyterian training ground soon embroiled in controversy over slavery. Beecher opposed slavery, yet in embracing "whatever was expedient as well as what was right" he, like Lane Seminary as a whole, could be called only moderately abolitionist — certainly in marked contrast to the radicals who in 1834 left Lane to found Oberlin College in northern Ohio.[19]

Beecher's views were largely shaped at Yale,[20] when that institution was developing into the leading stronghold of academic conservatism as well as the largest and most influential college in the United States.[21] There he had been, in turn, an outstanding student of the theologian Timothy Dwight,[22] himself the grandson of one of the most zealous of eighteenth-century latter-day "Puritans," Jonathan Edwards. Even so, Dwight in his early years — before he became president of Yale — was sufficiently unencumbered by tradition to belong to the "Connecticut Wits," the champions of an independent American literature in the years following the Revolutionary War. Indeed, if there was a single piece of writing that spoke to the condition of the people who founded Lake Forest, it was Dwight's book-length poem of 1794, *Greenfield Hill*.[23] There the vision of an ideal village was evoked that harked back in memory to English hamlets, while at the same time looking forward, in the hopeful belief that comparable real towns would materialize in America and spread across the whole country to the West Coast.

Dwight's dream can be read in some of the goals that drove the conception and organization of Lake Forest, but with significant qualifications. Certainly the Reverend Patterson and his colleagues would have agreed with the observation of the twentieth-century American historian Daniel Boorstin that "the Puritan beacon for misguided mankind was to be neither a book nor a theory

The Reverend Harvey Curtis (1806–62), pastor of Chicago's First Presbyterian Church. In 1858 Curtis left the city for Galesburg, Illinois, to become president of another Illinois Presbyterian-related institution, Knox College.

...[but] the community itself."[24] Thus the early Lake Foresters were motivated by some of the social and philosophical impulses, felt throughout America at mid-century, that led to the formation of small idealistic settlements restricted to people of shared values. At the heart of this phenomenon was a strong resistance to city life. Since commercial and industrial growth together with the new factory economy were part and parcel of the urban environment, their activity was regarded as the cause in that setting of impoverished living conditions and a dubious moral climate, the overall effect of which was seen as a threat to the traditional family structure that undergirded the virtuous life. But while sharing the idealistic and antiurban attitudes common to such famous utopian communes as Brook Farm in Massachusetts, Bishop Hill in Illinois, and New Harmony in Indiana, the founders of Lake Forest, good entrepreneurs all, were in no way moved by such agrarian, antimaterialist visions. If Chicago was not Elysium, and they knew full well it was not, it was nevertheless the place where business was transacted, and business was an indispensable part of

1850

1851

Chicago's population
reaches 28,000, the
majority foreign born.

Methodists in Evanston
establish what will become
Northwestern University.

their life and their quotidian affairs. They had in mind a domestic refuge, hardly a new way of life.

It was as a promising young churchman, and in a sense a dynastic heir, that the Reverend Patterson arrived in Chicago to found the Second Presbyterian Church. The year was 1842 and the city, incorporated only five years earlier, had a population of roughly 6,000.[25] Breaking with the more theologically and politically liberal views of First Presbyterian and following the moderate model of Lane Seminary,[26] Second Presbyterian during the next decades thrived under Patterson's pastorate, gathering to itself a congregation drawn from many of the growing city's leaders, wealthier citizens,[27] and figures prominent also in the slavery issue (among them Senator Stephen Douglas, the railroad engineer George B. McClelland — better known later as a general in the Union army during the Civil War — and, whenever he was in town, Abraham Lincoln).[28] Patterson's orations consisted of the

appropriate Presbyterian homilies, yet he was well aware that they were addressed to ambitious types who had left the East primarily to seek their fortunes in Chicago. Some, to be sure, had been forced to make the move west when the Erie Canal opened a route east for Midwestern farm produce, at the expense of New England agriculture and its economy.[29] Yet whether the Second Presbyterian parishioners came voluntarily or not, they saw no conflict between the faith they brought with them as they settled and the full, guilt-free mercantile advantage they gained from a city already showing signs of developing into the great commercial gateway to the American West — raw, clamorous, headstrong Chicago. Piety and profit: It was yet another paradox that the good folk could live with, in a good Protestant tradition.[30]

The clear distinction they made between living from and living in Chicago was further affected by local demographics. They were well aware that by 1850 the city's population had swelled to almost 30,000, more than half of whom were foreign-born.[31] More to the point, the largest ethnicities were the Irish and German immigrants, the former consisting of staunch Roman Catholics, the latter made up largely of liberals, as often agnostic as churchgoing, who had left Germany following the failed revolution of 1848. A three-way relationship took form, activated by a tension of shared and divided loyalties. The well-to-do Presbyterians identified the Irish not only with a faith foreign to their own but with the lower economic classes. Thus they regarded themselves as both different from and superior to the Irish, even as they were now and then fearful of them, since the rougher Irish youths often physically assaulted their Presbyterian counterparts on the city streets. The Irish and the Germans, meanwhile, took a more convivial attitude toward alcohol, even on the Sabbath, than

1855

**By January a train reaches north from Chicago as far as Waukegan.**

1856

**A Lake Forest Association is assembled to acquire property and sell shares.**

1856

**Sylvester Lind pledges land valued at $80,000 to launch the university at Lake Forest.**

did the decorous and temperamentally reserved Presbyterians, whereas the Irish and the Presbyterians jointly disapproved of the German religious free-thinkers. Then again, the Germans and the Presbyterians tended to share a belief in abolitionism, which the Irish feared on account of the threat posed to their employment opportunities by any possible emancipation of black slaves, who might move north.[32]

It had been apparent soon enough to the Presbyterians that the nagging intricacy of these relationships could be simplified and the problems attached to them circumvented by the expedient of creating a new community haven, comfortably removed from the city, with an institution of learning at its spiritual center.

Events unfolded with remarkable rapidity. On February 26, 1856, a meeting called at the Second Presbyterian Church "to establish an institution of learning of a high order in which Christian teaching would hold a central place"[33] led to the formation of the Lake Forest Association, which undertook the organized purchasing of land that had already been given a name. The Association's first president was Hiram F. Mather, whose background was altogether pertinent to the Lake Forest enterprise.[34] He was a descendant of Richard Mather, brother of Cotton Mather, the storied seventeenth-century New England Puritan preacher, and he himself had been educated at Yale, also under Timothy Dwight. Hiram Mather was a chancery judge, but the blood of the old orthodoxy flowed in his veins.

In March of 1856 the Association began selling shares. The income gained was used to buy tracts from earlier settlers who had left their shore land wooded, preferring to farm the open prairie to the west. The areas purchased came to some 2,300 acres in all, located on both sides of the Chicago & Milwaukee Railroad tracks. The wooded 1,300 acres to the east were subdivided into lots, with half given to the shareholders and half sold to the public to provide financing for the projected university and its preparatory schools.[35] Fundraising did not stop there. The Reverend Slocum, one of the five men on the bluff, had been in contact with a Mr. Gibson of Cincinnati, who offered $100,000 on the condition that the university be called Gibson University.[36] Gibson's wealth, however, came from distilling whiskey, a fact grievous enough in the eyes of the temperate Presbyterians to remove him, and his money, from consideration. Shortly thereafter a Chicagoan, Sylvester Lind,[37] destined to play a major role in the eventual development of the school, stepped forward with another pledge. Lind had already figured in the prehistory of the town. His business affairs had required his traveling by horseback along the old Green Bay trail between Chicago and Milwaukee, and he is reported to have suggested the place along the new railroad where the Reverend Patterson and his four cohorts disembarked from the train and made their historic walk to the lake.[38] In 1856 Lind promised to give the Lake Forest Association six acres of land in Chicago valued at $80,000, with the proviso that a sum of $100,000 be raised by the Presbyterian community of the city and earmarked for academic building on the new campus.[39] Since Lind was as religious as he was well fixed, he seemed an ideal benefactor, and his proposition was readily accepted and acted upon. On February 13, 1857, less than a year after the formation of the Association, the charter of Lind University was approved by the Illinois State Legislature. The document, which formally designated the community as Lake Forest, specifically projected

*Lind University Catalogue of the Literary, Theological, and Medical Departments, 1861–62* is the first such bulletin to be issued. The Medical Department, which was situated in the Lind Building in Chicago, lists fifty-one students. This program introduced the pattern (followed today by Northwestern University and the University of Chicago) of central-city branches of outlying universities.

1857

**The town is planned, platted (and formally registered in Waukegan), following innovative landscape designs by Almerin Hotchkiss.**

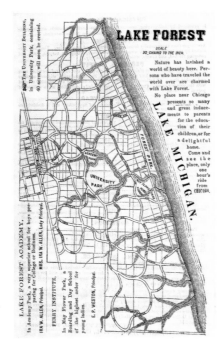

"a college and seminaries or departments devoted
to instruction in Theology, Law, Medicine, General or
Particular Sciences and Literature or the Arts."[40]

In view of the dispatch with which the Lake Foresters
were acting, it is ironic that the primary goal of their
enterprise, the University, would not become a lasting
reality until the mid-1870s, two decades later than
anyone could have anticipated. But the intentions of the
founders were clear. If the curriculum remained to
be formulated only in the future, the charter already
implied an institution of breadth sufficiently encompassing to qualify as a university. And while its theological
purpose was not affirmed in so many words, it was
quite certainly prescribed.[41] American higher education
in the middle of the nineteenth century was still taken
up with the issue of religious training and inculcation;
or, perhaps more precisely, the various major denominations were at pains to organize their own colleges and
universities. The Methodists had created Northwestern
University in 1851 in Evanston, a suburb closer on the
North Shore to Chicago. Although Presbyterian/
Congregationalist followers had established two down-
state colleges, Illinois College and Knox College, and
in Wisconsin, Beloit College, the Reverend Patterson's
Second Presbyterian Church version of the faith was

not represented by any institution within easy reach of
a rapidly expanding Chicago. And since each of those older
colleges had adopted an uncompromising stance on the
issue of slavery and abolition, the decision seemed called
for in Lake Forest to open a school essentially conservative in nature – doctrinally, politically, academically.[42]

That the curriculum eventually bore this out, moreover
in a manner aspiring to the highest possible intellectual
level, may be inferred from the 1878–79 catalog, published
shortly after the school became actually operative.
There the claim was lodged that the University "embraces
substantially the old and time-honored course of study
pursued in the best American colleges."[43] Confirmation
may be found in a report written in 1877 by the local
historian Elijah M. Haines. Reflecting on the curriculum
of the newly created Lake Forest University, which
included parallel Classical and Scientific tracks, Haines
described them as "substantially co-extensive with the
courses in Yale College."[44] (Earlier, in a similar vein, the
first catalog of nearby Beloit College had proudly
announced that its own standard course of study was
"drawn up exactly on the Yale plan.")[45]

However dedicated to tradition the early Lake Foresters
may have been, one of their decisions proved exceptionally innovative. Remarkably enough, it took on physical
rather than spiritual or academic form, albeit with
significant implications for the character and eventual
development of the University. By July of 1857 the
choice 1,300 acres of Lake Forest to the east had been
planned, platted, and formally registered in Waukegan.[46]
The designer was Almerin Hotchkiss of St. Louis,[47] whose
place in the history of American landscape architecture
has been lately reassessed upward, not least on account
of the originality of his Lake Forest plan. Hotchkiss
emerged in the early 1840s as one of the designers,
together with the well-known architect Richard
Upjohn, of the second phase of Green-Wood Cemetery in
Brooklyn, New York. That burial ground is remembered
as one of the first American public examples of a landscape
organized in picturesquely informal looping lanes and
paths, a form influenced by the traditional English garden
and energized by the nineteenth-century Romantic
movement as a whole. In 1848 Hotchkiss left Brooklyn

for St. Louis,[48] where he produced two versions of a comparably rambling plan, first for that city's Bellefontaine Cemetery, later, in 1855, for the Chippianock Cemetery in Rock Island, Illinois. He was then hired to configure the grounds of Lake Forest, an assignment he completed early in the summer of 1857,[49] following the same romantic approach. So doing, he created what was probably the first professionally designed landscape in the Chicago area and the first curvilinear street plan in the United States that clearly defined a central space.[50] Alexander Jackson Davis's Llewellyn Park of 1855[51] was similarly conceived, but it was a subdivision of Orange, New Jersey, not an independent urban entity. It is worth adding that a more historically renowned landscape architect, Frederick Law Olmsted, the designer of New York's Central Park, plotted the curving lanes of another Chicago suburb, Riverside, in 1869, more than a decade following Hotchkiss's Lake Forest plan.[52] Until recently, it was widely, and erroneously, understood that Olmsted himself had designed Lake Forest. That the Riverside plan remains better known even today is due to his fame and Hotchkiss's relative lack of it.

There was more than picturesquely winding streets to Hotchkiss's rationale, and by inference to that of the Lake Foresters who hired him. A business area was consciously omitted from his plan,[53] while the 40 acres that took up most of the central portion of the 1,300 acres accommodated Academy Park and University Park, their function obvious from the names.[54] "A town originally laid out as a park" was the proud citation offered up in the 1887–88 catalog of the University and seconded by virtually every later generation associated with the school. The few shops that did spring up were kept to the margin, lined along the far side of the railroad tracks that formed the western boundary of the town.[55] With the lake as the eastern edge, Hotchkiss organized the internal thoroughfares so that none of them except a service track to Half Day, Illinois, led in any direction out of town and no other roads were encouraged into it. Lake Forest was in effect a closed community, socially and residentially exclusive, convolutedly nestled around its educational core. (To this day its own citizens sometimes have trouble finding their way around in it.) The railroad

was meant to serve as an economic umbilical cord, a route to the nourishing materiality of Chicago, and, just as surely, a way of ensuring a necessary spiritual independence.

In retrospect, the early stages of the planning procedure appear to have been carried out rationally and expeditiously, all action based on the fundamental understanding that an academic institution of excellence was the ultimate objective of the community. The first building of any consequence in the town was a hotel erected a short distance from the railroad in Triangle Park, a space bordered on the south by Deerpath, the most prominent natural pathway in the area. Completed in the summer of 1858,[56] the Lake Forest Hotel served several purposes. It accommodated those, mostly from Chicago, who came up to inspect the land and negotiate property rights as well as lot boundaries, or simply to spend the summers in demonstrably more comfortable conditions than they would have endured in the city. During its first two winters the hotel provided quarters for the town's first operational school, Lake Forest Academy, a boys' school. Then, early in 1859,[57] the Academy's own building, Italianate in manner, was

Map of Lake Forest in 1861 by George Hale, county surveyor, showing the location of the estates of prominent residents concentrated along Deerpath, Academy Park (Lake Forest Academy), University Park (the University), and the Female Academy (Ferry Hall).

The Presbyterian Vision

finished at the southeast corner of newly named Deerpath Avenue and University Avenue (later Sheridan Road) after designs by the Chicago architectural firm of Carter and Drake.[58] The process of doubling up continued, a sign of a community eager, even impatient, to assemble itself, as the congregants of the First Presbyterian Church of Lake Forest met for the first time in the new Academy.[59] Probably in deference to educational priorities, they would wait until 1862 before acquiring a structure of their own. Meanwhile, a girls' seminary, headed by the Reverend Baxter Dickinson[60] and named after him, opened in 1859,[61] in another Italianate building nearby, at the southeast corner of Washington Avenue and Linden Avenue (the latter now College Road). (Dickinson, an 1817 Yale graduate who had taught at Lane with Lyman Beecher from 1835 to 1839, personified yet another Dwight-Beecher connection.)

Since a faculty had to be assembled and a curriculum determined for the Collegiate Department of Lind University (as it was formally designated, though it was always popularly known as Lake Forest University), that portion of the larger institution took somewhat longer to materialize. The first order of business, after all, was the education of the community's younger children in feeder schools for the projected university. Hence the earlier dates of the Academy and Dickinson Seminary – and even of a public school,[62] which, since it served mostly the servant class, was more modest in concept. Given circumstances, however, the public school is probably of greater immediate historical interest, since its particular situation happened to share in the impact of the slavery issue on even so socially conservative a town as Lake Forest. The following narrative bears much of this out.

Operational by 1860, the school was located just north of Triangle Park. Its principal teacher was Roxanna

Beecher, whose surname had already figured in Lake Forest's history and was about to do so again, directly.[63] She was the granddaughter of the Reverend Robert Patterson's teacher Lyman Beecher, and the daughter of William Beecher, probably the most resolute abolitionist of a family renowned for their united opposition to slavery. She was also the niece of the most famous of that extraordinary clan, Harriet Beecher Stowe. In 1836 the latter, daughter of Lyman Beecher and sister of yet another famed clergyman of the time, Henry Ward Beecher, had assumed the name Stowe when she married Calvin Ellis Stowe, at that time also a member of the faculty of Lane Seminary. Puritan in spirit, she found much to despise about slavery, but she did not express herself formally on the subject until the passage of the Fugitive Slave Act of 1850.[64] That notorious piece of legislation, which promised more profit to a legal officer if he returned an alleged fugitive to slavery than if he set him or her free, inspired Stowe to write her immensely influential novel, *Uncle Tom's Cabin* (1852).

While the local conventional wisdom that Lake Forest was a stop on the Underground Railroad has never been convincingly proved, there is enough provocative anecdotal evidence to warrant some speculation on the matter. Several living Lake Foresters remember playing as children in what they claim was always known as an Underground Railroad hideaway: a secret refuge concealed beneath a trapdoor in one of the town's early homes, on what is now Westleigh Road.[65] Others recall the conviction of a highly regarded member of the College's staff that her home near the northern edge of Lake Forest had also been a temporary sanctuary.[66]

Questionable as such lore may be, it is certain that other local residents, together with their friends, were actively involved in promoting escape routes. C. Volney Dyer, an

| 1858 | 1860 | 1863 |
|---|---|---|
| The first building of importance in town, a hotel designed by Asher Carter, opens on what is now Triangle Park. | In Chicago Abraham Lincoln is nominated as the presidential candidate of the Republican Party. | With the Civil War, the "Collegiate Department" formally organized in 1861 disbands and the University, obliged to cease post-secondary operations, is reduced to only the boys' preparatory program. |

early visitor to Lake Forest and one of the major forces behind the Chicago involvement in the Railroad, used his influence as an executive of the Chicago, Burlington & Quincy line to help slaves move north by train,[67] just as a number of newly settled Lake Foresters, Devillo Holt and Sylvester Lind notable among them, assisted in putting a variety of forms of boat transportation to similar use on Lake Michigan.[68]

That an identifiable black community had developed by 1860 southwest of University Park[69] is evidence that African Americans were on hand, illegally or not. In fact, by the end of the Civil War, there were black children in sufficient number to prompt the Presbyterian church to organize a Sunday School for them[70] in what had been Roxanna Beecher's school (her departure in 1863 coinciding with Emancipation).[71] At about the same time, according to village records, three African Americans were enrolled in the public evening school for illiterate adults.[72] It seems reasonable to presume that the blacks were employed in the spacious homes lately erected along Deerpath and University Avenue (and in their more remote stables) by such sympathetic citizens as Devillo Holt and Sylvester Lind and other men of substantial means[73] — like Charles Quinlan, Gilbert Rossiter (who entertained Lincoln during his presidential campaign),[74] and Harvey Thompson, whose barn at what is now 100 North Sheridan Road bordered the black neighborhood.[75]

Thus, apparently, arose another paradox characteristic of early Lake Forest.[76] The founders had intentionally created a closed, class-conscious community, yet they proceeded no less willfully to allow its penetration by blacks, fugitives or recently emancipated, a collective that would normally have been less than welcome in their midst.[77] Once again the eye for thrift and the arm of charity marked the domestic actions of those citizens, just as Calvinist tradition had united comfortably with frontier enterprise when the first generation moved west. Yet however much racial tolerance in an otherwise exclusionary town might have been tinctured with pragmatism, that would hardly suffice to account for the pride the University took in announcing, in the *Daily Commencement Bulletin* of June 7, 1901, that John G. Burns '04, an African American student, had received the highest grade in the Department of History: "In recognition of Mr. Burns's record [Professor W. L. Burnap] presented him with a handsome volume on the 'Causes of the French Revolution.'"[78]

If the Underground Railroad was a metaphor, its literal equivalent was a phenomenon of unparalleled importance in nineteenth-century American life.[79] Nothing approached the railroad as the instrument of the country's nearly obsessive expansion west across the plains and mountains to the Pacific Coast. To be sure, the North and the South were ideologically split on the issue of slavery, but the railroad and its expansion struck one of the economic sparks that helped to ignite the Civil War.[80] With the South eager to see the new western territories assume the identity of slave states, the passage of the Kansas-Nebraska Act of 1854 was meant as a compromise that would allow slavery in Kansas but not in Nebraska.[81] Yet that legislation turned out to be more a failure than a success. Disputes grew bloody and disruptive, while both sides chafed over the delay in freeing the railroad to extend itself westward.[82]

In the course of all this, Chicago's destiny was forged. Its early importance rested on a favorable location at the foot of the Great Lakes that led to the creation of a route of waterways eventually connecting the East Coast to the Gulf of Mexico. But with the growth of the railroads

1865

Lake Forest Academy builds a two-story building at the corner of Deerpath and Sheridan Road. In 1865 it was expanded as shown here. When in 1879 it was destroyed by fire, it was succeeded on the site by Durand Institute in 1892.

As told by Ralph Starkweather and adapted from the 1911 *Forester*

In 1860 the plan, proposed from the start, to develop a Collegiate Department in Lind University, took definite shape, and one young man named Heath seems to have been regarded by his fellows as of superior rank, that is, as the first freshman. But he did not continue in the institution, and it was in the autumn of 1861 that the first freshman class was definitely organized. The members of this class were the following:

Charles Velasco Chandler, Macomb, Illinois. Mr. Chandler entered the Army, served through war, was wounded, has long been a leading citizen of Macomb.

Frederick Chapman, in the Army. According to one report, lost his life there, another impression is that he survived for some years.

George Manierre Jr., Chicago. A prosperous businessman, now of Dibble and Manierre Real Estate, residing at 61 Bellevue Place.

William D. Price, Ottawa, Illinois. An attractive, brilliant fellow. Entered the Army, promoted to the rank of Lieutenant in 63rd Illinois Infantry, killed in Tennessee, October 5, 1863.

Ralph E. Starkweather, M.D. Entered Williams College as sophomore in 1862, was graduated in 1865, M.D., College Physicians and Surgeons, New York, 1868. Practiced medicine in Chicago until 1892. Resides at 1223 Grove Street, Evanston.

John C. Patterson. Went from Lake Forest in 1862 to Yale; did not graduate. Lawyer in Chicago… resides 1350 Wilson Avenue.

The studies of freshman year included Cicero's *De Officiis* and Livy, Xenophon's *Memorabilia* and Homer, Geometry and Conic Sections, with Declamation and English Composition. The requirements for admission were not greatly lower in quality than they are now, but it is interesting to notice that the collegiate age was lower, as students could be admitted at fourteen.

The College teaching was done chiefly by Professor W. C. Dickinson,[92] afterward pastor for a time of the church, and by the Principal of the Academy, S. F. Miller,[93] who a little later devoted himself chiefly to the College work and was succeeded in the Academy by Milford C. Butler. Mr. C. T. Dickinson,[94] a tutor, also gave instruction to freshmen. The work was limited in range, but of such a nature that Dr. Starkweather was admitted to level standing in Williams in the autumn of 1862.

The life of the school and community was in a manner primitive, but spirited. Enterprise was in the air, and everyone lent a hand to everything that was going. A half-holiday was granted now and then on condition that the students help shingle the church or grub stumps out of the "streets." The boys were invited to the village tea parties and were made to feel themselves partners in all activities, social and religious as well as educational. The life had all the zest as well as the hard work of that of pioneers.

The effort to maintain a College failed only because the Civil War absorbed all the energy that did not go into the industrial and commercial activity of the region. The student body at Lake Forest was thrilled with the fires of patriotism, which was heightened still further when that dashing and fascinating leader, Col. Ellsworth, came out here every Saturday for a number of weeks to conduct the Zouave drill. At least three of the little freshmen class went into the army, and the College idea was abandoned for a time, to be taken up again as soon after the war as was feasible.

Ralph E. Starkweather, Class of 1865.

that position became only more strategic. Chicago was soon the most important city of the rapidly growing Northwest as well as the rail capital of the entire country,[83] veritably the gateway to the West. It was in Chicago in 1860 that Abraham Lincoln was nominated as the presidential candidate of the Republican Party, founded four years earlier largely for the purpose of blocking the expansion of slavery westward. Lincoln's reputation derived from, among other things, his service as a prairie lawyer who argued in behalf of the railroads, and in fact the promotion of a transcontinental railroad was included in the 1860 Republican platform.[84]

Lake Forest, with its connection to the civic leadership of Chicago, played a role in these various developments. The relationship of Lincoln with the Reverend Patterson, who both preached to him and supported him, as well as the ties that bound Patterson to Lake Forest, have already been established here. The community was in Lincoln's camp, actively involved in his campaign.[85] It had both reason to want the railroads to succeed and the means to help in the achievement of that end, even if it meant war. Several personal examples illustrate this commitment. Harvey Thompson owned a big hotel in Chicago[86] that profited from the strengthening of the city as a rail center, and Devillo Holt, a lumber merchant,[87] could hardly help but see the rails as the best way of transporting his goods to the great infinity of land (and potential gain) that lay to the west. Of even greater eventual consequence than either of those men was John V. Farwell, an Eastern-born Chicago merchant who had been a regular summer visitor at the Lake Forest Hotel until he took up residence in the town in the late 1860s, on land purchased in 1857. In his mammoth warehouse, built in the mid-1850s in Chicago, wholesale dry goods were gathered and stored in such a volume that one of his partners and a majority of the leading heads of the city were persuaded that he would soon bankrupt himself. The prediction was skewed, to say the least. During the war the magnitude of his operation proved uniquely capable of distributing the goods required by the northern army. General Ulysses S. Grant's success in the West depended in no small measure on long supply lines kept intact largely by the ample materiel he would have been able to secure from the Farwell warehouse.[88]

If the war was felt less directly in Lake Forest than in Chicago, the town and its gradually developing University sustained their share of losses, both personal and collective. Colonel Elmer Ephraim Ellsworth, a soldier who had led students through military drills on the Academy grounds even before open hostilities began, was killed in 1861, the first Union officer to die in the war.[89] Other lives with closer ties to the town were inevitably lost. But a major casualty at the institutional level, grave enough to bear consequences that lasted into the 1870s and beyond, was Lind University itself. There college-level classes, with light enrollments but standards as exacting as those of the better Eastern schools, had been conducted in the Academy's building as early as 1859. With the Reverend William C. Dickinson (son of the seminary's Baxter Dickinson and Amherst graduate, mentioned in Emily Dickinson's correspondence) as its first professor,[90] the University appeared to have become a functioning entity, yet once the war was engaged, the older students gradually left to serve in the ranks.[91] The school was dealt what seemed at the time a mortal blow. By 1863 it had been reduced to the status of a paper corporation and obliged to cease operations.[95] Even a hopeful new Chicago-based medical program that had opened as a branch of Lind University disaffiliated due to lack of support from Lake Forest, which by then was too preoccupied with matters related directly to the war.[96] What had been a dream turned into a reality was obliged to return to a dream, and in that immaterial form it remained for well over a decade.

**The union of secular and spiritual objectives that** had marked the founding of Lake Forest in the 1850s remained intact during the years following the Civil War. Economically, the town had found the war a profitable enterprise, a development reflected in the values and habits of a new generation of citizens. Among the Chicagoans who moved to Lake Forest at the turn of the 1870s, two gifted brothers stood out. Charles B. Farwell and John V. Farwell were possessed of noticeably different temperaments and talents, but each was compelling in the way he fashioned his abilities and both rose to national prominence. Charles, the more freethinking and liberal-minded of the two,[97] made a career in politics, gaining status as the first important political boss of Cook County. Following the war, he rose

Right above. Charles B. Farwell (1823–1903) painted by George P. A. Healy. In 1864, Farwell took charge of J. V. Farwell & Company, arguably the most important wholesale dry goods warehouse in Chicago. More than just a successful businessman, Farwell enjoyed a distinguished political career, serving in Congress, first as representative (1871–76) and then as senator (1887–91). And for most of his career he was a trustee of the University (1864–96), which he was instrumental in founding.

Left center. Charles's brother, John V. Farwell, was an innovative and successful Chicago dry goods merchant and entrepeneur.

Right below. The estates of John V. Farwell (bottom) and Charles B. Farwell (top), constructed in 1870 and 1869 respectively, were located across the street from one another at the east end of Deerpath Road. Later, in Chicago, the brothers even built their town houses adjacent to each other on Pearson Street.

1865

A new state charter for the institution drops Lind's name and Lake Forest University becomes the formal – and familiar – title of a non-functional entity.

to the position of a U.S. congressman and, later, senator.[98] John, more observably conservative, especially in his religious beliefs, turned out to be, as already suggested, something of a mercantile genius.[99]

Shortly after they moved to Lake Forest, the Farwell brothers built houses opposite each other, on Deerpath Road between University Avenue and the lake. John's place, contrary to his customary conservatism, was an exuberant neo-Gothic affair, bristling with gables and finials, more stylistically self-conscious than anything theretofore erected in Lake Forest.[100] The greenhouse he built on the same grounds was an even more impressive structure, on a par with the most ambitious private horticultural conservatories in the country.[101] Charles's home, a free variation on the theme of the Tuscan villa, was comparably ornate. However large the Holt and Thompson homes of 1860 had been, their frame construction and measured decoration had kept them free of ostentation. (The Holt house was actually constructed of brick, with its clapboard cladding underscoring its owner's involvement in and commitment to the lumber business.)[102]

With the erection of the Farwell mansions — each was more grandiose than a mere house — building in Lake Forest had reached a level both quantitative and qualitative that served as a reminder that architecture is, in its own right, certifiably significant evidence of history.[103] The Farwell places were among the more obvious demonstrations of the town's intent to extend itself outward, centrifugally, farther from the old academic center and nearer the lake. In 1869 a new women's seminary — replacing Dickinson Seminary, which had been forced to close because of the ill health of the Reverend Dickinson — was opened on grounds at the east edge of University

Park. Financed by a bequest from the Reverend William Ferry of Michigan, Ferry Hall,[104] designed by the well-known architect O. L. Wheelock,[105] was another reminder of the wealth asserting itself more and more within the town's boundaries. The most arresting evidence of this came in 1871 in the form of a new hotel, erected, like Ferry Hall and the two Farwell houses, nearer the bluff. More luxuriously decked out than the modestly appointed first hotel, the new Lake Forest Hotel was meant to attract even more of the summer visitors whose appearance was becoming an annual local event.[106]

Prosperity was in the air, strengthened as more members of the Chicago merchant class took up residence in Lake Forest. Chief among these were Simon Somerville Reid[107] and Henry C. Durand,[108] both later to become important benefactors of the University, both having made the kind of fortune in the wholesale grocery trade that was typical of the men who drove the formidable Chicago commercial engine of the late nineteenth century. At the beginning of the 1870s Lake Forest was by consensus the most prominent suburb of the city, exclusive in a social as well as a geographic sense. Acceptance there was tantamount to acceptance in the best circles of Chicago society.[109]

This halcyon condition was no less dependent on a development in the religious realm, most of it traceable to the actions of one man. He was the redoubtable Reverend Patterson, who became even more widely known as "the Bishop of the Northwest"[110] when, in the late 1860s, with abolition no longer an issue, he confronted and played a central role in mediating doctrinal disputes that had simmered for years within the entire Presbyterian community of Illinois and the surrounding states. Patterson spent much of this postwar period

1869

A new women's seminary is opened on grounds east of University Park.

1870

UNIVERSITY.

The Lake Forest Hotel (historically known as the New Hotel) is built in affluent 1870, when, with the completion of the transcontinental railroad, Lake Forest becomes a fashionable gathering point for vacationing Chicagoans.

## Mary Eveline Smith Farwell: A Veritable Alma Mater

Lake Forest's alumni dispersed around the world were the "records of her great soul more enduring than monumental brass or cold marble," wrote John J. Halsey[120] in memory of Mary Eveline Smith Farwell after her death September 26, 1905, at the age of eighty. And well could this be said of the woman who provided the impetus for the permanent establishment of coeducational college-level work at Lake Forest in 1876.

Pioneer champion of education for women, Mary Eveline was fortunate in her own training, first as a girl tutored in the shadow of Williams College and later as a young woman enrolled, in its opening year of 1842–43, at Pittsfield (Massachusetts) Young Ladies' Institute (later Maplewood Seminary),[121] where she would conduct classes – in English in 1846 and in Latin and History from 1848 to 1850. After a further stint of teaching at Kinderhook, New York, she traveled to Chicago to work. There she subsequently met Charles B. Farwell, whom she married in 1853. It was in Lake Forest that she raised the three daughters who figure in this history: the precocious Anna (De Koven), for whom the University was refounded, Rose (Chatfield-Taylor), and Grace (McGann).

During her long lifetime, Mrs. Farwell bridged the gap (as her daughter Anna explained in her memoir of 1926, *A Musician and His Wife*, the principal source of information on her mother's life) from church-centered Puritan New England village life, through the idealized reproduction of it in the Lake Forest of the 1860s, to the culturally centered cosmopolitan world of the later Lake Forest, Chicago, and Washington, the last where her husband's political career took him, first as congressman and later as senator. Yet for a quarter century she was secretary to the Presbyterian Women's Board of Foreign Missions, true to her early experience of the church as the focus of spiritual and temporal life in a community.

Mary Eveline Smith Farwell (1826–1905) painted by Charles Highwood (fl. New York City 1848–53; Chicago 1863–85; studied in Munich under Peter Cornelius).

1871

1875

24

**The Chicago Fire.**

**Bankruptcy of the New Hotel returns the property to the Lake Forest Association, providing a logical site for the soon-to-be reincarnated university.**

consulting tirelessly with representatives of the various factions, softening ancient hostilities and eventually restoring an atmosphere of amicable communication among conservatives, moderates, and liberals. In this instance as in others, his motives were a mixture of moral commitment and practical endeavor, meant to advance the cause of a united Presbyterianism in the settling of the West.[111]

However, a price compounded of ironies had to be paid for this achievement, and it was incurred by the very institution, Lind University, that Patterson had labored so hard to bring into being. With a commonality of view newly secured among the Presbyterians, there now seemed a lack of urgency in the promotion of Lind University as an alternative to Knox or Beloit.[112] These schools already existed, in a form more substantial than paper, and as matters turned out, even paper registered loss in its own way. Since Sylvester Lind had suffered a series of financial reverses that prevented him from honoring the pledges he had made in the late 1850s, his name no longer seemed pertinent to the institution, and in 1865 Lake Forest University became the formal — and already familiar — title[113] of what was, curiously enough, a nonoperational entity. Thus, even though the creation of an institution of higher learning had been the principal goal of the founders of the town, it was the University that was consigned to oblivion, while the lower-level Academy and Ferry Hall[114] (the latter incorporated into the entire package in 1870) flourished. If the community mood at the turn of the decade was salubrious, the town's once lofty academic ambitions had grown problematic.

Both Lake Forest and Chicago passed much of the 1870s in similar frames of mind, due to their involvement in some of the same circumstances. Two events qualify as major, one of which was nothing less than historic. The Chicago Fire of 1871 was a holocaust in the classic sense of the word, one of the great urban disasters of modern times. Any simple measurement of it still fails to do justice to its scale and impact. It may be enough to recall here that Chicago's population of 300,000 marked it as one of the fastest growing urban settlements in the world, yet its physical substance was almost totally wiped out, nearly four square miles of it, in a matter of two days.[115]

The city restored itself with remarkable swiftness, thanks largely to the fact that the singular asset of its geographical location was unaffected by the fire.[116] A second reversal, however, followed shortly thereafter. The Panic of 1873, one of the more ruinous American recessions of the nineteenth century, affected nearly everyone, but its impact on Chicago, and thus on Lake Forest, was felt not only economically but politically. The downturn occurred coincident with an assortment of scandals that rocked and ultimately undermined the administration of President Ulysses S. Grant. Given that Grant stood for Illinois, it was Illinois that lost much of its erstwhile power and influence at the national level.[117] Soon enough, however, Chicago's special robustness helped it survive even this misfortune, and by 1880 it had established itself as the leading metropolis of the Midwest.

Nonetheless, in Lake Forest one of the surer signs of economic ill health in the 1870s could be read in the fate of the new hotel. It had opened on a note of high hopes in the same year as the Chicago Fire, yet its short life and unexpected bankruptcy were traceable to that very conjunction. Chicagoans in the process of rebuilding their city had little time and less reason to spend either the summers or shorter periods in a comfortable hostelry on the North Shore. After two years of operation, the new hotel had failed to turn a profit. In 1875 the owners deeded it with the grounds back to the Lake Forest Association for the remainder of their indebtedness.[118] Saddled with so large a building and conscious of an unfulfilled collegiate vision, the Association could hardly have overlooked the obvious, especially when, in one of those rare fortuitous concurrences, Charles B. Farwell happened to have a daughter who at the time was about to enter college. The congressman directly became the central figure in a transaction that effectively brought the University back to life in material form. Already made wealthy by his connection with his brother John's business, of which he had assumed leadership in 1864, he had both the means and station to establish the second founding of the institution. But the motive, if not to say the inspiration, was something else, traceable mostly to his wife, Mary Eveline

Smith Farwell,[119] an exceptional figure in her own right, whose commitments were perfectly attuned to the circumstances she encountered in Lake Forest after she married Charles Farwell in 1852. Her belief in liberal education and the values of a cultivated life stemmed from the private classical education she had received in her native South Williamstown, Massachusetts, where she had studied side by side with the daughters of the legendary educator (and president of Williams College) Mark Hopkins. This training was put to use in her brief career as a teacher. After she moved to Lake Forest, her awareness of the original rationale of Lake Forest University, combined with another of her passions, the cause of liberal education for women, and not least the fact that her eldest daughter had reached college age, prompted her and her husband to take the action necessary to revive the University.[122]

The Farwells wanted Anna to be educated near Lake Forest, where, it was understood, she would most likely make her home and form her standing circle of friends. Thus coeducation, a concept rare among elite private eastern schools until recent times, was added to Mary Eveline Farwell's convictions and instituted as part of the mission of Lake Forest University.[123]

In the fall of 1876 the University formally took over ownership of the defunct Lake Forest Hotel and turned its interior into classrooms and dormitory spaces.[124] The Reverend Patterson, having retired from the Second Presbyterian Church of Chicago to join the faculty at Chicago's McCormick Theological Seminary, retained the latter post even as he agreed to become Lake Forest University's first president. Classes began on September 7. Twelve students were in attendance, all of them, including Anna, graduates of Chicago's first high school and

all but herself granted scholarships by the Farwells. Courses were supervised by a faculty of three.[125] The seal,[126] adopted by Lind University in 1859 and depicting an open Bible lying atop another book, bounded by the motto *Christo et Ecclesiae* ("For Christ and the Church"), was affixed to all formal documents pertaining to a new institution already almost a generation old.

Thus Lake Forest University was founded a second time, on a note as hopeful as that which accompanied the first. What followed directly was less cheering. Since the hotel had been meant for summer guests, it had no heating system other than fireplaces in individual rooms, a circumstance that may have been responsible for the fire that almost totally consumed the building on December 16, 1877.[127] The following March, President Patterson, having reached the age of sixty-five, elected to retire and confine his services to McCormick Seminary.[128]

In view of all the obstacles fate had thrown in the way of the school over a twenty-year period, it is worthy of note that the remaining people who stood for it regrouped and pressed on as they did, with the Farwells' encouragement (and wherewithal) and with characteristic dispatch. Classes were moved to the old hotel, male students were housed in rooms in the Academy and women in local homes, and plans were undertaken to build an independent structure for the University in University Park. The site proposed was a parcel of land directly across University Avenue from the Holt house.

To mark the end of the founding era, the Lake Forest Association was dissolved in April of 1878, with its assets reverting to the new university. Construction on University Hall, as it came to be known (more latterly College Hall and eventually Young Hall), began at about

1876

1877

26

Under the leadership of the Reverend Patterson, Lake Forest University opens its now coeducational Collegiate Department in the wooframe lakefront hotel building made available by the Lake Forest Association.

The hotel burns. "We came with the enthusiasm and faith of pilgrim fathers and mothers. When our first Building burnt down I sat beside the ruins and wept... but we...got up Phoenix-like out of the ashes." Josephine White Bates, Class of 1880, in the June 5, 1903, *Stentor.*

the same time, and it was hastily but resourcefully carried out under the guidance of new Acting President John Hewitt, who brought to this key project the sound academic experience he had garnered earlier as acting president of Michigan's Olivet College.[129] Once drawings were completed by Chicago architect Leon Welch,[130] whose position in the office of O. L. Wheelock, designer of Ferry Hall, had acquainted him with the layout of Lake Forest, a deep hole was dug in the meadow of University Park, a few yards east of the site the building was to occupy. Clay was extracted and baked into bricks in kilns set up on the grounds.[131] Secondary materials were carted in by day and by night, until a five-story structure took shape, completed in the fall and composed largely of the very ground on which it stood, some 150 yards back from University Avenue. Stylistically, University Hall was for the most part true to the Second Empire manner whose widespread use during the 1870s stemmed from the popular notion that it was especially expressive of classical authority. Welch's use of a mansard roof with a truncated pyramidal turret at its center and two gabled roof pavilions on its flanks produced the desired note of

dignity, although the addition of several Gothicized pointed arches on the facade and a broad porch that ascended from the ground to the main floor produced a more vernacular hominess than the grandeur associated with the pure Second Empire style. Nevertheless, University Hall was a big, palpably institutional building, to this day the tallest structure in the town, owned and occupied solely by Lake Forest University. Most important, it was in place.

University Hall (later known as College Hall and in 1982 renamed Young Hall), built in 1878 from designs by Chicago architect Leon C. Welch and paid for by Charles B. Farwell, housed faculty and students, classrooms, chemistry labs, library, and chapel.

## College and Town Founder Lind, the Underground Railway, and Chicago's Unique "Underwater Seaway"

Explained in an 1890 article in the *Stentor*

When junior *Stentor* whiz reporter William Danforth, Class of 1891, wrote his May 1890 story on the "Underground Railroad: How the System Worked in Chicago," he was able to draw on a remarkable first-hand source in Sylvester Lind (1808–92), who lived then at what now is 550 East Deerpath, just west of the Presbyterian Church. In an account that sounds like an "as told to" narrative derived from Lind, Chicago's role in the wholesale movement to whisk escaped slaves away from the South and from the hands of federally protected slave-catchers is outlined in detail, with graphic examples. The Chicago group's clever method of secreting slaves onto boats and then shuttling them down Lakes Michigan and Huron to the St. Clair River just north of Detroit, close to Canada and to freedom, is told, taken down by a student and filed away on dusty library shelves – and hitherto unknown certainly in Lake Forest and Door County – for historians one day to uncover. Here is recounted one tale of a group of escapees showing up in Chicago and then being smuggled through the city to the harbor by Lind and a group of associates. Lind went ahead of the closed carriage to make sure the coast was clear for boarding his lumber steamer:

*Mr. Lind owned some lumber mills in the northern lake region, and he had two vessels plying between that region and Chicago. One of the vessels was waiting in the Chicago harbor for a favorable wind on the night in question. In reaching the lumber region these boats had to pass through a narrow channel which was called "Death's Door" near which was an island where all lake steamers took on wood. It was customary for the slaves to be left at this island until a boat came along which could take them down through the St. Clair River. The channel was so narrow in some places that the slaves could easily jump from the boat onto the Canada side before Detroit was reached. The slave owners could not find out at what point the runaways jumped off. The law on the subject was as follows: any lake captain who knowingly took fugitive slaves onto his boat in a United States harbor, was subject to a fine of $100,000; but if he found slaves on his boat after he had gotten out into the lake, not knowing when they came on, he was not obliged to turn them over to the law until he reached a United States port. Slaves furnished with money contributed by the underground committee could thus be put aboard a vessel unbeknown to the captain, and when the boat reached the middle of the lake, the money was paid over by the slave, who jumped off when he reached Canada, the captain winking at the performance but not responsible. Mr. Lind often had slaves put on his boats in this way. They were sent up to the wood station near "Death's Door."*

*When Mr. Lind reached his boat on the night in question, he found no one on board but the cook. The captain had gone ashore. This exactly suited Mr. Lind's purpose. The cook, being an anti-slavery man, the fact that the slaves were coming to the boat was made known to him. He promised to secret the negroes in the hold and give them food. Before morning they were safely on their way to Canada.*

Danforth also had interviewed former escaped slave Samuel Dent in the February 1890 *Stentor* issue, shortly before the beloved local liveryman's death, perhaps prompting Lind or his friends to suggest this follow-up story. The enterprising young reporter also covered a whistle-stop visit to Lake Forest by the African explorer Henry Stanley before being chosen as the *Stentor* editor for 1890–91 and then going on to a career in journalism at the *Chicago Tribune*.

Below right. William E. Danforth, Class of 1891 and editor of the *Stentor*, 1890–91.

Below left. Sylvester Lind, a wealthy Chicago banker and businessman, pledged a large sum toward the founding of a university named in his honor. When he lost his fortune shortly thereafter and was no longer able to meet his obligation. Lind University was renamed Lake Forest University in 1865.

# The Burgeoning University of Presidents Gregory and Roberts

chapter 2

With the coming of the 1880s, the leading citizens of Lake Forest felt increasingly secure in the belief that the communal ends their predecessors had set for themselves in the 1850s were well on the way to realization. The old Puritan ethic, which saw a causal connection between faith and worldly reward, seemed supported by the fact that the village with its 1,200 inhabitants included more millionaires than any other small town in the Middle West.[1] Social prestige came as a matter of course, not only grounded in the position of the townsmen in the Chicago commercial world, but apparent from the special breed of visitors who made their way to Lake Forest in the late 1870s and early 1880s. Among the more distinguished were Whitelaw Reid,[2] editor of the *New York Tribune* and later ambassador to Great Britain, General John A. Logan,[3] three times president of the Grand Army of the Republic and head of the Republican Party in

1878

President Rutherford B. Hayes is an overnight guest of the William Henry Smith family.

1879

A new English program, "a novelty in the American College," is introduced into the curriculum.

Illinois, and a pair of authentic Civil War heroes, General William T. Sherman[4] and General Philip Sheridan.[5] President Rutherford B. Hayes was an overnight guest of the William Henry Smith family in 1878.[6] No Chicago suburb of the time, surely none so modest in size, had attracted, much less entertained, a company of greater eminence.[7]

Yet the sense of community held fast. Lake Forest was small enough and its citizens sufficiently alike in tastes and sympathies that they made a civic celebration out of the return of Devillo Holt's sons, four of them, from the trip they had made around the world in 1878. Flags were displayed throughout the town and the gate of the Holt house was festooned with decorations.[8]

Such a show of neighborliness, to be sure, did not alter the social identities that continued to distinguish the landowners from those who served them. Among the former, the bond of status only reinforced the bond of community. Moreover, Lake Forest was nothing if not an orderly place. Local shops and stores, more of them in 1880 than a generation earlier, were still gathered, or more precisely sequestered, on the west side of the railroad tracks.[9] That separation would continue intact for years, consistent with the intentions of the founders of the town to preserve not only their collective privacy but their parklike landscape.

A kindred constancy of belief in the future of the University marked the local attitude of the 1880s. University Hall was the chief material symbol of an educational promise long assumed and newly resurrected, while the retirement of the Reverend Patterson led with little delay to the hiring of a successor. John Hewitt,[10] professor of Latin and Greek, acted as president for several months until a permanent president, Daniel Seelye Gregory,[11] was appointed in June of 1878, when the new catalog would announce that the Collegiate Department was at last "fully organized."

It might well have read "fully *re*-organized." For in the two decades following the chartering of the University, American higher education as a whole had been caught up in a process of change sweeping and long lasting enough to qualify as a revolution. The agency was a growing nationwide spirit of social democracy and utilitarianism,

whose effect upon a subculture as traditionally elitist as academia was most obviously manifest in the widespread founding of land-grant colleges and state universities.[12] Ralph Waldo Emerson had sensed this as early as 1867, when he declared, "The treatises that are written on University reform may be acute or not, but their chief value to the observer is in showing that a cleavage is occurring in the hitherto granite of the past and a new era is nearly arrived."[13]

Among the monuments swept away in the current of that new era was the Yale curriculum of 1828 that had long dominated American education. The force of the change was felt no less surely at Lake Forest University, where allegiance to the Yale model, reflected in the 1876 adoption of President Patterson's understandably traditional Classical and Scientific courses, was greatly modified during the administration of his successor, President Gregory, who had been brought to Lake Forest from a professorship at Wooster. The two presidents, Roberts and Coulter, who followed Gregory, were similarly responsive to the winds of change. Common to all three was their belief in a movement that spread throughout the American educational community at the time: the influence of German thought and the model of the German university, a further upheaval that redirected the thrust of higher education from the molding of character to a rigorous training of the mind, with emphasis on scientific methodology and new intellectual disciplines.[14]

Gregory's tenure revealed this and more, all of it a mixture of his own academic background and his adopted outlook. Well grounded at Princeton in logic, metaphysics, and language, during his first year at Lake Forest he oversaw the addition to the existent programs of two new ones—philosophical and literary or English. Of the latter, the catalog boasted that it was "in its extent, thoroughness and completeness, a novelty in the American College." Though it proved short-lived, it typified yet another noteworthy post–Civil War development that amounted to a form of cultural nationalism. English and other departments of language and literature were moved to a more nearly central position in college curricula, a shift apparent not only in Lake Forest University's new English program but in the new philosophical course, where German was substituted for Greek—so as to "lay

The Reverend Daniel Seelye Gregory (1832–1915) served as the second president of the University from 1878 to 1886.

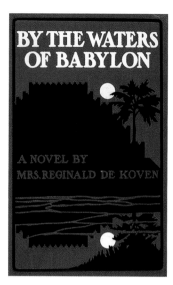

Published by significant Chicago-related publishers, two novels (from 1902 and 1895) by Anna Farwell De Koven.

the foundations for the requirements of a thorough knowledge of the best in German thought." Thus the growing authority of the German intellectual tradition went hand in hand with an increased interest in English and the English language.[15] Further evidence was provided by a new course in Anglo-Saxon introduced in the English curriculum and demonstrative of an elevated interest in Philology, another area of study imported from Germany. (Meanwhile, at the national level, the year 1883 witnessed the establishment of the Modern Language Association, which has remained the foremost professional organization in the field.)

If Gregory's career at Lake Forest began with these additions and alterations, it would end, in his final year, 1886, with plans for graduate study. Just as the larger eastern universities followed one by one the research model of the German university, where the Ph.D. degree was regarded as the ideal goal of the serious student, Gregory's position abreast these advances was evident in his projection of a first doctoral program, in Philosophy.

For all of that, and however devoted to these radical academic changes Gregory may have been, he also believed they were in full accord with his fundamental trust in the imperative of Christian education. Accordingly, students preparing for the ministry, or otherwise appropriately qualified, could avail themselves of work in Hebrew and Sanskrit. During his service the University trained proportionately more young men for the clerical life, indeed by a substantial margin, than any other institution of its kind in the country.[16] No president, before or since, ever found the motto *Christo et Ecclesiae* more relevant to the school's purpose and calling.

The first full-term graduation of Lake Forest University occurred in 1880, the second year of Gregory's presidency. A measure of poetic justice was meted out when Anna Farwell, the young woman who had inspired her parents to see to her education by giving new life to the school she would attend, was awarded valedictorian honors. She thus became living justification of the efforts of her mother, Mary Eveline Farwell, in establishing coeducation as one of the most important components of the original academic program of Lake Forest University. Despite the fears of Lyman Beecher ("This amalgamation of the sexes won't do. If you live in a Powder House, you blow up once in a while"),[17] by the 1870s, coeducation was fairly standard in the Middle West. Even Northwestern, in 1873, had instituted the Woman's College of Northwestern University, though history contends that many of the first women students, free to enroll in all the under-graduate classes of the university, confined themselves

1880

1880

**Interested University and Academy students meet March 10 to organize the Lake Forest Base Ball Association, with a ball ground on North Campus. The team wins its first game against Waukegan on March 17.**

**During the winter vacation the ravine behind Young Hall is dammed up to create a pond to accumulate water for the boilers; students look forward to a skating rink in winter.**

## Anna Farwell, Very Much Her Parents' Redoubtable Daughter, Speaks Out

In her book *A Musician and His Wife* (1926), Anna Farwell recalled a conversation with her uncle John V. Farwell, a man as strict in his religious beliefs as he was orthodox. In this regard he was quite unlike his brother (and Anna's father) Charles, who, as she recalled, "had not declared his faith, and of no church was he a member." Anna cared for her uncle but idolized her father, and her assimilation of Charles's more liberal views – not to mention what she had learned at Lake Forest University – was apparent in her argument with John on the subject of eternal damnation. In her own words:

*Not until the study of the New Testament in Greek, with the discovery that the word "unending" was never used in the original to designate the punishment of unbelievers, was the terror of my father's damnation lifted from my childhood. Well I remember my triumphant announcement of this liberating discovery to my uncle John, the evangelist, the Bible student. "Anna," he sternly declared, "you must believe in eternal damnation; the Bible teaches it. You will be punished if you refuse to believe."*

*"... But, uncle, the Greek word is not eternal," I insisted.*

*"I thank my Heavenly Father," he answered, "that I do not base my theology on a Greek word."*

*"And I, dear uncle," was my probably very irritating reply, "am thankful that I need not base mine on a translation."*

Anna's personal history warranted the attention she paid it in the book. While still in her twenties, she laid the groundwork for several serious literary journals, to which she contributed, and after leaving Lake Forest she and her husband traveled widely, living in New York and Florence, all the while enjoying the company of the international set on both sides of the Atlantic.

While her parents were still alive, she returned to Lake Forest for summers. During this later period she wrote a variety of books, including two novels, *A Sawdust Doll* (1895) and *By the Waters of Babylon* (1902). In 1913 her two-volume edition of the letters of John Paul Jones, undertaken in the spirit of the reform era – and true to her challenging nature – exposed significant forgeries by a previous biographer. Her efforts prevented the inscription of false quotations on a statue of Jones that was being mounted in Washington, D. C.

1880

Susan B. Anthony and Elizabeth Cady Stanton attempt unsucessfully to vote in a national election.

Anna Farwell, Class of 1880.

Womens Dormitories, University of Chicago.

to the study of literature and the fine arts.[18] Meanwhile, at Oberlin College, where coeducation was nationally launched in 1837, a parallel ladies' seminary continued in place, scholastically less rigorous but more popularly attended.[19]

In practice, the situation in Lake Forest also exemplified some of this ambivalence, quite likely a reflection of the sentiments of female students' parents. At Ferry Hall, a Ladies' Collegiate Course[20] was defined by the University catalog of 1879–80 in unmistakably seminarian terms, as "furnishing a thorough intellectual training, and yet not so severe as to exclude the ornamental and graceful." On the other hand, the University proper took self-conscious pride in characterizing its coeducational program: "It is the aim of the Trustees to furnish the young women of the North-West with opportunities for thorough intellectual culture, every way equal to those afforded to young men, and which cannot be furnished, without a ... curriculum of a College." The distinction as expressed seems clear enough, and the coeducational aspect appears strengthened by another passage in the same catalog, which listed among the University's advantages "a more thorough intellectual training than

can be obtained in any College exclusively for women." Yet within the following decade, a short-lived entity called Ferry College was formed adjunct to the Ferry Hall curricula and equipped to offer a B.A. degree – equal but alternative to that of the University. Notwithstanding the motives behind such an arrangement, Lake Forest University remained well grounded in its coeducational commitment.

Anna Farwell, whose valedictory address was appropriately titled "The Position and Opportunities of Woman in America," was not alone in validating the merit of the goals her mother worked so hard to achieve. The salutatorian of her graduating class was another woman, Josephine Louise White, Class of 1880, of Chicago, who went on to become a successful novelist and essayist.[21] Anna's description of her as "a brilliant girl" was evidently shared by the Chicago newspaper *Interior.* Reporting on the two honor prizes won by Farwell and White, who "presented essays which would have done credit to the ablest male graduates of any college in the country," *Interior* added, "it was practical proof of the success of the coeducation theory, so well illustrated in these scholarly and accomplished young ladies."[22] Anna herself not only went on to marry a composer of national importance, Reginald De Koven,[23] but made a solid literary career for herself as a biographer and thoughtful chronicler of the customs and mores of the world she knew.[24]

By the time Anna and Josephine graduated, together with the five men who rounded out the Class of 1880, the University's physical plant had grown to a point that the grounds it occupied qualified as a campus. Fire, that scourge of the 1870s, once again played a role both destructive and constructive, since in 1879 the frame structure of the Academy building burned to the ground and in 1880 a substantial four-story building was put up nearby to serve in its stead.[25] (Later catalogs would make a point of advertising "steam-heated" buildings.) The new Academy (later North Hall), located a few yards north of University Hall, shared with the latter the same material, common yellow brick, and the same architect, Leon Welch.[26] Stylistically, it was a study in vernacular classicism, less ambitious than

**Above.** Starting with President Gregory in 1880 and ending with President Nollen in 1918, this Second Empire building was known as the President's House (later Patterson Lodge). From the 1920s to the 1990s, faculty and students lived there, most notably Coach Ralph Jones in the 1930s and '40s. In more recent years it has housed the Admissions and Financial Aid offices.

**Center.** Lake Forest Academy was renamed North Hall when it was remodeled for use by Lake Forest University in the 1890s to serve as classroom, dormitory, and office space for the first half of the next century. In the 1950s it became the College's administration building.

**Below.** This view of the campus, first published in June 1880 shows the 1878 University Hall (right), the 1880 Lake Forest Academy Building (center), and (left) the president's house (1880). The small building at center rear is the wood-frame Academia, demolished in the 1960s.

The *University Review*, launched in January, 1880, for a three-year run, was the first official faculty-student voice, initially edited by Anna Farwell, assisted by Josephine White. Farwell's article "The Position and Opportunities of Woman in America" appeared in the June issue of the first year. The last issue came in 1883.

of content and literacy of style can be made out in articles as varied and informed as an 1881 discussion of the theology of the medieval visionary Hildegard of Bingen[31] (a "discovery" of the late twentieth century) and another essay of the same year on the system of electrical street lighting newly installed in London.[32] (The earliest commercially practical incandescent lightbulb had been invented only two years earlier, in 1879.) The first editor of the *Review*—the "editress"—was Anna Farwell,[33] and a promotional article by President Gregory appeared regularly on the back page. There he encapsulated his view of the twin purposes of the school in the phrase "the highest kind of Christian Collegiate education," taking further pride in the faculty ("a corps of ten professors ... made up of graduates of Princeton, Yale and other prominent institutions"), the local climate's freedom from malaria (like cholera, no small menace in the later nineteenth century and in fact one of the factors that attracted city dwellers everywhere to the presumably cleaner air of country suburbs like Lake Forest), and the town's prohibition of the sale of all intoxicating drinks ("so that the student is free from all the ordinary temptations which lure from study, lead to idleness and unfit [sic] for the duties of life").

the earlier structure but consistent with it.[27] Meanwhile, in the same year, 1880, two other buildings went up. The president's home, composed of yellow brick in small-scale Second Empire, and later named for Robert Patterson, was erected west of the new Academy, close to University Avenue,[28] while a modest effort in wood, meant as a dining hall (later known as Academia and razed in the 1960s), rose between and somewhat east of the Academy and University Hall.[29] A local landscape designer, William Gordon, was hired to organize plantings for the campus.[30]

The resultant scene was depicted in an engraving that appeared from time to time in the pages of a new periodical, *Lake Forest University Review*. Begun in 1880, the *Review* was intended as a university literary magazine, one of the first in the Middle West. Its contents ranged from papers by students and alumni to short but well-researched articles by faculty members on current events and historical and literary topics. By the standards of the late twentieth century, the *Review*'s seriousness

The Reverend Gregory remained in his Lake Forest post until 1886. His last year there was clouded by illness, but he recovered well enough to spend the rest of his career in pursuit of the same religious and intellectual objectives common to his Lake Forest presidency. For a time he served as pastor of a small parish in Minnesota, then moved on to New York City, where his exceptional competence in language study, one of the fastest-growing scholarly disciplines of the day, earned him the managing editorship of a major new American reference work, the *Standard Dictionary*, later *Funk and Wagnall's*.

1881

**At the start of the Fall term a professor meets with the College men to note some rules: (1) no smoking in rooms, (2) do not throw slops out of the windows, and (3) do not leave trash in the hall.**

1883–85

**Chicago architect William Le Baron Jenney constructs the first metal-framed "skyscraper," the Home Insurance Building.**

# The High-Rising Starrett Brothers

New York's Flatiron and Empire State buildings, Washington's Lincoln Memorial, Chicago's Northern Trust bank – what do these disparate buildings have in common other than being well known? All were built by the Starrett brothers, contractors extraordinaire, the leading two of whom, Theodore, Class of 1884, and Paul, Class of 1887, attended Lake Forest University. Together with their three brothers they came to dominate the field of skyscraper construction, Paul's 1938 autobiography, *Changing the Skyline*, bearing out their influence.

While in the early 1880s the boys' parents, a minister and a teacher, published a small magazine in nearby Highland Park, Theodore and Paul studied at Lake Forest, Theodore for four years and Paul (who according to his brother commuted to campus by freight train!) for only two, leaving when the family moved to Chicago. In reminiscences he wrote for the 1906 *Forester*, Theodore recalled how he "took particular interest in Logic which [he] studied under Dr. Gregory," who had written a standard text on the subject. "I got a foundation in this one study," he contended, "which was more than most men got out of four years of college life with all its joys."

By 1887 Paul had gained an entry-level job in the office of the architects Burnham and Root, at that time at the center of the developing Chicago School of Architecture, having completed the Rookery building on LaSalle Street in 1886. Eventually three of the five brothers to enter into the construction business passed through that office – in those seminal days a "school" itself – before going on to lead the dominant construction firms of the day, the George A. Fuller Company (Paul) and Thompson-Starrett (Theodore), and relocating to the East, where their major projects were realized.

The Northern Trust Building at LaSalle and Monroe streets, designed by Lake Forest and campus architects Frost and Granger, and built by Theodore Starrett's firm, was completed in 1906.

1886

Lake Forest University introduces its first doctoral program, in Philosophy.

The Reverend William C. Roberts (1832–1903), the University's third president, served from 1886 to 1892.

Gregory and his administration drew the praise of a man in a position to judge them. John J. Halsey, a historian who joined the faculty of Lake Forest University in 1878 and later wrote one of the first full-scale chronicles of the time, a 1912 history of Lake County, spoke admiringly of Gregory's "indefatigable and dauntless efforts for the institution," adding that "a high standard of work, the value of ideas in the face of a material world, careful and systematic thinking, and a close and personal relation between the president and every student, were the contribution of President Gregory to the traditions of Lake Forest."[34] While such language may sound platitudinous today, it meant something more substantive in Gregory's day, especially to Halsey. The danger of unchecked materialism was still a concern of some Americans, just as it had been of the founders of the agrarian communes, and it ranked among the intellectual priorities that distinguished most professors from most businessmen.

In fact, the late 1880s and the early 1890s were a time of tensions in Lake Forest that sharpened that distinction and precipitated academic disagreements lasting well into the future. The issues were defined by two events, apparently remote from one another, yet in an oblique and ironic way connected. In 1886 the Reverend William C. Roberts[35] was named the third president of Lake Forest University. In the same year, the Haymarket Square riot exploded in Chicago.

The riot was of such national consequence that it has long been the stuff of textbooks. Even so, since it involved Lake Forest interests, it deserves a brief summary here. During the 1880s the forces of labor had been pushing throughout the country for better working conditions, chiefly for an eight-hour working day. On May 4, 1886, a demonstration, for the most part staged by local anarchists,[36] drew about 1,500 people to Haymarket Square on the Near West Side of Chicago. After police were summoned to disperse the crowd, a bomb went off and outright rioting followed. Eleven people, including seven policemen, were killed, and over one hundred onlookers were injured. Eight of the anarchist leaders were jailed and indicted on grounds of inciting to riot. They were eventually convicted. Four were executed, one committed suicide, and three were finally pardoned by Governor John P. Altgeld. While historians later tended to the view that the punishment was excessive, since no evidence ever conclusively proved that the convicted men had made or thrown the bomb, the final verdict only attested to the intensity of passions surrounding the case at the time.[37]

The anarchists, it is pertinent to note, were mostly German immigrants of liberal persuasion, with connections to international socialism. In a political sense, then, they were the natural enemy of Chicago business leaders, just as, in a social sense, their immediate forebears had furnished the Presbyterians of the 1850s with a reason to leave Chicago and found Lake Forest. Significantly, the target of the Haymarket demonstration was the McCormick Reaper Works, whose director, Cyrus McCormick Jr., was a trustee of Lake Forest University. He had taken over the seat of his father, Cyrus Sr., a trustee himself from 1869 to 1884.[38] The junior McCormick was not the only Lake Forester who took sides in the labor wars common to the time. John V. Farwell offered his dray horses to transport the police assigned to subdue the Haymarket rioters, and he found no reason to quarrel with the verdict of the court. "I am very proud of our government," he wrote. "… it was left for our glorious America to teach … a lesson in how to exterminate this social vermin by chopping off its head, and thus kill the body of the movement."[39]

Even so, since the Haymarket riot was only the most recent in a series of disturbances, there was reason to suspect that more lay ahead. Countermeasures had already begun with an 1885 proposal offered in the councils of Chicago's Commercial Club, whose members included the most powerful businessmen in the city, to the effect that a military base should be built to protect against further disorders in the Chicago area. The leaders of the Commercial Club argued for it locally, while Senator Charles B. Farwell advanced the cause in Washington. In 1887, 632 acres of land just south of Lake Forest were transferred to the federal government by the Commercial Club.[40] The location was hardly accidental, since it promised direct security to a town whose citizens were collectively aligned with ownership rather than labor. The name Camp Highwood, as it was originally called, was changed in 1888 to Fort Sheridan.

Yet the issue of Germans, whose role in the Haymarket affair drew such deep hostility from Lake Forest businessmen, had, as we have already observed, taken a far different turn, intellectual rather than economic, in Lake Forest itself — at the University. The substance of it could be found not only in the catalogs of the school but in the pages of the *Lake Forest University Review* during its 1880 to 1883 run. Both sources were united in their unqualified admiration for the intellectual accomplishments of modern Germany.

The same spirit imbued President Roberts. A graduate of Princeton Theological Seminary, who read law during his vacations, Roberts was a handsomely educated man, conversant with all aspects of academic and church life, including administrative responsibilities. While still in his thirties, he had been appointed to trusteeships at Wooster, Lafayette, and Princeton, and he later served as elected president of the nationally important Presbyterian Board of Home Missions before accepting the presidency at Lake Forest. He was, in short, a practical believer, and foresighted enough, once at Lake Forest, to see the advantages of casting even more in the German mold the university he now headed. During his tenure, three professional schools in Chicago were brought under the aegis of Lake Forest University: a college of law, a college of dental surgery, and a medical college[41] — a second version of the medical school

whose first incarnation had ceased with the closing of Lind University in the early 1860s.[42] These institutions, with flourishing enrollments even at the outset, remained within the framework of the University until the turn of the century.

Meanwhile, however, there was no loss of focus on undergraduate studies. Catalogs carried Topical Statements of Work written by professors to describe their disciplines to the student, suggesting an emphasis on areas of study — rather than specifically required texts — that was itself something of an academic innovation.[43] It is especially worthy of further note that American literature (if only of the nineteenth century), while still a rarity in college curricula, was available along with the broader offerings in English literature.[44] German, of course, continued to be granted a central position. While the first two years of undergraduate work were prescribed, the last two provided for elective studies, "enough to afford a reasonable scope for the student's taste." Any such predilection, especially if embraced by better students, could be satisfied by "options" that included Sanskrit, Hebrew, Spanish, Italian, Arabic, Keltic, and Anglo-Saxon!

Under Roberts's guidance the graduate program was expanded, and he proudly announced that "the Philosophical Faculty corresponds in general to the Philosophical Faculty in the European universities." The educational reformation was now in full force, reflected in yet another movement that would shortly effect a change of substantial intellectual weight: Darwinian theory. However hotly contested that epochal view was, it was generally accepted throughout the country by the end of the century, when it found its way into the curriculum of even so doctrinally orthodox an institution as nearby Illinois College.[45] Thus it is not surprising to find the 1886–87 catalog of Lake Forest University listing readings, in the second year course of the postgraduate program in natural science, that included Darwin's *Origin of Species* and *The Descent of Man*, other texts on evolution, and even "Essays in the *Popular Science Monthly*," the last of these known to the widest lay public as a periodical devoted to the gospel of progress.[46] The catalogs of this period also highlight Apparatus and Cabinets [for fossil and other collections].

CATALOGUE
of
LAKE FOREST UNIVERSITY
1890-91

UNDERGRADUATE DEPARTMENT
LAKE FOREST COLLEGE
FERRY COLLEGE AND SEMINARY
LAKE FOREST ACADEMY
Located at Lake Forest, Ill.

PROFESSIONAL DEPARTMENTS
THE PHILOSOPHICAL FACULTY, offering
GRADUATE COURSES
Located at Lake Forest, Ill.

THE MEDICAL FACULTY, comprising
RUSH MEDICAL COLLEGE, CHICAGO
CHICAGO COLLEGE OF DENTAL SURGERY

THE LAW FACULTY
CHICAGO COLLEGE OF LAW

It was under President Roberts that a university-scaled institution took shape with three notable developments: the professional schools in Chicago, a separate identity for what had previously been the Collegiate Department, and a distinct but parallel four-year Ferry College for women.

So described, the academic situation at Lake Forest University might well have seemed felicitous by some standards, reflective of an institution secure in its mission, attuned to the most advanced educational theory, and eager to aspire to higher goals. As matters turned out, however, there were other standards in place, and other actions expressive of them. The first notable wedge was driven during the late 1880s between the values of the school and those of the community.

A single event, nonetheless of import, may suffice as illustration. In 1887 President Roberts appointed a promising young scholar, James Mark Baldwin,[47] to the chair of the Philosophy Department. Recently schooled at Princeton and European universities, Baldwin was the kind of new academic specialist—distinct from the more customary generalist—around whom Roberts wanted to build his faculty. He was already respected for the quality of his research and, as such, awarded by Roberts a lighter than normal teaching load.

This did not sit well with the trustees, whose objections Baldwin himself recalled: "I was soon brought up before the Board to explain why I was not giving full fifteen hours' instruction per week; and the explanation being found inadequate, I was assigned supplementary hours in another and completely remote subject. This I flatly refused to accept, and presented my resignation. It was only the personal stand of the good President Roberts that saved the day. He had to meet arguments like this—urged by

one of the trustees, a prominent merchant of Chicago— 'Let the professor go, and we will save money; I can get plenty of clerks, in my business, for twelve hundred dollars a year, while he is getting fifteen hundred.'"[48]

While the unnamed trustee's criteria were overtly economic, they were only a little less evidently colored by social attitude, not to mention a measure of anti-intellectualism. Insofar as Professor Baldwin stood for the research professional as distinct from the gentleman teacher-scholar, he could be seen, especially by his detractors, as representative of the influence of Germany, a symptom contrary to Lake Forest's traditional academic as well as theological, social, and political conservatism.[49] Nor was Baldwin the sole specialist of consequence on the faculty. During President Roberts's period of service, the nationally renowned (and stalwart local Presbyterian) Elisha Gray, whose claim to have invented the telephone is taken seriously by students of the subject, was a lecturer in Theoretical and Applied Electricity from 1887 to 1892.[50]

Thus a tug-of-war between Roberts and some of his trustees had started, and it signified a far-reaching difference of opinion between University and town that eventually bore upon the very nature of the former. To meet the expenses of his programs and assemble the kind of faculty he wanted, Roberts constantly pressured his trustees for money, and while they did not succeed in raising the $1 million he asked for, the University's endowment did rise sharply. Statistics from the Report of the Commissioner of Education at Washington, D.C., charting the financial state of "western" Presbyterian colleges in 1889, show Lake Forest University with a "productive endowment" of $803,000, a sum substantially higher than that listed for any other of the institutions cited. (Hamilton College, with an endowment of $284,123, and Lafayette College, with $272,303, were closest to Lake Forest, with the rest falling far below those figures.)[51]

If in coercing his trustees into financial action Roberts on occasion had threatened to resign,[52] in 1892 he actually did leave, to return to the Board of Home Missions, this time in the prestigious position of

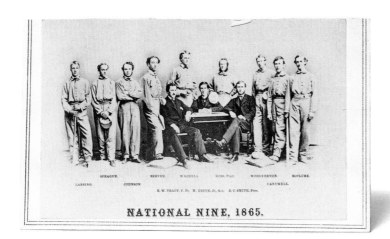

NATIONAL NINE, 1865.

40

chief of staff. (Even before departing Lake Forest he had served as moderator of the Presbyterian General Assembly, another significant post.)[53] In 1898 he became president of Centre College in Kentucky and, when he consolidated it with Central University of Richmond, president of the new Central University of Kentucky at Danville.

In sum, despite Roberts's academic reforms and overall financial success, his arguments with his trustees were persistent and serious. They might in fact have eventually proven fatal to the University, had it not been for the emergence of a man who, at least for a time, managed to ameliorate much of the ongoing contention. In the process, and gifted as he was in the art of persuasion, he not only recalled the classic model of the Reverend Robert Patterson, but secured himself a place as one of the special figures in the history of both the school and the community.

He was James Gore King McClure,[54] a man of the cloth and independently well-off, both identities quite in keeping with Lake Forest values. At the time of the Haymarket riot in 1886, he was already a resident of the town, having been appointed in 1881 to the pastorate of the local First Presbyterian Church.

Born in Albany, New York, in 1848, McClure traced his heritage back to the Mayflower. That his family had grown wealthy in the wholesale goods business was consonant with the way money was made in Chicago; indeed McClure himself seems to have shared with the Presbyterian founders of the town something of the same drive that carried them to fortune in the West. Following an undergraduate education at Yale, where he made an exceptional record for himself as a student and student leader, he attended Princeton

Theological Seminary, served for a time as minister in New Scotland, New York (the very name of the town recalling the origins of Presbyterianism), and, consistent with his own station, married Annie P. Dixon, the daughter of Nathan Fellows Dixon, a wealthy and influential congressman from Rhode Island. McClure was thirty-one when he and his wife, having completed the socially requisite yearlong tour of Europe, settled in Lake Forest. If he stood for God and wealth, he also represented the East, the part of the country that spawned the early citizens of Lake Forest and never ceased eliciting from them and their descendants a respect bordering on envy bordering on awe.[55]

His parishioners, meanwhile, continued to conduct their worship services in the Carpenter Gothic church they had erected in 1862 at Deerpath and University Avenue.[56] Several wings had been added in the years prior to the arrival of the Reverend McClure, who began his ministry with a campaign to finance the construction of a new sanctuary for the community. One of his special talents became directly apparent. He was an accomplished fundraiser, whose effort to create not only a bigger church but one handsome enough to represent everything the town stood for, gained all the support he needed. By 1886 the salvaged black-spotted blocks of limestone that had made up the walls of the old Second Presbyterian Church in Chicago (Patterson's old shrine, destroyed in the fire of 1871), had been purchased and brought to Lake Forest.[57] There they formed the base of an arresting new structure designed by Henry Ives Cobb and Charles Frost, both later residents of Lake Forest and already among Chicago's best-trained and most accomplished architects.[58] The Cobb-Frost building bore little resemblance in either manner or substance to any other institutional

George Kennan (1845–1924) lectured at the University in 1891 and 1892 about his travels in Russia. His nephew, Sovietologist George F. Kennan, who himself would speak at the College ninety years later, is the future President Hotchkiss's uncle.

1886

**President Roberts arrives for a tenure that will see implementation of three professional schools in Chicago and further doctoral work in Lake Forest.**

1888

**Professor Locy "has recently received ten Zeiss microscopes, costing $450, imported from Germany for his Biology class," the *Stentor* reports.**

edifice in the village. Not as tall as University Hall, it was patently more sophisticated, without a trace of the vernacular obvious even in that most ambitious of the University's buildings. Cobb and Frost had a generous budget at their disposal, and they responded with a piece of work conceived in the coolly but elegantly simple Shingle Style in vogue at the time among the better architects of the East.

The sermon marking the dedication of the church in June of 1887 was delivered – fittingly – by the Reverend Patterson,[59] who in effect passed the baton of leadership to the congregation's thirty-nine-year-old pastor. As the 1880s turned into the 1890s, James McClure became the idol of the town, a preacher whose personal charm matched his social position. He was a master moderator in all things, of getting on well with all the people he met and teaching them to get on with each other. If he officiated at the sumptuous wedding in 1884 of the unchurchly Charles B. Farwell's daughter Anna Farwell to Reginald De Koven, his sermons could also celebrate the ideal of the simple life and orthodox beliefs evoked by Timothy Dwight in *Greenfield Hill.* Serving from 1889 onward as a trustee of the University by virtue of his pastorate, he proved especially adroit in turning the attention of the town and the school away from issues that divided them toward ends they could share.

The construction in 1891 of the Henry C. Durand Art Institute was evidence enough of that. It was built for the Lake Forest Art Institute Club, an organization headed by Walter Larned, a local lawyer and the art critic of the *Chicago Daily News,* who oversaw the use of the building as a venue for lectures, art exhibitions, programs at the University, and appropriate social occasions.[60] In turn, its significance to the University was spelled out in the

school catalog: "It contains a large and finely appointed hall for Commencement and other public exercises, rooms for Art and Archaeological library and collections, lecture and class rooms. In grace of style, in perfection of material and finish, in location, this monument of Mr. Durand's generosity can not be surpassed."

Indeed, the Durand Art Institute was as architecturally ambitious as the First Presbyterian Church, which it faced, and symbolically addressed, rising from the same campus space on which the Academy had stood before the fire of 1879. It too was designed by Henry Ives Cobb, who in the same year, 1891, became the first architect retained by the newly re-created University of Chicago.[61] Cobb executed the Institute in red sandstone, employing the same rugged Romanesque manner that the distinguished Henry Hobson Richardson of Boston had turned into a veritable national style during the 1880s.[62] While Cobb's building is one of the best surviving examples in the Chicago area of the Richardsonian Romanesque, it is a no less compelling material reminder of James McClure's special ability to reconcile the purposes of town and gown.

By persuading Henry C. Durand to provide most of the money for the edifice named after him, McClure managed to return a degree of civic importance to the corner of Deerpath and University Avenue, nearer the location of the earliest institutional buildings of the town, while remaining equally mindful of the needs of the University and its campus a quarter mile south. In his capacity as a member of the University's board of trustees, he persuaded his fellow trustees to underwrite several additional structures, all done by Cobb & Frost in a variety of manners but in an abiding command of style that suggested an increase of urbanity in the overall

1891

The forty-voice-strong University Male Chorus presents a program of patriotic war songs on May 29, 1891 – the evening before Decoration Day and just a month after the official opening of the new gymnasium, where the program was held. (George W. Root was the well-known Chicago composer.) Pictured here is the announcement for a repeat performance in Waukegan.

Lake Forest College, Lake Forest, Ill. 24241

architectural image of the community. Two faculty residences executed in the English Arts and Crafts mode, one named for William Bross, a ranking member of the editorial staff of the *Chicago Tribune* (and president of the University board during the Roberts years), the other for the wealthy lumber baron Jacob Beidler, went up in 1889 and 1891, respectively, east of University Hall. In 1890 a new gymnasium, designed by Cobb and financed by Charles B. Farwell (soon to be the president of the board), rose on a space nearby.[63] A more modest example of the Richardsonian Romanesque than the Durand Art Institute, this last effort was equipped with an indoor swimming pool, at the time a rare recreational advantage for an athletic facility.

Nor did McClure's interest in the physical aspect of both town and academe end there. In 1892–93, upon the departure of the Reverend Roberts, he was named acting president of the University, whereupon he became the chief force in launching the biggest construction project yet undertaken in Lake Forest, the relocation of the Academy to a plot of land south of University Hall, on the west side of University Avenue.[64] Four separate structures went up — a substantial central unit called Reid Hall and three dormitories, the entire ensemble bearing another architectural signature of distinction, the firm of Pond & Pond of Chicago.[65] All the buildings were of brick, done in a hybrid English cottage style. Reid Hall dominated, a rather splendid, sprawling pile with a tall, gabled middle tract given over to a chapel and topped by a Tudor bell tower. The full complex, laid out by the

noted landscape architect Ossian Simonds[66] and embellished with a football field and several tennis courts, overlooked a campus comparably scaled and all in all as visible as that of the University. McClure had taken further pains to upgrade the Academy scholastically, granting it a faculty separate from that of the University, and reconstituting it in the Eastern preparatory mold, with Phillips Exeter Academy of Andover, Massachusetts, a school he himself had attended, as a model. The old Academy building meanwhile was transferred to the University and renamed North Hall.

These accomplishments, secular and clerical and in all cases ambitious, were effected while McClure remained pastor of the First Presbyterian Church. His influence in Lake Forest derived in large part from that position, which he negotiated expertly enough that the townspeople had seen no one better suited to the post of acting president of the University. In little more than a decade of residence in Lake Forest, he had become a man most highly regarded by a community that was — for the time being — reunited in the spirit of its founding fathers.

1892

According to the November 8 *Stentor* the Lake Forest Art Institute's principal subject for the season is to be the World's Columbian Exhibition, including talks by William LeBaron Jenny on its architecture and Larado Taft on its sculpture.

**Above.** Alexander M. Candee, Class of 1892, attended the University 1888–91, and graduated from Princeton in 1892. His scrapbook, comprising 250 items, provides a rich look at student life of the period.

**Center.** Pictured is his room, perhaps – as suggested by the transom – in College (later Young) Hall. Notable are the substantial work table, the guitar, and the many notes pinned to the door, some of which in time no doubt made it into his voluminous scrapbook.

**Below.** The Class of 1891 as freshmen. Among those pictured are Mary Allen Davies (back row, fourth from left), valedictorian; local resident Juliet Rumsey (third row, standing center); and 1891 football captain Neptune Blood William Gallway (back row, far right).

# The Catalytic
# President Coulter

1893—1896

In the history of Chicago, Lake Forest, and Lake Forest University, together and separately, no decade stands out more sharply in relief than the 1890s. All three communities experienced change of an order profound enough to affect their identities down to the present day.

In the course of those years Chicago could point to a striking number of achievements that accelerated its commercial momentum while adding a cultural dimension that prompted it to measure itself against the world and conclude that it deserved to be called a great city with a still greater future.

The perspectives of Lake Forest and its young University were necessarily more limited, but no less perceptibly altered by circumstance and intent, as both the town and the school that had grown up together were markedly transformed. The result was a more complex set of relationships within each and between both.

1891

The Chicago Orchestra, under the baton of Theodore Thomas, is formed. In 1912 it will be renamed the Chicago Symphony Orchestra.

1892

The University of Chicago opens, backed by the financial weight of John D. Rockefeller.

1893

Hiram Stanley (1857–1903), Class of 1881, the University's first full-time librarian, produces a printed catalog of the collection.

In 1893, the attention of the entire country was riveted on Chicago, as the World's Columbian Exposition opened along the lakefront on the city's South Side. Everything about the fair was outsized – its planning, its scale, its ambition, and its immediate and long-lasting influence. Seventy-two countries were represented, and on a 600-acre tract of reconstituted marshland laid out by Frederick Law Olmsted, no fewer than 150 buildings were put up, one of them, the Manufactures and Liberal Arts Building, advertised at the time as the largest building in the world. The Exposition was also noteworthy in the attitude it struck – uncommon for its day – toward women in American culture. The Woman's Building, the only major structure on the grounds that was the result of a competition, was designed by a young graduate of the Massachusetts Institute of Technology, Sophia G. Hayden, and embellished with a large mural by the renowned American expatriate Impressionist Mary Cassatt. Twenty-seven million visitors made their way through the gates of the Fair, a number equal to two-fifths of the entire population of the country.

In concept the Exposition was meant as a salute to America's nationhood on the 400th anniversary of the landing of Columbus (it was a year late in fulfilling that schedule). Many historians who regard it as as the beginning of the City Beautiful movement cite it as a historic model of urban order.[1] The Fair's supervisor, Chicago architect Daniel Burnham, shared that view, claiming that it might serve to inspire the replacement of what he called "the jumble of buildings that surrounds us in our new cities."[2]

Burnham was already one of the figures responsible for the growing global reputation of Chicago-based architecture and its innovations in the expression of the newest technology in building design. In 1889 the Auditorium Building, a massive edifice designed by the partnership of Dankmar Adler and Louis Sullivan as a combination opera house, luxury hotel, and office building, had drawn national attention to the city as well as to itself. The first tall structure built on a metal frame, a milestone in the evolution of the skyscraper, went up in downtown Chicago in 1884–85, after plans by William LeBaron Jenney.[3]

These were only several signs of a large-scale civic awakening. In 1893, the Art Institute of Chicago moved into lavish new quarters on Michigan Avenue, its hopes of taking its place among the country's leading museums based upon the patronage of a generation of commercially aggressive and newly wealthy Chicago collectors. Sponsored by local citizens with kindred civic ambitions, the Chicago Symphony Orchestra was founded in 1891. The following year witnessed the opening of the new University of Chicago, supported in large part by no less a financial heavyweight than John D. Rockefeller, and driven by the ambition, surprisingly swift in its realization, to take its place among the country's foremost academic institutions. As the century drew to a close, Chicago had become more than a large city with an exploding population. Its aspirations to become eventually the nation's premier metropolis could point to a record of apparent, even palpable, success.

Reverberations of the new Chicago were felt in Lake Forest, perhaps most obviously at the domestic level, where citizens could be seen taking a consciously active interest in the arts that went hand in hand with an increase in social ambitions. The town's residences were adorned with paintings and sculptures shown at the Columbian Exposition and esteemed because many of them presumably came from Europe, where, it was taken for granted, the best art had long been made.

In fact, the attraction of things cultural had already started earlier; the Fair only encouraged it. The programs at the Durand Art Institute had been going on since 1892,[4] and even in the late 1880s the tireless Anna Farwell De Koven promoted and contributed to two literary periodicals sponsored by her father, *The Rambler* and *America*. Her efforts, and those of her husband, Reginald De Koven, began to bear demonstrable fruit in the 1890s as his operetta *Robin Hood*, composed in 1888–89, was favorably received by international audiences.[5] This recognition led her to recall, by contrast, a conversation of the same years with her father and a banker member of the De Koven family in which both men, as she later wrote, "expressed the opinion that music should be considered a diversion and should not be seriously followed."[6] But it *was* followed seriously,

by De Koven himself, who, at the turn of the decade to the 1890s, wrote a series of articles in *America* that helped to pave the way for the founding of the Chicago Symphony.[7]

Clearly, a subtext is implicit in Anna Farwell's anecdote. Chicago, the erstwhile slough of crudity from which the early Lake Foresters sought refuge, had in certain crucial respects overtaken some of the later Lake Foresters — surely if cultural accomplishment counts for as much as mercantilistic striving.

Yet taken together, the Lake Forest townspeople were no longer subject so readily to one-dimensional characterization. A new generation was making itself felt in the mid-1890s, shortly after Anna Farwell's banker relative commented so demeaningly on music as a professional calling. The latter-day breed,

altogether ambitious enough, were motivated more by the self-conscious pursuit of fashion and social cachet than were their predecessors, who by contrast seemed on the outside more businesslike, on the inside more piously proper. The earlier emphasis on the home and family, on habits of temperance and close connections with neighbors — friends of similar station and Presbyterian faith, of course — had begun to give way to the predilections of people of more heterogeneous background, whose recent commercial success prompted them to take the summer air in Lake Forest while maintaining their winter homes in Chicago. They tended to jockey for social position among themselves, all the while evincing a new interest in the diversions and fancies of a far wider world than the older folks knew.

Many of them had already been abroad more than once, consorting with the social elites of Europe and the East Coast, and they yearned to imitate the life they had seen and to create a community based on their lately gained ideals. This ambition was most overtly apparent in their attitudes toward social pleasures and recreation. They cultivated golf,[8] a sport still foreign to Chicago and one that, if Scottish in origin, had hardly commanded the attention of older Lake Forest citizens like Devillo Holt, who already harbored, even nursed, a low opinion of cardplaying, theater-going, dancing, and other worldly frivolities.[9] The new socialites also grew interested in the game of polo,[10] which they associated with the aristocracy, and they wanted to play it themselves or see it played in Lake Forest.

It made only the best kind of sense that the Onwentsia Club was formed in 1895[11] as a social organization whose stress on exclusivity of membership caused other Chicago communities to pay the Club the kind and

1892–94

1893

George Holt (1852–1924), son of town and university founder Devillo Holt and secretary of the Board of Trustees (1892–94) at the time of the initial discussions with the University of Chicago about a possible merger, which Holt supports. Soon after discussions fail, Holt leaves the Board.

President Coulter arrives in Lake Forest and directly institutes an elective system for the curriculum – the last of the important academic innovations introduced by the school's early presidents.

Rose Farwell Chatfield-Taylor (1870–1918), Class of 1890, painted by Beaux-Arts trained English painter John Elliott. Among her post-college activities was a course of study in fine book binding in Paris, followed by the establishment of the Rose Bindery in the Fine Arts Building on South Michigan Avenue. On the lawn of the family's Fairlawn estate, where a small seven-hole course had been created as early as 1892, Rose learned golf, six years later winning the Western Women's Golf Championship.

English. There is only a touch of hyperbole in the comparison of Lake Forest at the turn of the century with a small but well-controlled social empire, especially as, in the next decade, the great estates and stately homes now associated with the community began appearing in and around it.

It was ever so much a changed community that Grace (Farwell) McGann, Class of 1888, reflected upon in a 1919 memoir,[12] and she deplored what she saw. Though the sister of Anna Farwell and the daughter of the relatively free-thinking Charles Farwell, she was a social conservative who did not cherish the changes in mores that were everywhere about her. Arthur Meeker, a perceptive social commentator writing in 1955, recalled her response: "Mrs. McGann, unfortunately for her peace of mind, lived on into another era, when the doughty patricians she knew were swallowed up by a horde of ambitious newcomers. She viewed, not with alarm — for whom had she to fear? — but with weary disgust the disaster she conceived had overtaken her beloved village, invaded by well-heeled climbers from the wrong side of the tracks, some of whom were Democrats or even, *horribile dictu*, Roman Catholics. Cassandra-like she brooded over the ruins, denouncing each fresh enormity of the Philistines with a kind of gloomy relish. I have heard her exclaim dramatically: 'They came to dig our ditches, and stayed to marry our daughters!' This, in a literal sense, was untrue, but somehow caught the spirit of the changing times."[13]

The contrary view had its own unapologetic corps of champions. If the Onwentsia Club was the physical embodiment of what the new class of Lake Foresters represented, Hobart Chatfield [*sic*] Chatfield-Taylor[14] was their most assertive leader and, in fact, the figure chiefly responsible for the founding of the Club. Unburdened by modesty, Chatfield-Taylor might well have agreed with Arthur Meeker's judgment of him: "doesn't the name *sound* like a snob's?"[15] He was fully content to take pride in the role he played in the life of the town as well as of Chicago. Born to money in the city,[16] he married Rose Farwell, Class of 1890, Grace and Anna's sister, and moved to Lake Forest, where he not only personified the values his sister-in-law detested, but endeavored to convert them into an enviable lifestyle. Chatfield-Taylor was well read, well

degree of respect the new Lake Foresters presumed they deserved. Onwentsia opened on the west side of the railroad, where there was room enough for a golf course, riding stables, and a clubhouse of appropriate size and elegance. Yet still more space was needed to accommodate a pastime that ranked highest in the new Lake Forest's emulation of things English: fox hunting. To this end some of the club members acquired land farther to the west and later to the north of the old town boundaries. Insofar as the building of Onwentsia was the first major deviation from the purposely closed space of Almerin Hotchkiss's 1857 plan, it affected physical movement around the town as well as social mobility within it. The belief in the simpler village life to which the citizens aspired in the earlier years was exchanged for an emphasis on the country life of a new landed gentry — "county," as it was called by the spoken, and well connected, and he, more than anyone else, knew it and savored it. His own self-image as well as the life he admired may be discerned from a passage in one of the numerous books he wrote,[17] *Cities of Many Men.* Recalling a ball he had personally staged in Adler & Sullivan's formidable new Auditorium Building in Chicago, as an event related to the Columbian Exposition, he wrote, "This task performed, [John Philip] Sousa, on a sign from me, raised his baton; whereupon the most imposing array of personages Chicago has ever beheld filed in slow procession into the Auditorium, to dazzle with gorgeous costumes, stunning uniforms, and glittering decorations eyes unaccustomed not only to the sight of Orientals in court-dress, but to that of stately diplomats as well, with orders on their breasts, swords at their sides, and cocked hats in hand."[18] Beyond testifying to Chatfield-Taylor's view of his own authority, the excerpt is a reminder that Chicago's very taste for pomp and circumstance was a sign of the distance the city had traversed since its days as a frontier trading town.

Meanwhile, Lake Forest University also seemed poised on the brink of an expanding destiny, as no less eminent a figure than John Merle Coulter,[19] president of Indiana University and by consensus well on his way to becoming one of the world's most distinguished botanists, was appointed in 1893 to succeed President Roberts. Coulter entertained many if not more of the same academic ambitions as his two predecessors, and it is safe to say that the service of the three men, as an ensemble, in a brief fifteen years encapsulated the sweeping changes that had affected American higher education over the previous half-century. Gregory and Roberts had introduced, after the German model, new undergraduate and graduate programs, with a growing emphasis on science, and the Chicago professional schools as well.

It was left to President Coulter to activate at Lake Forest the last and perhaps the most reorienting innovation: the elective system. Inaugurated by President Charles William Eliot of Harvard University (where Coulter, whenever he had the opportunity, worked with the leading scientists of the day),[20] the college curriculum as we now know it, a flexible program with a range of choice in departmental majors, was announced by Coulter himself in the Lake Forest University catalog issued shortly after his arrival:

*At the beginning of the academic year 1893–94 the College curriculum was reorganized. As the changes involved are somewhat fundamental they deserve a brief explanation. The earlier American curriculum prescribed work throughout the four undergraduate years, consisting mainly of Greek, Latin and Mathematics, with a modicum of Philosophy and textbook science, supplemented by various miscellaneous subjects. When the great subjects of Philosophy, Modern Literature, History, Social and Political Science, and the Science of Nature, assumed such form as to make them worthy of collegiate study, they were admitted in small amounts by reducing the time given to the older subjects. The number of subjects to be introduced presently became so great that it was no longer possible to divide the time among them and secure effective work. Relief was sought by distributing college subjects among two or three rigid courses; and still further by putting work into two categories, that which was required of all students in the prescribed courses, and that which was elective. It was still felt by many that too many subjects [were] being demanded of students, and too little time given to any of them for the best results. Prompted by this feeling the work of the College has been reorganized and attempted to secure both the advantage of few subjects and continuous work, and also the flexibility which recognizes individual aptitudes and tastes.*

Lake Forest University was ready for the twentieth century.

1895

**The University's first fraternity, Phi Pi Epsilon, is organized.**

1895

**Henry Ives Cobb and his wife, Emma, deed their 175-acre farm and house to the Onwentsia Club. The largest house in Lake Forest when it was completed two years earlier, it will serve handsomely as the clubhouse for more than thirty years.**

53

Questions arise directly: How had Acting President McClure managed to lure so renowned an academic as Coulter to Lake Forest? And why – in view of the tensions that he must have known had already arisen between the University's ambitious presidents and some of its more conservative trustees? Perhaps McClure himself was driven by the impetus that had so altered the course of the University during the immediate past. Certainly Coulter could only have been taken with the prospects generated by that momentum, which had reached full force with his predecessor's presidency. Reporting on conditions at the time of Roberts's departure from Lake Forest, Coulter's biographer Andrew Denny Rodgers III argues accordingly:

*Lake Forest's Board of Trustees had sought for some time to obtain Coulter's services. It was thought that if only Coulter could be induced to come the institution's problems would be solved, and Lake Forest could go forward with plans to make it one of the great universities of the West, indeed of the nation. Coulter had salesmanship, prominence, polish as a lecturer, the scholarship of a scientist, proven administrative ability, and was a churchman of high standing. He could raise money. He could promote the large ambitions of the university better than anyone of their knowledge. The University of Chicago was then a comparatively small institution of Baptist affiliations. Northwestern had not yet attained a ranking of large proportions and was under Methodist domination. Lake Forest University was to be the great school to provide the growing, great city of Chicago with educational facilities the equivalent of those had by New York, Philadelphia, and Boston. The board of trustees secured Coulter and then left him to his task.* [21]

Thereupon, however, Rodgers added a portentous note: "A large and almost impossible task it proved to be."

And so it did. Yet Coulter appears to have labored greatly to carry it through successfully, at least in the early phase of his eventually short-lived term. He turned out to be everything Lake Forest and its University might have expected of him, and then some, which included a knack for socializing with the townspeople as easily as McClure had. He opened his home to meetings of the townspeople of the local University Club, the forum at which lectures and discussions covering a wide variety of topics were standard fare in the 1890s.[22] His pioneering work in what would become known as plant

succession ecology made a lasting impression on the families of Lake Forest, particularly the women members, several of whom studied with him in a special summer session at the University.[23] Harriet Hammond McCormick, the wife of Cyrus Jr., was unsurpassed in her devotion, applying what she had learned about ecology from Coulter in the cultivation of property she and her husband had lately bought on the Lake Forest bluff overlooking Lake Michigan.[24]

Coulter, we may assume, knew enough to recognize and respond to the difference between a large state university like Indiana and a small, flourishing private one like Lake Forest. Yet he was before all else the professional scientist, as the program he lost no time in fashioning at the University reflected. He was, moreover, an articulate and persuasive speaker. In his inaugural address of June 15, 1893, he made a vigorous case not only for the imperative of learning as a whole but for the kind of logical thinking that is the bedrock of science. He was especially hard on what he regarded as superstition, identifying it in sweeping terms: "It permeates all business, makes demagoguery possible, and is the foundation of the most of religious cant."[25]

It is unclear how the Presbyterians in his audience reacted to this observation, which could be easily interpreted as casting aspersions on that double-sided ethos of Lake Forest, devotion to the Almighty and to commerce. But Coulter brought his speech close to an end with mollification enough: "Therefore, while all the varying beliefs and disbeliefs must meet here on perfect equality, as is befitting an intellectual community seeking for truth in every direction, we must all unite in *one* belief, that the only kind of life worth living is that one which is governed by the highest moral principles. As for myself, I find the best statement of these principles in the utterances of the great Nazarene . . . ."

Thus the new president, a son of missionaries, saw no conflict between genuine science and earnest religion. A Christian hungry for enlightenment could rest assured that the University had been entrusted to a man mentally well disciplined but also a man of faith. Coulter the botanist did not believe in miracles, but Coulter the Christian remained distrustful of the theory of evolution as late as 1878.[26] (He would help lead the national Young Men's Christian Association movement and later taught a men's Bible class at a Presbyterian church on Chicago's South Side, frequently occupying the pulpit.)[27] He had, furthermore, a good deal to say publicly about the relevance of religion to the kind of institution he headed in Lake Forest, and his trustees must have been gratified to hear him say, early in 1894, "It is easier to utilize denominational organizations than any others in the development of colleges, and such a method has its educational reason as well, in that it appeals to those of similar tastes, similar habits of thought, similar conceptions of education. The logic of the situation demands the development at Lake Forest of the strongest Presbyterian college in the west."[28]

Such sentiments would seem in accord with the intentions of the town's founding fathers, and Coulter followed

them up with proposals for new buildings on the Lake Forest campus.[29] Nonetheless, when he referred, as he regularly did, to Lake Forest *College*, he meant it as part of the total University, which consisted, as he also regularly made clear, of five other parts: Ferry Hall Seminary, Lake Forest Academy, Rush Medical College, Chicago College of Dental Surgery, and Chicago College of Law. His conscious commitment to the latter three institutions among the total of six further signified his long-standing dedication to professional and graduate education and, by inference, to the German model that had engendered the intramural debates of the 1880s.

Shortly after his arrival, Coulter could have cited ample reasons for believing that the institution he headed might well anticipate a hopeful future. The growing emphasis on science, which he favored, was both exemplified and enhanced by new faculty appointments that resulted partly from the new departmental organization he had supervised. By 1896, where once there had usually been one professor per subject, there were now two in German, three in English, two in Economics, two in Physics, two in Chemistry, two in Zoology and — unsurprisingly — three in Botany.[30] Enrollments had risen. The number of students in the customarily small doctoral programs showed a gratifying increase to about a dozen, while some 120 undergraduates doubled that constituency of the student population of the 1880s. The professional schools in Chicago, meanwhile, always well attended, enjoyed an enrollment of close to 2,000.[31]

These palpable assets notwithstanding, there were more than a few liabilities to match them. A measure of uneasiness continued in the minds of the Lake Forest townsmen and their confreres on the Board of Trustees who did not share Coulter's grand vision, and who had never surrendered the notion of a small baccalaureate

1895

Harriet Hammond McCormick (d. 1921), wife of Cyrus Jr. (shown in her wedding gown), is among the early Lake Forest residents to take a summer course in botany taught by President Coulter in 1895. In landscaping her lakefront Lake Forest estate, she utilizes principles of plant succession ecology that would be published in 1899 by Coulter's protégé Alfred Cowles of the University of Chicago. In this period (1892–98) the McCormicks are Lake Forest University's leading donors after Henry C. Durand.

## From the Coulter Years, Two Leaders in Medical Science: Charles Thom and Dean Dewitt Lewis

Even though Lake Forest had fewer than 200 students in the early 1890s, the biology/botany faculty grew to four members, plus President Coulter himself. One result of this extraordinary concentration was the training and calling of two biological scientists, each of whom would make significant contributions to the advancement of medicine as it moved away from its pre-twentieth-century practitioner-based speculations. These two alumni were Charles Thom and Dean Dewitt Lewis, both of the Class of 1895, with careers in antibiotics and surgery, respectively.

Thom (1872–1956) was not an M.D. but a Ph.D. in Biology – in 1899 the first degree in that field granted by the University of Missouri. This would not be his only pioneering achievement. As part of the reform era commitment to improving food safety, Thom testified in court cases about sanitary practices, eventually writing *Hygienic Fundamentals of Food Handling* in 1924. Also in the early 1900s, he began working on fungi at Cornell, an interest that had begun at Lake Forest under Professor R. A. Harper. This experience led to positions with the U.S. Department of Agriculture, where, working on the microbiology of cheese production, he became (according to a biographical sketch at the time of his death) "the world's undisputed authority on *penicillium*," the mold Sir Alexander Fleming used to usher in the period of modern antibiotics. In World War II, after retirement, Thom led the American arm of the effort to develop further such antibodies.

Dean Dewitt Lewis (1874–1941) received his M.D. degree from Rush Medical College in 1899, at the time when it was affiliated with the University of Chicago. Soon he was an assistant professor in anatomy there. After work in microscopic analysis and study at Leipzig, he advanced eventually to the rank of full professor. During World War I he served in emergency hospitals specializing in reconstructive and neurological surgery, for which he was decorated. He was the founding editor of the journal *Archives of Surgery*, participating in it from 1920 to 1940, and by the mid 1920s he was chief of surgery at Johns Hopkins, arguably the senior post in the land. While in that position he held a term as president (1933–34) of the American Medical Association.

1895

The *Stentor*, October 1, 1895: "The doors of the College were opened for a summer session the first time in the history of Lake Forest University, June 18.... Thirty students were enrolled, and carried on regular or special work with a zest and earnestness that would be hard to equal in the regular College year."

school free of graduate or professional involvements. A similar sentiment was entertained by some of the faculty as well. Hiram M. Stanley, Class of 1881,[32] a respected librarian and professor of English and, not incidentally, a member of an old Lake Forest family,[33] published an article in 1894 in *The Dial*,[34] expressing himself with open animus on the subject of science and its effects on the higher learning in America: "Just now *parvenu* science, crass, boorish, and overbearing, as the *parvenu* generally is, has got the upper hand in education. Hence we see in literary education, as everywhere else, the undue stress laid on the scientific method, and literature constantly and dominantly interpreted from the standpoints of anthropology, psychology, history, and philology." However immoderate Stanley's rhetoric, he captured the flavor of the academically conservative viewpoint that ran counter to many of the latter-day reforms. Despite Coulter's proposals, not to mention his demonstrable professional virtues and personal charm, the issue of the direction and compass of the University remained unresolved as the 1890s wore on.

The gravity of the situation finally impressed itself upon Coulter as he confronted two major disappointments: more burdensome administrative duties than he had anticipated and the growing weight of indifference to his academic efforts from many of the townsmen on whose financial backing he had counted when he accepted the presidency. (Some of that support may have been withheld because of the Depression of 1894 and the distractions created among the businessmen by the violent Pullman strike of the same year.)[35] By 1895 a crisis of sorts had developed, whose resolution turned on relations with the University of Chicago, specifically its bold new president, William Rainey Harper,[36] and, more distantly, its immensely wealthy patron, Rockefeller.

This circumstance too had a history, which began even prior to Coulter's arrival. Minutes of the December 23, 1892, meeting of the Board of Trustees of Lake Forest University note that Dr. McClure and Dr. Herrick Johnson had reported on the "substance of interviews" with Dr. Harper, and that Dr. Johnson then read the proposition by the University of Chicago for an "alliance" of the two institutions.[37] Following discussion, a motion was passed that a committee of five (Messrs. Farwell, McClure, McPherson, McCormick, and Bouton) be appointed to meet a comparable committee from Chicago "for the purpose of submitting this matter in clearer shape to the Board for its consideration...."

Coulter had not yet taken office when, in January of 1893, the "alliance" was more precisely defined by the subcommittee representing both schools.[38] Simply put, the proposals pertinent to Lake Forest were these: All the schools that made up Lake Forest University, undergraduate and professional, would be combined in a single university, the University of Chicago. Lake Forest College would be regarded as strictly an undergraduate institution, one of a number in the larger Chicago area – hitherto unrelated but now all on equal footing and subject to the authority of the University and the chancellor of the University.

In fact Coulter himself may well have had personal dealings with the University of Chicago while he was still at Indiana University. Once he learned of Harper's intentions to build a formidable university – with the no less redoubtable financial assistance of Rockefeller – his professional interest certainly could have been engaged. "It is said on good authority," biographer Rodgers reports, "that one of the reasons why Coulter was induced to leave Indiana University was a projected plan whereby post-graduate study was to be established at

Pertinent to financial matters at this time and mentioned in President McClure's 1898–99 budget report is the Jacob Beidler Endowment, which included this 1889 building at 530 and 532 West Madison Street in Chicago: "Eight-ninths of the income from this property goes towards the salary of the Jacob Beidler Professor of Physics and Chemistry, and the other one-ninth is used in assisting needy students who have in view the ministry of evangelical churches." The endowment then is $497,000, including $45,000 for this property and $100,000 for other real estate – roughly one-third of the total. With the decline of the Madison Street neighborhood in the next few decades, these properties' values may have shrunk enough to have affected earnings, especially by the late 1940s

# Herodotus on the Great University

In a lively example of sophomoric wit of the 1890s, a *Stentor* article, dated January 14, 1896, comments on the plan to merge with the University of Chicago.

"Speaking of universities," said Herodotus to a reporter for the *Gun:* "Did I ever tell you my experience in the educational line? I do not enjoy thinking it over, for it finally drove me from Greece, but as Vergil used to say 'vice versa.' There was an educational boom in Greece. A merchant grown enormously rich by raising the price of olive-oil gathered together about twenty talents and decided to start a university. He appointed me president and instructed me to make a big thing of it. 'It must be the biggest novelty in all Greece, Herodotus,' he said, 'and you are just the man to make it such.'

"So I went ahead, and in a few months the university was running full blast; but newspapers are costly things to buy up, so when the buildings were completed and the first year's salaries paid the talents were gone.

"Something had to be done. Another talent was coaxed from my friend of the olives and it went into 'ads.' There were all kinds of 'ads,' editorials, front-pagers, prospect 'ads,' great discovery 'ads' and puffs, till the name of the Great Athens University had penetrated into the farthest wilds of Boeotia. Then a happy thought came to me. I wrote to the three most fashionable nobles of Attica:

"Dear Sir: Accept our profoundest gratitude for your gift of thirty talents. Enclosed find receipt. Keep mum and oblige. Yours as ever, President H_____.

"The next morning's papers were filled with the account of the munificence of the aforesaid three gentlemen and that afternoon contributions began to flow into our treasury.

"The fashion had been set and all the would-be swells in Athens felt compelled to give. From that time on all was plain sailing. The money came so plentifully that we had to request donors to hand in their gifts at certain fixed times and finally we arranged it so that a talent came in every Saturday night in time for the Sunday morning papers. Yes, it was plain sailing. We had chairs of more things than one could think of, even had he a hundred lungs and a tongue of brass. There were chairs of theology and chiropody and amanuensis, of metallurgy and South African literature. Professorships in all the dialects of Greece and the Fiji islands, in fencing and gastronomy as well as millinery, in bovine anatomy, and naval architecture. We had five schools of metathesis, twenty-nine professors of music, and thirteen endowed janitorships.

"But, alas, those old times can never come back. How did it end up? Well that is rather a delicate matter to talk about, but the end was something like this: After we had affiliated every school within two hundred parasangs, and attained a membership of something within a million, I lost my head. The three original patrons and my olive-oil friend, who had considered themselves a general supervising board of trustees, wanted me to remove the head professor of domestic economy and I thought the time had come for me to assume entire control. So I dissolved the committee. The story of the thirty talents was given to the public and there was an explosion. The twenty thousand patrons of the university rose to a man and demanded my death, while the eleven hundred respective chairs were dragged one by one from the buildings, the 'isms' were dispersed, and in three hours the buildings had 'for sale' signs in their windows.

"The university was no more. That night I slipped out of the safe, where I was concealed, and left Greece for ever. But that was a long time ago, and there is very little left of the ninety talents I carried with me."

William Rainey Harper (right), founding president of the University of Chicago, walking with his famous benefactor, John D. Rockefeller.

the University of Chicago and undergraduate study at Lake Forest College, all under the supervision of Coulter...."[39]

That account rests partly on speculation. Another question, fetching to ask if thus far not certainly answerable, pertains to the extent to which the attractiveness of a merger may have been played by the coeducational status, unusual for its time, of not just one but both schools. These issues notwithstanding, the reactions in Lake Forest to the prospects of a merger are more reliably known. In a letter of January 9, 1893, written to the chairman of the Board of Trustees of Lake Forest University, Board Secretary George H. Holt wrote:

*My understanding of the present situation as now conceived as proposed by Chicago University is,*

*The Lake Forest Faculty, with the exception of Profs. Halsey, Thomas, and Dawson, incline to favor union.*

*The students, Alumni, and official Presbyterians generally, with such information as they have, deprecate it.*

*The larger Presbyterian public and outside public, and many of the faculty of the Chicago University and its students, favor union.*

*The objections are: 1. Baptist control; 2. Overshadowing importance; 3. Loss of individuality.*[40]

A number of documents in the Lake Forest College archives enlarge on Holt's summary.[41] In editorials and letters published by the student newspaper *The Red and Black* during 1892[42] (before Coulter arrived), the various factions expressed themselves, all consistent with Holt's findings. Albert E. Jack, Class of 1884 (soon to be named to a Lake Forest professorship), argued that "the fact that in less than two years, more than five million dollars

flowed into Chicago's treasury speaks well for Pres. Harper as a money getter. The indications are that still greater gifts are to follow. That Pres. Harper would use his influence to secure large gifts for us is highly probable...."[43]

On the other hand, student opinion, evident in an editorial, struck a conservative note based on a strong commitment to the idea of a college, a traditional one at that:

*But let us not forget the points in favor of a small college.... It should be borne in mind that the educational methods of Pres. Harper are radically different from those pursued here and in fact in the majority of educational institutions. Would it be well to substitute new and untried methods for those of known worth?*

*Consider then what [is] involved in this loss of our identity. The old associations would be changed and "college spirit" would become superfluous.*

And still more than that was at stake:

*Religious feeling also enters into the matter, for according to the charter of Chicago University its President and a majority of the Trustees must be Baptists.*[44]

Former President Roberts voiced his own concern. Recalling that in his inaugural address he had himself envisioned a university as a center of colleges connected with it, he added that he had never intended Presbyterian Lake Forest University to become a grouping of colleges of different denominations or "subject to the control of men of all denominations, or no denomination."[45]

The matter continued to be debated during Coulter's presidency, its conclusion forced by one overarching and highly symbolic development. Among Harper's

1896

**The *Stentor*, March 17:** "In a letter recently received from Dean D. Lewis, Class of 1895, he says: 'A multitude of medical facts is about all I have encountered since leaving Lake Forest. I was very sorry to hear that Dr. Coulter had decided to leave the institution. Of course the trustees will provide some good man and things will go smoothly.'"

1896

The trustees receive a report recommending that the institution drop its university status and "take its true position as a college."

achievements was a special endowment of $1 million intended to establish what promised to be one of the most important botanical laboratories in the United States. The chair of the Department of Botany was offered to Coulter, who accepted. On the occasion of this formal appointment, February 11, 1896, he resigned his post at Lake Forest University.[46]

Harper's gesture provided the Lake Foresters with a clear view of a cold reality that consisted not only of the vast financial resources Harper had at his command but of the dimensions of the academic plant that Harper, and Coulter, saw as constituting a modern university. The physical layout of the University of Chicago had been decided by 1893,[47] and the imposing buildings already up by 1895 on the Midway of Chicago's South Side[48] must have suggested an eventual facility of a size too huge for Lake Forest's landscape, too rich for Lake Forest's blood: in brief, an operation too expensive, too expansive.

Although Coulter's departure inevitably provoked a range of responses, any antagonism among them must have mellowed with time, given the later responses he made to invitations of the College.[49] Even so, the hopes on which he had based his presidency were, if not dashed, in large part frustrated. While he managed a far-reaching change in the College's curriculum, emphasizing science and easing the traditional grip of the humanities (though with his departure the five faculty members in Botany and Zoology were significantly reduced to *one* in Biology),[50] he accomplished little else of enduring substance to realize his ultimate ambitions. None of the buildings he proposed was ever built. More significant still – indeed its bearing on the future of the College cannot be overestimated – is an entry in the trustees' minutes of February 19, 1896, written slightly more than a week after the University of Chicago had announced his appointment. Under the heading "Recommendations," the following statement appears:

*First: Your committee recommend that the Institution abandon the claim to be a University and take its true position as a College, and to this end – (a) Terminate the connection with Rush Medical College, Chicago College of Dental Surgery, and Chicago College of Law, by giving to each six months notice before the close of the academic year, as provided by the terms*

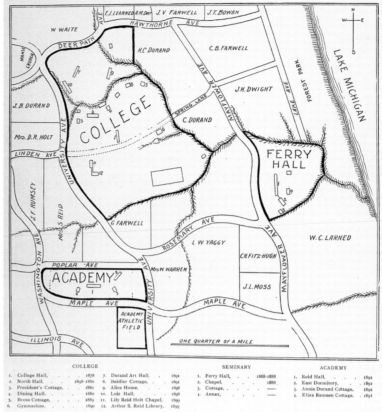

1899 map showing the three campuses and their relationship to the estates of some major donors.

*of agreements. (b) Apply to the next Legislature to change the name from Lake Forest University to Lake Forest College.*

Unstated but clearly understood was the definition of that college as a body small, unmistakably Presbyterian, and contained in an orderly and controlling fashion within Lake Forest proper. It would henceforward be an institution where gentlemen-scholars were distinctly more welcome than anyone primarily devoted to professional education[51] – something President Coulter himself had finally recognized. No less apparent, and momentous as well, was the difference that had developed during the 1890s between the determined reassertion of traditional values by the University's trustees (including such familiar names as Farwell, Holt, McClure, and McCormick) and the embrace of new commitments associated with high society by the town's club-oriented, ball-loving, foxhunting Chatfield-Taylor set. Years would pass before that gap was closed.

# The Herbarium: A Botanical Legacy

When President Coulter, editor of *The Botanical Gazette*, arrived on campus in 1893 he brought with him his world-famous 60,000-plant herbarium, having obtained plant specimens from around the globe. This collection was tended by an assistant, Mogens Christian Jensen, M.A. 1896. When Coulter left in 1896 to head the new botany program at the University of Chicago, he took the herbarium with him.

The plant loss in 1896 distressed the Lake Foresters and plans immediately got under way to replace this research and teaching tool. Jensen, remaining on the Lake Forest staff, began to collect new specimens. This 1896–97 project forms the valuable nucleus of what today is known as the Elizabeth Lunn Herbarium, a 5,000-plant collection of specimens, most of them local, housed in the Johnson Science Center. The collection is named for the late Professor Lunn, chair of the Biology Department in the 1950s, who undertook the preservation and expansion of this resource.

Much of that work was carried out by George La Roi '58, whose senior thesis, in the College archives, provides a Lake County plant list, including the remounted 1890s specimens and also the later ones. The Lunn Herbarium stands as a benchmark of known Lake County plants of the 1890s and, especially, of the 1950s, and as such is invaluable for future students of the local environment seeking information about native plants. For example, the collection has been consulted in conjunction with restoring the east end of the Mellody Farms estate, now the property of Lake Forest Open Lands, which Jens Jensen, known for using regional native plants, had landscaped in the first two decades of the century. The Herbarium helped researchers in their effort to determine which "native" plants might have been original to the "Middlefork Savannah," and which might have been introduced there, by Jensen or others.

This specimen was sent back to his alma mater by Cornelius Betten '00, then a graduate student at Cornell University, where, after teaching at Lake Forest, he later became dean of the faculty.

THE LAKE FOREST COLLEGE HERBARIUM

Scientific Name  Caltha palustris L.
(B+B-52)

Locality  Cornell Heights, Ithaca, N.Y.

Habitat

Descriptive Notes

Date  5-  1904       No.

Collected by  Cornelius Betten

Identified by  Cornelius Betten

# The Early College Campus

Clearly, the fortunes of the University in the early decades of its existence had depended first and foremost on actions taken by its administrators and by people close to it in spirit but physically apart.

Yet there remained a constituency — the students — who by the turn of the new century were playing a role surely as important to the history of the school as shifts in the educational philosophy of its presidents, the fiscal decisions of its trustees, and the influence of academic developments elsewhere. Indeed, throughout the country college students, almost unwittingly, had come to exert an unprecedented influence on the conduct of campus affairs. Just as the American university was shaped in the period following the Civil War, the modern college itself was assuming a new form at the very time Lake Forest chose to concentrate its attention on undergraduate education.[1]

1880

"Farewell! Oh happy college days, farewell!" The College is entertained by its first graduating class's song.

1882

*University Review*, May 1882: "The young men of the Senior Class, much to the astonishment of numerous small boys, made their appearance a few mornings since, decked out with the gaudiest of hats. They are made of brilliant red material, trimmed with black velvet, giving them a most dignified and at the same time captivating appearance."

In many respects the transformation was a response to the state of the national economy in the closing decades of the century. An increasingly affluent society was in a position to send its children to college, but if the parents anticipated an educational benefit for their young, many of them were inspired even more by the prospects of the social prestige such an experience was likely to bestow upon their sons and daughters and themselves. Unsurprisingly, this generation of students all too often proved lacking in the motivation that had driven their predecessors, the majority of whom had attended schools where preparation for the ministry or the professions made up the bedrock of the curriculum. More in the spirit of the times was the presumption that America owed its increasing wealth to the robust kinship of capitalism and individualism. The elective system introduced at Harvard by President Eliot and endorsed so enthusiastically by President Coulter at Lake Forest[2] was in part, paradoxically, a reflection of both factors: the attitudes of the latter-day students seen in the context of the value newly placed on individualism. The emphasis of the elective system on freedom of choice, with its corollary assumption of the sovereignty of the student to act as judge of his own best educational interests, was meant to engage the new uncommitted student body. Yet as matters turned out, the move exacted a twofold price, not only leading to the overthrow of the classical curriculum that had long governed American higher education but issuing a challenge to the very tradition of academic authority.[3]

With students more inclined to pursue careers in business and less disposed to follow the traditional disciplines, friendships – "connections" – formed in college were regarded as advantageous to later life. Bonding with one's peers in an interplay of shared social interests took on an importance in academe that had little precedent. Given these circumstances, it was only a short step to the institution of extracurricular activities, in their familiar, multifaceted form.[4]

To be sure, the shift here described hardly took effect at once. Many of the old habits and traditions mingled with the new, and some would remain in place for decades. Nonetheless, from the 1870s on, student customs and mores, student life in general, came to occupy a place

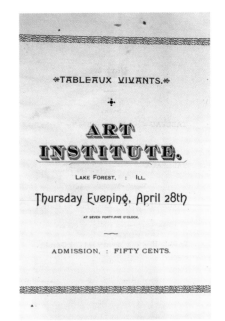

*Tableaux Vivants* program, held at Durand Art Institute, 1892. The tableaux included the "Ten Virgins," "In Love," and "The Country and City Courtship."

integral to the very identity of American universities and colleges. Lake Forest was no exception.[5]

As mentioned earlier in the account of the possible merger of Lake Forest and the University of Chicago, the students of President Coulter's College already identified closely with the school they were most immediately part of: they belonged to the College before they belonged to the University, and they were quick to point with pride to "college spirit" as both cause and effect of their allegiance.[6]

Evidence that the new values had grown appealing even earlier can be read in many of the romantic, markedly sentimental expressions of friendship and loyalty to comrades, classes, and various student organizations that were commonplace in the opening years. Composing poetry was the indulgence not of a few but of virtually all students on campus. Doggerel it may have been, but it was easy to understand, mindful of meter, and it always rhymed. The Class of 1880, the College's first graduating class, published its own class song, with words by the highly regarded salutatorian, Josephine White, and music by her classmate Charles F. Ward, Class of 1880. ("Farewell! Oh happy college days, farewell!/How bright so e'er the mystic future be/Our hearts can never feel a stronger spell/Than that which binds their love, their life to thee.")[7]

Campus activities had proliferated. Concerts were frequent, with performances usually by glee clubs; banjo, guitar, and mandolin bands; individual singers; and solo instrumentalists. Some concertizing was more than a little exotic by today's standards: ladies' and gentlemen's whistling quartets, a so-called "voluntary missionary band," and in a curious transcription, a solo trombone rendering of the baritone aria from Wagner's *Tannhäuser*, "Song to the Evening Star."[8] Wagner, in fact, and Mozart, Schubert, and Moritz Moszkowski were popular composers, with Mendelssohn more beloved still. (There is little mention of Bach or Beethoven.) Yet the classics shared space and time with minstrel shows and college sing-alongs, the latter often given over to patriotic and war songs. Generous use of the stage featured drama, *tableaux vivants*, and skits (e.g., "The Last Day of Skule"), often written by the students themselves.

One of their earliest initiatives, the formation of a literary society, followed a national trend that had begun at Yale in 1753.[9] Bearing the name Athenæan Literary Society,[10] the Lake Forest group was assembled in November of 1876, the inaugural year of the University. Its purposes were most comprehensively outlined in its constitution, which defined its "literary exercises" as "essays, declamations, orations, papers, impromptus, and discussions regular and sentimental." While the society by its very

nature functioned as an extracurricular group activity, it is well to note that the object listed as primary to its purposes — "the mental and moral improvement of its members" — was more nearly in keeping with the traditional Christian values of the institution during the 1870s and early 1880s than with the more socially minded outlook that so impelled students a generation later, at the turn of the century. Indeed, the College bulletins of the 1870s and 1880s put it in writing that students of that early period were expected to join a literary society.[11]

In 1880 two similar groups were formed: the Zeta Epsilon,[12] made up of men alone, and the Alethian,[13] only of women (thus leading the Athenæan itself to change from a membership of both sexes to males solely). Moreover, in the same year the *Lake Forest University Review* was published for the first time, its overall excellence testimony to the editorial talents of Josephine White's valedictorian classmate, the ever-versatile Anna Farwell. Quite evidently the common bond of these activities, united in their cultivation of verbal skills, was as intellectual as it was social, more nearly cocurricular than extracurricular.

Even so, for all the earnestness of the literary societies and their journalistic collateral descendants, the student newspapers *The Stentor* and *The Red and Black* (begun in 1887 and 1892, respectively), there is ample record of an opposite but compatible spirit of light self-entertainment. The official program of the "Grand Annual Flunk"[14] of the "Athenæan Literary (?) Society" listed a "Disorder of Exercises" that began with an address "written for the Society, by one of the Professors some years ago, [to] be warmed over and trilled forth by the figurehead of this clique of assassins of good English," and ended with the note that "infants in arms must positively be disarmed before they enter the house."

If the humor is sophomoric, that very word is an apt reminder that students, not just sophomores but freshmen, juniors, and seniors, identified themselves with their respective classes, engaging in an assortment of intramural rivalries[15] as fierce as they were good-natured. Each class, as well as the various societies

66

**Above.** The Athenæan Literary Society, organized in 1876 as the first such student group, was coed until 1880.

**Center.** Members of the all-male Athenæan Literary Society in 1890.

**Left below.** George W. Cable, an important New Orleans local-color author, came to the Ferry Hall campus January 30, 1892, to present a program sponsored by the Athenæan Literary Society.

**Right below.** Zeta Epsilon's constitution, 1890.

Ferry Hall, Lake Forest.

SATURDAY EVENING, JANUARY 30, 1892.

READINGS FROM HIS OWN WORKS

...BY...

Mr. Geo. W. Cable

UNDER THE AUSPICES OF THE

ATHENAEAN LITERARY SOCIETY

OF LAKE FOREST UNIVERSITY.

PROGRAM.

PART I.

1. Narcisse's Discourse on his "Handwritings."
2. Borrowing Scene. John and Mary Richling and Narcisse.
3. The Widow Riley and Narcisse. More borrowing.
4. Mrs. Riley and Richling discuss matrimony.

PART II.

1. Mrs. Riley changes her name.
2. Narcisse announces the "melancholic intelligens" of Lady Byron's death.
3. A Sound of Drums. Death of Narcisse.
4. Mary's Night Ride.

CONSTITUTION

—AND—

BY-LAWS

—OF THE—

ZETA EPSILON

LITERARY SOCIETY

—OF—

LAKE FOREST UNIVERSITY,

LAKE FOREST, ILL.

ADOPTED JANUARY, 1880.

REVISED APRIL, 1886.

REVISED OCT., 1890.

Ζητοῦμεν Ἐπιστήμην.

CHICAGO.

The Red and Black.

Left above. The *Stentor*, first issued monthly in June 1887, has been the school's longest running student publication. That it was the voice of the community as well as the campus for at least a decade, until the founding of the local newspaper *The Lake Forester* in 1896, reflects the diverging interests developing between the University and the community.

Right above. *The Red and Black*, an ambitious and university-wide weekly organ, published concurrently with the *Stentor*, was printed in Chicago and attempted to provide coverage of both Lake Forest and Chicago-based programs. Perhaps too ambitious, it survived only one year.

and clubs, had its own colors, its own motto, sometimes even its own yell (composed as often in Latin or Greek as in vernacular English).[16] Now and then the mottos, even if borrowed from outside sources, were more ingenious than simple-minded: *Verus amore, more, ore, re* ("True in love, character, word, and deed").[17]

If the literary societies reflected in large part the older values of the institution, it was only a matter of time before newer ones were manifest in athletics, an activity especially appealing to students in organized form. Pickup games of baseball presumably had provided casual entertainment in the 1870s (given the existence then of an academy ball field), but the formation of official intercollegiate teams in baseball and football occurred in 1886 and 1888.[18] Since President Roberts had taken office in 1886 – and he was the first president to make conscious reference to Lake Forest College as distinct from Lake Forest University[19] – there is reason to suspect that the school's intercollegiate program enjoyed his personal support and encouragement. In fact, a football

team had been assembled as early as 1882, but an item in the *Lake Forest University Review* of that year reporting that "the football eleven are thirsting for gore!" added that "after depriving themselves of many of the luxuries and even necessaries of life to buy uniforms, they are unable to scare up a team to play with them."[20]

The desire to compete on the field was obviously urgent. At the time, football was still a relatively new sport, especially in the Midwest.[21] Since the first intercollegiate football game, between Rutgers and Princeton, had been played just thirteen years earlier in 1869, it is not surprising that the first opponents "scared up," even after the Lake Forest team had gained official status, ranged from neighboring local high schools to universities as large as Northwestern and Wisconsin.

Baseball had originated earlier than football – though not by more than a few decades – yet it was the latter activity that captured more of the College's fancy, not least because it was commonly considered the more manly sport. Football "heroes" were so designated and readily admired, enough, in fact, to prompt the *Chicago Record-Herald* to run a feature in 1913 that celebrated Lake Forest College's football prowess (". . . when the University of Chicago first opened its doors, Coach [Amos Alonzo] Stagg's football team found Lake Forest one of its toughest customers"), citing Marion Woolsey, Class of 1896, as the College's "greatest football player," and naming Fred Hayner, Class of 1895, as "the fiercest man to down another in the West. It was he who introduced or rather invented that flying tackle which never failed to stop a man in his tracks."[22] (Especially in this context, contemporary readers may be interested in the contrast of Hayner's dimensions – six feet two, 158 pounds[23] – with those of the gridiron mastadons of the present day.)

1886–88

Official intercollegiate teams in both baseball and football are organized.

1888

An article in the May *Stentor* calls for student "representation at Faculty meetings" and for "an organization of the students themselves."

It needs adding, nonetheless, that the very Woolsey-Hayner Lake Forest College team so worthy of Coach Stagg's respect was whipped by Chicago twice running, 34–6 in 1894 and 54–0 in 1895. *The Forester*, the College's yearbook, did not shrink from the fact, but neither did it falter in its loyalty or its willingness to make a lot out of a little:

*It took a long time for Lake Forest, proud of her great record in the early nineties, to learn that she was not a great university, and with her hundred and fifty students could not hope to cope with the teams turned out by universities ten to twenty times larger in numbers. That the teams of this period, which even went through one season without scoring, were nevertheless a great credit to their Alma Mater is significantly shown by a remark in a newspaper write-up of a game in which Notre Dame rolled up a 37 to 0 score on us, to the effect that the Lake Forest team was the gamest ever seen at South Bend, and that at its weight (it was outweighed thirty pounds to the man by Notre Dame) it was undoubtedly the best team in the Middle West.*[24]

Meanwhile, basketball had been invented in 1891, on the heels of the opening in the same year of the College's gymnasium, an up-to-the-minute facility, but one ill-equipped to accommodate the new game. That, however, did not stop students, men and women alike, from playing it there, just as they used the space for baseball and even football.[25] An indoor track was more functionally suited to the building, although track and field were best pursued out of doors during the warmer months. (The times, lengths, and heights achieved by the winners of the various contests are worth a brief aside: the 100-yard dash was usually won in about 10 seconds, the long jump [called the running broad jump] at about 19 feet, the mile run in about 5 minutes, the high jump at slightly less than 6 feet.)[26] By 1898 two instructors had been hired in Physical Education, the name given a year later to a department of the faculty.

**Basic to the evolution of the American campus** experience were the conditions of residential life: where this new generation of students lived, dined, and formed friendships at the nonacademic, strictly social level suggested above. Following the construction of University Hall in 1878, a number of men occupied dormitory rooms in the upper reaches of the building, while most of

the women were housed and fed in Ferry Hall. In 1881, Mitchell Hall, the former Dickinson Seminary, located on the southeast corner of Linden Avenue (now College Road) and Washington Road, was remodeled and put into service as a dormitory for some of the women.[27] Students of both sexes meanwhile took rented quarters in local residences and ate with the families who lived there, while the humble frame house called Academia served as a dining hall for male students billeted on campus.

Two events of 1895, the formation of the Phi Pi Epsilon fraternity[28] and the founding of the Onwentsia Club,[29] also had a bearing on housing at the College and, as matters developed, on far more. That Phi Pi Epsilon was the first fraternity at Lake Forest University (to be followed in 1896 by Kappa Sigma)[30] is arguably less significant than the school's decision to allow its very existence. Though established as early as the 1820s, social fraternities had long been frowned upon by most American colleges and universities,[31] especially by those with religious affiliations, on the grounds that they were secret societies anointed with Greek names and given to mysteries and rituals alien to the Christian tradition. The Lake Forest University catalog of 1879–80 and subsequent issues specifically proscribed any such student organizations. In the words of the famed academician Mark Hopkins, "the influences of fraternities have been evil. They create class and factions, and put men socially in regard to each other into an artificial and false position. . . . The alienation

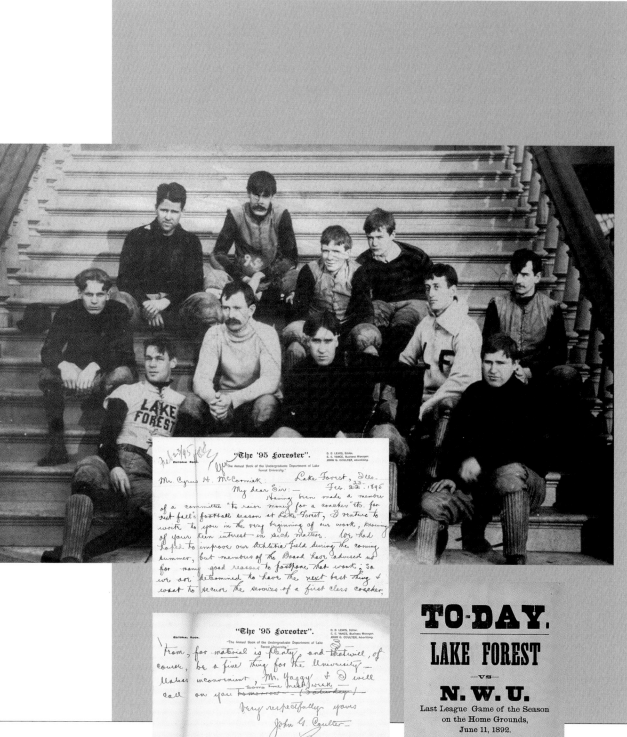

The 1895 football team and letter from John G. Coulter to Cyrus H. McCormick, and an 1892 game bill.

**Above.** The 1895 football team. Pictured front row, from left: Charles G. Smith, Charles O. Parish, John H. Rhys, Charles B. Moore (Class of 1896, trustee 1916–29, and brother of Herbert Moore, College president 1920–42), Edward E. Vance, Charles M. Thom (contributor to the development of antibiotics), and Frederick S. Mellen. Back row: John H. S. Lee (later a trustee), Fred A. Hayner (inventor of the flying tackle), Dean Dewitt Lewis (later president of the American Medical Association), and John G. Coulter (son of the president at the time).

**Center.** In 1895 young Coulter wrote this letter to trustee Cyrus McCormick Jr., soliciting funds to hire a "first class coacher" for the football team, which had not had one in the previous season, because of tight Depression budgets. Coulter noted that the team hoped to find five men to give one hundred dollars each, and that Lake Forest resident and Northern Trust Bank founder Byron L. Smith had agreed to be one of the five.

**Below.** In 1892, Northwestern was a larger institution Lake Forest still aspired to athletic as well as academic parity.

70

TO-DAY.

LAKE FOREST

— vs —

N. W. U.

Last League Game of the Season on the Home Grounds, June 11, 1892.

TO-DAY.

GAME CALLED AT 2:30 P. M.

of feeling and want of cordiality thus created are not favorable to a right moral and religious state."[32]

Yet the American college fraternity had proven itself an ideal medium for offering students not just a special sense of fellowship, but pleasures – drinking, smoking, singing, partying – that made the solemnities of the religious school seem lackluster, tedious, and even forbidding by contrast. This condition grew naturally out of the increasingly secular, student-oriented character of the new American college. Thus the fraternity's attractiveness to students could not continue to be long opposed or ignored by institutions of higher learning, the majority of which were finally obliged to recognize and make room for it.[33] Even Lake Forest University, devoted as it was to Christian habits, by 1888 had modified its restrictive clauses to the admonition that no secret society might be established except with the consent of the faculty. An opening wedge had been driven that was widened by an accompanying weakening of literary societies both locally and nationwide.[34]

In a way, Lake Forest's Phi Pi Epsilon (which was local rather than national in its identity) could be regarded as a training ground of sorts for any pointedly exclusive social club, in this instance Onwentsia. Since social intercourse, sports, and elegant dining, all held together by shared status and personal loyalties, were the essential ingredients of the Club – a number of whose members had begun to send their children to Lake Forest University – the consonance of values is obvious. Nor did the easy availability of Onwentsia's golf course and polo field detract from the equation. Once Phi Pi Epsilon was accepted by the College, its well-to-do membership enjoyed the school's new elite physical counterpart of Onwentsia: a separate house and independent dining facility, located two blocks west of the campus on what is now Illinois Road.[35] The shared values of the memberships of the fraternity and Onwentsia further reflected the changing nature of both the college and the town and the growing complexity of their relationship. For both entities were served by citizens as high in the ranks at Onwentsia as they were spiritually distant from the founding generation of Lake Forest, whose own descendants were nonetheless still party to the governance of school and municipality.

Given the shift of priorities in American colleges of the late nineteenth and early twentieth centuries, it should be evident that Lake Forest University was for the most part true to the national norm, although in one respect it was fortunate to miss a significant shaping development. For in many instances throughout the country, largely prior to the Civil War, tensions had grown between professors and students that occasionally erupted into violence.[36] The student, historically subordinate to and dependent on the professor, and the professor, called upon in turn to "civilize" his young charge, were in some regards natural enemies. Even as the century wore on, the gulf between the two factions remained, especially as the disciplines of the old order broke down. In fact, part of the rationale for the elective system was the hope that it might actually lead to a more companionable relationship between instructor and instructed, an expectation that was, all in all, only partially fulfilled. But Lake Forest University, earlier and later, escaped any such acrimony, perhaps because it began operations after the period of the greatest turmoil. Although the school's archives contain documents of skits written by students that occasionally poked fun at professors and even trustees and local citizens, they seem to be in the nature of spoofs, more gently satiric than pointedly critical, and in all recorded instances, free of perceptible hostility. Student scrapbooks even included numerous genial references to teachers, and student yearbooks were regularly and formally dedicated

Pictured here in academic procession for the 1908 Commencement is the faculty group that within a decade would bring Lake Forest University recognition as one of the leading liberal arts colleges nationwide. Pictured from right to left are: Prof. M. Bross Thomas, Biblical Literature; President John S. Nollen; Charles L. Hutchinson, president, Art Institute of Chicago; Frederick W. Crosby, trustee; W. H. Wray Boyle, trustee and minister of Lake Forest Presbyterian Church; Charles D. Norton, trustee; Albert B. Dick, trustee; Edith Denise, dean of women and first woman member of the faculty; Prof. Walter Ray Bridgman, Greek; Prof. John J. Halsey, Political Science; Prof. Lewis Stuart, Latin; Prof. Malcolm McNeill, Mathematics; Prof. Frederick W. Stevens, Physics; Prof. George W. Schmidt, German; Prof. William L. Burnap, History; Prof. Ralph H. McKee, Chemistry; Prof. John M. Clapp, English; Prof. Cornelius Betten, Class of 1900, Biology; Prof. Frederick C. L. van Stenderen, Romance Languages; Robert H. Crozier, Class of 1893, assistant to the president; Frances L. Hughes, principal of Ferry Hall; William Mather Lewis, Class of 1900, headmaster, Lake Forest Academy.

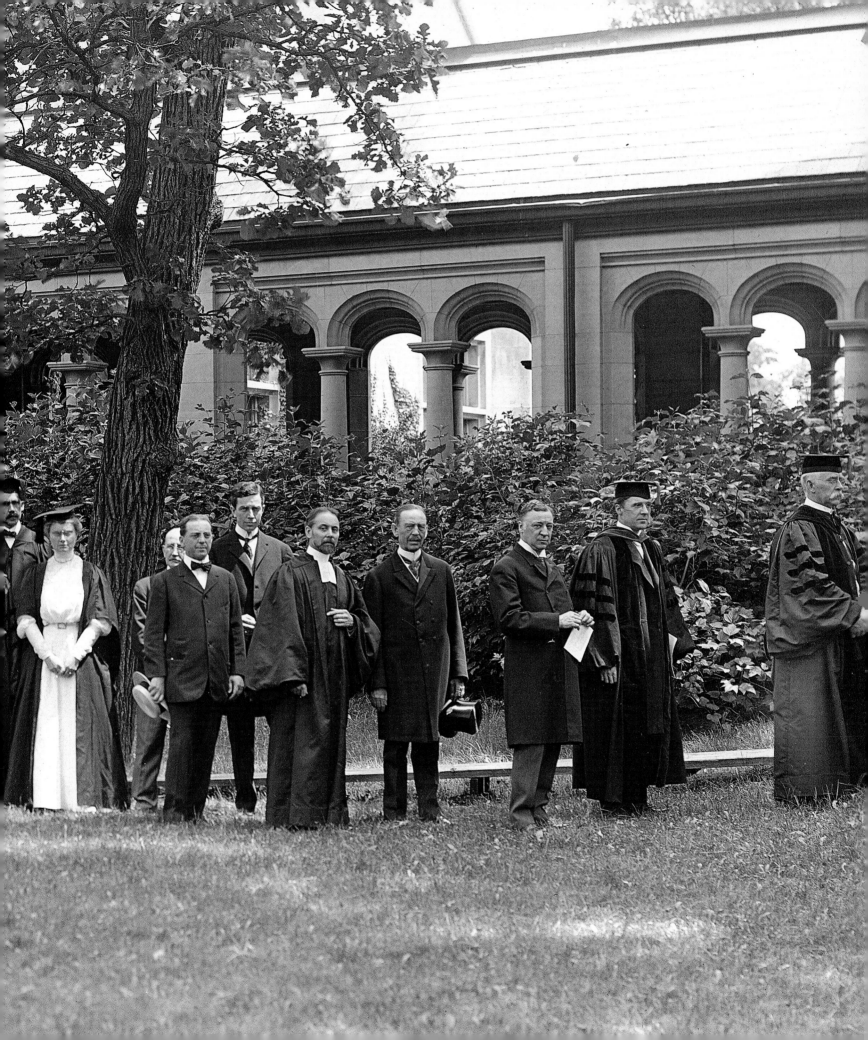

to presidents or deans.[37] Nor is there any startling evidence of the reverse, of any special disrespect directed by the faculty toward the students.

Indeed, the faculty as a collective appear to have had cause to be satisfied with their own lot, and in a majority of cases, deserving of the satisfaction. While the values of some of the Lake Forest townspeople had from time to time run counter to the policies of the institution's three academically ambitious presidents, the faculty assembled by those leaders during the 1880s and 1890s had earned the respect of the community that led by 1889 to three named professorships and two ample houses constructed on campus as residences for two of the chair-holders: Bross House for the Bross Professor of Biblical Literature and Beidler House for the Beidler Professor of Physical Science, with the D. K. Pearsons Professor-ship established for a professor of Political Science.

Such reputations were not purely local. With the rapid growth of American universities during the last decades of the nineteenth century, scholars moved with pro-portional frequency from position to position, the best of them attracted to prestigious schools, especially those notable for their graduate programs. Given these circum-stances, any reading of the record suggests that the Gregory-Roberts-Coulter administrations put together a faculty impressive in talent, training, promise, and accomplishment. A substantial number of Lake Forest instructors performed handsomely enough to be appointed later to posts in firmly established larger uni-versities.[38] No fewer than four professors in Biology followed such a route of promotion: William Albert Locy (in residence 1887–96; Ph.D. University of Chicago), to Northwestern; Robert Almer Harper (1891–98 [who taught Botany as well as Biology]; Ph.D. University of Bonn), to Wisconsin and later Columbia; James George Needham (1898–1907; Ph.D. Cornell), to his alma mater; and, of course, President Coulter himself, to the University of Chicago. In Greek and Latin, former Acting President John Haskell Hewitt (1875–81; M.A. Yale) went on to Williams, and Francis Wesley Kelsey (1880–89; Ph.D. Rochester), to Michigan. Mathematicians Edward Parmelee Morris (1877–79; L.H.D. Williams) and Fred Newton Willson (1879–80; M.A. Princeton) moved to Yale and Princeton, respectively, while Fernando Sanford (1890–91; M.S. Carthage) of Physics (who earlier had studied with the polymathic scientist Hermann Helmholtz in Berlin) left for Stanford, and Ralph Harper McKee (1891–1914; Ph.D. University of Chicago), of Chemistry, for Columbia.

Given the academic goals and personal specialty of President Coulter, it should come as no surprise that the Department of Biology boasted a group of scholars unsurpassed among the ranks of the Lake Forest faculty. Coulter's career, already discussed here, speaks for itself, while his colleague Professor Locy attained a place among the preeminent zoologists and animal morph-ologists in America. Author of numerous articles and two major books, Locy served for a time as zoological editor— a position of consequence—of the New American Supple-ment of the *Encyclopædia Britannica*.[39] An even more distinguished record was fashioned in Psychology and Philosophy by James Mark Baldwin, the very man, as noted earlier, so poorly valued and insolently remarked upon by a member of the Lake Forest Board of Trustees.[40] Having earned a Ph.D. at Princeton, Baldwin went on to study at four European universities in the course of a career that included, in addition to his 1887–89 stint at Lake Forest, tenure at Princeton and Johns Hopkins, honorary doctorates from Glasgow and Oxford, and books translated into four languages.

In sum, the early Lake Forest faculty were educated at first-class American institutions, and more than a few of

1890

At the June 17th Junior Class "Oratorical Exhibition," William H. Humiston, Class of 1891, plays an organ solo, "Forest Murmurs," from Wagner's *Siegfried*. Humiston later will serve as assistant conductor of the New York Philharmonic Orchestra.

1892

*The Forester* yearbook appears for the first time.

them, like Baldwin and Harper, received additional training abroad, most memorably at such elect German universities as Berlin, Munich, Göttingen, Tübingen, and Leipzig.[41] Further awareness of their distinction as a whole derives from a lengthy list of publications and honorary degrees as well as the inclusion of several of their company in *Who's Who in America*[42] and *The Dictionary of American Biography*, with two mentioned in the new (1999) *American National Biography*.[43]

It is worth noting, meanwhile, that a number of these professors, who collectively sought and gained various forms of national recognition, departed Lake Forest about the time the University reconceived itself as a college. Yet in the course of that transformation they shared space with a group of colleagues who stayed on, their contribution more local, their term of service often longer, but their value to both town and gown sufficient to earn them an honored place in the history of the Lake Forest community.[44] Mathematician Malcolm McNeill (Ph.D. Princeton), who joined the faculty in 1888, remained for thirty-five years, apparently unmatched in the personal esteem he commanded from students and alumni. According to the *Stentor*, "almost the first question asked by a Lake Forest alumnus upon returning to the campus was, 'How is Little Mac?'" The Reverend M. Bross Thomas (M.A. Williams) occupied the Bross Chair of Biblical Literature from 1888 until 1920, while Walter Ray Bridgman (M.A. Yale) held a professorship in Greek from 1891 until 1930. Albert E. Jack[45] (Class of 1884, M.A. Lake Forest, 1887, Professor of English 1893–1906) and Hiram M. Stanley[46] (Class of 1881, M.A. Lake Forest 1884, Librarian 1887–1903) were two of the most widely published alumni.

Yet in respect to unqualified devotion to the institution and the town, not to mention versatility, no professor quite matched the illustrious and indefatigable John J. Halsey,[47] who served on the faculty from 1878 until 1919, a term of forty-one years, during which he taught History and Political Science before and after heading the English Department; gained the D. K. Pearsons chair in Political Science; served as acting president in 1896–97 and 1906–7; spent a leave of absence as a guest professor at Stanford University; and managed to find time to serve Lake Forest as alderman and president of the Board

of Education. In 1912 his *History of Lake County, Illinois* was published, a work still widely respected for its scholarship. At the time of his retirement, the city of Lake Forest, fully aware of the role Halsey played as surely in its history as in that of the College, honored him by putting his name on one of its public schools, a building that was ultimately taken down in the 1950s.[48]

This account of an institution whose growth encompassed broadened academic programs, an expanded faculty, and burgeoning extracurricular activities points to a commensurately enlarging student body. From the first fourteen students who matriculated in 1876–77, undergraduate enrollment proceeded to average between 50 and 60 during the 1880s and between 90 and 110 in the 1890s, rising as high as 191 in the following decade.[49] If these figures as a whole seem low by contemporary standards, it should be remembered that college and university populations were much smaller in the nineteenth century than in the twentieth. In 1830, for instance, Yale had 324 undergraduates, Amherst 211, Dartmouth 128, Princeton 43 (a downturn year), and Dickinson 62. By 1860, when Lake Forest's first (albeit short-lived) collegiate classes convened, Yale's enrollment was 502, Amherst's 235, Princeton's 300, DePauw's 266, and Williams's 224.[50] Between 1876 and 1890, Northwestern granted only 388 baccalaureate degrees, and in 1890

**Above.** John J. Halsey, on the faculty from 1878 to 1919, was Lake Forest's first career faculty member and the institution's primary historian, serving also as acting president in 1896–97 and 1906–7.

**Below.** Malcolm McNeill, professor of Mathematics and Astronomy, joined the faculty in 1888 and became one of the best-beloved campus figures.

# Anna Freeman Davies, Pioneer Social Worker

In 1898, when the founder of Hull House, Jane Addams, suggested to Anna Davies, Class of 1889, M.A. 1894, that she join the staff of the fledgling College Settlement in Philadelphia, the call was unsettling for the able young Lake Forest alumna. Although at the time Davies held a post in a southern ladies' seminary and, about to complete her Ph.D. at Chicago, would have had a promising scholarly career, a year later found her the "head worker" at the Settlement and soon to embark on a reform career that would change not only her life but that of the College Settlement and inner-city Philadelphia as well.

Davies was recalled by a young college volunteer at the Philadelphia Settlement as "always cheerful, energetic, resourceful and oh, so greatly loved by all the people of the neighborhood" – those to whose welfare she devoted herself for over forty years. With a missionary philosophy "that people were fundamentally good and would respond to the finer things in life if subtly shown the way," she worked hard to provide those "finer things," crusading for kindergartens, playgrounds, better housing, visiting nurses, libraries, and honest government. Eventually from the modest start of a simple, poorly located row house, she achieved on a better site seven buildings to serve her purpose, as she became a widely recognized pioneer in community services and a consultant for other social workers.

Anna's courage, self-confidence, and dedication came no doubt from the religious and missionary background of her family. But Lake Forest University, in that period a potent training ground and networking base for church workers, must have played a role too. Early on she could well have met the Reverend John Manning Linn of the University staff, the brother-in-law of Jane Addams and father of John A. Linn, Class of 1893. Davies graduated as valedictorian in 1889, choosing for her address "Agnosticism." After college she studied not only at the University of Chicago but in Berlin, Freiburg, and Göttingen. All in all, her alma mater could well be proud of this impressive and admirable daughter.

Anna F. Davies, Class of 1889 (d. 1942).

there were 383 students in its college classes, 387 in those of the University of Illinois. In 1894–95, the enrollment at Lawrence was 77 and at Illinois College, 89.[51]

Despite such comparatively small class sizes and a year-to-year tendency toward fluctuation, the ratio of men to women in the early period at Lake Forest ran roughly three to two. (That proportion evened out when the new century began.)[52] Numbers notwithstanding, it is clear that at the outset women performed exceptionally well, especially against the backdrop of a male-dominated society. In fact an article in the *Chicago Tribune* of July 2, 1893, took note of the achievement of the Adams sisters, heralding Rebecca, valedictorian of "the largest [class] ever graduated out of the undergraduate department of the university," and Annie, who had been selected to deliver the salutatory oration. "From a total of six young ladies and sixteen young men in the class," the *Tribune* summarized, "the girls won all the scholarship honors."[53]

While the Adams sisters came from Chicago, where their father was involved in missionary work, the city provided relatively few recruits to the University after the first few years of its steady operation. The student body came mainly from small Illinois towns, especially communities with strong ties to the New England/Presbyterian tradition. It was only after 1900 that enrollments from beyond adjacent states rose (from thirteen in 1901–2 to thirty-four in 1910–11) and the number of students hailing from the town of Lake Forest dropped off,[54] a shift probably reflective of the disputes, more local than national, and yet to be recorded here, over the role and place of fraternities at the College.

In the nineteenth century, male students were inclined to prepare for a life either in the church as pastors or missionaries, or in education,[55] while women tended to concentrate on a career in teaching.[56] Yet inevitably, exceptions prove the rule. While there were such distinguished early Lake Forest alumni as the Reverend Newell Dwight Hillis,[57] Class of 1884, successor to Henry Ward Beecher and Lyman Abbott at Brooklyn's famous Plymouth Congregational Church, William Mather Lewis,[58] Class of 1900, president of Lafayette College, and social worker Anna Davies,[59] Class of 1889, head of College Settlement in Philadelphia, there were also noteworthy scientists, like Dr. Dean Dewitt Lewis,[60] Class of 1895, professor of Medicine and chief of surgery at Johns Hopkins Medical School, and Dr. Charles Thom,[61] Class of 1895, a ranking researcher at the U.S. Department of Agriculture, not to mention the intriguing Starrett brothers (Theodore, Class of 1884 and Paul, Class of 1887),[62] contractors extraordinaire. Similarly, the new century, with its nationwide tendency toward academic secularization, would produce more businessmen than clerics, but that generalization too does not always apply to the College's memorable alumni. If Everett D. Graff[63] '06 was president of the Inland Steel Company and John Orr Young[64] '10 cofounded the Young & Rubicam advertising agency, Paul W. Linebarger,[65] Class of 1892, was a federal judge in the Philippines, who wrote a biography of Chinese President Sun Yat Sen, Akira Izumi[66] '07 (one of the College's few foreign-born students from the early twentieth century) served as professor of International Law at Keijo Imperial University in Tokyo and was author of legal treatises, and William H. Humiston,[67] Class of 1891, gained distinction as a musician, musical scholar, and assistant conductor of the New York Philharmonic Orchestra.

1900

From the 1901 *Forester*, published by the Class of 1900:

**Ode to Lake Forest**
No woodman's ax e'er touched these stately trees, No yokel's plow the virgin soil e'er turned, Here hill and dale in nature's beauty please, And commerce and her noisy hum are spurned....

1903

By 1903 student art is finding its way into the annual's pages. This cover by Richard Harvey Curtis, Class of 1900, who already was embarked on a career with the *Chicago Tribune*, reflects the sophistication of book illustration in Chicago at the turn of the century.

# Everett D. Graff: The Early-Century Ideal of a Lake Forest Liberal Arts Graduate

Everett D. Graff '06 (1885–1964) exemplified the early-century ideal of a Lake Forest College liberal arts graduate: rising to both corporate and cultural leadership in Chicago and making a lasting scholarly contribution as the preeminent collector and preserver of Trans-Mississippi Americana and providing for a bibliography of his collection.

Graff's birthplace, Clarinda, Iowa, was typical of the Midwestern origins of many Lake Forest students of his day. Active in College life as a member of the Kappa Sigma fraternity and the 1905–6 tennis team, and business manager of the 1906 *Forester* staff, Graff upon graduation (major: English) joined Ryerson Steel as an office boy. From this start he rose in classic Horatio Alger fashion to the presidency of Ryerson when it became a subsidiary of Inland Steel in 1937, eventually becoming chief executive of the parent firm.

Early developing a passion for collecting books, journals, art, and ephemera of the American West, by the post–World War II period Graff had, under the guidance of Chicago master bookseller Wright Howes, assembled a remarkable collection that led scholars into new findings about the West. For example, researcher Mae Reed Porter (a contributor to historian Bernard De Voto's 1947 classical study *Across the Wide Missouri*), pursuing the neglected painter of the fur-trade era, Alfred Jacob Miller, found many of Miller's canvases, salvaged from a Scottish castle, preserved in Graff's Winnetka home (designed by architect Stanley Anderson '16). Graff's collection brought him into associations with key Chicago cultural institutions, in all of which his organizational ability destined him ultimately for presidencies. These included the book collectors' group the Caxton Club, the Art Institute, and the Newberry Library. It was to this last that most of his book collection was donated, to the care of Lake Forest alumna Gertrude Loop (Woodward) '17, curator of rare books. Not only did Graff endow his collection there for future purchases, but he set aside funds for it to be professionally cataloged. That thick volume has, for a generation, been the standard reference in the field for scholars and collectors.

Graff also was loyal to his alma mater (which awarded him an honorary doctorate in 1955), donating both his Napoleonic and Canadiana collections to the College library along with an endowment fund for annual purchases. This bequest has allowed the College to acquire a wide range of items relating to his collecting interests. From office boy to the board room, from Reid Library study tables to a niche at the Newberry, Graff indeed epitomized the goals of the College leaders who reengineered the institution as a quality liberal arts college a century ago.

Everett D. Graff '06.

# The New College
# of Presidents
# McClure, Harlan,
# and Nollen

chapter

Anyone familiar with the College's chapel, a building completed in 1900, may recall a leaded glass window along the south wall, adjacent to the pipe organ. In retrospect, the inscription "L.F.U./1901" may be regarded as a valediction of sorts, symbolically marking the year in which the trustees voted to follow the pivotal "recommendations" of February 1896.[1] Thus five years had been needed before a decision was formally reached not only to "abandon [the institution's] claim to be a university and take its true position as a College" but to "terminate the connection with Rush Medical College, Chicago College of Dental Surgery, and Chicago College of Law." By 1903, the basic transaction had been completed.[2] Lake Forest College had divested itself of the professional schools and begun a new chapter as an undergraduate institution.

1901

1902

The Reverend Richard Harlan arrives, the first president appointed for the College, as the institution enters its new stage.

The window at the east end of Holt Chapel is designed by New York's Tiffany Studios.

While this lengthy procedure was worked out, life at the school went on at a brisk pace. More than a little of what transpired on the campus as distinct from the chambers of the trustees, had its own effect on the shift in the College's identity. The students and the faculty pressed on, their ends, means, and mutual relationships already recorded here, while within the administration, the achievements of two men stand out.

As the old century gave way to the new, Professor John Halsey continued in his capacity as the leading professorial voice in the school's affairs as well as a trusted and respected figure in the town. He was the logical choice to be acting president of Lake Forest University after John Coulter resigned in 1896,[3] although it is probable that part of the confidence he inspired throughout the local community was traceable to his unfailing opposition to the merger with the University of Chicago.

With the University temporarily in the hands of Halsey, the Board undertook a search for a permanent president. To all appearances, the rejection of an invitation extended to John Huston Finley,[4] the president of Knox College, eventually proved a stroke of good fortune, since the Lake Forest faculty, led by Halsey himself, nominated their own candidate, petitioning the trustees to appoint "one man," as they put it, recognizable to all concerned as the Reverend James McClure.[5]

McClure took over the presidency of Lake Forest University in 1897[6] and forthwith conducted himself as Halsey and the faculty evidently felt sure he would. As was true earlier as acting president, he assumed his responsibilities most naturally. Everyone local knew him; everyone respected him. Maintaining his place in the pulpit, he was in a perfect position to advance the University toward its collegiate goal while retaining the support of the citizenry and even widening and deepening it. With Lake Forest donors willing and eager to memorialize or be memorialized, he saw to the construction of several campus buildings that, as individual edifices, bespoke long-standing local values, and, as a group, abided by the scale identified with a small college. The first of these was a women's dormitory put up in 1898–99, a short distance south of Durand Art Institute, and named for Lois Barnes Durand, mother of Henry and Calvin Durand (and herself a descendant of Elihu Yale, the founder of Yale University).[7] Built in brick in the Tudor Gothic manner, the building was the first direct architectural

manifestation on campus of the English influence so traditionally dear to Lake Forest hearts. The designers were Charles Frost and Alfred Granger,[8] a newly formed partnership destined to add tellingly, and rapidly, to the school's overall architectural makeup. Between 1899 and 1900 the firm erected a pair of buildings close to University Avenue and Linden Avenue (now Sheridan Road and College Road) that had the contextual effect of completing a semicircle begun by Patterson Lodge, North Hall, and University Hall. One of the two new structures was the Lily Reid Holt Chapel, the other, joined to it by a cloister, the Arthur Somerville Reid Memorial Library. Both were named for deceased Lake Forest alumni and financed by their mother, Mrs. Simon Reid.[9] Since the material used for chapel and library was Bedford limestone and the style Collegiate Gothic reinforced by the cloister, the combined effect of the pair further reflected the English tradition and, especially, the architectural ambition associated with McClure's presidency. (One of the chapel's most distinctive features was the stained-glass window over the altar, designed by the renowned Tiffany Studios of New York.)[10] The fourth building was a hospital, built with funds from Mrs. Henry Clay Durand as a memorial to her sister, Alice Bursdal Burhans.[11] It was finished in 1899, from designs by Frost and Granger, at a site close to Durand Institute and Lois Durand Hall. Constructed of the more modest materials of wood and stucco (with a touch of Tudor ornament), but meant to serve school and town alike, Alice Home, as it was locally called, typified McClure's steadfast, conscious identification with the total community.

The Reverend James G. K. McClure (1848–1932), president of the University from 1897 to 1901, pictured in 1891, a year before he became acting president following President Roberts's departure. He also continued to serve as minister of the Lake Forest Presbyterian Church throughout his university career.

together with its preparatory schools, all the while serving his Presbyterian congregation. He had rekindled much of the goodwill of the townspeople toward the College, which in its own right had cause to return the affection.

This much achieved, and the good repute that went with it, it was time by 1901 for him and his fellow trustees to turn the leadership of the College over to a successor. The Reverend Richard Harlan,[16] like McClure a graduate of Princeton Theological Seminary, was chosen as the sixth president and the first of the newly designated Lake Forest College.

The Reverend Harlan had forged a sound reputation as a clergyman. On both sides of a tour of study in Berlin, he had served as the minister of important Presbyterian churches in Rochester, New York, and New York City, and had preached at least once in Lake Forest as well.[17]

Even so, his five years of presidential service at Lake Forest cannot be discussed without reference to the fact, and its effect upon him, that he was the son of John Marshall Harlan, an associate justice of the U.S. Supreme Court.[18] Widely known as a dedicated political and social liberal and heralded as "one of the most forceful dissenters" in the history of the Court, the elder Harlan is still remembered for his famous dissent in the *Plessy v. Ferguson* case of 1896 that certified the practice of "separate but equal" facilities for African Americans. "Our Constitution is color-blind," Harlan had asserted, "and neither knows nor tolerates classes among its citizens."[19]

Justice Harlan's son inherited his father's outlook, and the policies he followed at Lake Forest College showed it. That they would result in occasional sharp disagreements with conservative members of his constituency, arguments surely more contentious than anything associated with that apostle of moderation, James McClure, seems obvious enough. Some of Harlan's ambitions were fulfilled, some not, and the difference between his successes and failures exceeded the range of anything comparable in the

By 1901, then, the campus extended from Durand Institute on the north to the new chapel and library at the southern edge. Twelve buildings of substance had gone up since the late 1870s.[12] An athletic field and a group of tennis courts were adjacent to the gymnasium, and a man-made pond lay southeast of University Hall (fittingly renamed College Hall). With the completion of Lois Durand Hall, Mitchell Hall, the former women's residence, was sold and moved to a location east of the Academy's property.[13] Students belonging to the two fraternities, Phi Pi Epsilon and Kappa Sigma, lived in their own houses off campus,[14] while independent men, lodged in dormitories atop North Hall and College Hall, continued to take their meals in Academia.

Some measure of the importance of President McClure's efforts may be discerned from the fact that he was directly or indirectly responsible for the construction of more than half the buildings of the College and Academy together.[15] These tangible signs in turn had intangible counterparts. McClure had presided over the reorganization, one might say the reengineering, of an institution of higher learning

1903

1903

**Lake Forest College has divested itself of the professional schools in Chicago and has begun a new chapter as an undergraduate institution.**

**William Mather Lewis '00 joins the faculty and founds the group which becomes the Garrick Players in 1904.**

99 PEARSON STREET.

Dear Professor Bridgman

I am sending to the college library by express some books which I hope will make a good addition to the collection of books already there — My husband valued them but he needs them no longer and I think I am making the best use of what is possible

for me. I like to think of the enduring usefulness of a well cared-for library. It may be doing its work when all of us are gone. And so it is with great pleasure that I donate these books —

Yours most sincerely

Mary E. Farwell

March 22nd 1904

Early 1900s

84

Received by the new Reid Library are major donations of rare books and documents from Adeline Rossiter Judd (including a letter from Mary Todd Lincoln), Mary Eveline Farwell, and Hobart Chatfield-Taylor.

administrations of the College's early presidents. Certainly, his most significant moves aroused a degree of opposition proportional to the spirit of reform with which he invested them.

At the outset of his tenure Harlan's assignment was seen by the trustees, and by McClure, as the academic consolidation and administrative implementation of the college-scale model the school had assumed for itself. To this end he sought to bring the College to the attention of the public at large — a marketing strategy, in more contemporary terms, meant to add to the school's image of quality by reinforcing its reputation among the townspeople, the students and faculty, the alumni, and a more far-flung Presbyterian community.[20]

The approach of the College's semicentennial, in 1907, provided a focus to this multifaceted endeavor. While an alumni association had been created in 1893 and a listing of graduates appended to the 1901–2 catalog, by 1904 Harlan had organized alumni clubs in Chicago and New York, with others later added in Logansport, Indiana, and Ottumwa, Iowa, the very sort of Midwestern towns from which the College customarily drew many of its students. (By 1915 similar groups were formed in Portland, Oregon, and in Los Angeles and Pasadena, California, as enrollments became more national under both Harlan and his successor.)[21] Harlan also made a point of soliciting writings by alumni, gathering them together and, in his first year of service, allotting them a separate shelf in the College library.[22]

While his attentions to the alumni were constant, he extended the hand of the College to others as well. In 1897 one of the trustees, William Bross, had bequeathed to the school a considerable sum of money with two expressed aims: to provide a prize for the publication of books bearing on Christianity and to finance a series of lectures by Christian religionists but open to a variety of subjects.[23] Indicative of the effect of Bross's generosity was the appearance in 1903 of the first of a group of distinguished visitors, the Reverend Francis L. Patton, president of Princeton Theological Seminary, who delivered a series of talks on "Obligatory Morality."[24] The *College Bulletin* extolled Bross's gift:

*The list of Bross Lectures will contain some of the ablest men in the world, including representative Christian scholars from Europe. The Lake Forest authorities, wishing to give the people of*

*Chicago the benefit of such a remarkable series of lectures, purpose to arrange for their repetition . . . at some central point in that city, and to extend a cordial invitation to the general public to attend them. It is hoped that the Bross Prize, the Bross Lectures and the Bross Library [a compendium of the published lectures] will prove of interest and service to English-speaking Christendom.*[25]

Provision was also made for complimentary copies of the volumes of the Bross Library to be distributed to a number of libraries throughout the United States and other countries.

During the early phase of President Harlan's administration, these and other long-range components of his plan were supported by his trustees, especially by fellow Princetonian and board chairman Cyrus McCormick Jr. and fellow Princeton seminarian McClure. Soon enough, however, several crises of assorted nature arose, fired largely by the fact that Harlan's pursuit of his more controversial goals was interrupted by the loss of those two important allies. In 1902 McCormick took over the leadership of New York financier J. P. Morgan's new farm implement trust, International Harvester, and retired from his Lake Forest chair.[26] In 1905 McClure moved to Chicago to assume, at McCormick's behest, the headship of the McCormick Theological Seminary. Harlan enjoyed the backing of McCormick's replacement as board chair, David B. Jones,[27] yet another Princeton alumnus, but Jones served only until 1904. By 1905 the president found himself with as many

When this anticipated series of annual debates between Lake Forest and Illinois College was launched in 1901, McClure was president of Lake Forest University and Clifford Barnes, spouse of Alice Reid Barnes (Class of 1886), was president of Illinois College. The subject of this debate, in a Reform vein, was the efficacy of trusts, with the Lake Foresters, unsurprisingly, taking the side of the Rockefellers and McCormicks. The Lake Forest team was led by George W. Rogers '02, in time an attorney and trustee, 1927–60.

adversaries as advocates, since Jones's two successors, alumnus Delavan Smith,[32] Class of 1884 (1904–5) and stockbroker Alfred L. Baker[33] (1905–8), struck positions that ranged, depending on the issue, from neutral to openly antagonistic.

One specific issue was central to the shift. Among Harlan's most cherished goals, toward which he steadily strove as he settled into his office, was to unite the College residentially. To this end he worked to require the fraternities to move from their independent houses to facilities on campus, where a dining hall was to be built that would accommodate them and other male students. This proposal, conceived as a way of promoting a kinship of college spirit, was clearly egalitarian in motive and effect and on that very account it met with hostility. Given the circumstances, it is safe to presume that the two fraternities were especially resistant. Certainly they would have found their most powerful voice in the remonstrations of several trustees and alumni, notably meat packer Louis Swift,[34] whose son Nathan Butler Swift[35] belonged at the time to Phi Pi Epsilon, and

the latter's fraternity brother William Mather Lewis '00,[36] a young faculty member whose middle name points to his own family social connections. (Lewis, who married a daughter of Calvin Durand, was a man of formidable self-assurance, soon to assume the headship of the Academy and later the presidency of Lafayette College.) Harlan encountered further strenuous opposition from faculty who on one ground or another felt they had cause to challenge his authority or his capacity for leadership. In 1905 the highly regarded alumnus Albert Jack, Class of 1884, went so far as to resign his professorship and chairmanship of the English Department, and there was talk around campus of other possible defections.[38]

Nonetheless, on the singular issue of turning Lake Forest into a fully residential college, with fraternities located on campus and dining facilities built to accommodate them, Harlan effectively won the day, albeit at considerable cost. He did not remain in office long enough to see his plans achieved in the manner and to the degree he wished, but in 1906 he was sufficiently confident of his administration and its role in the College's future to preside over the creation of a campus master plan. New York architect Benjamin Wistar Morris[39] and Boston landscape architect Warren Manning[40] (Cyrus McCormick's personal landscape architect) were commissioned to produce a plan the ambition and sophistication of which are evidence of its secure appropriation of Beaux-Arts organizing principles. College Hall, North Hall, and several smaller structures would have been taken down, the pond filled in, and the campus greatly recomposed, with a women's campus — actually so designated — to the north and a men's campus extending to a border just slightly north of the Academy. Two intersecting tree-lined malls would have occupied the center of the grounds, one addressing a two-part administration building from University Avenue, the other leading from a set of men's dormitories diagonally northeast to a court commanded by a large academic hall. Another dormitory

1907

1908

**Lake Forest College celebrates its Semi-Centennial.**

**Glen Rowan, designed by Howard Van Doren Shaw, is built for Clifford and Alice Reid (Class of 1886) Barnes, west of Middle Campus.**

## The Princeton Connection?

President Harlan's ultimate victory in democratically recentering the College's social life by forcing campus residence and dining on its elitist fraternities had repercussions for him personally as well as for his school, just beginning to establish its collegiate identity. But this liberal thrust may have had even wider historical ramifications, for at the very time that Blackstone and Harlan halls and Durand Commons were rising in 1906–8 as the physical symbols of Harlan's success in reining in the fraternities, Princeton was launching a high-profile but similar struggle on the same question of social equity. Like Harlan slightly before him, Princeton President Woodrow Wilson took a determined stand, in his case on the issue of the powerful eating clubs that had replaced the University's fraternities, abolished in 1877: "an organization which introduces elements of social exclusiveness constitutes the worst possible soil for serious intellectual endeavor."[28]

Were these two idealists separately reflecting current "progressive" attitudes? Perhaps – but it is interesting to note that two of Wilson's trustee supporters were David B. Jones (Princeton Class of 1875) and Cyrus McCormick Jr. (Princeton Class of 1879), both of whom had served, only a few years before, as presidents of the Lake Forest Board of Trustees, when they had championed Harlan's policies. And Jones (president of the Lake Forest Board 1903–4) in 1907 went on record in protest against pressure by Princeton alumni to thwart Wilson's egalitarian moves. "I shall be infinitely most sorry to see the University dominated by the club men of New York, Philadelphia, and Pittsburgh."[29]

After three years of fighting the establishment on the matter, a frustrated Wilson left Princeton to run for governor of New Jersey in 1910 and then, in 1912, for president of the United States.

Although in this respect there is almost no mention of Lake Forest in the published Wilson correspondence,[30] it is still intriguing to speculate on whether the College might indeed have played a peripheral role in what has been described as "the finest of all struggles between aristos and demos in the American college"[31] – and to wonder whether Wilson would have become the country's leader (and, ironically to the Lake Foresters, a force for the reenactment, in 1913, of an income tax!) had he carried the day as did Harlan.

Cyrus McCormick Jr. (1859–1936) succeeded his father as trustee of Lake Forest University in 1884 and became president of the Board in 1901. Two years later, when taken up with the presidency of the new International Harvester Trust, he resigned as University Board president but stayed on as a trustee until 1914.

Blackstone and Harlan halls.

would have been built on the women's campus, with a third mall flanked by fraternity houses meant for the eastern edge of the campus.

While nothing that monumental was ever realized, Harlan enjoyed sufficient patronage to see a modest materialization of some of the components of the Morris-Manning plan. Aided by the influence his father wielded at the national level, he sought and obtained financial assistance from Andrew Carnegie, chiefly for the purpose of putting up a building to be devoted exclusively to the sciences. (Designed in brick Collegiate Gothic by Frost and Granger, it was not completed until 1908.)[41] Closer to home, the president's most dedicated champion was Mrs. Timothy Blackstone, the widow of the Chicago railroad baron. It was she who provided most of the money for two men's dormitories crucial to the goals of uniting the College at the residential level, going even so far as to insist that if one of the buildings was to bear the Blackstone name, the other should bear Harlan's.[42] These structures, done in a red brick treatment of Collegiate Gothic, were completed in 1907.[43] Though they occupied the same site proposed in Morris's plan, the architects were again Frost and Granger, who kept both buildings minimally ornamented, partly in the belief that dormitories should defer to the symbolically higher authority of the limestone chapel and library.[44] The men's dining hall, long since known as Calvin Durand Commons and rendered in a style reminiscent of English Tudor models by a leading Chicago architect resident in Lake Forest, Howard Van Doren Shaw,[45] was also realized,

in 1908. "With the addition of these buildings," declared the College's 1907–8 catalog in a mood of triumph, "Lake Forest College has an unusually complete equipment for the best type of College work, and offers her students, both men and women, ideal conditions of residence. All the students live in College Dormitories and Commons on the Campus."

By that time, however, the ill-fated Harlan's time had passed. Following a period both notable and fascinating for the variety and intensity of its intramural political and financial quarrels, the trustees finally and corporately decided that he had failed to inspire sufficient confidence either as a manager of the College's fiscal affairs or as the leader of a united faculty. On December 1, 1906, he resigned.[46]

**While the atmosphere surrounding his departure** obviously left a shadow over his name, history would eventually assess him more affirmatively, especially as his tenure is regarded in the light of several intertwined national trends occurring at the time he served at Lake Forest.

The urbanization and industrialization of the United States following the Civil War had led to a serious socioeconomic conflict in which corporate wealth was pitted against the national workforce. As a new affluence grew, labor-unionism grew with it, leading in the last generation of the nineteenth century to a series of eruptions most dramatically evident in the Haymarket Square riot of 1886 and the Pullman strike of 1894. This discord produced its own reaction, which took the form of a movement directed at raising national awareness of a serious social problem. Progressivism, as it came to be called, stood for a mostly middle-class expression of conscience directed by moral objectives, principally the hope of lessening the conflict between rich and poor. With the turn of the twentieth century, progressivism became increasingly responsive to the misery of slum and tenement life, to the cause of the immigrant, and to the deleterious effect of political machines and unrestrained corporate monopolies. Settlement houses, among them most prominently Hull House in Chicago under the direction of the famed Jane Addams, were a tangible outgrowth of the reform spirit.

Seen against such a backdrop, Harlan's endeavors to equalize residential conditions at Lake Forest and thus further the democratization of the student body take on a more historic significance. Much the same can be said of the opposition he encountered among citizens intent on retaining their status of privilege. Yet in its attitudes toward

GENERAL PLAN
OF
LAKE FOREST UNIVERSITY

Proposed by

Benjamin Wistar Morris, Architect, New York.
and
Warren H. Manning, Consulting Landscape Architect, Boston.

Scale, 1inch = 50 ft.
Date, June 1906.

**Above.** As president of Chicago's Merchants Club (later merged into the Commercial Club), Charles Dyer Norton convinced Daniel Burnham to undertake the well-known Chicago Plan of 1909. He also was the main force behind the creation of the College's own "city-beautiful" Manning Plan of 1906, pictured here. Architect Benjamin Wistar Morris of New York and landscape architect Warren H. Manning of Boston submitted this plan, the main Beaux-Arts axis of which, focusing on Lake Forest Academy, was never implemented, but is recalled in the striking Harlan-Blackstone gate.

**Left and right below.** Calvin Durand Commons (1908), designed by Howard Van Doren Shaw, was an elegant dining facility (said to be modeled on the dining hall of Kings College, Cambridge). It was meant to accommodate all men, commingling the wealthy residents of the former fraternity houses with scholarship holders.

At center, President John Scholte Nollen (1869–1952), fishing at his camp in Excelsior, Minnesota, with trustee Charles H. Ewing and Edson C. Van Sickle '21. Though seen here in a relaxed moment, German-trained modern language scholar Nollen enjoyed a decade-long tenure (1907–17) at Lake Forest, a period known for its significant academic achievement.

College's most sanguine periods, unique in the forever intricate interrelationship of town, gown, and city. For the first time the three entities were bound by links not only commercial and fiscal but intellectual. Each experienced a form of aesthetic awakening, and while they did not necessarily share a common vision, a special closeness grew among them, between artist and patron, academic and amateur, campus and community.

At the age of thirty-eight when he was inaugurated at Lake Forest in 1907, Nollen was reassuringly old enough and promisingly young enough. Born in Pella, Iowa, in 1869, he had taken his undergraduate training at the State University of Iowa, where he was elected to Phi Beta Kappa. His Ph.D., from the University of Leipzig (1893), bore the most radiant international luster. He was a specialist in modern languages, chiefly in German, and his member-ships in the Modern Language Association, the Goethe Gesellschaft, and the American Bibliographical Society only added to an impressive set of credentials. Until his arrival in Lake Forest, he had been on the faculty of Indiana University, where he headed and greatly strengthened the Department of German, accomplishments carrying the reminder that the same school had now provided the College with two presidents.

social reform, the community of Lake Forest, traditionally conservative, was not monolithic. In 1895 Jane Addams (whose nephew John A. Linn[47] was an 1893 graduate of the College) had spoken at Ferry Hall,[48] to an audience surely made up of members of both sexes, and in a remarkable gesture a year earlier, the Reverend James McClure had invited the controversial Socialist leader Eugene V. Debs to present his point of view on the Pullman strike to the congregation of the Presbyterian Church.[49] In short, President Harlan, the case against him notwithstanding, left an indelible imprint on the campus life and institutional values of Lake Forest College. Moreover, he made it easier for later presidents to preserve those ideals as well as to pursue others of their own devising.

Harlan went on to Washington, D. C., where he super-vised The George Washington University Movement, a project that sought to raise an endowment sufficient to carry out the will of the nation's first president and thus to establish George Washington University.

The search for his successor at Lake Forest was undertaken directly upon his departure, with Professor Halsey once again acting in executive capacity until the trustees decided on a permanent president.[50]

John Scholte Nollen[51] must have seemed heaven-sent. A model education had been followed by a career in academe in which he had distinguished himself not only in teaching and scholarship but in that precious capacity, administration, which the trustees, following the parlous Harlan years, regarded as a prime presidential asset. And indeed his decade of service at Lake Forest would comprise one of the

Like Coulter with his "New Curriculum," Nollen inaugurated his presidency by publishing "The New Catalogue," in which he sketched the outlines of his academic projections. He described the changes in the Statement of Require-ments for Entrance (to match standard national practice)[52] and in the Course of Study. There concentration on a single major was replaced with a so-called Group System ("recently adopted by the strongest colleges"), clusters of related courses undergirded by general education require-ments and elective choices. Moreover, presaging a future emphasis on vocationalism, he also initiated pre-professional studies, encouraging students to spend one or two years at Lake Forest before undertaking specialized training, in the belief, as he put it, that "some experience of the life of a good college will have great value for students who will complete their preparations for their life work under the condition of the technical and professional school." He doubtless had such "experience" in mind when he added the Chronicle of College Events to the catalog, a list that annually recorded the speeches and programs that took place on campus. Among them the importance and prestige of the Bross Lectures could be inferred from the appearance in 1911 of Josiah Royce of Harvard,[53] a distinguished philosopher who figured prominently in the social-philosophical debates that livened the day.

Yet perhaps more significant than these innovations of the Nollen years was a reorientation of the curriculum that had been quietly evolving even prior to his arrival in Lake Forest. President Coulter's tenure, as already noted, had been marked by a stress on the sciences that reflected his own professional specialty as surely as it did his overall educational philosophy. A shift in priorities occurred after he left, with the humanities and the social sciences raised to a stronger position during the Harlan years. Nollen the humanist did nothing to alter this curricular hierarchy. Any reading of the College catalog during the first decades of the century cannot fail to take note of the preference assigned the humanities in the order and quantity of courses listed.

This focus was in concert with intellectual currents stirred in part by the broader progressive movement cited earlier. They affected the College chiefly through the two outer worlds historically closest to it, Lake Forest the town and Chicago the city. A new spirit was abroad in which social concerns of one sort or another found their voices in the arts, even if the themes expressed were inspired by different muses.[54]

For while the momentum of aesthetic reform grew after 1900, it was apparent already in the culturally crucial decade of the 1890s, when Chicago enjoyed a flowering of literature that lasted well into the new century. The novels of Hamlin Garland, Robert Herrick, and Henry Blake Fuller, foreshadowing the American realist-naturalist school, dealt with subjects closely related to plebeian life in the roisterous metropolis that already dominated what Garland called "the middle border" of the country. Following the turn of the century, this creative development accelerated, spawning a generation that included the

realist novelists Theodore Dreiser, Willa Cather, and Sherwood Anderson, poets Vachel Lindsey, Edgar Lee Masters, Harriet Monroe, and Carl Sandburg, and editors Monroe and Margaret Anderson. Monroe was passionate in her promotion of a poetry that could deal even with life in the slums of the city and that was free enough to be expressed in innovative verse forms. Certain that she and her colleagues in Chicago were fashioning a new tradition, she was echoed by Dreiser, who found words of his own to celebrate the extraordinary prairie urban world in which he lived: "To me at this time Chicago seethed with a peculiarly human or realistic atmosphere. It is given to some cities, as to some lands, to suggest romance, and to me Chicago did that hourly. It sang, I thought, and ... I was singing with it."[55]

This was an era unmatched in Chicago's literary history, uniquely golden in contrast with the inner city's very tarnish, and if its writers responded accordingly, so did those who published them. The new literature was the stuff of a

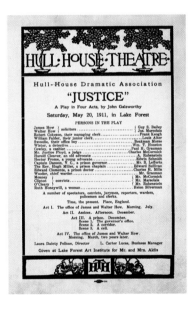

1911

A number of College students are guests at a Saturday night party in January at Lake Forest's Winter Club. The evening features ice skating, tobogganing, and dancing.

1915

Lake Forest's Garrick Club premieres Chicago playwright Kenneth Sawyer Goodman's reform play "Back of the Yards."

1916

Philosophy professor Henry Wilkes Wright's book, *Faith Justified by Progress*, is published on the Bross Fund.

number of lively journals, principally Monroe's *Poetry*, Anderson's *The Little Review*, and *The Chap-Book* (the last of these published in the 1890s), and of several important and nationally respected Chicago publishing houses, notably A. C. McClurg,[56] Stone & Kimball,[57] and Way & Williams.[58] The sobriquet Chicago Literary Renaissance was coined to describe this phenomenon, which was taken seriously beyond the city limits, earning its most enthusiastic praise from H. L. Mencken, who, writing in *The Nation* in 1920, called Chicago "The Literary Capital of the United States."[59]

Mencken's designation would seem to leave literary Lake Forest of the same period removed to the provinces. In view of the village's history of wealth and the space it consciously kept between itself and the soot of the Chicago streets, it was largely indifferent to the progressivist movement and any of the gritty art that reflected it. Just when the Chicago writers were celebrating the lustiness of the city, Lake Forest was building an estate culture consisting of grand mansions and formal gardens west of the railroad tracks, built on acreages substantially larger than those owned by the town's founding fathers. No less a figure than Frank Lloyd Wright, well known at home and abroad for his advanced residential designs, submitted to Harold Fowler McCormick and his wife Edith Rockefeller McCormick a proposal for an estate in Lake Forest that, if built, would have been unsurpassed in scale among his Prairie Style efforts. Significantly, in view of Lake Forest's tastes, it was rejected, in favor of a comparably lavish but decisively more traditional design by Charles Platt.[60]

Yet at the same time, some of the new gentry looked toward a cultural tradition of their own, genteel if not tough-minded, that had a newly projected place for intellectual values and artistic expression. It is fair, then, to say that the arts that did flourish in Lake Forest after the turn of the century produced a local Renaissance with, as it were, a small "r," that in some ways overlapped and in others turned away from developments in Chicago.

By 1911 the village had begun to play a role in the growth of theater in the city. The Arthur Aldis family,[61] chief among them Mary Reynolds Aldis, wife of a developer active in the building boom that drew worldwide architectural attention to the city, were a local cultural force in themselves. Mrs. Aldis not only set up one of the first community theaters on her own Lake Forest estate,[62] but partook significantly in the creation of the highly successful Little Theatre in Chicago. In the latter capacity she worked hand in glove with the director of the theater, the British-born Maurice Browne,[63] who lived at the Aldis compound in Lake Forest, where over the years many artists and literati came as guests: Masters, Monroe, and Eugene Field among them.[64] Mrs. Aldis also invited a group of players from Chicago's Hull House to perform at Durand Institute in 1911,[65] and later led local amateur productions that included members of the College's faculty and student body.[66] Nor was she alone in her efforts to cultivate drama in Lake Forest. The family and friends of Howard Van Doren Shaw staged their own amateur pageants on his spacious Lake Forest estate, Ragdale,[67] designed by Shaw earlier and elegantly in the Arts and Crafts manner. Thus the theatrical arts, aided and nourished by what amounted to artists' colonies in Lake Forest, grew in the Chicago area at about the same time that Harriet Monroe was busy with the publication of the first issue of *Poetry* in 1912.

And it is here that Hobart Chatfield-Taylor, the personification of such "cross-cultural" developments, resumes a place in the narrative. As ubiquitous as Anna Farwell De Koven—who at the time was writing decorous novels addressed to her own social set[68]—Chatfield-Taylor would cut a perceptibly wide swath throughout the entire Chicago region. No less proud than Anna of his social position, and inspired by it as well, he acted, among other things, the role of patron—moreover inventively—as he proposed the sale of subscriptions to Monroe's magazine (an idea soon seized upon by the Little Theatre). According to her biographer, Monroe acknowledged the importance of this concept by asserting that she dated the beginning of the magazine from June 23, 1911—the day Chatfield-Taylor suggested his imaginative financing scheme,[69] one that would gain the support of such Lake Foresters as Chatfield-Taylor himself, Howard Shaw, Arthur Aldis (the first three subscribers), Alfred Baker, Cyrus McCormick Jr., and Samuel Insull.[70] In short, Chatfield-Taylor was among the first to devise a system of shared patronage, a way of financing artistic enterprises that has become customary throughout the country.

Not content with that, he labored to familiarize the growing base of Chicago theater audiences with French drama, in the process involving himself with student and faculty life at Lake Forest College. His translation of Moliere's *The Physician in Spite of Himself* was performed in 1907 by the

# GARRICK CLUB — FARCES

## THREE ONE-ACT PLAYS

Dispatches for Washington

The Point of View *My Play !!*
*translated from French*

Peter Pumpkin Eater

=== AT ===

The DURAND ART INSTITUTE

## FRIDAY, NOV.

Admission 25c 8:1

---

The GARRICK CLUB of
LAKE FOREST COLLEGE

Presents THREE PLAYS

"A Quarter of an Hour"—Louie R. Stanwood
"Back of the Yards"—Kenneth Sawyer Goodman
"East and West"—Adapted by John Milton '16.

UNDER THE AUSPICES of the
NEW TRIER DRAMATIC CLUB

New Trier High School Auditorium
Friday, Evening, March 19, 1915

---

*The Point of View*

# FOUR ONE ACT PLAYS

Written and Translated by College Students
UNDER THE DIRECTION OF C. C. MATHER

THE THIRD NUMBER IN THE SERIES OF ENTERTAINMENTS GIVEN BY

## THE NEIGHBORHOOD THEATRE
### DURAND ART INSTITUTE

COLLEGE CAMPUS          LAKE FOREST, ILL.

## FRIDAY EVENING, FEB. 9, 1917

Curtain at 8:15

General Admission, 25c     Reserved Seats, 50c

# Lake Forest College: Academically Top-Notch

A 1913 article as it appeared in the *Forester*

While we have always had a private idea that Lake Forest amounted to something, after all it did us good to know that the United States Bureau of Education thought so, too. When its report on the classification of the universities, colleges, and technical schools of the country was made public in January, Lake Forest took a place in the lists that is a source of interested satisfaction to all who are friends of the college.

This report is based upon thorough investigation of the merits of each institution, the efficiency of the faculties, the records of graduates, the condition of equipment, the class of educational preparation offered, and this information has been obtained through a personal inspection or reports of the state boards of education and investigations by the Carnegie Foundation.

According to the report, the three hundred and forty institutions classified are divided into four classes upon a basis of the value of their B.A. degree to their graduates who would enter a strong graduate school. All those in Class I would have their degree accepted at par, that is graduates would be fitted to take up without further preparation any graduate work. The degree of an institution in Class II might be discounted at about 10% to 15%, according to the report; those in Class III about 25% and those in Class IV about 50%. Of the whole number there are only fifty-nine in Class I, made up of thirty-seven universities and technical schools and twenty-two colleges. Institutions of Class I are divided geographically as follows: – in the North Central States, 13 universities and 5 colleges; the Southern States, 5 universities and 1 college; the Western States, 6 universities and no colleges; the North Eastern States, 13 universities and 16 colleges. Consideration of the map indicates that there are but five colleges of Class I in all the territory from the Alleghenies to the Pacific Coast. Those five are Beloit in Wisconsin, Grinnell in Iowa, Oberlin in Ohio, and Knox and *Lake Forest* in Illinois.

Such a classification is a great honor to Lake Forest, but it, at the same time, imposes a demand for a strong and continued effort on our part.

**Below.** Close town-gown ties are evidenced in this affectionate caricature of Lake Forest faculty and staff from the 1909 *Forester,* drawn by immensely popular *Chicago Tribune* cartoonist John T. McCutcheon, who had a weekend place in Lake Forest. Playing the presiding fool (left) is history professor William L. Burnap with Edith Denise, dean of women and assistant professor of French, the campus custodian Johann Dorn; professor of Philosophy Henry Wright, professor of Political and Social Science John J. Halsey, professor of English John M. Clapp, and President John S. Nollen.

1916

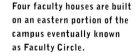

94

**Four faculty houses are built on an eastern portion of the campus eventually known as Faculty Circle.**

players of the Garrick Club,[71] a group begun in 1903 by faculty instructor (and Chatfield-Taylor's fellow Onwentsian) William Mather Lewis[72] that was destined for a vital place in campus history. In 1906 Lewis was succeeded as Garrick director by Professor John Mantel Clapp (in residence 1906–16, M.A. Amherst), who is remembered not only for the effort he devoted to nurturing theater,[73] but for other activities at the College and in the city – in a way establishing himself as the campus equivalent of Chatfield-Taylor. It was Clapp who came to Lake Forest with the support and largely at the behest of the wealthy and powerful Durand family;[74] Clapp who had been the faculty member chiefly in charge of the recruitment of President John Nollen in 1906;[75] Clapp who went on to be a player of consequence in the theatrical life of Chicago as well as of Lake Forest;[76] Clapp who was especially close to a major College trustee, Charles Dyer Norton,[77] in his own right a figure of influence on both the 1906 Morris master plan of the campus and the celebrated 1909 Burnham Plan of Chicago; Clapp, in short, who quickly and firmly assembled a weighty set of social, artistic, and institutional credentials that stood him in exceptionally good stead on the campus, in Lake Forest, and in Chicago.

Clapp's friend Norton further figures in the story on account of his connections with the East. He was married to Catherine McKim, niece of architect Charles Follen McKim of McKim, Mead & White, the famous New York firm that had been greatly responsible for the Beaux-Arts Classicism of the 1893 World's Columbian Exposition.[78]

The career of yet another Lake Forest faculty member, Frederick van Steenderen[79] (1907–36; Ph.D. Iowa), extended beyond the campus by virtue of a link with the multi-faceted Chatfield-Taylor. Besides his translations of Moliere, the latter's major literary accomplishment consisted of a pair of ambitious biographies, one of Moliere, in 1906,[80] the other of the eighteenth-century Italian dramatist Carlo

Goldoni, in 1913.[81] The national vogue for Goldoni that followed the book's publication[82] was significantly enhanced by the fullness of a bibliography[83] compiled by van Steenderen, which helped to make Goldoni's work accessible to more Americans than ever before.

As the College entered the second decade of the new century, it must have been with an increasing sense of confidence. And in 1913 there would be national recognition of accomplishment when a report of the United States Bureau of Education ranked it in the highest category of college and universities, one among only five colleges of the north central states and twenty-two colleges in the whole country.[84] It naturally followed that preparations were later underway for making application (subsequently unfulfilled)[85] for a chapter of Phi Beta Kappa, another measure of academic excellence. In that same year, 1913, President Nollen had supervised a major fundraising campaign,[86] the success of which was symptomatic of the high regard the community as a whole felt toward the school. In fact, trustee Louis Swift, who would have been among the severest critics of President Harlan's decision to unify the College's residential facilities in 1906, was the principal donor of the money needed to build four faculty houses in 1916 on an eastern portion of the campus eventually known as Faculty Circle.[87] The architect was Howard Van Doren Shaw, busy at the time refining his design of Lake Forest's patrician shopping center, Market Square,[88] which was itself a further sign of the town's prosperity, its friendliness toward the arts, and the desire to dress itself up.

Nor did the cordiality end there; at the College it found further favor at a curricular level. In 1916 a group of summer courses in landscape gardening was put into the catalog, inspired by the formal inauguration several years earlier of the Lake Forest Garden Club.[89] The College program was directed by Ralph Rodney Root,[89] regularly on the

1914

1916

1919

Dance cards that belonged to Dorothy Cooper '17, a Theta Psi, and Margaret Horton '19, *Stentor* editor and Garrick member, both of whose extensive scrapbooks are now in the College archives.

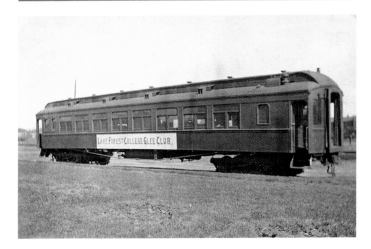

SANTA FE.
# Lake Forest College
## GLEE CLUB
### "Chicago to Los Angeles"

Nonetheless, to the degree the conflict made itself felt locally, Lake Forest had cause to be more aware of it than most neighboring communities, flanked as it was by two major military encampments, Fort Sheridan and the Great Lakes Naval Training Station. The former particularly attracted attention from the town and the College, since the faculty were engaged in teaching the Fort's officer-trainees, and troops frequently marched just south of the campus, along the thoroughfare now known as Sheridan Road.[92]

In the spring of 1917, the marching took on a far more serious meaning and the war grew closer indeed with the formal entry of the United States into the fight. While the College reacted to the event fully conscious of the tight times necessarily imposed by the loss of a portion of the male student body (a situation that never grew as grave as it had in 1863), it remained for the aftermath of the war to exert an impact on the school that affected its scholastic fortunes to a degree totally unforeseen by anyone.

**Above.** In 1911 the Glee Club went on a cross-country trip to Los Angeles with stopovers and performances in, among other places, Newton, Kansas, Albuquerque, New Mexico, Kingman, Arizona, and Barstow, California.

**Right.** The fourth annual Lake Forest Day (1911) began with a parade through town followed by a sack race, a hammer throw, an egg and spoon race, and a pie-eating contest in front of Durand Institute.

faculty of landscape architecture at the University of Illinois, who enjoyed such success in his first summer at Lake Forest (drawing people from vast distances) that a four-year independent program in landscape architecture was proposed for the College.[90] A similar endeavor in another art, music, was conceived at about the same time, again in the form of an autonomous four-year program.[91]

In the meantime, World War I, which had been raging in Europe since 1914, was largely perceived in much of the Midwest as safely remote from Chicago and inland America.

1917

**In Russia, Czar Nicholas II abdicates in March, and in November Bolshevik troops occupy Moscow. The United States enters World War I in April.**

1917

**President Nollen assumes a nonmilitary post, serving with the YMCA in support of American forces in Italy.**

# Quiescence and Amiability with President Moore

chapter

6

1921–1942

One of the most far-reaching ironies in the history of Lake Forest College unfolded as the 1910s turned into the 1920s, and it was related to developments of moment in Lake Forest and Chicago. Following the hearty Nollen years and the celebration of the nation's military victory, euphoria in Lake Forest lasted only briefly. Within months of the November 1918 armistice, the community and the College, for that matter Chicago itself, had lapsed into a far grimmer frame of mind than might be normally expected of a promising institution of higher learning and a militarily triumphant people.

The country as a whole endured a period of social and economic turmoil after the war. Strikes and troubled race relations on the domestic front were matched by a widespread popular disagreement over the extent to which America should become further involved in international affairs.

1916

1918

From the May 12, 1916, *Stentor* report on Professor Wright's Bross lectures on "Faith Justified by Progress": "It is a proud day for Lake Forest College when she is able to place her professors against all comers and find that her professors are adequate…. There is just one thing we have regret about those lectures": that they were poorly attended by students who "took it for granted that they would not understand what was said."

Varsity letter sweater once worn by Leon N. McFerran '18.

Two issues of the day made themselves especially felt in Chicago and, if anything, even more emphatically among the leading, traditionally conservative citizens of Lake Forest. One was a slump in the nation's postwar economy[1] and the other, an event of global consequence, the Russian revolution of 1917, accompanied by fears associated with the international Communist movement. Both developments had sent a shiver of anxiety through the collective mind of the American wealthy classes, the elite of Lake Forest among them.[2] The effect of all this on Lake Forest College was traceable partly and more directly to a single incident in 1919 that seemed, surely to the man responsible for it, an ethically requisite gesture rather than what it also turned out to be, namely the most administratively disastrous act that had ever befallen the school.

Professor Henry Wilkes Wright,[3] the head of the College's Department of Philosophy and a distinguished scholar, who had come to the College in 1907, was named acting president when John Nollen left for Europe in 1918 to direct wartime activities of the YMCA in Italy.[4] Wright was a liberal, given to a point of view that he made clear in a speech delivered in the College chapel in April 1919. The war, he declared, had obliged the citizenry to conform to a patriotic unity on most major social and political issues, but the war was over, and the time had come for men of good social faith to resume, when appropriate, the critical attitude toward capitalism and monopoly that had occupied the reformers of the progressivist movement before 1917.[5]

Most of the College trustees had obviously not taken the trouble to examine in detail Wright's prewar book, *Faith Justified by Progress* (published in 1916 by Scribner's on the College's Bross Foundation Fund, no less!) in which he had expressed similar views on social justice.[6] But they could hardly fail to read the front page story in the *Stentor*, which reported his chapel lecture.

As a body they were in no mood for the speaker's sentiments. The fact that the economy was down affected most of them, but two in particular had been hit hard by judgments that seemed to them outgrowths of the politics espoused by the College's acting president. Despite a contemporaneous resurgence of laissez-faire economic policies, Louis Swift's meatpacking company had been targeted for harsh and extended criticism in a three-volume report issued by the Federal Trade Commission shortly after the armistice.[7]

Several years earlier, Board vice president A. B. Dick's mimeograph firm had engaged in business practices which, though adjudged legal by the Supreme Court, had drawn the full fury of the antimonopolists, muckrakers, and social reformists of the day, contributing to the passage in 1914 of the Clayton Anti-Trust Act.[8] Another College trustee, Board president Clayton Mark, had watched his own steel company endure a sudden, sharp drop in profits in the immediate postwar economic recession.[9] Market forces affected the historic Farwell wholesale company as well, leading to a decline that only worsened in the 1920s, when the firm was obliged to surrender more and more of its business to such direct retailing firms as Sears, Roebuck and Mongomery Ward.[10] These assorted financial reverses among people connected with Lake Forest, together with their shared belief in the menace of a worldwide Bolshevist takeover, produced a compound reaction, part economic, part ideological, and totally ill-disposed toward sustaining the warm relationship that happened to exist between the College and its townspeople during the Nollen years. In this response they were not alone, for nationally with the secularization of colleges and universities, ever larger numbers of businessmen had become involved in academic affairs as trustees, at the very time that faculties had begun to challenge many of the social and economic attitudes represented by these overseers.[11]

All of this took place locally with stunning swiftness, in little more than half a decade. Nor did the new estrangement settle only on the campus. By the early 1920s many of the major participants in the Literary Renaissance, Chicagoans and Lake Foresters alike, had departed the larger community. What those among them who embraced the creed of social justice had regarded as idealistic criticism and enlightened self-examination underwritten by supportive wealthy neighbors was now seen by many of those very patrons as subversive, more deserving of withdrawal or outright resistance than of approval. Joseph Medill Patterson—grandson at once of the founder of the *Chicago Tribune* and of the first president of Lake Forest University—whose own early left-leaning views can be inferred from the title of an autobiographically self-critical essay, *Confessions of a Drone*, left Lake Forest for New York.[12] So did another Lake Forester, Ernest Poole,[13] who had won the first Pulitzer Prize for fiction (in 1918) and published a novel about labor strife, *The Harbor*. Earlier Poole had lent assistance to Upton Sinclair when the latter published his exposé of grossly unhealthy conditions in the Chicago meatpacking houses, *The Jungle* (1906), a book that had surely done little to stir Louis Swift's sympathies. Moreover, since the arts of the Literary Renaissance were in some cases joined at the hip with reformist causes, even enterprises free of political over-tones, like the Little Theatre, were deprived of the Chicago patronage they had earlier taken for granted.[14] The cultural climate chilled, abruptly. Ironically, by the time Mencken had written his aforementioned salute to Chicago as the nation's "literary capital," the city's writers and theatrical people had left or were in the process of leaving, Margaret Anderson, Sherwood Anderson, and Maurice Browne[15] chief among them. With the departure of the redoubtable Chatfield-Taylor to California following the death of his wife Rose in 1918,[16] it might have seemed that even providence had deserted the cause of cultural cordiality and communal well-being. In 1920 Alphonse Capone arrived in town from New York, and within a few years the city's flamboyant mayor, William Hale (Big Bill) Thompson, was better known for his verbal tirades against England than for his efforts to combat the gangs Capone came to stand for. Chicago, whose self-image had grown and prospered almost steadily since the golden 1890s, would see its reputation

in the eyes of the outside world drastically transformed. By the end of the decade it was known everywhere, even to itself, more as "the gangster city" than as a metropolis with reason to be proud of itself.

While the College was free of such a stigma, its future was in any case uncertain. Professor and Acting President Wright persisted with his liberal views, but not for long. During the 1920 Commencement activities, he invited to the chapel podium a graduating senior who echoed Wright's criticism of capitalism.[17] That, however, was the last word on the subject.[18] By mid-1920 Wright, having failed to gain local support for his views or even find another academic appointment in the United States, had left Lake Forest for the University of Manitoba. The trustees, meanwhile, exasperated by developments abroad and at home, found themselves faced with the question of what to do with a College whose role seemed suddenly to have shifted from that of an enriching, faithful complement to the community to one of an unreliable partner and irritating critic—and all this at a time of financial exigencies.

The ambivalence at Lake Forest was shortly subjected to a resolution that, however, did little to restore amity to the relationship of all parties involved and instead exerted serious repercussions on the future of the College. The trustees began their efforts by seeking the advice of several outside consultants,[19] including former President Coulter, who was convinced, as he put it in his "suggestions" to the trustees, that "insidious bolshevist ideas which are more dangerous than poison gas" constituted a major threat to the education of the young in America[20] (a fear no doubt seen as evidenced at hand by Wright's student supporter). In thus upholding the views of the trustees, Coulter resonated further with the sentiments of another major conservative figure, the literary critic Paul Elmer More, who in the Bross Lecture of 1921 used the occasion to deliver an attack on the "philosophy that preaches social dis-content as the means of progress."[21] Meanwhile, discussions

1918

1919

**On November 11 Armistice brings to a close the four-year European war, the end jolting the war-mobilized U.S. economy.**

**With wartime and postwar enrollments down, a crisis develops as Lake Forest's trustees consider a reorganization as a women's college.**

within the councils of the Board led to a recommendation that found special favor among some of the trustees, namely, that the College be transformed into a women's school.[22] Such a move, its proponents hoped, would attract admissions in the poor postwar economy and, equally important, ensure a genteel institution more in the nature of a traditional female seminary. Furthermore, the change to such a decorous educational model would, presumably, justify a new kind of curriculum, one that might diminish the threat of social criticism associated with the academic brotherhood at large.

Nevertheless, no sooner was the notion of a woman's college proposed than it encountered opposition from another constituency, the alumni, who were united in their desire to maintain the local coeducational tradition.[23] (In this stance some of them might have been energized by Wright who, in his waning days on campus, took issue with such a possibility.)[24] In yielding to that wish, the trustees were prepared to shift more of the responsibility for the College's operations to the alumni, whose ranks did in fact provide most of the Board chairmen from the 1920s until as late as the mid-1940s.[25] And in the course of this, the local trustees began to distance themselves from an institution that, if intended originally to educate their young, was now serving a substantially different clientele.

Of comparable consequence, the Board and the alumni agreed to organize and implement what amounted to a historic change in the character of the school. In their own eyes, they had cause, traceable in part, once again, to the words of Professor Wright, a man in whom they could easily find a common opponent. In the 1911 College yearbook, addressing himself to the purpose of higher education, Wright had written: "While it is the duty of the [American] college to prepare its students for life under modern conditions, we should not go to the extreme of regarding the college as merely a training school for a business or professional career. The college will not perform its mission best by adopting the methods of business or reproducing the conditions of professional activity."[26]

Under these circumstances, it is hardly surprising to find the Board adopting a position exactly opposite that espoused by Wright, especially since at the national level the collision between the belief in free enterprise capitalism

and the perceived Bolshevist threat abroad prompted a heightened awareness of, if not to say devotion to, American business. Vice President Calvin Coolidge, ever in character, wasted no words: "This is a business country … and it wants a business government." Writing in *The Independent* in 1921, Edward E. Purinton had more to say, more exultantly: "What is the finest game? Business. The soundest science? Business. The fullest education? Business. The fairest opportunity? Business. The cleanest philanthropy? Business. The sanest religion? Business."[27]

Such attitudes were not lost on the College and the Board, especially in view of the response of the second invited consultant, Samuel P. Capen, president of the American Council on Education.[28] After considering the conversion of the school into a women's college or a restructuring of the traditional liberal arts college model, Capen proposed an alternative that appeared to him more viable and least expensive to achieve: *The college might be partially reorganized to train men and women for positions in the executive and administrative departments of business and commercial enterprises. . . . Many conferences with representatives of industry and commerce have developed the fact that employers do not expect or desire from the graduates of collegiate institutions much specialized technical training. They are chiefly concerned with a fundamental*

## LAKE FOREST WILL CONTINUE AS CO-EDUCATIONAL COLLEGE

### Dr. Henry W. Wright Resigns the Acting Presidency

That the Trustees have definitely given up the plan of turning Lake Forest into a girls' school and will devote their efforts to developing it as a co-educational institution was officially announced by Dr. Wright in Chapel last Friday morning. At the same time, he said now that this question was finally decided, he had tendered his resignation as Acting President of the College, to take effect at the end of the present school year. He thanked the students for their patience and loyalty thru the period of indecision as to the fate of the college.

In conclusion, he spoke briefly of the place of the small college in education. He quoted the statements of teahers in large universities to the effect that in these larger schools, there is so great a variety of courses with so little correlation, that the graduate, although perhaps a specialist in one line, is merely confused with a mass of diffuse information, outside his own field. The small college avoids this by having fewer courses, related so as to make for a well rounded education. Thus he sees a bright future for the small college, doing a work of immense value to society.

Let us pause here for a moment to consider what Dr. Wright has done for Lake Forest. For two years, he has

shouldered the burden of the presidency in addition to his regular class work. Through the most trying and dangerous times the College has ever seen, he has piloted us safely. On at least one occasion, his courage and decision alone saved the College from becoming a girls' school. We owe him our deepest gratitude.

1920

When Acting President
Wright leaves to teach phi-
losophy at the University of
Manitoba, alumnus Herbert
Moore, Class of 1896,
becomes acting president.

Lake Forest College
BULLETIN

Volume 1        MAY 1922        Number 22

Department of
Business Administration

"Boost for a Bigger and Better Lake Forest"

LAKE FOREST COLLEGE
ALUMNI NEWS-BULLETIN

VOLUME I                    FEBRUARY, 1920                    NO. 1

### The Proposed Halsey Memorial

ALL friends of the college, upon the campus, in the
local community, and in the wider alumni circles,
are interested in the plan for providing a suitable
memorial for Dr. Halsey, whose life and work remain the
most complete embodiment of the spirit of Lake Forest.

For such a memorial sentiment in Lake Forest favors
an alcove in the College Library, to be known as the John
J. Halsey Alcove, which shall contain a collection of books
in the general field of history and political and social science.
Such a collection of books would constitute a singularly
appropriate memorial of Doctor Halsey, suggesting his own
literary proclivities, the direction of his scientific inquiries,
and his interest in his student's reading.

Furthermore, the al-
cove, with its growing
number of books, central-
ly located in the College
Library, would through
its usefulness to students
and citizens stand through
coming generations as a
tangible token and living
symbol of the respect and
admiration given to a
great teacher and an in-
spiring friend by his
students and fellow
townsmen.

A sum of not less than
two thousand dollars
should be raised to provide
for the accumulation of books. The hope is that half of
this sum will be given by the college alumni, and the other
half by the citizens of Lake Forest.

The editor of the News-Bulletin would like to hear
expressions from the alumni as to the type of memorial
which would be most likely favored, and suggestions as to
the method of financing the project. Such communications,
addressed to the editor, will be published in a later issue
of the News-Bulletin.

### Alumni Student Campaign of Last Summer Successful

AT a meeting of the General Alumni Association held
shortly after Commencement last year, eight of the
older Alumni pledged among themselves a sum of
$1,500 to be used in a campaign for new students for Lake
Forest College.

Through the efforts of these eight alumni, fifteen additional alumni made contributions to the fund; which
brought the total above the originally pledged figure.

(Continued on Page 2)

### The Kind of a Man I Would Select for President of Lake Forest

BY AN ALUMNUS

THE man must be of a distinctly and positively
Christian type.

His scholarship must be of such a high grade as to
command the respect of a strong faculty and of the educational public with whom he comes in contact.

He should be a man of ability as a public speaker.

He should have a constructive, creative type of mind
along educational lines and an ability to connect education
with present day needs.

He must have convictions, vision, fore-sight.

He must have executive and administrative ability.

He must be an out-
standing man who will
come to Lake Forest not
because he thinks im-
mediately that it would be
a promotion, but a man
who must be shown that
there is an opportunity in
Lake Forest for a big
man—a big man's job.

He must lend distinc-
tion to the school im-
mediately, rather than
have the school as it stands
appeal to him as lending
him distinction. In other
words we do not want to
waste time considering any
mediocre timber.

He must be big enough to see the vision of a greater
Lake Forest, to execute it, and command the respect and
the hearing of any one he may approach with this larger
future for Lake Forest in mind. We are not striking out
at the same level as the average small college, but striking
at a very much higher level than anything we have thought
of before for Lake Forest.

He should be not over fifty years of age—preferably
under forty-five.

The man we want will be very difficult to get. He
will have to be shown the possibilities of the institution,
which will tax his capacities and energy.

The Board of Trustees is now looking for a suitable candidate for the presidency. If you know of a
man who seems to meet the requirements, write and
tell us about him. We will suggest his name to the
Board of Trustees.—Editor.

education; such an education as may be given in a college of arts and sciences without extensive additions to its staff or equipment. Apparently the colleges of liberal arts will be called upon more and more in the coming years to meet this particular demand for training.[29]

Capen then briefly outlined a program that would combine study and practical experience by initiating cooperative relationships with neighboring industrial and mercantile firms, arguing that Lake Forest College, thirty miles north of Chicago, would be in an especially favorable location to undertake such a plan, which, if proven useful, would likely engender the financial support of that business community. And indeed a dramatically altered curricular direction was highlighted in the 1921 catalog, where, for the first time, the offerings leading to a bachelor of arts degree in Business Administration were listed. Among these were classes in accounting, marketing, finance, banking and the bond business, and actuarial, statistical, and even secretarial work. Later in the year a separate catalog of a Department of Business Administration was published.

One of the most urgent passages in Capen's memorandum had been his exhortation that whatever plan the College decided on required the leadership of a "man of reputation and possessed of a policy. It is essential that the policy should be a matter of conviction to the President." And he later reiterated the point: "In very self-defense the college must select for its President a man of force...."

No such choice was made. The man finally brought to campus to oversee the implementation of its goals was the Reverend Herbert McComb Moore.[30] As matters would have it, he was a Lake Forest alumnus (Class of 1896), the first and to this day the only graduate to ascend to the presidency, a post he formally assumed in 1921, after a one-year trial period as acting president. Upon his graduation from Lake Forest, Moore had attended McCormick Theological Seminary until 1899, following that with a year of study at the United Presbyterian Theological Seminary in Edinburgh; in his inaugural year he was awarded a D.D. at the University of Pittsburgh. His first professional appointment took him to Colorado's Cripple Creek region, where federal troops had been summoned to put down a series of bloody insurrections by local miners.[31] Moore's task was to preach in Goldfield, the town sheltering the troops encamped there under orders to protect the owners and their property.

After pastoral service and Presbyterian campus ministries in Wisconsin and New York State and a stint with the YMCA in France during World War I, he returned to his alma mater, where he would occupy the presidential chair until 1942. That twenty-one-year term would be far longer than any served by his predecessors, and the vocationalist direction the Board and the Moore administration established was destined to endure for almost forty years. That, in fact, was roughly the same amount of time that had elapsed since the University/College's 1876 opening, a span during which all its presidents or deans had been well-trained, well-informed men devoted to keeping the school abreast of the most advanced practices in American higher education. (Lake Forest, for example, in choosing John Coulter, was among the earliest institutions of its kind to hire a nonclerical president.)[32] Leadership, whether at the College or among the local citizens who supported it, had been the vital element in the school's success.

Yet with the accession of the new president, the momentum implicit in that asset stopped, at an especially crucial time. For the Reverend Moore brought next to no appropriate academic experience to his job and, accordingly, little understanding and appreciation of the character, cause, and polity of a liberal arts college, let alone one in search of a new identity. The Board apparently chose him because his own politics seemed close enough to theirs and his educational goals intellectually unadventurous and amenable to the newly countenanced objectives. He was, that is to say, manageable and reliable. In his letter of acceptance of the presidency, he had written to the Board, "It is my purpose

**Opposite.** President Herbert McComb Moore (right) (1876–1942), Class of 1896, presenting Harold L. Ickes (center), secretary of the interior, an honorary Doctor of Laws degree in 1933. (Ickes's granddaughter, Barbara Ickes, would graduate in 1955.) Professor Fletcher B. Coffin is pictured on the left. Moore has been the only alumnus to become president of the College, serving more than two decades, from 1920–42.

**Left center.** The Department of Business Administration was formed in 1921 "to meet the imperative demand for the thorough and specialized training of those men and women who plan to enter business." This curricular development could be seen in part as a response to the perceived challenge to business by postwar leftist sentiments.

**Left below.** Since February 1920, when Volume 1, Number 1 of the *Lake Forest College Alumni News-Bulletin* first appeared, the College has issued, at regular intervals, communications to its alumni and friends. This periodical continued into the 1960s, when it was succeeded by *Spectrum*.

1921

1924

**Dr. McClure, speaking at President Moore's inauguration in November, praises the faculty's role in the community: its "plain living and high thinking" counteracting giddy flapper-era materialism.**

**New rule: "During parties, women students are not permitted to be in automobiles outside the building, nor to go off campus except by permission."**

to give the utmost of myself to develop and maintain whatever plans and purposes are suggested by you for Lake Forest."[33] The Reverend McClure may have sensed something of the new president's uncommonly strong desire to please his superiors as the minister delivered the principal address at the First Presbyterian Church of Lake Forest on the occasion of Moore's installation in 1921.[34] It was a historical speech, notable for its plea to the trustees and friends to remember the College's unique place in the community and the singular role of the faculty in promoting the original educational mission of "plain living and high thinking." Not content with that, McClure spoke on behalf of a liberal theological position meant to embrace any and all religions founded on generosity and on what he called "Christlike-ness." (Judging from the record of Moore's administration, the new president followed his Board's older tradition of worshiping a more pragmatic and Calvinistic God.)

In his letter to the Board, cited earlier, the newly appointed president addressed the reconstituted course of study he had outlined for them at their last meeting, writing "that practical courses in Business Administration might be provided and that the business houses in Chicago might be used as laboratories where the students could have actual

contact with the conditions of industrial and commercial life." Were those words not reminiscent of Capen's? Yet if Moore had Capen's report in hand,[35] he did not, as matters turned out, have it in mind or heart. Courses were proposed that, among others, envisioned in the Department of Mathematics, "Mathematical Theory of Investment"; in the Department of Psychology, "Psychology of Advertising"; and in the Department of Biblical Literature, "Principles of Sociology." But the cooperative programs with Chicago institutions that were at the crux of Capen's recommendations[36] would not be assembled until some twenty-five years later, under another president's administration. What might have been a program sufficiently innovative to compensate for the loss of the College's traditional focus was forced in turn to give way for two decades to a model of uninspired vocationalism overshadowing the liberal arts.[37]

A further irony is observable in these developments. When Wright had expressed his opposition to specialized business education, he had had no doubt about the appropriate alternative: "[The college] will ... continue to do its most valuable work in training young people for business, profession, or calling, not by accustoming them to its methods and mechanical routine, but by giving them such breadth of interest and depth of thought as will enable them to distinguish the fundamental and enduring from the accidental and transitory in life.... After all, the chief purpose of the college is to inspire ... the ideal of a higher self and a larger life which represents the realization of all that is best in human nature."[38] Once again, a Lake Forest leader, speaking in 1911, had shown himself among the first to articulate a set of academic values, anticipating here positions historically identified with an exceptional period in the history of American higher education, a phase as alive with ideas as the ideas were complex in their interrelationships.[39] The 1920s and 1930s were marked by shifts in educational philosophy notable at once for innovation, reevaluation and even aggressive entrenchment, all played out in an atmosphere of vigorous debate: the scientifically oriented Germanic university model would be matched by a revitalized collegiate emphasis on the humanistic values immanent in the English tradition; the free-choice elective system would yield to a belief in general education, with a more prescribed curriculum and even common core courses in Western civilization; an honors program, initiated at Swarthmore College to benefit the most gifted students, would soon be widely copied, while other colleges, like

Antioch (with its famed work-study schedule), Reed, and Amherst, would propose new programmatic concepts; and of course the impact of John Dewey[40] and the Progressive Education Movement would create schools like Bennington, Sarah Lawrence, and Bard. Professor Irving Babbitt of Harvard,[41] whose New Humanism was in keeping with the sentiments expressed by Wright, was only one of a number of exceptional figures who bestrode the period. These included professors, to be sure, but even more memorably, a powerful group of college and university presidents: Alexander Meiklejohn at Amherst[42] (later director of the experimental college at Wisconsin), Nicholas Murray Butler at Columbia,[43] Robert Maynard Hutchins at Chicago,[44] Virginia Gildersleeve at Barnard,[45] and Frank Aydelotte at Swarthmore,[46] to name but a few. Indeed former President John Nollen, following his service in Italy, returned to America to assume the deanship and later the presidency of Grinnell College during a vital phase of that school's ascendancy.[47] It was a period, in sum, remarkable for the fecundity of its ideas and the brilliance of their sponsors.

While these exercises were enlivening the atmosphere of institutions after which the College had earlier modeled itself, Lake Forest had subsided into its own quiescent existence (where, it needs to be noted, it did weather the dark decade of the Depression). Now and then more vocational majors were created, in Speech and Education, and for a time a program in Aviation was instituted.[48] (For years a biplane was suspended from the ceiling of a laboratory in Carnegie Hall, then known as Physics.) Eventually opportunities for independent study and provision for graduating with honors were added, but, all in all, the environment remained more passive than active, well removed in spirit from that of either the educational elite or the pedagogical avant-garde.

In only one respect did the College mirror what was occurring nationally, as it followed a trend so widespread and so universally popular that no American institution stood apart from it: the continued, even growing emphasis on collegial student life.[49] The flapper mentality of the 1920s was reflected in the rising national popularity of campus fraternities and sororities[50] and an unprecedentedly keen interest in intercollegiate athletics. These several factors, each fully compatible with the others, provided a fitting response to the social needs of a homogeneous student body. Whatever may have been otherwise true of Lake Forest College, in the 1920s and 1930s it was, to those it served, a haven of sorts, confined in both size and ambition but on an interpersonal level perceptibly hospitable.

The composition of the student body accounts for this as surely as did President Moore's educational outlook. Indeed the two factors reflected each other. In the late 1920s enrollment had risen from about 300 to 425,[51] a number made up mostly of a clientele whose practical career ambitions drew them to the vocationalism, the low costs, and the availability of scholarships that characterized the College's program during the Moore years.[52] Some of the students, drawn from the community's service population, lived locally, while others commuted from nearby towns.[53] The remainder were housed in limited campus residence facilities. As a group they came from modest, middle-class backgrounds, and often they were the first of their upwardly mobile families to attend college. Accordingly, they remained well beneath the social station traditionally associated with the town. That fact warrants special note, since it is a further measure of the changes that overtook both communities after World War I. Whereas the College had once drawn upon the children of the Presbyterians who created it, a new local citizenry, their continuing wealth only highlighting their detachment from the school following the Harlan and Wright episodes, chose, as earlier noted, to send their young off to the more prestigious Eastern schools. As the separation from the town gradually widened, the campus effectively withdrew into itself.

1924

**The Prince of Wales visits Lake Forest.**

1925

**The College severs its ties with Lake Forest Academy and Ferry Hall.**

1926

**The Lake Forest Garden Club organizes the Foundation for Architecture and Landscape Architecture, housed at the College.**

**Above.** Kappa Sigma Tau fraternity room, 1929.

**Center.** Theta Psi sorority room, 1929.

**Below.** Members of the Phi Pi Epsilon fraternity burning their paddles in 1936, when fraternities abandoned this particular hazing ritual. From left: Albert Perry '36, T. Jae Reinier '40, Richard O. Vycital '39, William W. Penrod '36, Albert J. Nortman '37, and Edward H. Hoffman '36.

Membership in fraternities and sororities peaked in the late 1930s, when on average four out of five students were Greeks.[54] Football continued throughout the period to command the most concentrated attention, but basketball, baseball, men's tennis (and later women's tennis, women's baseball, and volleyball) hardly lacked their own followings. Homecoming, with its traditional bonfire and parade, and the junior prom, ruled by a campus king and queen, were the social highlights of the year, each as much an extravaganza as an event. Variety shows, formal dances, special occasions like the midwinter dinner, and assorted parties filled out most of the remaining school calendar. Nothing better illustrated extracurricular student life than the standards and induction rituals of the Iron Key Club, a group of senior men recognized as the combined social and academic leaders of the campus.[55] Once a year, as several robed and hooded members of Iron Key circulated deliberately and ceremoniously through a student audience, one of their number would suddenly tap a junior male on the shoulder and shout, "You!"

Given these various activities and circumstances, the College's graduates developed into alumni with fond recollections of the classmates they had spent their days with, the coaches they had played or cheered for, and the professors they had studied with, who, not insignificantly, lived on campus too, sometimes in the same buildings that served as student dormitories.[56] And while in retrospect this social amiability may have exacted a price in the form of the decline of the high academic standards to which the College had aspired in its earlier days,[57] the fact remains that many Americans present and past who have gone to college, not just Lake Foresters, judge their experience more by nonacademic than academic criteria.

In any case, it warrants remarking that the College of the Moore years, even with its circumscribed academic goals, produced its own list of successful alumni, one recent enough, in fact, to be known to living memory. An assortment of

fields is represented in it: in business by J. Howard Wood '22, who gained distinction as the publisher of the *Chicago Tribune*,[58] and Frank L. Spreyer Jr. '35, executive vice president of Jewel Foods; in publishing by Arnold W. Carlson '28, vice president of *Time-Life*;[59] in the arts by Robert E. Wallenborn '27, concert pianist and professor of music at Washington University, and Winfred (Win) Stracke '31, well remembered as a pioneer television personality, singer, and scholar of folk music who founded Chicago's Old Town School of Folk Music; in the military by Edward K. Cleveland '31 and Elmer J. Maiman '39, career officers, respectively, in the army and navy; in education by Robert King Hall '34, who had a distinguished career as an international authority on schooling in the Middle East and Far East, Stephen W. Gray '36, professor of anatomy at Emory University, and Harold F. Bright '37, provost at George Washington University. Women graduates who similarly rose to eminence include, among others, Angelina Pietrangeli '26, the first tenured woman on the faculty of Foreign Languages at the University of Illinois, and Mary Longbrake '35,[60] the first female vice president of the Northern Trust Company. Worthy of special mention is

**Above.** A lively moment of women's basketball in the venerable 1891 Gymnasium, in 1936–37.

**Below.** Though they were able to field a large team, the 1933–34 women's volleyball team played only interclass tournaments. From left: Wilma Westerman '35, Janice Hagerty '37, Janet Hardsocg '37, Lois Wilson '37, Margaret Clark '37, Ruth Hackley '36, Reva Kamper '36, Coach Mildred Travis Murphy, June Webster '37, Margaret Holty '35, Helen Heyworth '36, Eleanor Thompson '36, Margaret Shoemaker '37, Marjorie Ingram '36, Jane Crawford '37, and, kneeling, Virginia Throgmorton '37.

1926

1926

**Noted author Anna Farwell De Koven, Class of 1880, returns to campus to receive an honorary degree at the celebration of the fiftieth anniversary of the College's re-establishment in 1876.**

**Lake Forest's football team defeats Michigan State at East Lansing by a score of 6–0.**

philanthropist Irvin L. Young '26 (for whom College Hall would later be renamed), the archetypal example of a successful alumnus of the Moore years, who as a student walked around campus clutching a Bible and the *Mechanic's Handbook*, and who later made a hefty amount of money from his inventions, one of which was a hot dog–labeling machine.

Even more widely – indeed internationally – recognized are Herbert Block '31 (Herblock),[61] known for his trenchant political cartoons (his talent already observable in the wit and technique of the drawings he did for *The Forester* yearbook of 1930) and for his long and illustrious term of service at the *Washington Post*; and Richard Widmark '36,[62] who achieved a memorable reputation among American motion picture actors of the post–World War II generation. Widmark, in fact, served briefly on the College's drama faculty following his graduation, when the Garrick Players performed well enough to attract, as little else the College did, the attention of the townsfolk.

If not distinguished as an educational leader, President Moore personally is warmly recalled by more than a few of the alumni who knew him, and the faculty had its own roster of worthies. Records of local note were assembled by Harold Curtis (in residence 1926–52, Ph.D. Cornell) in Mathematics and Sterling Price Williams (1927–49, Ph.D. Chicago) in Philosophy and Psychology, with Roscoe Harris[63] (1925–46, Ph.D. Chicago) in Physics having somewhat broader recognition for his pioneer work in television. But the individuals best remembered were those whose fields were in closest accord with the school's curriculum. No professor of the time was more respected and more popular with students than Ernest Johnson (Ph.D. Northwestern), an economist and a stalwart of the Business Administration program. And while Johnson later rose in the ranks to succeed Moore as president in 1942, during his faculty tenure his reputation was matched by Russell Tomlinson (B.A. DePauw), director of the Garrick Theater,

an enterprise close to the extracurricularly oriented hearts of the student body. Finally, during the time in question and in fact in the entire history of the College, no name stands out more prominently than that of Ralph Jones,[64] the head football coach from 1932 to 1949.

Jones is a story unto himself, not merely because his Lake Forest teams consistently outplayed their competition, but because he has entered the record books as one of the most important innovative spirits in the history of football. He is credited with the addition of the man-in-motion to the T formation, a strategem that added such weight to offensive play that it has long been a crucial, even elemental,

Opposite. May Day exercises, an annual event from the teens and twenties, with Queen Mary Ruth Hendrickson '21, at center. In 1928 she married J. Howard Wood '22, late publisher of the *Chicago Tribune* and a trustee of the College.

Above. Perhaps no graduate in the history of the College has been as loyal in supporting alumni activities as Mary Longbrake '35, shown here at a 1970 event. The also-loyal gentlemen are, from left: Charles L. Thayer Jr. '16, Dan'l H. Brush '51, Dr. Edward C. Holmblad '16, and William L. Powell '51.

Below. On the left is pictured at the 1962 Commencement Irvin L. Young '26, the archetypal Moore-era student, who later made possible the renovation of the 1878 five-story College Hall, named Young Hall in his honor in 1981.

1929

Sigma Eta honor society is founded.

Quiesence and Amiability

# Block-Buster!

A three-time Pulitzer Prize winner, dubbed by *Time* in a 1960 cover story "the foremost editorial cartoonist in the U.S.," political cartoonist Herbert Block '31 honed his artistic and intellectual skills in two years at Lake Forest, 1927–29. Herblock, as he is known professionally, drew cartoons for the *Stentor* and illustrated the 1930 *Forester* yearbook. And in a *Stentor* interview in October 1968, he observed, "A school publication is the greatest place in the world to begin to learn how to draw or write for the public, to see how pictures reproduce in print and how people react to what you have to say."

But at Lake Forest Block didn't learn only to draw. His 1930 *Forester* contributions included six caricatures of professors who were important to him, for as he acknowledged, "One of the great things about Lake Forest was that the professors would meet with you and talk with you individually." One of those pictured was David Maynard, a professor in Block's major of political science, who got the young man "interested in international affairs, in the role of the United States throughout the world.... Maynard and I got to talking about politics more and more on an informal basis.... "

Former *Washington Post* publisher Katharine Graham has noted of her distinguished staff member that Herblock's ability to focus and crystallize issues of right and wrong "often influenced the course of events in Washington. " His championship of individuals' freedoms led him to coin the term "McCarthyism" and also to be granted the honor of designing a commemorative postage stamp for the 175th anniversary of the Bill of Rights in 1966. Since the early 1950s he has published several books, prompting one commentator to declare, "[Herblock is] a triple threat. He can think, he can draw, and he can write like nobody's business.'"

Herbert Block, if too busy to finish his degree, did stay in touch – directly and indirectly – with his alma mater and it with him, awarding him an honorary degree in 1957 and honorary Phi Beta Kappa membership in 1962. More significant is a legacy, tangible and intangible, from the College that has indeed remained with him: the little man, traceable to the 1930 *Forester* figure of a debater shouting his head off, who evolved into the cartoon representation, familiar to those who know his work, of "the vast multitude of folks that Herblock attempts ... to push into some sort of involvement with the world." For Herblock himself, as he described it, this engagement began at Lake Forest, especially in those conversations with Professor David Maynard.

Herblock's cartoons as they appeared in the 1930 *Forester*: upper left, Professor David Maynard; upper right, Harold Curtis; center, F.C.L. van Steenderen; lower right, Russell C. Tomlinson, lower middle, Ernest Johnson; and lower left, Walter Bridgman.

1935

The campus literary maga-
zine *Tusitala* is launched by
Stephen Gray '36 and Netta
Steinhaus '36.

component of the game. (Jones introduced it in 1927, when he coached teams at Lake Forest Academy.) Nor were his major accomplishments confined to tactical theory. Following his Academy years, he was head coach of the Chicago Bears professional team from 1930 to 1932, when he put together a record surpassed in the glittering annals of that franchise solely by the team's owner and first and later head coach, George Halas. That the College was fully aware of his importance not only as a national figure but as an athletic role model in the kind of undergraduate school President Moore had seen take shape is reflected in the attractiveness of the invitation from Moore that coaxed him back to Lake Forest. His annual salary in 1933 – in the depths of the Depression – was $4,000, an amount not only hugely above that of the average or even the best-paid academic faculty member,[65] but one greatly at odds with Moore's normally parsimonious approach to the College's economy. For in that period more than a few faculty members were paid minimal salaries and granted emoluments in the form of free living quarters – on campus, of course – and free meals, provided they were taken in the College's dining facilities.

As Lake Forest the college and Lake Forest the town passed through the 1920s and 1930s, even the Depression did little to reconcile or balance the respective fortunes of the two worlds – one the home of a coterie of very rich people, the other the site of a frugally run institution whose earlier academic bloom had faded. Prior to the 1929 crash, the town had experienced an economic rush that more than matched the nation's recovery from the post–World War I downturn. While the reputation of Lake Forest as a locale of mansions built on large plots of land by men of commercial importance goes back to the founding days, it increased substantially in these decades, just as the town's population more than doubled,[66] ushering in a new cluster of prominent citizens that included the Armour,[67]

Swift,[68] Reed/Schweppe,[69] and Donnelley[70] families and such nationally recognized financial figures as Samuel Insull,[71] public utilities tycoon, Edward A. Ryerson,[72] president of Inland Steel Company, Alfred Hamill,[73] investment banker, Albert Lasker,[74] advertising magnate, and Robert J. Thorne,[75] chief executive of Montgomery Ward & Company.

This narrative has already established that the early pieties of the Presbyterian fathers gave way to a growing cosmopolitanism when the Onwentsia Club was organized in the 1890s; but the swift acceleration of the village's social prestige two to three decades later may be measured by the fashionable new quarters the club put up for itself in 1927 and just as surely by the appearance of two more country clubs, Shoreacres in 1921 and Knollwood in 1924.[76] These additions in turn reflected the rising wealth of the owners of the grandiose residential compounds built in large numbers for this new generation, who, unlike their immediate predecessors, would make Lake Forest more than just their summer home.[77]

A number of architects, gifted and socially well connected, were quick to descend upon such an attractive scene, proving themselves more than equal to the generous budgetary means of their clients. Although Howard Van Doren Shaw was forced by failing health to curtail much of his practice in the 1920s,[78] the traditional building styles beloved of a conservative community were masterfully realized by a company of younger men, most notably David Adler,[79] Harrie T. Lindeberg,[80] Edwin H. Clark,[81] and Walter Frazier.[82] Their efforts were matched in turn by a comparably talented group of landscape architects, led by Jens Jensen,[83] Warren Manning,[84] Rose S. Nichols,[85] Ellen Shipman,[86] and the Olmsted brothers.[87] Taken together, the body of work these designers left in Lake Forest has since turned the townscape into a cynosure of national architectural historians.

1938

**President Moore mounts a campaign in the 1930s to expand campus facilities, including the 1938 remodeling of Reid Library (1900) to accommodate more books by adding a second floor. The modest nature of the** **fund-raising effort (made up of small donations, some collected in little metal coin banks like this) is in marked contrast to the original one-donor gift of the building.**

**Above.** Iron Key Society of 1933–34. Pictured from left: Alfred James Wennermark '34, George Eaton '34, Professor Ernest Johnson, Frank L. Spreyer Jr. '35 (later trustee), William H. J. Schultz '34, Milton E. Morgan '34, Rudi H. Kroetz '35, Robert Bade '35, and Sampson Parsons '35. The traditional Iron Key tapping ceremony was held in the Chapel at the end of the school year.

**Center.** Ralph R. Jones, directing men's athletics from 1933 to 1949, is remembered as one of the great innovators of football, coaching the Chicago Bears prior to coming to Lake Forest. Jones perfected the T formation, and while at Lake Forest continually experimented with protective gear, including shoulder pads.

**Below.** Jones's undefeated 1938 "Jaybirds" football team.

1940

112

**Lake Forest's football team is undefeated for a second time.**

It also provided a setting for a continuing tradition of lavish entertaining, its estates worthy of such visitors as Great Britain's Prince of Wales, who enjoyed the hospitality of Louis Swift in 1924, and, two years later, Crown Prince Gustavus Adolphus and Princess Louise of Sweden, who were guests of Mr. and Mrs. Charles Schweppe.[88] This was the Lake Forest immortalized by the novelist F. Scott Fitzgerald, himself an occasional visitor.[89]

In short, Lake Forest's social and corporate destinies were in sure hands on the eve of the Depression. While the town was affected, like the rest of the country, by the financial catastrophe that followed, its economic power saw it through with relatively minor losses. But with the growth of its population, its citizens continued to become correspondingly more heterogeneous in their interests. More than ever, social groups diversified and cliques took form, each with its own special agenda, seldom mindful of the principal missions of the founding fathers, central to which had been the College and its preparatory schools.[90]

Ever ironically, then, as the town looked confidently outward to the world, the College had turned almost totally inward and apart, not always managing to keep even its own campus boundaries free of disagreements with a community already grown both aloof and unsympathetic. For in 1925 the College had decided to sever its ties with the Academy and Ferry Hall—a move, interestingly enough, that consultant Capen had cautioned against several years earlier. Since most of the wealthy had children in the latter two schools (if no longer at the College), the stipulation that the College would receive $200,000 from each of the other two institutions added a sense of grievance toward it.[91] That this contretemps may have marked a low point in the relationship between town and gown seems to have been underscored a year later, when the College, in observance of the fiftieth anniversary of the matriculation of its first class, persuaded Anna Farwell De Koven to travel from her home in Florence, Italy, to receive an honorary doctorate.[92] The records show that the event was indifferently attended by her Chicago and Lake Forest social peers.[93]

If there was a definable moment of grace that lessened the impact of the cross purposes of town and gown, it followed the organization in 1926 of the Foundation for Architecture and Landscape Architecture.[94] Assembled by the elite Lake Forest Garden Club, which was influenced at the time by the City Beautiful aesthetic, the foundation arranged to rent the College's facilities during the summers.[95] It

furnished its own faculty and enticed the top architecture and landscape architecture graduates from each of a group of Midwestern universities to live and work on the College campus. There they were instructed in the exemplary combinations of built and landscaped environments that had been realized on the neighboring great estates. The project prospered. Armed with a talented and promising student body, it eventually drew students from as far as Harvard University,[96] in the process garnering a national reputation that prompted President Moore's proposal to build a separate structure for the foundation and incorporate it formally within the College.[97] After six years, however, the Depression intervened, and the concept, as well as another master plan for the campus, prepared in the 1930s by the Chicago architectural firm of Puckey & Jenkins,[98] never materialized. While Faculty Circle was enlarged by four one-family houses in 1927 and four duplexes in 1937, no academic buildings were erected during the twenty-one years of the Moore administration, a time during which most American colleges and universities were busy with construction projects that reflected burgeoning programs. In the late 1930s, as the world stood poised on the brink of World War II, instead of becoming a first-rate institution of higher learning working in close rapport with its immediate community, and even with the business world of Chicago, Lake Forest had retreated into its own small sphere, all too self contained. For the very recollection of a distinguished history had evaporated. In effect, the College had lost track of its own past.

The faculty at a hobo party on February 16, 1934, in Durand Commons. First row, seated, from left: Mrs. Tomlinson; Mrs. Wood; Mrs. Curtis; Mrs. Johnson; Mildred Murphy (Physical Education – Women); Mrs. Davey; Mrs. McPheeters; Bruce Lineburg, (Biology); Solly Hartzo (Political Science); and Russell C. Tomlinson (Speech and Drama). Second row: Mrs. Coffin; Mrs. Hartzo (nurse); Elizabeth Teter Smith (Lunn) (Biology); Miss Sloan; Mrs. Sleight; Mrs. Williams; Mrs. Harris; Mrs. Jones; and Mrs. Lineburg. Third row: Mrs. Hall; Louis Keller (Economics); Eldon Hill (English); Edward Perry (History); S. P. Williams (Philosophy and Psychology); Ernest Johnson (Economics and Business); President Herbert Moore; Mabel Powell (librarian); and Mrs. Logan. Fourth row: Mrs. Smith; Warren Hall (business manager); Walter Armbruster (Music); George Wood (History); Fletcher Coffin (Chemistry); Roscoe Harris (Physics); Ralph Jones (Physical Education – Men); Victor Davey (Romance Languages); Harold Curtis (Mathematics); William McPheeters (dean of the college, English); G. Johnson (coach); Robert Logan (Economics); George Sleight (Education); and F. C. L. van Steenderen (Modern Languages).

# From Floodlights to Klieg Lights
## with Richard Widmark

It was one of those electric moments of the silver screen: An utterly cold, laconic killer quietly catapults an old woman in a wheelchair down a flight of stairs – and catapults himself into cinematic history. The movie was *The Kiss of Death*; the year, 1947; the actor, Richard Widmark '36. From this breakthrough leading role in a classic *film noir* more than fifty years ago to a retrospective showing of his movies on British television in 1998, Widmark's has been a notably sustained career on stage, screen, and television, distinguished nevertheless from that of many other long-term Hollywood stars by the simple fact that he has always been a thinking person's actor. However much his intelligent – often sardonic – projections are a purely personal dimension of his talent, his alma mater would like to believe that his education and early career at Lake Forest played a part, too.

For a leader on campus, Widmark's extracurricular activities ranged from the football team, under the legendary Coach Ralph Jones, to a variety of theatrical roles under Garrick Director Russell Tomlinson, mentor to many who went on to show business careers. Perhaps even more significant, his incubation at the College included a two-year postgraduate stint backing up the veteran Tomlinson and directing plays on his own – this before taking off for New York to seek a future on the stage that soon led him to the West Coast.

Well documented in the College archives are the records of Widmark's visits to campus in the 1950s and 1960s, at the height of his career, when he invigorated Garrick performers of the day with his presence. His very identifiable voice can be heard, too, narrating a 1965 student venture into filmmaking. Appropriately, in recognition of his achievements, he would be presented with an honorary degree.

A 1934 Garrick production of *Smilin' Through* with, on the right, student Richard Widmark '36, who played two roles.

1940

114

**Epitomizing the amiable tone of the Moore era, the year's *Forester* is dedicated "to the spirit of friendship at Lake Forest ... on campus, in the classroom ... in fraternity and sorority...."**

# Stirrings and Renewal Under President Johnson

chapter **7**

1943—1959

In the years immediately prior to World War II, the role of Chicago in the impassioned debate between the isolationists and interventionists was greatly sustained by the conservatism of the powerful *Chicago Tribune*, a position shared by most leading Lake Forest citizens. Although the formal declaration of war following the Japanese attack on Pearl Harbor late in 1941 settled that issue, the United States had begun peacetime conscription in 1940, an action that left colleges and universities throughout the land confronted with the depletion of their male student populations.

At Lake Forest College, with its enrollment then at a level well below 400, this development amounted to a threat to its very existence.[1] Once again war was to play a major role in the College's fortunes. The Civil War had effectively closed the school down in the 1860s, and events triggered

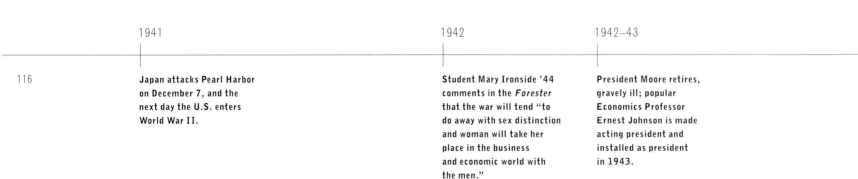

1941

**Japan attacks Pearl Harbor on December 7, and the next day the U.S. enters World War II.**

1942

**Student Mary Ironside '44 comments in the *Forester* that the war will tend "to do away with sex distinction and woman will take her place in the business and economic world with the men."**

1942–43

**President Moore retires, gravely ill; popular Economics Professor Ernest Johnson is made acting president and installed as president in 1943.**

by World War I had led to major alterations in its educational direction.

A sense of desperation may be apparent from the addition of a program in secretarial training, including credit courses in beginning shorthand, to the curriculum in 1941.[2] Yet the crisis only deepened when President Moore resigned in February 1942, due to ill health, and died three months later,[3] leaving the College with not only a major enrollment problem but the need for a new president to deal with it. The trustees elevated a member of the faculty, Professor of Economics and Business Administration Ernest Johnson, who had already taken on the acting presidency prior to Moore's death.[4]

One of Johnson's earliest decisions, the appointment of Robert Amaden as the College's first director of admissions,[5] contributed signally to increasing the enrollment. In 1942, initiating a campaign to recruit students by visiting high schools in northeastern Illinois and southeastern Wisconsin, Amaden succeeded in bringing to campus 173 new students (an increase of 18 percent over the previous year), with the 26 percent increase in women enough to keep the school for the moment financially viable – even as many of the men left for the services.[6] Blessed with a naturally optimistic, outgoing personality and an exceptional gift for relating easily to all types of people who comprised the College family, Amaden was to remain on campus in a variety of capacities for four decades, remembered by virtually everyone who had contact with him as one of its most beloved and productive figures.

Johnson's early strategy also included a concentrated effort to reach out to local industry. Early in 1943 he developed a working relationship with the local building materials firm of Johns-Manville that led to a program of scholarships notable for its merger of educational and business interests.[7] (Thus the recommendations made to the College by Samuel Capen[8] were fulfilled in spirit, at least partially,

some two decades after they had been made.) Thirty female high school honors students from across the nation were offered a free education at Lake Forest, with their own choice of majors, in return for which they were expected to put in work hours twice a week at the company offices in Waukegan, then to assume full-time responsibilities for a respectable period after they graduated. The "Manville Girls,"[9] as the group came to be called, added to the quality of the women's enrollment, which held numerically steady during the war. Males obviously constituted a more worrisome issue, but substantial relief arrived late in 1943, when negotiations with the federal government sent to the College approximately 400 men of the Army Specialized Training Program (ASTP).[10] These soldiers, enrolled in subjects essential to their candidacy as potential officers, remained in residence for little more than a year, but by the time they left in 1944, other means had been found to make up for their loss. A summer school began operation in 1942,[11] and an evening session, initiated in the fall of 1942, was expanded in the winter of 1943 to include eleven classes in Lake Forest and three in Waukegan, serving a total of 177 students.[12] These programs had the double advantage

1943

**Four-hundred ASTP men arrive on campus. Among them is Arthur Dubin '49 of Highland Park, who, after service in the Pacific, would become a Chicago architect and expert on passenger rail travel, giving the College in the** late 1990s his collection of railroad photographs. Accounts of all who served in the military are to be found in a volume published after the war, *Lake Forest College World War II Military Records.*

of offering credit courses to students of nonconventional standing and of providing extra wages for the regular faculty.

Meanwhile, another development of the war years pertinent to student recruitment calls for special notation here, partly because it was exceptional for its day and partly because it was the first instance of organized cultural diversity on the campus. It involved a small group of Nisei students, college-age men and women of Japanese ancestry whose families had been interned in California but who were considered patriotically "reliable" enough to allow the American Friends Service Committee to sponsor them at a number of Midwestern schools, Lake Forest among them.[13]

Thus, just as the beginning of the war had nearly brought on the ruination of the College, the end found it not only functioning but hopeful of better times. Johnson's role in saving the school and fueling its hopes for the future would eventually be judged among the proudest achievements of his presidency.

By 1946, the College as well as Chicago and the town of Lake Forest looked out upon a world that suddenly seemed to bear little resemblance to the one that had preceded the war. For a time, the nation's attention was fixed on the University of Chicago as the locale where research had led to the harnessing of nuclear energy and the development of the atomic bomb, the weapon most decisive in bringing an end to global hostilities. Yet with the years, that extraordinary accomplishment became more and more associated with the past than with the present, and in other respects the city's postwar fate added up to a mixture of loss and gain, frustration and success. The airplane and the automobile replaced the railroad as the prime means of moving people and goods from place to place, and Chicago lost a special position it had owned, and relished, for nearly a century, as the nation's transportation hub. Communications were similarly affected. For a short time following the war, the city became a regional center of television programming, but as the medium went national in the 1950s, the magnetic power of the long-standing centers of the entertainment world was strong enough to pull Chicago talent into the commanding embraces of New York and Los Angeles.

Yet several traditions historically associated with the city did remain intact. Chicago's role as the nation's convention center was reinforced with the construction of the mammoth McCormick Place exposition hall in 1960. Moreover, postwar industrial production increased, underscoring one of the city's ancient strengths and reinforcing its importance as one of the country's chief commercial, financial, and shipping centers.

Meanwhile and relatedly, Lake County and the northern suburbs prospered from the addition of the Johns-Manville company, already noted, and such major health care companies as Searle, Abbott, Baxter and American Hospital Supply. The response of Lake Forest itself to the postwar economy took the form of changes in its social makeup. Middle-class real estate developments rose south and west of the village, and the ranch house became the standard form of residence serving a citizenry of young executives and professional careerists. Wealthier townspeople, affected by the high income tax rates instituted during the administration of President Franklin Delano Roosevelt, found it more difficult to create homes equal in splendor to the great estates that had made the town famous in the days prior to the New Deal.[14]

Nonetheless, the American economy as a whole flourished in the late 1940s and 1950s and in one major respect prosperity, mixed with the optimism of a victorious nation, produced a benefit to colleges and universities that more than made up for the earlier loss of manpower to the war. One of the most important legislative acts of the time, historic in its buoyant effect on the younger population, was the federal GI Bill of Rights, which assured many returning veterans effectively cost-free college education. Enrollments swelled throughout the country, especially among men, and in turn schools were obliged proportionally to take on more faculty. For academia at large, it was a time of explosive growth.

If all these developments foreshadowed a new phase in the history of Lake Forest College, they did not amount to a revolution. The school continued to grow from Presbyterian roots, and Business Administration still dominated a curriculum nominally given to the liberal arts but weighted with elements of vocationalism. Johnson's own position was illustrative of the state of affairs. He was a moderate, committed at once to custom and to change. His own professional background and his fidelity to the interests of business can be read in the effort he devoted to the creation in 1946 of the Industrial Management Institute.[15] The IMI, organized as part of the College but separated from the regular curriculum, offered a nondegree program of two years (later extended to four) to students drawn from middle

Opposite above. Of the 400 soldiers brought to campus by the Army Specialized Training Program, 200 were headed for Europe and 200 for the Far East, to participate in what would be for this group the more costly invasions of Leyte and Okinawa. At a welcome-home dinner in April 1946, President Johnson honored Lake Forest College's 1,085 men and women who served in the war: "They took part in every landing; they manned the ships on every battle line at sea; they piloted bombers and fighters . . . ." Of this total, 74 gave their lives.

Center. In 1944, the Economics Club led by Professor Louis Keller included two Japanese-Americans, Nobby Arata '47 and John Tachihara '47.

Below. Irene Himmel '52 (foreground) in the process of moving into what is now Moore Hall on South Campus, ca. 1950. It was a family affair, with mother, father, and sister helping out.

management positions in Johns-Manville and two other nearby companies, Fansteel and Abbott Laboratories. This was further evidence of the College's growing relationship with the business community. (Among several later instances of that same cordiality, the James S. Kemper Foundation established its own Lake Forest College scholarship, the first recipient of which was David B. Mathis '60, who went on to become chairman and CEO of the Kemper Corporation itself — and who is expected to be elected chairman of the College's Board of Trustees in 2000, the first alumnus to hold that position in more than fifty years.)[16]

Yet at roughly this same time, Johnson also oversaw the establishment of the Department of Art in 1944,[17] an addition obviously meant to strengthen the humanities and underscore the College's commitment to its liberal arts identity. Meanwhile he maintained his staunch personal involvement with the church even as he remained loyal — *qualifiedly* loyal — to the school's formal Christian mission. In 1943 the Board of Christian Education of the Presbyterian Church had issued a set of standards requiring among other things that all faculty members in Presbyterian colleges be regular members of "some evangelical Christian Church which affirms its loyalty to Jesus Christ as the divine Lord and Savior." Johnson offered his own response to that mandate, as reported in the Faculty Minutes of October 10, 1944: "He ... stated that we should make an effort to cooperate with the Presbyterian Church, but that we should not permit it to dictate our educational policies. Dr. Johnson expressed the opinion that the phrasing of this statement [on church membership] is unfortunate and that it would not mean that the Church is to determine the kind of teachers that would be selected for Lake Forest College."[18] But while throughout the 1950s the directives implicit to many in the motto *Christo et Ecclesiae* would be as often as not observed in the breach, that was not enough for the faculty, who concertedly pressed for the elimination of all such denominational restrictions.[19]

The collective force behind this latter-day spirit was the younger instructional staff appointed directly following the end of the war. Most of them had never been acquainted with President Moore, who was known among the staff of his day as looking every inch a daunting executive and behaving like one too, a man capable of intimidating his subordinates.[20] His successor, Johnson, who projected a mild manner and an academic outlook amenable to compromise, was obviously more approachable. Yet that very fact, together with the fresh academic drive that moved most of the new faculty, only granted them greater latitude in forwarding their own agenda, which was stirred by a more purist attitude toward the liberal arts than was the ecumenicism of Johnson. Thus in the context of the late 1940s they were in effect innovators, another irony, since the ideals they espoused were those of the College of the Nollen

**Opposite.** Professor Joseph Nash's art class (1947) with model Lila Spannenberg '48. From left the artists are William D. Hollis '48, Shirley Parnell '50, and Lynn Beidler '49.

**Above.** Christmas cards illustrated by art students Helen Gayle '46, Mary Pope '45, and Lenore Linder '47. (Top left) the Blackstone-Harlan gates, (top right) College Hall, by this time missing its wooden porch and (bottom) the entrance to the Chapel.

mid–1940s

1946

**Woman's Athletic Association Trophy.**

**As enrollment reaches an all-time high of 754, new wings are approved for Blackstone and Harlan halls.**

# David B. Mathis, Modern-Day Horatio Alger

The Kemper Corporation recouped its investment tenfold when one-time Kemper Scholar David B. Mathis '60 was promoted to Kemper's executive team in 1982. Now the chairman and chief executive officer of Kemper, a major Long Grove, Illinois, firm dealing in insurance, risk management, and reinsurance, Mathis provides a model case of the way the Kemper Scholar program serves both students and the corporation.

The Kemper Foundation, established by James Scott Kemper, awards scholarships at seventeen institutions including Lake Forest College. In addition to receiving financial aid, Kemper Scholars spend their three undergraduate summers working within Kemper.

Mathis, a committed high school basketball player, was recruited to Lake Forest when his high school coach told him that he was an excellent candidate for the Scholar program. After his selection as a Kemper recipient, he participated fully in College life during the school years and then worked during the summers in Kemper's San Francisco property/casualty insurance operations. The relationship proved to be a good fit. Mathis returned to that office after graduation, worked his way up to sales manager, and then won an assignment in Europe with another division of Kemper, where the adaptive training of his liberal arts background must have been an advantage.

Now, as the head of Kemper, Mathis enjoys the opportunity to "give back" both to the College and to the Kemper Foundation. His role as a trustee of Lake Forest College and its anticipated first alumnus Board chair in fifty years gives him ample opportunity to continue to nourish the relationship between these two worlds.

Phi Delta Theta's intramural football team, 1958: Front row: Jim E. Dudley '58, Richard J. Bond '60, Randolph G. Koser '58, John W. Thomas '60, Alton M. Bathrick '60, E. James Newell '58, and David H. Jacobs '59. Back row: Bruce H. Altergott '59, David B. Mathis '60, and John E. Bostock, '60.

years, now three decades past but an integral part of a history that was by this time little more than a record moldering in the files. The young faculty were driven simply by the desire, nationally widespread among educational liberals of the time, to improve the academic tenor of the school that had hired them, concentrating their energies on traditional liberal arts disciplines and methods associated with them.

The year 1946 itself was eventful in the annals of the postwar College. With enrollment at an all-time high of 754,[21] and a waiting list for women,[22] new construction became imperative. Wings were added to Harlan and Blackstone halls, following the designs of the Chicago firm of Naess & Murphy and intended to match the style of the two earlier buildings.[23] In May 1946, the main building of Lake Forest Academy was destroyed by fire, and in the following March, the Academy elected to move to new quarters west of Lake Forest, in the former J. Ogden Armour estate. Its trustees signed over the 1890s campus to the College to forgive the debt still outstanding from the separation of 1925.[24] Despite this acquisition, President Johnson was reluctant to assume control of so substantial an increase in the school's infrastructure, and in 1948 he commissioned the local landscape architect Marshall Johnson to devise a campus plan that would have added several needed buildings to North and Middle campuses, thus confining the College to those two spaces and enabling it, if it chose, to sell off the old Academy campus.[25] However, the concept never materialized, and the newly acquired area was converted into South Campus, providing dormitory space for incoming students in three of the remaining Academy buildings, East House, Annie Durand Cottage, and Eliza Remsen House.[26] At the same time two smaller structures were taken over by the departments of Music and Art,[27] and Hixon Hall, formerly a garage of an estate designed by Howard Van Doren Shaw, was transformed into a dining facility.[28] In 1950 the Alumni Memorial Fieldhouse was put up close by, following designs by Naess & Murphy.[29]

The acquisition of physical facilities was matched by the call for new faculty. Following the appointments of Harald C. Jensen to Physics in 1942, Richard W. Hantke to History in 1942 as well, and Madeline Ashton to French in 1945,[30] no fewer than six of the College's new breed of instructors arrived in 1946: Rosemary D. Hale in Economics, Edwin C. Reichert in Education, Walter W. Pese in History, Robert L. Sharvy in Philosophy, and two who returned after the war, Elizabeth T. Lunn in Biology and Arthur W. M. Voss in

English.[31] In the course of the Johnson years (with hiring overseen less by the administration and more by departments and department chairs, who made a point of looking afield for promising candidates), they would be joined by Franz Schulze in Art, Charles D. Louch in Biology, John W. Coutts in Chemistry, H. Murray Herlihy in Economics, Harold R. Hutcheson, W. Gordon Milne, Rosemary E. Cowler and Ann Louise Hentz in English, Marvin C. Dilkey in German, Lindley J. Burton in Mathematics, Ann D. Bowen in Music, Ronald H. Forgus in Psychology, and Donald E. Bartlett in Religion.[32] The increased mobility of the faculty brought on losses as well, most notably Miller Upton in Economics, to later studies that led eventually to the presidency of Beloit College; Esther Pese Wagner in English, to Pitzer; and J. Edward Dirks in Philosophy, to Yale.

All of the above-mentioned who stayed on carved out long and memorable careers at Lake Forest, traceable in part to the efforts of their number to loosen the grip of business and Business Administration on academic affairs. In this regard they had a strong ally in the person of the dean of the College, William Dunn,[33] whose devotion to the cause of the liberal arts was unsurpassed by anyone else in the Johnson administration. Notwithstanding Dunn's support, many of the new faculty were active on their own, setting in motion a debate whose briskness replaced the relative academic somnolence of the prewar years. Further evidence of their initiatives took the form of the founding, yet again in 1946, of the Lake Forest chapter of the American Association of University Professors (AAUP), a national organization – effectively a professional educators' union – that provided a forum for collegial discussions of educational topics and advanced faculty fiscal and professional

Tri Beta national biology honorary fraternity in 1956. Standing, from left: Richard H. Baughman '63, A. William Magnuson '57, Charles A. McNeil '58, John F. Stremple '57, Frederick H. Harvey '58, Ronald M. Kleim '56, John W. Gray '57, and J. Angish. Seated: Professor Elizabeth Lunn, Margot Perusse '56, and instructor in Biology Archibald Sharer.

welfare, including the establishment of guidelines governing tenure.[34] Soon enough, the AAUP group was regularly issuing recommendations and even challenges to the administration — one of which urged formal dropping of the aforementioned requirement for faculty of Christian church membership[35] — and, with the passage of the 1950s, the faculty gradually established itself as the reigning constituency of the College. A new emphasis on scholarship ensued, marked by proposals to establish sabbatical leaves and provide reimbursement for professional travel.[36] Regular meetings took place in which instructors shared their latest research with their colleagues.[37] Classroom responsibilities were no less seriously addressed, as a special committee was assigned the objective of assisting in the overall improvement of teaching methods.[38] Equally characteristic of the spirit of the times was the reorganization of the faculty in 1954 into three divisions, Humanities, Social Sciences, and Natural Sciences, headed by a trio of the activists, Arthur Voss, chair of the Department of English, Richard Hantke, chair of the Department of History, and Edward North, chair of the Department of Chemistry. The curriculum was commensurately altered, with the adoption of new general education requirements, including core courses in world literature and, later, world history.[39]

As these various actions reflected a revamping of the faculty's educational priorities, President Johnson turned his

attentions elsewhere. If he remained true to his reliance on Business Administration and the more vocationally oriented departments to keep the school's economy manageably healthy and the enrollment up (even, at critical times, introducing cooperative programs with professional schools in the Chicago area),[40] he commenced to devote himself more than his predecessor Herbert Moore ever had to resuscitating the long-dormant relationship with the Lake Forest community.

In that regard there was plenty of room for improvement, and Johnson drew upon his younger faculty to assist him. The mid '50s saw the establishment of a program of "fireside seminars" in which townspeople were invited to join in informal discussions of topics drawn from the disciplines of the participating professors.[41] Since these sessions took place in Lake Forest private homes, a bond developed between hosts and instructors, and by extension the village and the College, that contributed to the restoration of the interaction and mutual respect that decades earlier had been taken for granted.

The traffic of that revived amity did not move on a one-way street. A number of townspeople, most of them women, had approached the College earlier in the decade with proposals for cultural events, principally art exhibitions, to be organized in tandem with the faculty and staged for the most part in Durand Institute, in the process reviving part of that building's original function. The women, chief among them Suzette Morton Zurcher (Davidson), Mildred Fagen, and trustee Frances Odell, knew their audience well enough to recognize that Lake Forest took its culture in Chicago, its society locally; hence each of the events they planned began with dinner parties and only then moved on to the campus, to the anticipated exhibition, lecture, or concert.[42] Out of this collaboration one townswoman emerged who became a storied figure in the College's history. In 1953 Ruth Winter, who would be instrumental in setting up the fireside seminars, was given an office on campus,[43] where she spent the next quarter century luring highly reputed artists, musicians, and especially scholars to the campus for memorable performances or lectures, and in the process further cementing relationships with the town. She brought a unique gift to bear on the luminaries on whom she set her sights, persuading them somehow to believe that a trip to Lake Forest would be as attractive to them as it would be beneficial to the College.

The intensity of local interest in postwar politics is reflected both in General Douglas MacArthur's 1951 visit to Lake Forest and the campus, following his removal by President Truman from command in the Korean War (left and below), and in the support for Republican presidential candidate Dwight D. Eisenhower in the 1952 and 1956 elections (above right). On both latter occasions Eisenhower defeated Adlai E. Stevenson, a local friend of the College.

1946

Temporary war-surplus buildings are put up east of Farwell Field (the site today of Halas Hall) as housing for faculty, married students, and returning veterans.

**Above.** Hurtling ahead of Elmhurst's best, Neal J. Martin '60 has his eye on the prize. A calendar change in the 1970s ended track and field – a sport in which Forester excellence reached back to the 1890s.

**Below.** Alumni Memorial Field House was dedicated on December 6, 1950, a facility made possible by small donations from hundreds of alumni. At this game in 1956 the attendance was 3,973.

Winter's endeavor was both symptomatic of change and catalytic. One of the more significant developments of post-war Lake Forest was a conjunction of the growing middle-class population cited earlier, a lowering of the sense of privilege among the possessors of old money, and a perceptibly more sophisticated, more prestigiously educated College faculty, with the combined result contributing, as has been noted, to an increasingly friendly town-gown commonality. Nothing underscored that condition more than local reaction to a development that bore grievous implications at the national level, Senator Joseph McCarthy's notorious anticommunist campaign, which in the early 1950s damaged the lives of more than a few American liberals, including academics, before it collapsed under the weight of the failure of its own allegations. Yet

it touched no one at the College and caused no break in relations with the surrounding community. (One cannot help recalling how massively different the situation was when local response to the Red scare following World War I almost destroyed the College — though two decades later, in the early 70s, the perceived radicalization of the campus would alienate some significant donors.)

Meanwhile, within its own walls the school continued its traditional close-knit social existence. Although the day of the automobile and its ownership by the average citizen had long since arrived, a fact that made Chicago's cultural offerings more accessible than ever, the inertia of the College's inward-turned living habits kept most faculty and most students close to their quarters. The school continued to draw its students mostly from Chicago and cities or towns within a 150-mile radius. Commuters made up a large percentage of the enrollment, which had grown to 799 by 1957.[44] Since nearly all the faculty lived on campus, largely because of the unaffordability of nearby real estate, everyone knew everyone else, with the interaction appropriately, and necessarily, limited to a small society that comprised a recognizable community.

Entertainment was still centered on campus social affairs and sports, especially football, and self-consciously intellectual professors cheered as lustily as the students seated next to them at the Farwell Field games that highlighted autumn weekends. These gridiron events were outwardly casual, considering that children and dogs sometimes wandered freely onto the field of play, yet in another sense, that very ease of collective demeanor was a sign that the College family found much to like in sports and regarded them with proportionate seriousness. In 1949, John Breen and Wally Lemm left their coaching positions at Carroll College to take over similar posts at Lake Forest — Breen as athletic director and Lemm as head football coach — and together they produced teams that were steady contenders during the 1950s for the championship of the athletic College

1947

Shown here are two varsity letters of Robert L. Bibbs '47.

1947

Lake Forest Academy elects to relocate west of Lake Forest and to relinquish its property – now South Campus – to the College.

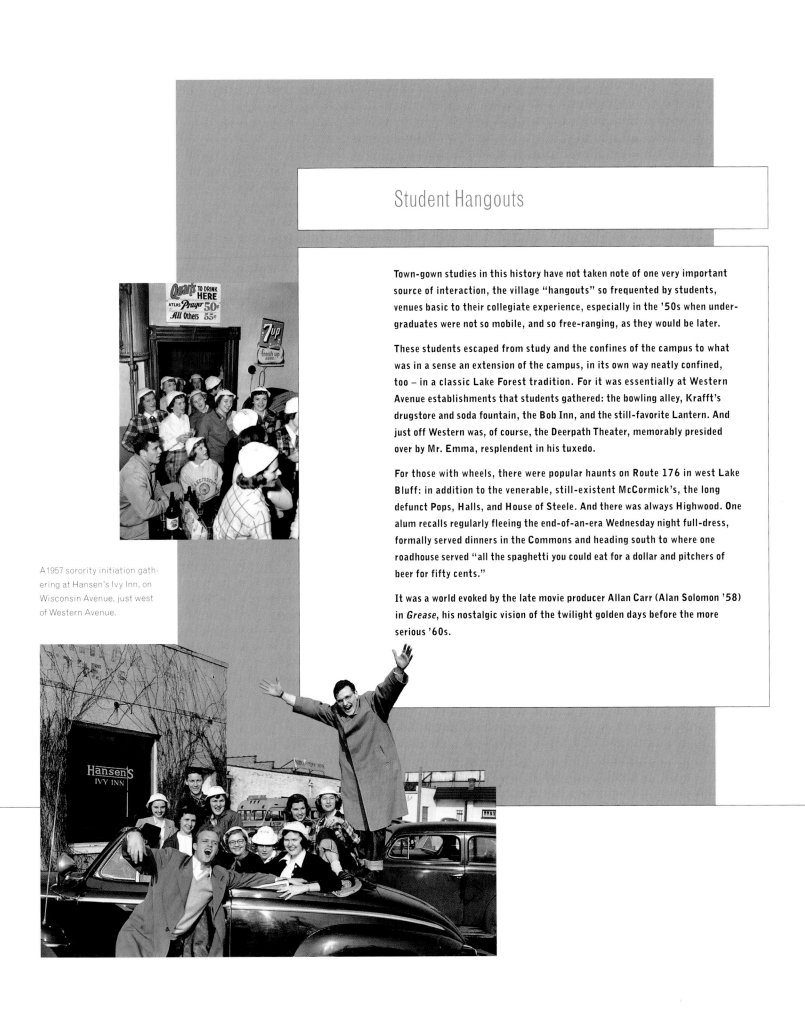

## Student Hangouts

Town-gown studies in this history have not taken note of one very important source of interaction, the village "hangouts" so frequented by students, venues basic to their collegiate experience, especially in the '50s when undergraduates were not so mobile, and so free-ranging, as they would be later.

These students escaped from study and the confines of the campus to what was in a sense an extension of the campus, in its own way neatly confined, too – in a classic Lake Forest tradition. For it was essentially at Western Avenue establishments that students gathered: the bowling alley, Krafft's drugstore and soda fountain, the Bob Inn, and the still-favorite Lantern. And just off Western was, of course, the Deerpath Theater, memorably presided over by Mr. Emma, resplendent in his tuxedo.

For those with wheels, there were popular haunts on Route 176 in west Lake Bluff: in addition to the venerable, still-existent McCormick's, the long defunct Pops, Halls, and House of Steele. And there was always Highwood. One alum recalls regularly fleeing the end-of-an-era Wednesday night full-dress, formally served dinners in the Commons and heading south to where one roadhouse served "all the spaghetti you could eat for a dollar and pitchers of beer for fifty cents."

It was a world evoked by the late movie producer Allan Carr (Alan Solomon '58) in *Grease*, his nostalgic vision of the twilight golden days before the more serious '60s.

A 1957 sorority initiation gathering at Hansen's Ivy Inn, on Wisconsin Avenue, just west of Western Avenue.

 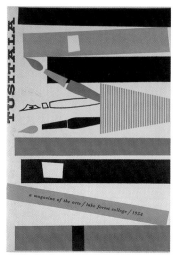

Tusitala, the campus literary magazine, begun in 1935, was edited in the 1950s by Ralph Mills Jr. '54, later a well-known poet, critic and academic.

Conference of Illinois. In 1957, they both left the College, and a year later Nicholas Wasylik was appointed to the combined position of athletic director and head football coach.[45]

At the time, the College's principal indoor come-one-come-all gathering place was the coffee shop on the ground floor of College Hall, a humbly furnished two-room space with little to distinguish it except the noisy crowds of students and faculty that assembled there during the morning class breaks. What passed for a student center was a one-story structure behind College Hall that was known to everyone as the "doghouse," having served earlier as a kennel on the grounds of the Korhumel estate when the foxhunt was still a favored sport of the local gentry.[46]

All in all, social life bore a perceptible resemblance to its counterpart of the Moore years. Activities were sponsored not only by the fraternities and sororities but by a wide-ranging assortment of clubs, committees, councils, boards, and other such organizations. Some of these oversaw single events like the traditional Junior Prom and Homecoming, College Day, the Women's Athletic Association Annual Banquet, Religion and Life Week, and the Student-Faculty Variety Show. Others consisted of continuing groups,

several with regularly occurring special events: honorary and departmental societies, glee club and band concerts, the Garrick Players, contests ("most typical," "ugly man," and, of course, intramural sports), and publications — The Forester yearbook, the weekly newspaper, the Stentor, and the journal of extracurricular writing and art, Tusitala.[47]

The fraternities and sororities remained, as always, the predominant agencies of social life,[48] although an incident of more than passing consequence took place in 1953–54, when Anthony H. Banks '57/'72, one of the most popular members of a growing contingent of the College's African American students (thirty-two in all), pledged Phi Pi Epsilon. The chapter was directly confronted with threats by a number of the fraternity alumni who vowed to withdraw their financial support. Although Banks agreed to give up his pledge pin, the controversy smoldered, but did not die. The resolution reached (to eliminate discriminatory practices) was, in fact, less a conclusion than a prelude, foretokening the disputes over racial discrimination that engulfed the College's fraternities and assailed the rest of the nation in a variety of ways in the 1960s.[49] That part of the story remains to be told.

As for their academic caliber, the students of the period were in most respects true to the national norm, although the College did enact several noteworthy changes in an effort to elevate their level of performance and responsibility. In the course of the 1950s, College Board tests were instituted as criteria for admission to the school,[50] and by the end of the decade the first class of promising students known as Patterson Scholars was enrolled in special sections of core courses and in a number of honors classes.[51] If there was one overall trait that distinguished the motives of the 1950s group from those of their predecessors of the 1930s and 1940s, it was the inclination, especially among the best of them, to identify with the ambitions of the faculty rather than with the values of the administration. Just as the faculty of the same period had begun to win

1947

**Shirley J. Flood's '47 Girls' Athletic Association varsity letters.**

**Above.** The College Hall Coffee Shop, in this 1947 photo, reflects a warm and informal campus atmosphere. The dog, well known to all students, was Zeke.

**Center left.** In the 1950s and 1960s variety shows were highlights of the campus year, opportunities for the community to see campus "wheels," administrators, and faculty more often out of character than not; this from 1959.

**Center right.** In 1952 the College gained a new student union building, always known familiarly and affectionately as the "doghouse." Here Mrs. Korhumel, in best *noblesse oblige* fashion, cuts the ribbon for the building's new role, with President Johnson looking on.

**Below.** The cast of the 1955 Garrick production of Moliere's *The Miser,* with the five students pictured here, from left: Ronald H. Voigt '56, Alan Solomon '58 (later known as Allan Carr, for whom the campus theater is named), Shirley Boccaccio '56, Barbara Hansen '56, and Gail Olson '55.

# True to His Text: Sigvard Gissler, Newspaperman

Headlines such as "Fraternities and Sororities Face Discrimination Issue" and "Discrimination and Society" began to appear in the College newspaper in 1954 and 1955 – a period in collegiate history hardly remarkable for political or social activism. Yet in those years, Sigvard "Sig" Gissler '56, American Civilization major, football player and gymnast, and member of the oldest fraternity on campus, Phi Pi Epsilon, as editor of the *Stentor* was grounding himself, philosophically and practically, with the experience that would take him to a distinguished career in journalism.

Starting out on the nearby Libertyville *Independent Register*, where he was news editor, Sig spent four years, from 1963 to 1967, as executive editor of the *Waukegan News Sun*. From there he went to Milwaukee to join the *Milwaukee Journal* staff as editorial writer, later assuming the post of editor and officer of the parent company from 1987 to 1993. Then after almost forty years as a newsman in a very localized area of the Middlewest, he moved to New York to become professor of journalism at Columbia University, even serving as an acting dean there.

What might indeed seem a major career shift, geographically and professionally, was actually not such a transplanting or grafting. For from those neophyte years on the *Stentor*, from those earliest undergraduate editorials, issues of race and diversity have proved an overarching focus for Sig, continuing hallmarks of his work. So if in 1991 he was launching in Milwaukee a year's newspaper coverage of such matters, the late '90s at Columbia would see him undertaking a program entitled "Let's Do It Better: The Columbia Workshop on Journalism, Race, and Ethnicity." He obviously has remained true to what he always has believed important – that which must be brought to public attention.

1947–48

From the period, a scholastic medallion (from a national honor society for freshman women) and a sorority pin: the Alpha Lambda Delta medal awarded to Shirley J. Flood '47 and the Alpha Delta Pi sorority pin worn by Margaret A. Flood '48.

Sigvard Gissler as a student.

Fulbright instructional fellowships – Milne and Voss to Germany and Coutts to Pakistan – a student, Nancy Phillips (Chandler) '52, was awarded a Fulbright to England.[52]

And the students did produce their fair share of alumni who found distinction in a variety of ways: in academe, Glen G. Cain '55, professor of Economics at the University of Wisconsin at Madison, Anita Chen (Li) '51, professor of Educational Psychology at the University of Calgary, Sanford E. Marovitz '60, professor of English, Kent State University, Glennette Tilley (Turner) '55, student teacher supervisor, National-Louis University, and Robert A. Waller '53, dean of the College of Liberal Arts at Clemson University; in the arts, Allan Carr '58, theatrical producer, and Ralph J. Mills '54, poet and professor of English at the University of Illinois at Chicago; in the church, Bruce O. Larson '49, pastor of the University Presbyterian Church, Seattle, and Lloyd J. Ogilvie '52, chaplain of the U.S. Senate; in journalism, Sigvard G. Gissler '56, editor of the *Milwaukee Evening Sentinel* and professor at the Columbia University Graduate School of Journalism, and Louis E. Porterfield '51, publisher of *Cosmopolitan* magazine; in science, Anna Thomas (Standard) '45, public health physician and professor at Howard University, and Martin I. Morad '59, professor of Pharmacology at Georgetown University; in sports, William C. Bartholomay '55, chairman of the Atlanta Braves major league baseball team; and in business – their number (to name but a few) reflecting the curricular emphasis that dominated most of the Johnson years – Wallace B. Askins '52, executive vice president and chief financial officer of Aramco, Richard T. Hough '48, chairman and CEO, Chemcentral, John H. Krehbiel '59, co-CEO of Molex, Harry G. Meadows '44, chairman, W. R. Meadows, Willliam F. Souders '52, both executive vice president of Xerox and CEO of Emery Air Freight, and Howard C. Shank '42, president of Leo Burnett.[53]

**For all the easy camaraderie on campus and the** sustenance of the habits it stood for, there was at last no stopping the momentum of academic change, and aside from the Tony Banks incident, no better illustration of the confrontation of old and new than the events of the several days the faculty spent together at a retreat in Williams Bay, Wisconsin, immediately prior to the academic year of 1955–56.

The purpose of the occasion was to take stock of the academic, business, and public relations departments of the College,

to help new instructors get to know one another, but, more significantly, to assemble the faculty in a conference sponsored by the Danforth Foundation for the purpose of discussing the question, "What does it mean to be a Christian college?"[54] The very issue took for granted Lake Forest's religious tradition, and, appropriately, the meeting, which was held in the George Williams Bible Camp on the shores of Lake Geneva, featured the singing of hymns by all assembled and a panel that addressed an essay by a member of the McCormick Theological Seminary faculty.

Much of the meeting proceeded expectably, but the collective inclination of the newer instructors was expressed freely enough to underscore yet again that old-time religion was no longer a guiding impulse in the College's endeavors. Among the statements best remembered from the conference's panel discussion were those of Professor Lunn, who affirmed that Christianity played no role in her courses in Biology, and Professor Hutcheson, who reminded his colleagues of Cardinal Newman's writings on education, in which the great nineteenth-century churchman emphasized the value of learning for its own sake above any primarily religious concern.

**Above.** Crescent Dream was the theme of the Gamma Phis' rush party in Durand Institute, 1950–51. The *Forester* that year recalled how the elaborate decorations transformed this familiar setting.

**Below.** This photo of a seminar led by Philosophy Professor Robert Sharvy illustrates how the circle arrangement around a table engaged students more actively than had the traditional lecture setting. Pictured on Sharvy's left is George F. Chlebak '58, himself later on the faculty of Lyon College in Arkansas. In this period, class-centered activities began to supplant extra-curricular campus pursuits.

Commission, met for the first time under the chairmanship of trustee Elliott Donnelley, a man destined within a decade to become the town's most active and generous supporter of the school.[59]

The campus plan favored by Booz, Allen & Hamilton had been drawn up as early as the late 1940s by Naess & Murphy in collaboration with Chicago landscape architect Chance S. Hill.[60] Based on Beaux-Arts principles and faintly reminiscent of the 1906 Morris-Manning plan, it featured a long mall that would have extended from the Middle Campus entrance at College and Sheridan roads east through the lateral axis of College Hall to a newly proposed field house (as distinguished from the one later built), with a second crossing mall connecting Harlan and Blackstone with North Hall and Patterson Lodge. Like the Marshall Johnson plan, this proposal also failed to materialize. All that came of it was the construction of a single building, Deerpath Hall, a women's dormitory designed in 1956, on a shoestring budget (that was all too apparent from the looks of it), by Naess & Murphy.[61]

The movement continued apace. Just two years later another conference was staged, whose title, "The Proper Function of the Liberal Arts College," revealed more than a little about the shift in academic direction that followed a national trend among denominational schools, steadily away from a strictly Christian mission toward ends more secular.

**The further importance of the second conference may** be judged by the fact that it was one of the major events of the College's 1957 centennial celebration.[55] Plans had been in the making since late in the 1940s to cope financially with the reality of a school both larger than and different from its prewar counterpart, and the centennial was envisioned as the symbolic linchpin and climactic moment of the projections. In the late 1940s, $2.1 million had been targeted, with half the total meant for buildings, half for endowment.[56] In 1953 the College mounted a major capital campaign that depended on assistance from two major outside sources, the Chicago firm of Gonser & Gerber, hired to oversee fundraising,[57] and the management consultants Booz, Allen & Hamilton, appointed to reorganize the College's administration and recommend yet another campus master plan.[58] Meanwhile, the College's own improvement program, the Development

The gap that had historically separated hope from fulfillment opened again in 1959, when one more master plan, this one the product of the Chicago architectural office of Perkins & Will, expired almost as soon as it was commissioned. It deserves note for little more than its reflection of the contemporaneous shift in taste from historical styles to the more informal modernist idiom already evident in the flat roof and undecorated facade of Deerpath Hall.[62] The sole architectural project of any scale that did see the light of day was a science building, proposed in the late 1950s, and even so, it did not open until the early 1960s, by which time a new administration had taken over completing the fundraising. All in all, the architectural and fiscal fortunes of the College's centennial were only modestly encouraging. Two new buildings had gone up, but three campus plans never advanced beyond the paper stage. By 1959

1949

1950

**The publicity office prepares a list of "Outstanding Faculty," along with a disclaimer that lack of time and facilities preclude large-scale research.**

**In the name of school spirit, the College issues a set of three 78 r.p.m. records of College songs, among them "Alma Mater" and "Varsity Song," directed by Professor Arnold Thomas.**

# Ma Lobdell and Mother I

Despite their common sobriquets, Mrs. Lobdell the College dietician and Mrs. Ingram the College housemother shared nothing but, importantly, the reality of their memorable presences on the campus of the late '50s and early '60s. And there was definitely nothing common about either of them, especially in their professional roles.

Ma Lobdell (Ethel) presided – the right term, though she ruled from the sidelines – over her dining hall. If she projected the aura of a tough bird, she had surprisingly opulent tastes. Turning a blind eye to the budget, she lavished on the students and fortunate faculty of the day spectacular meals – the holiday roast suckling pig dinners, the ice-sculptured weekend buffets.... They were indeed halcyon days for man and beast (in fact it required a special student bouncer to evict daily the town-gown throngs of canine gourmets, among them the ever present **Boots Reichert** and **Zeke Keller** but also **Lily**, the neighborhood whippet, and **Sherlock**, the aristocratic basset). And when she wasn't dreaming up feasts in the kitchen, Ma could often be found sequestered with a group of Phipe brothers in a friendly game of poker.

Meanwhile, Mother I (Mary Ingram) was dispensing sherry and advice at **East House**, the men's dormitory, where she was a reigning presence, too. She was hardly a typical housemother (actually none of the College housemothers was that), this elegant "Lake Forest" matron who inspired such respect and affection from "her boys." One of them, **Frederick A. Krehbiel '63**, vividly recalls her:

*She was always full of fun, always game for a practical joke or a good time but ... good manners had to prevail. If you had a problem with the administration or the faculty she was always ready to go to bat for you. She went out of her way to help you with your parents by assuring them how hard you were working. She would say, "Well now, we have your parents convinced, how about turning it into reality by getting your grades up?" She was also very helpful ... when it came to finding a job. She would get on the phone to old friends and sing your praises while lining up an interview. Sort of Auntie Mame with a more practical bent ... and every so often for a great achievement or celebration, out would come the sherry. Never a lot, but a glass or two never hurt anyone! Living at East House under the watchful, but far from strict, eye of Mother I was lots of fun and she was tops.*

Christmas dinner 1956 included a brace of trussed pigs, one of the many lavish offerings from Ma Lobdell's kitchen. Left to right, Margaret Neely (Wilhelm) '58, Ma Lobdell, and Edith and Ernest Johnson.

**Above.** Typical Man and Typical Woman Michael E. Dau '58 and Paula Ernst '58 were a perfect couple, as they also are today as active alumni, with Mike coaching handball and serving as assistant for offense in football. The idea of "typical" resonates with the feel of the '50s nationally, the era of the classic study of large-corporation behavior entitled *The Organization Man*.

**Center.** In May 1953 three competitors for the title of Jane Forester were (from left) Geraldine Larson '56, Patricia Clark '57, and Shirley Boccaccio '56.

**Below.** In 1958 intramural bowling for men and women reflected the national popularity of the sport. The men's match pictured is between the TKEs and Delta Chis, with Warren T. Strong '60 bowling for the TKEs.

1953

1953

J. Saunders Redding, author of the pioneering critical study *To Make a Poet Black* (1939), is writer-in-residence.

Homecoming button featuring the Forester lumberjack mascot.

the endowment had doubled, yet that boon was directly countered by a period of inflation. The 1950s, in sum, were notable less for bricks and mortar and the money necessary to assemble them and more (happily more) for accomplishments in the academic realm.

As the decade neared its conclusion, matters of moment drew to a climax. Ernest Johnson was stricken with leukemia and died in 1959,[65] a man, a professor, and a president who had won the respect and affection of all who knew him: the townspeople, who had grown to appreciate his efforts to restore their interest in the College's affairs, the students, whose individual names he, like his predecessor James McClure, invariably remembered, and the faculty, who recognized his genuine commitment to the College and his willingness to negotiate with those who took views opposed to his own. With his passing, many of his responsibilities were assumed by John Howard, the College's business manager, who, having already proven himself a skilled administrator, made it clear he aspired to the presidency himself. But Howard was not an academic, and in view of the persistent campus drive to regain the College's liberal arts status, his belief in the curricular centrality of Business Administration met with substantial resistance.[66]

Much of that came from the faculty, but not all of it. The Board of Trustees had undergone a parallel change of outlook since the 1940s. Clarence W. Diver '05,[67] Waukegan attorney, and one-time president of the Illinois State Bar Association, had served as chair from the late 1920s until the end of the war – the Moore years – when he was succeeded by Joseph Fleming,[68] a Lake Forest resident who practiced law in Chicago and had long been president of the Chicago Public Library Board. Fleming occupied the chair until 1960, when the trustees had become dominated by a nonalumni group, including prominent citizens such as Lilace Barnes[69] (the College's first woman trustee, appointed

At the groundbreaking ceremony for Deerpath Hall, 1956, were (left to right) Ernest Johnson and trustees Joseph Fleming, J. Howard Wood '22, and Elliott Donnelley.

in 1944), George Beach,[70] Francis Beidler,[71] Phoebe Bentley,[72] Elliott Donnelley,[73] Francis Farwell,[74] James R. Getz,[75] Daggett Harvey,[76] Frances Odell,[77] Frank Read,[78] Carroll Sudler,[79] and Ernest Volwiler,[80] who were determined to encourage much the same kind of advancement of the institution that had motivated the faculty.

It was no accident that the two bodies shared in taking on one of the most crucial issues of the day, the establishment of a College chapter of the Phi Beta Kappa national honor society. Such an achievement would be unsurpassed in the prestige it was sure to confer upon the school as a ranking undergraduate institution of the liberal arts (joining an elite group of only 164 throughout the country), and none would more reliably certify that the loss of scholastic respectability had been regained. The lapsed memory of its past heritage prevented the College in the late 1950s from knowing that President Nollen's administration had also sought

1956

The College celebrates its centennial and issues this commemorative Wedgwood plate depicting Lily Reid Holt Memorial Chapel.

1956

English Professor W. Gordon Milne's biography of nineteenth-century literary figure George William Curtis apparently is the first scholarly book published by a faculty member since 1919 (a monograph on Goldoni by Professor Van Steenderen).

The continuity of interest from the years of the founding families onward is demonstrated by this picture from the centennial year, 1957–58. In 1957 descendants of Dr. Robert W. Patterson, the first president of the continuing College, attended a Founder's Day dinner on February 11. Pictured from left: granddaughter Marion Patterson Phillips (Evanston), great-grandson Robert Patterson Cross Jr. (Hinsdale), grandson Stewart Patterson (Chicago), great-granddaughter Josephine Patterson (Chicago), and granddaughter Isabel Patterson Phillips (Evanston).

the B.A. degree in Business Administration, the Speech major, and a B.S. degree in Medical Technology that had been instituted as one of President Johnson's assorted expedients to raise the enrollment in the early 1950s.[84] It was a rather daring move, since the College had long depended on those vocationalist disciplines to keep its fiscal head above water. (In 1955 the majors in Business Administration, Economics, and Speech totaled 243, more than half of all the students who had declared their concentrations, and in fact a percentage higher than any from the Moore years.)[85]

And there was more, in the form of a prospect that not only increased the likelihood of acceptance by Phi Beta Kappa (which was granted in 1961) but signified something of potentially greater consequence. The College launched a national search for a new president – the first since it had undertaken to find President Nollen in 1906–7[86] – and the conclusion reached justified the effort. When William Graham Cole[87] was installed in 1960 as the tenth president of Lake Forest College, he brought with him a nearly ideal dossier, including a Ph.D. from Columbia University, a high-ranking position as a faculty member and dean of freshmen at Williams College, a record as a publishing scholar, and, not least, a background in divinity that marked him as a man of the cloth without disguising his fundamental academic liberalism – in short, the kind of first-rate, appropriately multifaceted Eastern pedigree that virtually everyone in Lake Forest, town and gown alike, found next to irresistible. What Cole himself found was a well-oiled machine with parts reconditioned but already running, waiting only for a determined driver to shift it into a higher gear.

to gain membership in Phi Beta Kappa, only to fail in the wake of the storm that followed Acting President Wright's unfortunate and ill-timed speech of 1919. But some forty years later a new day had dawned, and the opportunity was addressed afresh. The most recent applications for membership had been turned down again by the Society, for a variety of reasons, including the College's meager endowment, commensurately low faculty pay scale and insufficiently funded library, and, significantly, the heavy concentration of majors in such vocationally oriented subjects as Business Administration and Speech.[81]

Although it was Business Manager Howard himself who proposed a substantial across-the-board salary increase,[82] the principal impetus for applying again to Phi Beta Kappa came from the Board, led by its new chair, Carroll Sudler.[83] The College could now point to its concerted fund drive and the affirmative effect it would have on raising the endowment. The faculty reacted promptly, dropping

1958

**Graduating seniors begin the tradition of selecting a "Great Teacher" from among the faculty to address them at the spring honors convocation; their first choice is History Professor Richard Hantke.**

# President Cole
# and the Camelot
# Years

chapter 8

1960—1969

In almost all respects pertinent to culture – political, social, economic, aesthetic, indeed academic – the 1960s qualify as the most revolutionary decade of the twentieth century. Of violence there was more than enough. The period is fixed in memory inseparable from the horrors of the Vietnam War, the assassinations of President John F. Kennedy, black activist Malcolm X, Senator Robert F. Kennedy, and Dr. Martin Luther King Jr., and the reactive riots that broke out in major American cities, leaving whole neighborhoods burned out and uninhabitable. Less consistently physical but no less profound in their eventual national effect were the long-term struggles over civil rights, the shifts in sexual mores, the ascendancy of youth culture and popular culture at the expense of traditional standards in the arts, and more. No one was left unaffected. The impact of the 1960s was felt not only in Chicago, which in many respects turned

1961

1961

Phi Beta Kappa, the national honorary society recognizing academic achievement, grants a chapter to Lake Forest. Installation of the chapter follows in 1962.

In the early 1960s Art Professor Franz Schulze designs a new seal for the College, a view of a forest, carrying a new motto proposed by President Cole:

*Et veritas liberabit vos,* "And the Truth Shall Set You Free" (John 8:32) – biblical in its derivation but more universal in its meaning.

into an urban battleground, but, after their own fashion, in Lake Forest and at Lake Forest College as well. Inevitably, much that occurred at the College mirrored events and developments far beyond the limits of the campus, and not least among these was the massive transformation of the national mood from hope and idealism at the outset of the decade to doubt, suspicion, and conflict at the end of it.

Chicago's fortunes graphically illustrated the direction and pace of the turnabout, from the high points to the low ones. Much of the city's former importance as a transportation center was restored with the opening in 1960 of O'Hare International Airport, and several new superhighways drew an abundance of ground traffic into, through, and around the Chicago area. National leadership in architecture, lost during the 1920s, returned to the city in the 1960s, due largely to the influence of Ludwig Mies van der Rohe, the modernist master who had earlier emigrated from Germany to Chicago. Buildings of historic consequence, many bearing the Miesian mark and produced by such distinguished offices as Skidmore, Owings & Merrill, C. F. Murphy Associates, Loebl, Schlossman & Bennett, and Perkins & Will added significantly to the cityscape. Chicago jazz also regained much of its former renown, helped in no small way by the impact of another major national figure of popular culture, Chicagoan Hugh Hefner, founder of the *Playboy* magazine empire.

Yet behind the city's handsome skyline, racial segregation continued unabated. The policy of urban renewal, moreover, though intended to provide better housing for the underclass, had the effect of replacing old slums with new slums—the "projects," as they came to be called. Riots followed the assassination of Dr. King in 1968, and in the same year, the Democratic National Convention was jolted by several days of civic disruptions. With the approach of the 1970s Chicago, which liked to refer to itself as "the city that works," had lost more than a little of its luster in the nation's eyes.

American academe as a whole followed a similar pattern. In the early 1960s, as children of the baby boom reached college age, the effect on post-secondary schools was as encompassing as it was exhilarating. Enrollments ballooned everywhere, and following them, programs and ambitions: Normal schools took on the name of colleges, while colleges, expanding to include graduate schools, became universities. A strong national economy led to a burgeoning

of agencies awarding grants and fellowships. For institutions of higher learning throughout the country, the early 1960s were years of hope and optimism. Yet by the end of the decade, that condition, subjected to the shocking events that intervened, had been exchanged for one of acute disenchantment, as the academic world, like the nation at large, made war upon itself.

Consistent with the character of the decade, Lake Forest College greeted the 1960s on a note of euphoria. President Cole found the campus in a state of high excitement when he arrived, all parties anticipating an administration that would advance and expand the changes that had been proposed and even enacted in the late 1950s. He in turn had ideas of his own that were consistent with those of his new constituents. In short, the time was right for him, and he for the time.

Within a matter of several years, the student body and student life, the faculty, the curriculum, the physical plant, the building program, the fiscal condition, and the College's relation to the surrounding community underwent changes that qualitatively altered the core image of the school. Cole made a point at the very outset of setting the stage for what transpired. In his initial address to the faculty, in January 1960, he affirmed his personal identification with them corporately and individually: "The teacher of quality is the *sine qua non* of the college of quality," he declared, adding

**Above.** Physics Professor Bailey Donnally shares work on a research project with Thomas G. Clapp '65, during the summer of 1963.

**Opposite.** The spirit of the beginning of the decade is evident here as students gathered in the College Hall coffee shop in 1961–62 to join in folk songs with guitar accompaniment.

his belief that the differences between a Christian college and a purely secular one "do not include either a cramped conception of truth or a revival meeting disguised in cap and gown!" These remarks, which won him the faculty's confidence, were followed by others that earned him even more: applauding the increase in salaries that President Johnson and John Howard had negotiated, he added that wages "must continue to rise, fringe benefits must increase, teaching loads must be reduced, and provision must be made for sabbatical leaves."[1] Thus the new president began, as he would continue, very much a faculty's president.

Having assumed his duties in August of 1960, by the end of the calendar year Cole was clearly well launched, with evidence already growing that the College family as a whole was united in its willingness to accept his leadership. An increasing enrollment was already symptomatic of new potentialities: Of every seven students applying for admission to the class of 1964, only three were accepted, and they represented a change in the design of the student body.[2] The College now sought deliberately to enroll more

students than ever before from eastern preparatory schools. The motive was partly to bring to campus a more urbane and heterogeneous group, and in retrospect one may already see the move as one of the signs of Cole's conscious intention to turn the College from a local to a national school. Again, the times worked to nearly everyone's advantage. With Eastern colleges unable to accommodate an expanding pool of the students normally applying to them, Lake Forest launched a concerted recruiting campaign, engaging a new director of admissions from the East[3] and making the most of the connections Cole himself had established as dean of freshmen at Williams and a veteran of preaching on the Eastern boarding school circuit. The subsequent increase in the number and quality of students gave rise to a need for more faculty, then for more buildings, yet again for more money to finance the whole operation. The College's change in direction was matched by the swiftness with which events took place, and some sense of their volume, rapidity, and importance may be evident from an abbreviated summary list of developments in the first five years of the decade. Individually and in sum, they reflect a working out of the president's vision: to enlarge the student body to an academically viable size (of 1,000 residents and 250 commuters), in the process diversifying it geographically, socioeconomically and racially, and to provide these undergraduates an exciting educational environment, with a first-rate, also diversified faculty, expanded and updated facilities, and a strong program of studies bulwarked by engaging extracurricular activities.[4]

In 1960: Ground was broken for the Ernest A. Johnson Memorial Science Center. Annual giving reached a new high of well over three-quarters of a million dollars. The Class of 1964, 255 strong, was the largest ever to enter the College to that date. A new, three-term, three-course calendar was adopted. The standard weekly teaching load for faculty was lowered from fifteen to twelve hours, necessitating the addition of some ten new positions. A faculty sabbatical

1963

1964

**Betty Friedan publishes**
*The Feminine Mystique.*

**An omnibus federal civil rights law bans discrimination in voting, jobs, and public accommodations.**

leave program was created and regulations for academic tenure outlined. Plans were made for the construction of a new president's house, to be designed by William Brubaker, principal in the firm of Perkins & Will, which had already been commissioned to put up the new Science Center. The trustees approved construction of a student union building on Middle Campus and faculty housing on South Campus.[5]

In 1961: Of the record 900 students in the day school, one-third of the applicants were from independent schools and two-thirds from out of state. Fifteen students from twelve foreign countries were enrolled. The trustees approved the building of new coed dormitories on South Campus. A new grading system, consisting of honors, high pass, pass, and failure, was put into effect. A revision of the College curriculum was passed. A tuition benefit program was set up for faculty children going off campus to college. When the decision of the Phi Delta Theta fraternity to pledge a Jewish student resulted in the suspension of the chapter by the national organization, the faculty unanimously passed a resolution to the effect that the College would recognize only those social organizations that had "complete authority in the matter of selecting their local membership," and, moreover, that no local chapters would be permitted to impose restrictions on membership for reasons of "race, color, religion or national origin." A substantial adjustment in faculty salaries raised the College to a wage scale equal to that of the top twenty-five liberal arts colleges in the country. The United Christian Fellowship was estab-

lished to coordinate the efforts of a growing diversity of religious clubs. A soccer team was formed. Comprehensive senior examinations in the major were instituted that would later become a graduation requirement. Ground was broken for the new student union, to be added to Durand Commons after designs by Perkins & Will. A new community government constitution was devised. The trustees approved a record $2.3 million budget. One-third of the senior class would proceed to graduate school, with several of its members awarded graduate fellowships and one a Woodrow Wilson fellowship. The College adopted a new seal, with a new design and a new motto, *Et Veritas Liberabit Vos* ("And the Truth Shall Set You Free"), replacing *Christo et Ecclesiae*.[6]

In 1962: Following a thirty percent increase in applications (and 2,400 inquiries – a reflection not only of the College's growing reputation but of a national academic prosperity), the enrollment rose to another record, of 1,066. The Phi Beta Kappa chapter was installed. The Ford Foundation awarded the College a major matching grant of $2 million on condition that the school raise $4 million more. The trustees selected a site on Middle Campus for a $1 million library. A psychological counseling center for students was established. In athletics, the College withdrew from the College Conference of Illinois, and the physical education requirement was lowered to one term. The College was one of forty-eight American institutions newly merged in a scholarship program benefiting students from Africa. A conference "Understanding the New Africa" was staged, with Adlai Stevenson as keynote speaker.[7]

In 1963: Ground was broken for the new library and South Campus dormitories. College Board achievement as well as aptitude tests were added to conditions for admission. Another major faculty salary increase lifted the College's rating to a level equal to the highest scale of any institution of higher learning in the country. The enrollment rose yet again, to 1,172, leading to another record in the size of the faculty, now expanded to seventy-three, as twenty new members were appointed. A major conference took Latin America as its subject. "The Crisis in Race Relations" was made the theme of a fall conference on religion and contemporary literature. A student tutoring program was established to help underprivileged public school children in Chicago and Waukegan. A Jewish Activities Group was organized. A commencement symposium considered the place of the creative arts in the last half of the twentieth century.[8]

The Johnson Science Center (1962), Lake Forest's first new academic building since Carnegie was erected in 1908, an appropriate setting for stimulating new efforts – often with National Science Foundation funding – toward scientific education and knowledge. This timely addition to the campus reflected the serious concern over American scientific training after the late 1950s' launching of the Russian satellite *Sputnik*.

**Above.** The students sporting traditional freshman beanies in this 1966 New Student Week snapshot in the new Commons (built in 1962) reflect vestiges of the usually lighthearted hazing that dated from the College's earliest days.

**Center.** In 1962 President William Graham Cole enthusiastically opened the bowling alley in the new Commons with, from left: unidentified man; Howard Hoogesteger, dean of men, John Munshower, business manager, and Dorothy Siebert.

**Below.** Broadcasting returned to campus in 1964 with WLFC, reaching out "exclusively" to students via a closed-circuit system. The quality of this signal was so poor that a decade later, in the spring of 1972—just a half-century after an original WABA had begun as an experimental station— work started on a campus FM station, WMXM.

In 1964: A new fine arts center was planned, leading to an architectural competition won by Edward Larrabee Barnes of New York (whose design, however, was never realized). Retirement supplements for emeriti were passed. Another conference, "Focus on India," took up the subject of Indian politics and culture. The College was awarded a second Ford Foundation grant for a pilot project, "Operation Opportunity" (later "Program II"), a unique experiment undertaken in conjunction with Allegheny College and Colorado College (later joined by Bates, Florida Presbyterian [now Eckerd], and Pomona) to provide selected students with four full years of independent study supervised by Professor Donald Bartlett and overseen by College preceptors. A house system for nonfraternity, nonsorority students was established. A campus radio station went on the air, using the call letters WLFC. Another conference on race relations, "Next Step," was held. The first in a series of foreign study programs was created with headquarters in Spain. Others in Dijon, Berlin, and Athens would follow later in the decade. The constitution of a Catholic Guild was approved. A major in International Relations was added. The evening school was disbanded.[9]

In 1965: The new library, a gift of the Donnelley family, opened. The College acquired two historic Lake Forest residences, the Devillo Holt House (The Homestead) and the Simon Reid House (The Lilacs), located across from Middle Campus at the corner of Sheridan and College roads. Trustee Lilace Barnes, who lived in the Barnes estate (Glen Rowan, designed by Howard Van Doren Shaw) immediately south of the Reid place, sold the property to the College, which turned it into a conference center and guest house. Lutheran and Quaker student groups were formed. The old library, now Arthur Somerville Reid Hall, was transformed into an academic departmental building. Bross House, Beidler House, and Academia were taken down. Following the razing of Eliza Remsen House and Annie Durand Cottage, the four new South Campus dormitories (named for former

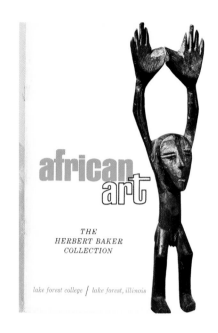

**african art**

THE
HERBERT BAKER
COLLECTION

*lake forest college / lake forest, illinois*

College presidents Gregory, Roberts, McClure, and Nollen) were completed. The South Campus faculty housing units were also finished. The Industrial Management Institute became an independent entity, adopting the name Advanced Management Institute but maintaining its South Campus quarters. The national AAUP recommendations defining faculty tenure and guaranteeing academic freedom were adopted. The Ford Foundation Challenge Program exceeded its goal of $4 million, making 1965 the greatest year for gifts in the College's 108-year history. The members of the class matriculating in September brought with them scores and secondary school ranking that earned them a place in the top ten percent of all students entering colleges and universities in the United States. As the 1965 Commencement program expressed it, "Put first-rate professors together with first-rate students and give them

1966

As reported in the *Forester*, the three-year-old student-volunteer program serves over 130 students in five Waukegan schools and on Chicago's west side.

1967

*Tusitala*, usually appearing annually in the spring, has been a showcase for student, faculty, and often alumni writing and art. In 1967 it carries this cover – with its stylized version of the new seal developed in the Cole years and redesigned for the occasion by Professor Franz Schulze.

# Back on Track with Elliott Donnelley

Though historically the College's Board of Trustees had included major regional as well as local resident figures, such as Senator Charles B. Farwell, Lt. Governor William Bross, the two Cyrus H. McCormicks, A. B. Dick, and Louis Swift, by the early 1940s this no longer was the case. But soon after Ernest Johnson became acting president in 1942, Elliott Donnelley, son of printer Thomas E. Donnelley, joined the Board, again a representative of a leading Chicago business and philanthropic family. With Donnelley's leadership over the next decades until his death in 1975, a sea change in relations between the College and the Chicago–Lake Forest establishment took place. As he gathered to the Board a new generation of trustees, his own generosity, which made possible the Donnelley Library (1965) and the Sports Center (1968), provided models for other benefactions.

So of course Elliott Donnelley is recognized and remembered for his obvious gifts to the campus, but there is another dimension of his involvement with the College that few were aware of – his very genuine concern for the students, as revealed in two anecdotes of the last several years of his service. First, President Hotchkiss has recalled Donnelley's hands-on intervention with students in the difficult 1969–70 academic year between the tenures of presidents Cole and Hotchkiss himself. As young men were embroiled in disciplinary proceedings in that year of national turmoil, miscreants were sentenced to the next Saturday morning at Mr. Donnelley's, helping with his miniature train spread at his Waukegan Road estate. After a morning of working on oiling and servicing the little engines and surveying the tracks around the grounds, as noon approached, Donnelley would stutter only a few words to the effect that the young men would try harder, wouldn't they, to stay out of sight the next week. The message: the young men were important to the College even of personal interest to the Board chair – whom they wouldn't want to let down, would they?

The second anecdote is of Donnelley's last Commencement week, in 1975, when a couple of nights before graduation, he and Mrs. Donnelley invited the entire senior class – well over two hundred young people – for a barbecue picnic and train rides. The event was memorable for all who were on hand, and in its warmth as generous and affirming as any larger, more tangible gestures to the College.

A final legacy was Elliott Donnelley's collection of railroad history books to the Donnelley Library, given by his family. Over a quarter-century this collection, nationally known, has been cared for by a string of student curators, beginning with John G. Allen '80 (Ph.D. in transportation planning from M.I.T., and a planner with the Chicago Transit Authority) and including among others, Eric J. Northern '87 and Wesley B. Phillips '89.

Left. The Donnelley Library as sketched by Alice Moulton in 1982.

Right. The College's library for the first two-thirds of the twentieth century was a memorial to Arthur Somerville Reid, Class of 1897. It was opened in 1900 and was presided over by two librarians, Mabel Powell (1901–42) and Martha Biggs '29 (1943–72). Here the somewhat crowded interior is shown. Reid was vacated at the end of 1964 when the collection moved to the new Donnelley Library.

the library and laboratory and learning materials that they require, and you are not very far from a first-rate college, which is what Lake Forest is trying hard to be."[10]

**Anyone taking stock of the College in the middle of the** decade would surely have judged its fortunes on a steady upward swing, an assessment as likely to come from national as well as local observers. Cole's educational agenda, including especially his goal of turning Lake Forest into a national college, was meeting with conspicuous success, some of which can be ascribed to his own personality and style. If he was a minister by training, he was no less an academic evangelist, a true preacher, in fact, who in those early years of his administration delivered countless formal lectures and informal talks throughout the Chicago area, explaining and championing the ends and means he envisioned for the College.[11] That he was free to be away from campus so much he owed to the continuity and steadfast administrative support provided by William Dunn, dean of the faculty, and fellow Johnson appointee Howard Hoogesteger, dean of students. Another long-term staff member, Registrar Marie Meloy, whose tenure extended back to the Moore era, retired early in the decade, to be succeeded by Ruth Christensen Volpe (Sproat) '52 and then by Ruthane I. Bopp '60 – who in turn would become over the years a campus stalwart.

Meanwhile, the school's reputation was drifting beyond the limits of Chicago, driven by more than its president's mastery at the podium. News of the exceptionally generous salary schedule was hardly lost on the academic world at large, and the recruitment of students from highly regarded Eastern preparatory schools called further attention to the College's name, not to mention a degree of reflected academic luster.

On campus, the air of anticipation had already led to a sense of achievement, matched in turn by the almost palpable atmosphere of liberalism and secularity that replaced the College's more homegrown latter-day tradition of religiosity in union with commercial business. When, in the early 1960s, the Christian Education Board of the Presbyterian Church insisted that the College abide by the rule that faculty belong to an "evangelical faith," Cole openly refused to accept the restriction, whereupon the Board itself decided to give up all efforts to enforce it.[12] Meanwhile, the president, together with his gifted wife Doris, who shared his liberal sentiments and academic interests (she participated in the 1963 Selma, Alabama, civil rights march and over the years taught several curricular courses),[13] actively entertained townsfolk, visitors, and faculty, making good use of the new presidential residence, where alcohol was not regarded as a foreign substance. Indeed, it was the faculty who collectively in 1960 welcomed the Coles at a cocktail party that probably had no precedent.[14]

In keeping with this new mood, the College as a body abandoned its former inward-turned self-sufficiency in favor of an attitude that reached outward to its immediate world. As if in rhythm, the Lake Forest community responded. More and more local citizens regarded the prospect of seeing their youthful relatives in attendance at Lake Forest College as worthy of the sort of aspiration most of the townspeople of the 1920s and 1930s could scarcely have envisioned.[15] Indeed the ancient connections were not

1967

1967

**"Protest songs and food boycotts produced a major shake-up in the ... food service as well as an extra steak dinner," reports the _Forester_.**

**Typical of _Forester_ senior entries of the period, is this whimsical one by Carol Danielson: "The mind ought sometimes to be amused, that it may the better return to thought, and to itself. Phaedrus."**

only reestablished but tightened, in an unprecedented two-way traffic pattern. The increase in the size of the faculty together with the upgraded salary schedule enabled tenured professors as much as it required them to move off campus and purchase houses in and around Lake Forest. In turn, the town's residents were drawn to the enriched intellectual climate at the College, especially to the voluminous program of extracurricular activities that was another distinguishing mark of the 1960s. No fewer than 405 men and women well known in their fields came to speak at Lake Forest at the time. The list is far too long to be enumerated here, but by contrast with any of its counterparts in the College's previous periods, much too distinguished to be reduced to a few names. Even the following roster represents only a little more than 10 percent of the total number:[16]

Philosophers Mortimer J. Adler, Hannah Arendt, and Suzanne Langer; novelists Nelson Algren, John Barth, Catherine Drinker Bowen, James Dickey, Ralph Ellison, Joseph Heller, Aldous Huxley, Isaac Bashevis Singer, and Kurt Vonnegut; poets Gwendolyn Brooks, Robert Creeley, e. e. cummings (appearing in Chicago under the cosponsorship of the College), alumnus Ralph J. Mills '54, Howard Nemerov, and Stephen Spender; critics Germaine Brée, Erich Heller, Elder Olson, Kenneth Rexroth, and Harold Rosenberg; artists Ivan Albright, Leon Golub, and Jules Feiffer; photographers Eliot Porter and Arthur Siegel; musicologist Otto Luening; classicist H. D. F. Kitto; educators George Beadle, Robert Maynard Hutchins, and James Phinney Baxter; journalists Lerone Bennett, William F. Buckley Jr., Hedley Donovan, and Tom Wicker; theologians Martin Marty and Paul Tillich (the latter in conversation with President Cole on one of his many visits to the campus); economists Milton Friedman and Paul Samuelson (together in conversation), George Steigler, and Barbara Ward Jackson; historians Henry Steele Commager, John Hope Franklin, Hans Morgenthau, and Peter Viereck; psychologists Bruno Bettelheim, Erich Fromm, Rollo May, Karl Menninger, and B. F. Skinner; natural scientists Albert Crewe, Irenaeus Eibl-Eibesfeld, and Loren Eisley; political figures and statesmen Julian Bond, Jesse Jackson, Ferenc Nagy, Charles Percy, William Proxmire, Donald Rumsfeld, Adlai Stevenson, Norman Thomas, and Kurt von Schuschnigg.

Senator Proxmire's lecture and its reception characterized something of the new mood alive on the campus. Though Proxmire represented the state of Wisconsin, he had grown up in Lake Forest during the Moore years, when the College was not held in high regard by the townspeople. At the time he visited Lake Forest in 1963, he was content to read from a canned speech on which he had labored little if at all, only to encounter, as he later recalled it, a series of strongly challenging questions from the students that set him back on his heels. The College, he added wryly, was quite evidently a new college, changed substantially since the days when his original opinion of it had been formed.[17]

The list of musical and dramatic performers who appeared in the 1960s is shorter in number than that of the speakers, but worthy of mention:[18] individual singers Adele Addison, Odetta, Nina Simone, and Josh White; group vocalists the Lost City Ramblers, the Staples Gospel Singers, and the Wanderers Three; harpsichordist Dorothy Lane; pianists Ruth Laredo, Vronsky and Babin, and alumnus Robert E. Wallenborn '27; violinist Sergiu Luca; sitarists Ustad Ghulamhusain and Brian Silver; flamenco guitarist Carlos Montoya; classical group instrumentalists the Fine Arts Quartet, the New York Camerata, and the Chicago Woodwind Quintet; jazz and blues groups the Contemporary Jazz Quintet and the Junior Wells Blues Band; the Pomare Dance Group; dramatic groups the Chicago City Players, the National Theater of the Deaf, and Ossie Davis and Ruby Dee. Some of these performers appeared as part of the programs organized in connection with the College's series of conferences. To their number may be added, among an extensive list of art and photography shows, an extraordinary exhibition of Old Master paintings (from the sixteenth through the

Cultural Office Director Ruth Winter pictured with student members of the off-campus cultural board for 1962–63.

**Above.** Student photographer Stephen R. Logowitz '70 captures the essence of close student-teacher working relationships as Art Professor Michael Croydon casts a critical eye over a work-in-progress by E. Jan Gates '71.

**Below.** A highlight of president Cole's inauguration in mid-November of 1960 was the Old Masters art exhibit in the Durand Art Institute. Pictured are Everett D. Graff '06, Martha Sudler and Carroll Sudler, trustee Board chair, admiring a painting by G.B. Tiepolo.

THE EXHIBITION WILL BE SHOWN IN CONJUNCTION WITH THE INAUGURATION OF THE TENTH PRESIDENT OF LAKE FOREST COLLEGE, DR. WILLIAM GRAHAM COLE. IT WILL HANG IN HENRY C. DURAND ART INSTITUTE, NORTH CAMPUS. FROM NOV. 14 THROUGH NOV. 20, 1960. HOURS: MONDAY THROUGH THURSDAY, 10-10; FRIDAY, 10-5; SATURDAY AND SUNDAY, 10-1.

BAGLIONE
BASSANO
BIBIENA
CARIANI
CHAMPAIGNE
VAN DYCK
FLINCK
GOYA
VAN GOYEN
GUARDI
MILLET
PIRANESI
STROZZI
TENIERS
TIEPOLO
VERSPRONCK
DE VOS
WATTEAU

THE DEPARTMENT OF ART
OF LAKE FOREST COLLEGE PRESENTS

*Old Masters*

PAINTINGS AND DRAWINGS, 15TH - 19TH CENTURIES.

A LOAN EXHIBITION

FROM PRIVATE COLLECTIONS

IN THE CHICAGO AREA.

nineteenth centuries) borrowed from Chicago private collections and mounted in 1960 as part of the ceremonies marking the inauguration of President Cole.[19]

Since the flood of names of the guests invited to the College is a sign of the brisk pace of the decade, the numerous faculty who arrived in the period deserve listing, for they joined the solid core of Johnson faculty in setting the academic tone for the next decades. Even more than their predecessors, they were long on scholarship, and they brought proportionate professional distinction to the campus. Of the appointees (a few among them moving on to eminent positions elsewhere), the following stand out:[20] in Art, Alexander F. Mitchell and Michael B. Croydon; in Biology, Frederic A. Giere and Kenneth L. Weik; in Chemistry, William B. Martin, M. L. Thompson, and Laura Kateley Klingbeil; in English, Kenneth C. Bennett and Robert M. Greenfield; in French, Jean-Luc Garneau; in History, John G. Sproat (later to the University of South Carolina), Nathan Huggins (later to Harvard University), Carol Gayle, and Arthur Zilversmit; in Mathematics, Ralph L. Shively and Robert J. Troyer; in Music, Frank E. Kirby; in Philosophy, Forest W. Hansen and Abba Lessing; in Physical Education, Michael E. Dau '58; in Physics, Bailey L. Donnally, T. H. Jeong, and Roger J. Faber; in Politics, Robert J. Steamer (later to the University of Massachusetts at Boston) and Jonathan F. Galloway; in Psychology, Charles F. Behling (later to the University of Michigan), Phylis M. Frankel, David L. Krantz, and Robert B. Glassman; in Religion, Dan P. Cole; in Sociology, Mihaly Csikszentmihaly (later to the University of Chicago), Jerry Gerasimo '52, and George T. Mills; in Spanish (and later the College administration), George L. Speros.

In several respects the faculty hired in the 1960s were more heterogeneous than their counterparts of previous decades. They had acquired their undergraduate and graduate education in a wider assortment of American schools, and some

of the foreign-born among them had taken degrees in first-rate institutions abroad. Now situated in the Midwest, most of them took substantially more advantage of the expanding cultural resources of Chicago than was common among the town-bound instructors of the Moore and Johnson periods.[21]

**The counterpoint of intellectual give-and-take within** the faculty can be read in the relationship that developed during the 1960s between teachers and students, each group, despite developing alarums and excursions, generally attracted to the other, and each gaining commensurately in the process. The College's students as a body are remembered as having been not only better schooled than their predecessors when they arrived on campus, but uncommonly eager to pursue their undergraduate training and, in a relatively large number of cases, to continue on to graduate school. An unusually creative and innovative group, they could collectively produce an original film about the College[22] and a stunningly clever variation on the yearbook that they called *The Yearbox*,[23] while supervising publication of several years of issues of the *Stentor* that rank among the liveliest and most literate in that newspaper's history.

*The Forester* yearbook first appeared in 1892 and, through most of the twentieth century, followed the format into which it settled cosily soon after its founding. So it was natural that by 1969, when students were questioning established expectations on all fronts, they would challenge the yearbook concept. Less to be expected, perhaps, was the creativity and verve of the result, a "yearbox" in place of the traditional bound volume. This contained a collection of printed ephemera and realia, including a memorable poster proclaiming the new diversity in the long-time Presbyterian college. Inspired by the innovative graphics of *Aspen Magazine*, Stephen R. Logowitz '70 provided the creative spark for this singular production.

1968

During the Democratic National Convention in Chicago, on August 28 a full-scale riot pitting police and National Guardsmen against youthful antiwar protesters captures the attention of the world.

1968

At a special fall conference on the generation gap, Chicago author and personality Studs Terkel observes that the Nazi officers he had seen in photos always were neatly groomed and depicted as well-disciplined and obedient to authority.

## "And Gladly Wolde He Lerne, and Gladly Teche"

Chaucer's memorable depiction of the Clerk of Oxford is a reminder that at the very heart of the undergraduate experience are the teachers whose effect on their students is the stuff of education. No listings – no faculty roster – can suggest the individuality of their roles and impact. Certainly the recent decades of College history could offer up to campus readers a kaleidoscope of images and sounds: Harold Hutcheson rushing late into class to mesmerize his students with *King Lear*; President Cole as Mega Professor holding forth in the faculty lounge to his favorite audience; Murray Herlihy striding across campus, followed, like a mother hen, by his departmental chicks; Franz Schulze and Bob Sharvy in relaxed moments, guitars in hand, offering up "The Ballad of Espinose" around a beach fire; Art Zilversmit answering students' demands after Kent State with a reminder that those manning the barricades at the Bastille were not protesting for course credit; Gene Hotchkiss on his bicycle pedaling his way to North Hall; George Mills, gurulike, epitomizing the '60s for his sociology students; the sonorous voices of Alex Mitchell and Michael Croyden, the "charisma boys" of the Art Department, emanating from darkened, slide-lighted rooms; Jack Coutts standing tall in a faculty meeting to defend the classics when President Cole was proposing cutting the number of majors; Bailey Donnally's very, very, very measured southern cadences; street scenes with Ed Packel, Bob Holliday, and Mike Dau jogging furiously and perhaps passing a bemused Chuck Miller on his perennial bicycle; Roger Faber on the roof of Carnegie offering up the heavens to his enrapt stargazers; Ann Hentz rivetingly reaching the last line of Sylvia Plath's *Daddy*: "Daddy, daddy, you bastard, I'm through." The account could continue as long as the faculty lists, from which alumni will pick out at least one individual who made a difference, one figure engraved in memory.

Student-Faculty Variety Show, 1961. For a skit based on Carrie Nation, these Flora Dora "girls" wore costumes created by a faculty member's mother. Left to right: Rosemary Cowler, English department, Ann Hentz, English department, Ruth Christensen (Sproat) '52, Registrar's office, Ann Bowen, Music department, Blanche Ott Coutts, development office, and Dorothy Daydiff, business office.

Obviously, the generation of the 1960s was an assertive lot, and strong-minded, in rough proportion to their intellectual inquisitiveness, and this was especially evident in the approach they took to their personal lives as well as to the major social and political issues of the day. When the new coed dormitories were going up on South Campus, the students for whom they were meant were less taken with the familiar plan of units ranged along a common hallway than with a design made up of four-person, two-room suites, each with its own exterior access. The preferred arrangement, which was carried out, granted greater autonomy to the residents. While apartments had been reserved for housemothers or faculty residents, the increase in individual student entries represented a clear break with the collegiate tradition in which a single entryway could be overseen by one dormitory official. By the end of the 1960s the gatekeeper function was on the wane, though adults continued to live in assigned suites after the turn of the 1970s. The timeless parietal rules likewise disappeared and, with them, much of the role of the College *in loco parentis*.[24] Significantly, it was during the 1960s that the Counseling Center was instituted.

Meanwhile, on the larger scene, the students' independence of spirit was manifest in the concern they took increasingly in the politics of a period that was, after all, notable in its own right for a heavy dose of domestic strife and international tension. Soon enough in the course of the decade, as we shall see, relations between some of the students and many of their elders commenced to curdle, but in the early and mid-1960s, and even in some respects steadily throughout the decade, the College's undergraduates were an accomplishing lot who made a singularly memorable record for themselves.

Indeed, the alumni from the period went on to distinction in a number of areas: in the arts, Richard D. Armstrong '71, of the Carnegie Museum of Art, Arthur Q. Davis Jr. '69, of the New Orleans Jazz Heritage Festival, Christine Lund '66, television anchor, Ingram D. Marshall '64, composer, Frederick F. Phillips '69, architect, and John L. Preston Jr. '69, author; in business, J. David Brock, '66 of the Northern Trust Co., Judith Simpson Corson '64, of Custom Research, Thomas H. Jacobsen '63, of Mercantile Bancorporation, Hiroshi Iwamoto '61, of Japan's NHK International Division, Frederick A. Krehbiel '63, of Molex, James M. Micali '69, of Michelin North America, Yasuhiro Moriuchi '68, of Hitachi Information System Group, Ann Welton '69, of AXXYS Pharmaceuticals, and Nicholas J. Pritzker '69, of Hyatt Development; in education, Alden S. Bean '61, of Lehigh University, Robert P. Emlen '69, of Brown University, Walter A. Hill '68, of Tuskegee University, Donald S. Monroe '61, of Francis Parker School, Alfred A. Moss '65, of the University of Maryland, and John C. Virden '69, of Hotchkiss School; in journalism, Marcia Gillespie '66, of *MS.* magazine and Robert W. Verdi '67, of the *Chicago Tribune*; in the sciences, Thomas L. Babb '64, of the Cleveland Clinic and Ford Ballantyne '65, of the medical school of the University of Wisconsin.[25]

There was, however, another aspect of this dynamic scenario that involved a widespread negative response of alumni, especially those old enough to remember the altogether different College that obtained during the Moore and the Johnson years. Gone, it seemed to them, was the school they had known and loved. A new breed of students, faculty, and administration had taken over, with none of whom the old alums could readily identify. Even the built environment of the campus was changing. Many felt dispossessed.

Much, but not all, of their alienation grew out of the dispute over the fraternities and sororities, specifically over the issue of chapter autonomy, that consumed so much of the College family's attentions in the early '60s. Some groups went local,[26] some disbanded, others continued without restrictive clauses and, as interest at the College waxed

1968

1968

**In early October students protest an Air Force recruiter on campus.**

**Dr. Martin Luther King Jr. is assassinated.**

**Above.** The emergence of soccer reflected changes in athletics, responding to a broader College constituency that included Eastern as well as international students.

**Below right.** As the scale of the College expanded, both the new and old sports could be supported – each with its own constituency. Here a picture of the enthusiastic, full-scaled 1964 football team with coaches Nicholas Wasylik, left, and Alvin Hanke, right.

**Below left.** The shifts in campus life occasioned by the arrival in numbers of Eastern prep school graduates in the early Cole years resulted in the importation of further East Coast athletic preferences, notably among them ice hockey. Here in February of 1963 an early men's team is pictured. Quickly the College established itself in this new sport and began playing major institutional opponents, such as the Air Force Academy.

**Above.** Vietnam demonstration in downtown Lake Forest on May 24, 1969, as recorded by Mark S. Hertzberg '72, one of Ellen Mosey's student-photographers.

**Below.** Chicago Seven Trial demonstration in downtown Chicago (February 22, 1970), depicting Jesse Jackson, photographed by Thomas H. Livermore '70.

and waned, all of them felt the impact of the national rejection of exclusive social societies increasingly marginalized by larger issues. An editorial in the *Stentor* of September 20, 1968, had this to say: "We have passed beyond the years when fraternity weekends and football games occupy most of our extracurricular time. These are important, but only as a means of release *from* constructive activity...." In addition, the alumni saw the disappearance of still other customs, activities, and traditions they fondly recalled: Iron Key ceased to exist,[27] and even academic distinction through "shield honors" gave way to Phi Beta Kappa elections. Nothing was sacred, not even sports. Time-honored rivalries were dissolved when the College, unwilling to lower its new academic standards to attract less qualified athletes, dropped its membership in the College Conference of Illinois.[28] How altogether foreign the whole scene now appeared, when an enthusiastic audience of students and faculty gathered on a Saturday morning outside the Memorial Fieldhouse to watch soccer matches in which the College's African players performed so expertly barefoot that opposing coaches soon insisted that all participants be shod![29] Furthermore, if it was not soccer that looked unfamiliar to Midwestern eyes long accustomed to football, it was lacrosse, a sport more exotic still.

In some respects the disparity between the new and the old Lake Forest College was a subject unto itself, yet in retrospect it can be seen related to a growing national crisis. Certainly the optimism so patently characteristic of the first years of the Cole administration crested in mid-decade

and began an erratic but inexorable descent into the darker, less hopeful state of mind that spread throughout the country at the end of the 1960s. In 1965 the United States started air raids on North Vietnam, thus taking the fatal step that initiated this country's full-scale active involvement in that conflict. The fact was pertinent to the fortunes of the College for a variety of reasons, not least among them the effect of the war on the students, who recognized that they were vulnerable to many of the life-threatening demands that a country at war would impose on them. That it was a monumentally controversial war only intensified American students' attitude toward it nationwide, which, as the nation's military action in southeast Asia led from one frustration to another, turned rapidly from disapproval to overt protest and occasionally even open antiwar violence. No single incident provided a more dramatic example of the issues dividing the country than the explosive 1968 Democratic National Convention, which shook Chicago and, not incidentally, both attracted and involved students from the College.[30]

Just as the myriad actions and events of the early 1960s had worked in uncanny concert for the good of American academe and, by extension, Lake Forest College, nearly everything that occurred in the second half of the decade seemed to have conspired, no less interactively, to overshadow what had been so hopefully achieved. The struggle over civil rights generated its own turbulence, even as the rise of a vigorous popular culture, with which the young identified, drove a wedge between the generations. By the late 1960s a cause that came to be known as the counterculture, one of whose watchwords was "Don't trust anyone over thirty!" had enlisted the sympathies of so many students all over the country that America as a whole approached the new decade in a state of uncertainty and intermingling animosities.

The story of the College in the late 1960s and early 1970s is best related with the students rather than either the faculty or the administration in the lead role. In an affirmative sense, that view can be regarded as evidence of a harvest of all that had grown out of a communal effort to create a quality school serving a quality student body. But that very body was changing within itself. On October 1, 1968, President Cole addressed the faculty on the mood of the American campus, so exceptional, as he saw it, that it called for "measures out of the ordinary." Reminding his audience that trustees and administrators had been, until very recently, "unconscionably slow" in taking faculty into collegial partnership in policy and decision making, he tried to place in perspective the current aspiration of students to "a similar participatory role and privilege." Urging faculty and administration to take a common stand in the matter, he made a proposal that would have been virtually unthinkable a generation earlier. The students, he suggested – the responsible and sensible majority, that is – should be consulted and heeded in curricular planning and course evaluations, on which instructors, moreover, could be judged – not on their scholarly competence, of course, but on their ability to share their knowledge with their students.

The faculty offered a qualified response. When they granted students permission to address them in faculty meeting, they denied the further request that interested undergraduates be allowed to attend these meetings. But they passed a motion declaring that each faculty committee should consider methods of improving communication with the appropriate student committee.[31] President Cole followed this with the report that the Board of Trustees planned to invite the chairs of the two elected faculty committees and the president and vice president of student government to attend Board meetings (without voting privileges).[32]

Given this measured accession to student wishes, Lake Forest managed to avoid the turmoil and violence that occurred in many of the country's colleges and universities. In 1966 a chapter of the militant Students for a Democratic Society had been organized on campus,[33] but the fundamental relationship between the faculty and the student body was close enough to keep the latter from viewing the former as their enemy. In fact, there was an innocence of sorts in the protests and demands the students did issue in the late 1960s and the turbulent spring of 1970. They would boycott a class – on principle – then want to know when the instructor planned to make it up. A demonstration at Fort Sheridan was preceded by a phone call to the military announcing the intention to march, followed by indignation when the procession, once arrived, found the gates of the compound closed to them. Wonderfully ironic too were the collective responses to speeches delivered at a college-wide gathering in May 1970, at which the question of the closing of the College following the American military incursion into Cambodia and the killing of students by the National Guard at Kent State University was debated. One faculty presentation, a powerfully reasoned plea to keep the school in session, in recognition of the political privileges and cultural obligations of an open society, was met with a standing ovation. The very next speaker, a student, who framed a diametrically opposite opinion in blazing rhetoric, brought the same audience to its feet, in shouts of agreement. A later effort to set up an alternative student revolutionary government was never taken very seriously[34] and a so-called Free University[35] that featured a few faculty members supervising such courses as "Being," "Ethnic Cooking," and "Fundamentals of Rock Climbing" scarcely proved a threat to the standard curriculum. Classes continued throughout the period to be conducted without any real interference.

1969

In turbulent times, an early June blaze – origins to remain unknown – destroys the interior of the North Gym, "Old Ironsides."

1969

The Woodstock Music Festival, August 15–17, provides an extreme and highly visible symbol of the generation gap.

# The Mosey Boys – Campus Photographers

Director of Publicity from the 1950s to the 1970s, Ellen Mosey, memorialized by Michael Croydon's sculpture *Wounded Angel* after her sudden death in the mid-1970s, nurtured a generation of College student photographers who together produced a remarkable archive of lively photographs. This period, which marked the greatest change in campus life since the Civil War, fortunately was recorded well by the group.

The "boys," with one "girl" (before 1971 students didn't come of age until twenty-one), shared a darkroom on the fifth floor of College Hall. The woman, according to Stephen Logowitz '70, was Lata Sochynsky '73. The men included Thomas Davies '65, Douglas Donaldson '67, Edwin (Ted) Adriance '67, Ronald Pownall '69, Thomas Livermore '70, Jonathan Atkin '71, Mark Hertzberg '72 and Bruce C. Read '73 . The College provided the darkroom and supplies, with the students on piecework for their time, Mrs. Mosey paying them around two dollars per contact sheet and fifty cents per print. But her astute eye and sympathetic ear were ultimately more significant payment for these novices. She encouraged them, mentored them, and they learned from each other.

If Steve Logowitz claimed that Ron Pownall showed him the ropes in the darkroom, Ron in turn credited what he knew to Ted Adriance and to hard experience – as a favorite anecdote testifies. Hired by Michael Dau to film football games in the coach's first teaching year and never having run a movie camera, he started out his first day by shooting eight important reels of – NOTHING. In bed the next morning, he had a call from Dean Hoogesteger warning him to get out of his room and quickly before Coach Dau found him. He escaped then but at an end-of-season banquet, had a box of eight unwound reels emptied over his head.

That experience was just a prelude for even headier ones. In the summer of 1968, Ron's friend Robert Verdi '67, just having secured a position on the *Chicago Tribune*, arranged for him to work as a photographer in what promised to be a busy time, with the Democratic Convention coming up in the August of what was proving a volatile year. Ron recalls that with his youthful mobility he shot riots by day and rock stars by night – among the latter, Janis Joplin and Jimi Hendrix most noteworthy. One of his Convention confrontation shots included a young man being clubbed by a policeman, a picture that went around the world by wire service. In a November 1968 exhibit of photographs in Durand Commons, the young man was identified as Rennie Davis (one of the Chicago Seven defendants) by his girlfriend in the audience.

It was a memorable period indeed, marked by great student initiative and imagination, with one of the crowning campus achievements the brilliant Yearbox masterminded by Steve Logowitz, also editor of the *Stentor.* Given these various campus – and off-campus – capers, it is not surprising that careers were carved out of them. Steve today is a graphic designer while Ron, Jon, and Mark have continued with photography, Ron for fifteen years shooting for *Rolling Stone,* and currently among other things doing record album jackets, most recently one for a retrospective for Eric Clapton. Another campus photographer, from a slightly earlier period, James Bengston '64, also turned his student job into a profession, in which he is well established in Norway. He and classmate Ingram ("Butch") Marshall '64, now a distinguished composer, have collaborated on a video *Alcatraz*, where sound and sight interweave strikingly.

Campus scenes recorded by Steve Logowitz '70, one of Ellen Mosey's student photographers.

Considerably less guileless, however, was the unhealthy relationship that developed between the counterculture and the growing dependence on drugs. There was a segment of the student body whose use of narcotics went hand in hand with a markedly hostile view toward many of the forms and values of what they perceived as the Establishment, and this group made themselves felt in trashing furniture and equipment in Commons and the dormitories, no longer the controlled environments they once had been.[36] As substance and alcohol abuse began to take on the dimensions of a major campus concern, a fire destroyed all of the interior of Old Ironsides – the North Gym – on June 4, 1969.[37] While it was never determined whether the cause was arson, the occurrence during a period so driven by mutual hostilities lent it a symbolic significance that produced yet another cloud on a darkening horizon.

**That much said, more than a little evidence of promise** and hope continued to be active and visible: In 1967 a program cosponsored with the Whitney Museum of American Art took art history students to New York to study with major figures of the Manhattan art world,[38] and a year later a poet-in-residence program brought nationally respected poets to the campus on an annual basis.[39] Another major feature of 1968 was a conference, "Between the Generations: The Confidence Gap,"[40] that addressed one of the most pertinent issues of the day. Further, at the academic level, the Department of Physics in 1969 gained national recognition for research efforts in which students, having worked together with faculty, were listed in publications alongside their supervisors.[41]

In 1968 the largest building put up during the 1960s, the Sports Center, opened on South Campus.[42] Most of the money needed to carry out the design (by Loebl, Schlossman & Bennett of Chicago, with Edward Dart in supervising capacity)[43] was provided by Elliott Donnelley, who in the course of the decade had become the College's principal benefactor.[44] A Computing Center was established in College Hall a year later,[45] when enrollment hit a new high of 1,350.[46]

Evidently enough, assets were stacked against liabilities as the decade came to a close, yet on balance the College's overall state of health was less than heartening. The faculty were no longer so unified in their academic visions nor so much in concert with the administration. Schisms had developed among the students. And just as portentous, a sense of financial unease had taken hold. After the lavish expenditures on salaries, programs, and buildings, the report in the faculty minutes of October 7, 1969, from the Committee on Admissions and Financial Aid was preceded by the sobering statement that "the faculty of Lake Forest College recognizes the limitations of the College's present resources and that expenses cannot long exceed current income." This was followed by a request that the Board of Trustees review all budgetary items in hopes that the College could maintain its leadership and standard of excellence in all its efforts, with particular concern for financial aid, where any reduction might "seriously impair further growth and ... affect adversely our present stature."

If these notes of disquiet were not enough, President Cole struck another disconcerting one, in his letter of resignation, read to the faculty on March 4, 1969. The decade had opened propitiously with the president-elect's words of high good cheer to his teaching staff, but it would end on a different, decidedly more ambiguous chord. Although about half of his remarks were given over to explaining his reasons for leaving – that it had always been his intention to remain about ten years and no more ("prolonged presidencies are on the whole injurious to institutions and unwholesome for individuals")[47] – he fixed much of his attention on a problem whose seriousness was equal to the College's failure up until that time to solve it satisfactorily. He addressed the matter with appropriate concern, but by bringing it up coincident with his resignation, hence

The John Hancock Center, at 1,127 feet in height, epitomizes the Chicago skyscraper building spree which by 1974 will produce the Sears Tower, its 1,450 feet making it taller than the heretofore highest 1931 Empire State Building (1,250 feet, constructed by Paul Starrett, Class of 1887).

1969

**A Computing Center is established in College Hall.**

157

leaving it to be tackled by a leaderless faculty, his decision to step down produced an effect absent of conclusion, much less of closure, and notable mostly for irresolution.

The issue at hand was the place and role at the College of its African American students. There had long been a purposeful effort to recruit black students, dating back to the Johnson period,[48] and in that regard the College had been even more persevering during the Cole years,[49] beginning in 1962 with the faculty setting up a Coordinating Committee on Black Recruitment[50] and in 1968 adding a course in black history to the curriculum.[51] In the same year, the College organized Soul Week, a concentrated effort to illuminate the African American heritage.[52] It was at this time that Dr. Martin Luther King Jr. was assassinated, and the effect on Chicago was especially incendiary, since King's earlier visit to the city, spent in an effort to alleviate segregation at the level of public housing, had met with un-yielding resistance. Thus the urban rioting that followed, laying waste whole sections of Chicago's West Side, was partly in reaction to King's failure.

Events were moving with dizzying swiftness as the issue of civil rights took on an increased national urgency. The response of Lake Forest's African American students was a drive not only to pursue their rights more vigorously than ever on campus but to seek the power to regulate them. A delegation of Black Panthers appeared on campus in 1969,[53] adding a measure of militancy to an already tense and uneasy atmosphere. Black Students for Black Action was formed at the same time, a group that called for the hiring by the fall term of 1970–71 of African American faculty in proportion to the number of full-time African American students on campus – "even if it necessitates the creation of new positions" – and the right of the students to bring African American candidates to the campus at the College's expense, moreover to take part in the interviewing process.[54] By early June 1969, subsequent to Cole's resignation, the faculty had complied, not fully but in principle, with most of the students' demands.[55]

Whether the faculty's actions, not to mention those of the outgoing president, amounted to capitulation to unrealistic demands or a redress of legitimate social grievances – or both – was open to debate then as now, but there seems no denying in retrospect that with the end of the 1960s, the College's Camelot years had run their course.

1969

**A delegation of Black Panthers appears on campus.**

1969

**Enrollment reaches a record high of 1,350.**

# Continuity and Consolidation with President Hotchkiss

chapter 9

1970—1993

"It is hard to find the right name for what followed the sixties. Backlash, conservative reaction, hard times, times of trouble – none of these quite captures the danger to academic life and the need for sober attention to difficulties old and new." This passage, taken from a 1999 article by Hugh Hawkins in a section appropriately subtitled "After the Sixties: Sobriety and Managerialism,"[1] pertains to Lake Forest College as surely as it does to the national academic environment that Professor Hawkins took as the subject of his study.[2] For Lake Forest indeed felt the lash of the "hard times," like many another quality liberal arts college, although the progress it had made in the 1960s helped it see its way through the two especially lean decades, the 1970s and 1980s, that witnessed the foundering of more than 150 private four-year American colleges.[3]

1970

In January Chicago Seven
defense lawyer, William
Kunstler, speaks on campus
in the same month that
a federal jury acquits
his clients.

1970

In April astronaut (later
trustee) James Lovell
guides home safely an
endangered Apollo-Saturn
13 moon mission.

Within a few years of the turn of the 1970s it was apparent, as we observed earlier, that the self-assurance of American academe as a whole had given way to doubt and uncertainty about the future. Financial problems loomed with increased federal aid carrying a price in the form of added governmental regulations (on such new issues, for example, as racial and gender discrimination) and reactive academic bureaucracy. These various concerns would have an expanding impact on a society whose litigious tendencies affected not only academic budgets but the intangible traditions of community. College administrations grew in size and strength, perforce, and academic programs were often obliged to assume a position of lower institutional priority. Faculties began to feel new stringencies in tenure requirements, a tightening job market, and loss of real income in an inflationary period. There were pressures everywhere to undercut the old, easy academic collegiality.[4] Hawkins's reference to "sobriety and managerialism" fits the period altogether accurately.

**During the prosperous, high-flying 1960s, Lake Forest** had made no plans to prepare itself for the possibility of any serious financial downturn.[5] In the very achievement of many of its goals, the College had catapulted itself into a position of lofty expectations, but there proved to be insufficient time in which to consolidate its gains and reinforce its new reputation. If the hopeful momentum of the 1960s was sustained briefly, the more restrictive mood of the 1970s was not far behind. In 1969 the enrollment had reached a record high of 1,350,[6] as noted earlier, and applications for the following year increased five percent.[7] Moreover, the graduating classes of 1969, 1970, and 1971 are still remembered as among the strongest intellectually of any in the College's history. Nevertheless, all too soon the school's problems turned from latency to actuality[8] and the chief responsibility for coping with them—for salvaging the very destiny of the school—fell to the president who succeeded William Graham Cole.

Eugene Hotchkiss III, chosen in another national search, took office in 1970,[9] after Dean William Dunn had served as acting president and Professor Donald Bartlett as acting provost.[10] After growing up in neighboring Highland Park, Hotchkiss did his undergraduate work at Dartmouth and got his doctorate in student personnel and guidance at Cornell. His experience prior to the Lake Forest appointment was administrative, with tours as dean of the college at Harvey Mudd (of the Claremont colleges) and executive dean at Chatham College in Pennsylvania.[11] Thus he was well

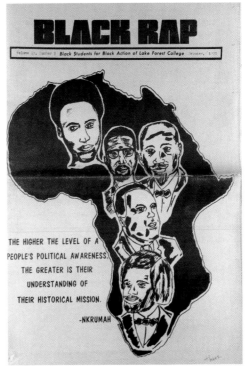

schooled and appropriately armed to take on the kind of assignment that would become pressing in the 1970s. His awareness of the problems facing the College was one of the prime professional assets that won him the presidency, although he added the element of courage to it when, in the course of his interview by the search committee, he took issue with Board Chair Elliott Donnelley's overly sanguine assessment of the College's financial condition. He had done his homework, and he knew better than Donnelley that some serious effort had to be made to repair the fiscal leaks he had discovered before even being offered the job.[12]

His exchange with Donnelley and the committee adumbrated the direction of the administration that he would oversee for the next twenty-three years. This was apparent as early as November of 1970, when he delivered to the faculty a report that stood in stark contrast to the ebullience of President Cole's address to the same audience just ten years before. More mindful of problems than of potentialities, Hotchkiss identified the major points of concern: finances first and foremost, followed by the interests of the College's African American constituency, the ongoing problem with drugs, the need for a beefed-up campus security force, and a full-scale review of the curriculum.[13]

**Left.** The increased self-awareness of African American students on campus is evident here in an issue of *Black Rap*, a publication produced by Black Students for Black Action. BSBA was an early residence hall purpose unit, always in Roberts Hall, with a lounge dedicated to its activities.

**Right.** As the campus explored the "far out" aspects of life in the early 1970s, nostalgia for an earlier, still-remembered simpler existence in the 1950s became a national vogue. This 1974 Winter Weekend scene in the Sports Center shows the broad appeal for this return to the carefree innocence of that pre-'60s time. Here a peg-jeaned, leather-jacketed student typifies that "look."

Events beyond Lake Forest did more to exacerbate than alleviate the crisis Hotchkiss foresaw confronting the school. Shortly before he was installed, American academe as a whole was rocked by the disruptions that followed the Kent State killings in May 1970. Furthermore, the College found its earnest commitment to the hiring of African American faculty doubly handicapped by the modest number of available candidates and the competition for their services waged by other schools throughout the land.[14]

Yet these incidents and circumstances paled next to another development that carried the most injurious implications for the College's future: the decision of its most powerful rivals, the traditional private Eastern colleges and universities, to turn coeducational and expand their facilities to accommodate larger student bodies.[15] That move was made mostly in response to changing social conditions, but at Lake Forest, faced already with a dwindling pool of post–baby boom applicants, it had the further grievous effect of surrendering to the Eastern schools many of the very students who shortly before would have applied to the College. Added to this burden was the problem of attrition among those undergraduates already enrolled. As student mobility increased nationally, transferring to other schools became more common than ever before.

Nor was the gloomy outlook confined to extramural factors. Lake Forest's endowment was still small at about $3 million, which meant that the school's finances continued to be largely tuition-driven. And twenty-five percent of the students were on financial aid.[16] Yet the monetary support necessary to carry on in the face of these conditions could no longer be counted on from the town, whose historically conservative citizens now recoiled at what many of them perceived as a radicalized institution.[17] Politics aside, those locals who were ready to send their children off to college found the newly coeducational Eastern schools more attractive than ever and worthy of their renewed allegiance.

One may reasonably wonder why Eugene Hotchkiss accepted a position that in many respects was more a burden than a boon. But he did take it on, not least because he had the administrative skills that were vital to the solution of the problem, and he went on to prove himself as resourceful — and as dogged — in keeping the College on course, and then some, as Ernest Johnson had been.

Hotchkiss's first decade was taken up with stabilizing the school, and nothing was more important to that end than tackling the budget, which had shown a deficit for three years running, beginning in 1967.[18] This meant imposing austerity measures wherever they seemed appropriate, while at the same time it was no less important that the College be made as attractive to students as possible, especially since by 1972, 254 fewer students were enrolled than two years earlier.[19] In curricular and related matters, the College devised a number of changes in an effort to cope with threatened losses. A committee appointed by Hotchkiss and cochaired by professors William Martin and Arthur Zilversmit proposed a completely new system of governance, which was adopted (and has endured), in which the increased role of students in the decision making process reflected demands of the 1960s.[20] The faculty acted in similar vein, removing all general course requirements from the curriculum, seeking instead to rely on an advising system as the ideal method for guiding students while granting them some authority over their individual programs.[21] This effect was accompanied by others similarly motivated, including a group of seminars prepared especially for incoming freshmen;[22] expanded course offerings in studio art and music;[23] and the promising College Scholar Program, which offered advanced work in self-directed study with individualized faculty assistance.[24] Two off-campus programs were initiated, one to West Africa,[25] the other, in marine biology, at Chicago's Shedd Aquarium and in Florida.[26] A revised calendar, the so-called 3-2-3 plan, featured a shortened winter term,[27] with students provided

1971

The twenty-sixth amendment to the U.S. Constitution, lowering the voting age to eighteen, is ratified June 30 – altering forever the relationship between administrators and students.

The introduction of the Continuing Education program by Arthur Zilversmit and Carol Gayle in the mid-1970s brought nontraditional-aged students into regular classes. Shown here is a perennial CE-student favorite, Franz Schulze, giving an art lecture, with Women's Board member Barbara Gardner in front.

readier access to the off-campus internships[28] that were taking shape throughout the nation as a major educational experiment of their time and that, in fact, had already been established at the College by Professor Rosemary Hale in the Department of Economics. A cooperative arrangement with nearby Barat College, a four-year Roman Catholic liberal arts institution located a mile south of the College, enabled students of each school to take courses at the other.[29] In an innovative step by Librarian Arthur Miller that effectively expanded the resources of Donnelley Library, Lake Forest in 1980 became the first among national liberal arts colleges to share automated book circulation with several major libraries around the state.[30] President Hotchkiss also took the lead in fashioning a program meant to differentiate the College from its rivals in an era of renewed competition, the Wood Institute for Local and Regional Studies.[31] This was the first in a projected series of "institutes," whose basic theme was internship requirements, all of them meant to generate career opportunities.[32] Despite a lack of anticipated funding, the Wood Institute was effective for its some ten years' duration, having helped to produce a city manager for Lake Forest, and a village manager for Lake Bluff. The one other realized institute, in health sciences, enjoyed only limited success, in part because the faculty had had little directly to do with its formulation.[33]

Meanwhile, like many another college in similar circumstances, Lake Forest, pursuing all possible ways of swelling its enrollments, turned to students of nontraditional age.[34] That had been President Ernest Johnson's strategy earlier when he created the evening school, subsequently phased

out with the rise of local community colleges. This time the effort was made to attract women to the day classes: those who had left campuses for marriage during World War II or others, with children now grown, for whom college training would once have been less accessible.[35] Thus, the College began its Continuing Education program,[36] following it in 1977, at the behest of President Hotchkiss, with an important innovation in adult education, an interdisciplinary graduate program leading to a Master of Liberal Studies degree. Developed by Professor Arthur Zilversmit and notable for its team-taught seminars, it included in its requirements appropriate electives drawn from the regular undergraduate courses. As well as introducing serious students to classes where their presence often marked them as role models for their undergraduate colleagues, this measure had the secondary beneficial effect of adding numbers to undersubscribed upper-level courses. The College's M/LS plan was the first in the Chicago area of a kind that has since proven increasingly popular, both locally and throughout the country.[37]

Beyond the attention to academic improvement, concern was directed to extracurricular life, as the new administration contended with what the faculty minutes of March 2, 1971, referred to as the "general malaise that permeates our campus."[38] Unrest over political and social issues was still a factor in the thinking and behavior of the student body. Indeed, one of the reasons that President Hotchkiss had called for a full-scale security force was the continued threat of campus disorder.[39] Action was taken on some of the more pressing problems by a committee of trustees, faculty, and students that convened in 1971 with the express purpose of discussing College life, its substantive discontents, and their possible amelioration.[40]

Shortly thereafter, in 1972, an unprecedented event, conceived by Professor Michael Croydon of the Department of Art, injected new life and a more buoyant spirit into the social calendar. Taking its name "Ra" from the ancient Egyptian sun god, it was a festival celebrated shortly before the end of the school year – a rite of spring unique to Lake Forest College in which members of the faculty joined 600 students in donning masks and costumes and marching through the town.[41]

If the frolic of Ra boded well for the future, the present was still heavily burdened. The sudden switch from prosperity to enforced frugality that marked the onset of the

1970s affected no constituency of the College more than the faculty, especially since they had become fully persuaded that they *were* the College and, as such, accustomed to being appropriately well compensated. When Hotchkiss was compelled early in the decade to freeze salaries, it did little to win him friends among his teaching staff, nor did relationships improve with another administrative decision that reduced the College's contribution to retirement benefits for new faculty. A period of national inflation only imposed added pressure on salary schedules.[42] Younger instructors, unable to purchase houses in Lake Forest in an exploding real estate market, more and more took to commuting from nearby towns, while their spouses, responding to circumstances that extended nationwide, often entered the workforce. The sense of close community, whose erosion had begun during the Cole years, was further diminished, as provisions were made to include in faculty meetings probing and occasionally challenging questions prepared for the administration by the local AAUP chapter.[43] Following AAUP guidelines, a faculty grievance committee was organized in 1972.[44]

For all of that, however, the new president had set his sights on maintaining the excellence of the faculty despite dwindling enrollments. The new curriculum led inevitably to different departmental allocations and provided for reductions in personnel, though an adequate ratio of faculty to students was retained and compensation kept as high as conditions allowed.[45] This effort to preserve quality if not quantity is apparent in a list of the major instructors hired during the 1970s, all of them destined to become role players of consequence in the history of the school: in Economics, William Moskoff (who served from 1970 to 1972 and returned in 1982) and Robert A. Baade; in English, Nance van Winckel (later to Eastern Washington University); in German, Clayton Gray Jr.; in History, Michael H. Ebner, D. L. LeMahieu, and Steven J.

Rosswurm; in the Library, Arthur H. Miller; in Mathematics, Edward W. Packel; in Physical Education, Anthony L. Fritz; in Politics, Paul B. Fischer, Christopher Mojekwu (a distinguished African jurist whose death in a 1982 automobile accident cost both the College and the town a valued presence), Charles A. Miller, and W. Rand Smith (later to serve as an associate dean of the faculty); in Psychology, Claire F. Michaels (later to the Free University of Amsterdam) and Stephanie Riger (later to the University of Illinois at Chicago); in Religion, Ronald H. Miller (later to serve as dean of students); in Sociology, Arlene Eskilson and Leo van Hoey; in German, and later the Writing Center, Gertrude Grisham.[46]

**If Hotchkiss's academic objectives required action** within the College, they were no less dependent on the reestablishment of the erstwhile unity with the town, lately lost on account of the school's politicized image and its sluggish efforts in the raising of funds. One of the president's first appointments was that of a new director of development, who took over the position in January 1971.[47] Shortly thereafter a Women's Board was assembled, whose purpose was to support campus activities and sponsor programs that would foster the College's purposes.[48] Hotchkiss on his own recognized that despite the constant and unstinting generosity of Elliott Donnelley and his family, his son James R. Donnelley[49] following him on the Board, the participation of other local citizens was vital, not only to the College's fiscal soundness but to the restoration of its historic ties to Lake Forest. Among the townspeople and nearby residents who contributed most materially – and spiritually, too, believing as each of them did in the liberal arts mission of the school – were leaders like Wesley Dixon[50] and Arthur Hailand,[51] who had joined the Board of Trustees in the later 1960s, and newer appointees, including most prominently Prudence Beidler (Mrs. Francis Beidler III and great granddaughter of President Coulter),

Edward W. Packel, chair of the Mathematics and Computer Science Department, has balanced teaching and scholarship, in the 1970s conducting a course on games and gambling (a.k.a. probability theory) and in the 1980s making enjoyable the department's expanded mission in computer science.

1971–72

1970s

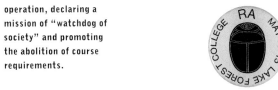

**A Provisional Revolutionary government, complete with "El Presidente" and a "Minister of Information," takes over from the traditional student-council-type** operation, declaring a mission of "watchdog of society" and promoting the abolition of course requirements.

**Ra buttons**

# Ra, Ra, Ra!

The 1960s with their intense political and social upheavals had seen many college traditions and organizations fade away. Campus life was left with few formal structures and punctuations in the calendar other than vacations, exams and paper deadlines, a newly casual Commencement, and the Great Lakes weather. Into this vacuum in the spring of 1972 Art professor and sculptor Michael Croydon injected a vibrant new tradition: the Festival of Ra, named for the Egyptian God of the Sun.

Starting that May as an arts festival, this late–spring term weekend of release was to continue through the rest of the century. At the outset it gave the appearance of a hybrid of Haight-Ashbury and a Parisian Left-Bank Mardi Gras: colorfully costumed parading students and faculty, with a student-work art fair to benefit the Art Department's fund for studio equipment, a film-dance-music festival, and a druidic bonfire. Through it all drifted a fog of incense, or worse.

Strikingly recalled by the Mosey Boys' photography, Ra Weekend, as it came to be known, has grown more staid with age but still remains as it was originally, a festival to the return of sunshine after what always seems a long winter, even with a calendar now richly filled.

These three photos from May of 1972 capture the spirit of the first Ra parade into town and around Market Square, led by pharaoh Michael Croydon – with the aid of both a fencing foil and a bullhorn.

Clarissa Chandler (like James Donnelley, a grandchild of Lake Forest patriarch T. E. Donnelley), Augustin and Margaret Hart (a granddaughter of the Reverend McClure), Charlotte Simmons, Hugo Sonnenschein '44, James Vail, and Board chairs Charles Meyer, James Gorter, Russell Fisher, and Geoffery Shields.[52] Soon a $20 million capital campaign, "The Cost of Quality," was launched, ending on a peak in 1982[53] and followed in 1985 by a new drive that aimed at raising $40 million.[54] Meanwhile, efforts to add diversity to the Board, which had begun with the appointment in 1969 of the prominent Chicago lawyer Jewel Lafontant[55] (later the first woman Solicitor General of the United States), continued, as several other African Americans were added in the 1970s and 1980s.

While credit for attracting so dedicated a group of trustees and friends is owed primarily to Hotchkiss, it belongs as surely to his wife, Suzanne, a devoted help-meet[56] and a woman of elegance in her own right. As a couple they became more than the College's president and his wife; they were in short order members of the community. Together, in fact, with Charlotte Simmons, the Hotchkisses were primarily instrumental in the formation of the Women's Board.

As the College's 100th anniversary of its refounding in 1876 approached, it was more and more apparent that Hotchkiss's efforts had begun to reverse the school's downward momentum. Under Director of Admissions Francis (Spike) Gummere, recruitment of students, extending now to small Midwestern towns and rural areas as well as major cities and the two coasts, was producing results in enrollment,[57] strengthened by the federal support for student financial aid in the capable hands of Gordon White.[58] In October of 1976, the president could report that the College had the highest percentage of growth among comparable liberal arts colleges in the Midwest[59] (and by 1985, its largest incoming class in ten years).[60] A special measure of what was being accomplished can be inferred from the invitation extended the College in 1974 to join the Associated Colleges of the Midwest, a consortium that included among its members such elite schools as Carleton, Colorado, Grinnell, and Lawrence.[61]

While the institutional prestige attaching to that association was reminiscent of the College's fortunes in the 1960s, the new students were noticeably different from their immediate predecessors in both their attitudes and ambitions.[62] One of their most distinctive traits was a preoccupation with material matters that stood in striking contrast with the idealism that had inspired the students of the '60s to fix upon their star and follow it. During the '70s, however, an economic cloud obscured the heavens, limiting the outlook of the young to issues and things immediately around them, especially those that touched them personally. In a period of stagflation, the historic American presumption that each generation could normally expect to achieve greater security than the one previous, was suddenly subjected to doubt. Accordingly aware of this, students (and their parents) reacted by concentrating on ways and means of reaching a respectable – or better still, profitable – livelihood.[63]

Academe could not help but be affected by these developments, and in the course of the '70s, vocationalism resurfaced in the offerings of many colleges. At Lake Forest, the number of prelaw and premed students rose, along with the number of those keenly interested in other marketable futures.[64] By 1979, a Computer Science major had been added to the curriculum and the Business major – with formidable enrollments – reinstated.[65] Further evidence of altered perspectives was manifest overseas as well, where internships, already increasingly popular for the Chicago area, were made key elements in the College's Paris and Madrid programs.[66] With new interest in Asia, a Pacific Rim program was assembled, reinforced by prestigious grants from the Hewlett and Mellon foundations.[67] To help develop

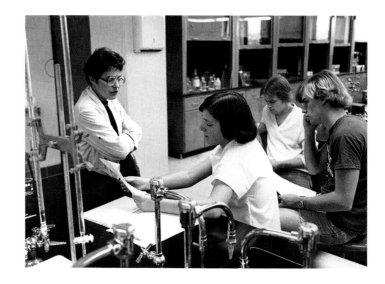

Instructor Laura Kateley Klingbeil with students in a chemistry lab, 1978.

# Publish and Prosper

One of the signs of the College's growing academic reputation in the last decades has been the distinction of its faculty, reflected in a record of valuable publications, with a number of books achieving national recognition: D. L. LeMahieu's *A Culture for Democracy: Mass Communication and the Cultivated Mind in Britain Between the Wars* (1985), winner of a national award of the North American Conference on British Studies; Edward Packel's *The Mathematics of Games and Gambling* (1985), winner of the Mathematical Association of America Book Prize; Franz Schulze's *Mies van der Rohe: a Critical Biography* (1985), winner of Honorable Mention, Alice Davis Hitchcock Award of the American Society of Architectural Historians; Michael Ebner's *Creating Chicago's North Shore, A Suburban History* (1988), winner of the Matson Memorial Award for Non-Fiction, Friends of Literature, and Rosemary Cowler's edition of the major prose works of Alexander Pope (1986), winner of the British Academy's international Rose Mary Crawshay Prize and declared an Outstanding Academic Book of the Year by *Choice*, the American Library Association's review of current books. This last honor has also been given to several later faculty works: *The Idea of Progress in Eighteenth-Century Britain* (1990) by David Spadafora, dean of the faculty and later president of the College; *Creating Chicago's North Shore* by Michael Ebner; and *Max Weber's Society of Intellectuals* (1992) by Ahmad Sadri. Included in the American Library Association's list of 50,000 books essential to any college library are Arthur Zilversmit's *Lincoln on Black and White* (1968) and Schulze's biography of Mies van der Rohe.

Faculty authors Franz Schulze, Steven Rosswurm, and William Moskoff at a 1988 reception honoring Rosswurm's new book.

new course offerings, eight faculty members made a tour of the major countries of the Far East, and subsequently classes in Japanese language and literature were introduced into the curriculum along with others in Asian history, art, and philosophy.[68] An exchange arrangement established with Waseda University in Tokyo[69] was related to the reinstatement of a program dating from President Johnson's years, when the Grew Foundation shared with the College the costs of educating gifted Japanese students. The plan had later been cancelled due to budgetary considerations, but with the Asian thrust of the 1980s, the College resumed its partnership with the foundation.[70]

And all of this coincided with the onset of the computer revolution that was central to the new technology, itself so much a part of American life in the 1970s and 1980s. By 1983 public-access PCs had been made available on campus.[71]

The new emphasis on the practical and experiential, though disturbing to some academics at the time, was put to use in one program that proved especially effective in combining the careerist priorities of the period with traditional liberal arts values. This was the Richter Apprentice Scholar Program, begun in 1987 under the direction of Dean of the Faculty Bailey Donnally, which provided a small group of topflight underclassmen with a set of lively intellectual opportunities that encouraged them to consider life work in research and teaching. Added to a special interdisciplinary seminar on "Ways of Knowing," taken during the freshman year, and later weekly faculty-student colloquia, a focal component of the Richter program was the students' summer experience as apprentice scholars – junior collaborators, as it were – working one-on-one with faculty members and, in the process, becoming acquainted with some of the rewards a scholar's life might offer.[72] The Richter program, recalling both the Patterson Scholars of the Johnson era and Program II of the Cole years, represented the

renewed concern for academic quality, as did the 1988 establishment of a chapter of Sigma Xi, a national science honor society.[73]

The import of these various developments could be felt in campus life, but in ways that were neither always such clear reflections of national norms nor consistent characteristics of the College's student body. The Richter scholars, true to their intellectual direction, formed an organization called the Red and Black, which had its own dormitory area where faculty members were invited to speak on subjects of academic and cultural interest.[74] Other students, anticipating careers that might ultimately prove more necessary than satisfying or edifying, often acted on the presumption that their school years could provide their last, best opportunity for a life of pleasure and camaraderie, relatively unfettered by adult responsibilities. Hence fraternity life, following a brief resurgence in the early '70s, which saw also the rise of housing purpose units, like the black students' House of Soul,[75] was revived yet again in the late 1980s with a return

Even as new internship programs in Paris and Madrid, and later Chile, combined traditional foreign-study interests with new practical priorities, and as membership in the Associated Colleges of the Midwest expanded off-campus options for students, the long-established Greece and Turkey program continued to be the popular choice among Lake Forest's own overseas offerings. This 1973 photo by Alexander Lotocki de Veligost '74 shows students engrossed in a lesson in Athens below the Parthenon on the Acropolis.

1971

With the events of 1969–70 eclipsing traditional Greek activities, this Class of 1971 memento symbolizes the exception rather than the rule of the day.

1972

In sweeping reforms the faculty eliminates distribution requirements and approves a new governance plan guaranteeing student participation in decision-making.

Above. House of Soul members in the late 1970s. Back row, left to right: Phil Bates '81, Deleria Rice '80, Sandra Upchurch '81, Walter Lumpkin '80, Wesley Winfrey '79, Deborah Towns '80, Debbie Morgan '79, Viola Maxwell '80, Deidre Vincent '80, Lynn Jackson '78, Jocelyn Burton '80, Tony Green '78, Paula Stepter '80, Gary Chatmon '79, Trudy Hardin '80, and Pam Williams '78. Middle row: Tony Ferguson '80, Katrina Young '81, Duplain Gant '80, Joyce Jones '81, and Rodney Stewart '80. Front row: Fred Carter '81, Jocelyn Willis '80, and Johnathan Colbert '80.

Below. This 1981–82 view of the Lake Forest chorus in rehearsal pictures Dean of Students Eric Reidel, (top, second left) chiming in with student singers.

the majority of the students reserved their most enthusiastic response for such guests as George Plimpton, the society intellectual who had made a name for himself by writing on sports,[78] and the movie star Robert Redford,[79] who spoke when he was in Lake Forest directing the Academy Award–winning film *Ordinary People*. Another lecture series, equally reflective of the careerist values of the period and fittingly sponsored by the A. B. Dick Fund,[80] focused on entrepreneurial issues and featured such speakers as the television magnate Ted Turner[81] and the department store executive Stanley Marcus of Neiman-Marcus.[82]

All in all, then, the College provided a social and intellectual environment that accommodated a wide range of tastes and interests. If in the mid-'70s an enterprising student could singlehandedly fashion a minitheater in Commons called *Commonplace*, where one-act plays, readings, and other creative-dramatic forms of entertainment were staged,[83] a decade later professional comedians and pop musicians would be customarily hired to perform on campus.[84] Big weekends, most notably the one given over to the steadily successful Ra celebration in the spring, were part of a campus scene in which students also requested a bagpiper to add zest to Commencement ceremonies by leading the graduates' march to the podium.[85] For a time the basement of Commons, which had earlier housed a bowling alley, was turned into a pub when the state drinking age was lowered to nineteen in 1975. With the later return of the age limit to twenty-one, the pub was turned into a pool hall, and finally, in the early 1990s, into the Coffee House.[86]

And, lest it be forgotten, note should be taken that the national vogue of streaking in the early '70s produced (in the enterprising spirit of the College) a racing figure of one of the campus leaders, best cloaked here in anonymity.

On the other hand, if that zany fad was short-lived, student devotion to sports was anything but. Athletics moved at a brisk and lively pace in the 1970s and 1980s that reflected,

to national affiliations that pointed to a renewed appreciation of bonding rituals.[76]

In such a varied social climate, poetry readings could continue to flourish, especially in the early 1970s, although with the passage of time the pace of cultural programs so typical of the 1960s slowed (the more so because required attendance at many events had been dropped during the 1969–70 academic year) and the overall intellectual level was lowered somewhat. By the late '70s, the schedule of lectures was largely confined to weekly convocations.[77] There

1974

**The Student Government Association elects its first woman president, Susan Hendry '75.**

1974

**Lake Forest joins the Associated Colleges of the Midwest (ACM), a consortium of respected peer institutions collaborating on an extensive array of programs.**

A leaflet made up later of Dr. Seuss's memorable address also provided an illustration in his famous style. The poem was widely published and is a perennial favorite of U.S. journalists doing commencement stories. For its twentieth anniversary, the Class of 1977 donated a boulder on which a copy of the poem is mounted for all present and future Lake Foresters to digest.

# Dr. Seuss's Celebrated Commencement Speech

**On June 4, 1977, Theodore Seuss Geisel (Dr. Seuss) delivered what may have been the shortest commencement address ever given. It was certainly the briefest (and most sage?) in Lake Forest history.**

*My Uncle Terwilliger on the Art of Eating Popovers*

**My uncle ordered popovers**
**From the restaurant's bill of fare.**
**And, when they were served,**
**He regarded them with a penetrating stare ....**
**Then he spoke great Words of Wisdom**
**As he sat there on that chair:**
**"To eat these things," said my uncle,**
**"You must exercise great care.**
**You may swallow down what's solid ...**
**BUT ... you** *must* **spit out the air!"**
**And ... as you partake of the world's bill of fare, that's darned good advice to follow.**
**Do a lot of spitting out the hot air. And be careful what you swallow.**

1977

**The Master of Liberal Studies (M/LS) program is introduced, the first such interdisciplinary graduate offering in the Chicago area.**

as did so many aspects of the College's affairs, the interaction of traditional and changing values. An Athletic Hall of Fame was dedicated in the Sports Center in 1974,[87] shortly before the arrival on campus of the Chicago Bears professional football team, which used the school as its summer training camp and in 1979 built Halas Hall as its headquarters adjacent to Farwell Field.[88] Meanwhile, soccer found an eager audience[89] as it grew into one of the major success stories of the American amateur sports scene of the last quarter of the century. The College's own handball teams under Coach Michael E. Dau '58 reached a level of success unmatched by any other sport in the school's history, winning the national intercollegiate championship twelve times in the 1970s and 1980s (sharing the title with the University of Texas in 1971 and 1981).[90] The College took comparable pride in the exceptional record racked up by the women's swimming team of the period.[91] A generation earlier, in the 1950s, the prime sports time of the week, Saturday afternoon, had been given over solely to the football game. While football as both a participating and spectator sport continued to be popular (even energized by the annual appearance of the Bears), it progressively faced competition, not only from soccer, handball, and ice hockey (soon enough the latest "niche" sport),[92] but from another, ultimately more consequential source. Title IX, the program passed by federal legislation in 1972, obliged all colleges and universities to devote as much money and attention to women's sports as to men's. The ruling altered athletic activities at the College as surely as it increased them.[93] Women's basketball and volleyball, especially, came alive;[94] indeed the effect of Title IX could be felt in all facets of the sports program.

The appointment of Jacqueline Slaats, the women's basketball coach, as the school's athletic director in 1992[95] was further evidence of the higher place of women in College affairs. Among the students, the 1970s had seen Susan Hendry '75 elected the first woman president of the Government Association,[96] while the '70s and '80s were marked by a national competition for able women educators that recalled a comparable demand for African American instructors during the 1960s.

The character the College had latterly taken on can be further discerned from the list of alumni who went on to distinction, frequently representing business interests. Among the more notable were John Rutledge '70, of Rutledge & Co., Susan C. Gordon '76, of Viacom International; David J. Miller '78, of Minnetonka Moccasins; Robert L. Lawrence '75, of Jacor Communications; Stephen S. Cole '76, of Cash Station; James C. Foster '72, of Charles River Laboratories; Carlotta R. Mills '88, of the Kresge Foundation; Kai K. Ichikawa '88, of Microsoft; Philmore Anderson IV '86, of Atlantic Records; Doni Dahm (Fordyce) '81, of Bear Stearns Asset Management; and Michael J. Hennel '81, of Silvon Software. Other alumni comparably deserving of recognition covered a wide variety of fields: in education, Gayle R. Pemberton '70, of Wesleyan University and Philip A. Klinkner '85, of Hamilton College; in medicine, Emmett B. Chapital Jr. '74 and John S. Blanchard '75; in television, ABC network commentator (and earlier swimming champion) Diana Nyad '73 and production figure Scott Goldstein '71; in the arts, Peter S. Reed '77, of the Museum of Modern Art; in journalism, Katherine Q. Seelye '71, of the *New York Times*; in public service, Peggy A. Lautenschlager '77, U.S. attorney for the Western District of Wisconsin, Holly Fujiye Clemons '79, judge of the Circuit Court, Champaign, Illinois, and Brian W. Ellis '88, assistant U.S. attorney for the Northern District of Illinois.[97]

Many of these careers and others of this generation of undergraduates — as well as their lives in general — were shaped not only by the campus experience just reviewed, but by the College's increased use of the city of Chicago as an educational tool. Given a student body which, as we have seen, often reflected national traits of pragmatism and neoconservatism, the school strove to make available to them experiences that might widen their horizons. The internship program that drew students into businesses and nonprofit

**Left.** The College fielded its first handball team in 1968 and three years later won the NCAA championship under Coach Dau. The four-player team consisted of brothers Wesley '72 and William Yee '72, David A. Smith '72, and Steven N. Jamron '72.

**Right.** In 1979 the ice hockey team won second place in the NCAA Division II championship.

172

**Above.** This mid-1970s shot of Michael Dulaney '78 (with the ball) shows the vigorous continuation of men's sports and the significant support of fans.

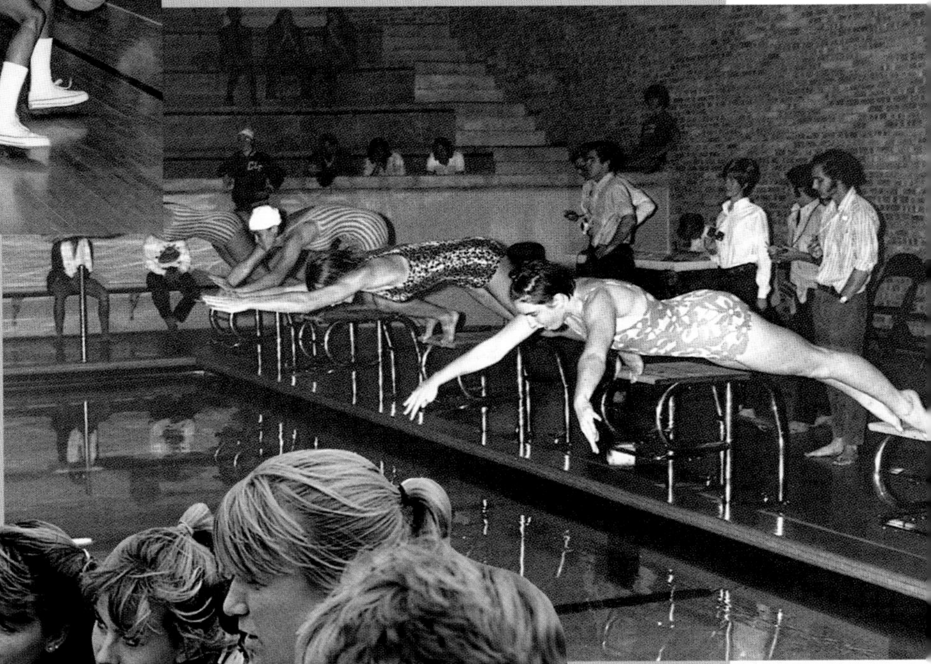

**Center.** The major innovation in athletics at Lake Forest and elsewhere in the last third of the century was 1972's Title IX, which required that resources for women's teams should equal those for men's in sports offered by colleges. This quickly ushered in an expansion of women's participation in intercollegiate sports, and by the 1990s led to outstanding teams in soccer, basketball, and volleyball. Already women swimmers had distinguished themselves in the Olympic-scaled pool in the 1968 Sports Center. Pictured on the right in the foreground is Laurie Finke '74, with Sharon Wichman '74 next to her, diving into the pool.

**Below.** The women's soccer team with coach Sue Trefny, 1986.

At the same time, Chicago was in the process of regaining a sense of itself as the dark days of the late 1960s receded into the past. Its uniquely famous political scene, following the unexpected death of Mayor Richard J. Daley in 1976, witnessed the jockeying for position by his several colorful successors, among whom Jane Byrne helped to expand the national political role of women and Harold Washington did much the same for African Americans. Moreover, at the cultural level, the city experienced a remarkable theatrical awakening, generated largely by the success of the Steppenwolf Theater Company, which had had its origins in a church basement in Lake Forest's neighboring community, Highland Park.

Indeed, one of the most important demographic developments of the 1970s and 1980s, again with consequence to the North Shore in general and the College in particular, was the effect of the growth of the suburbs and Chicago's collar counties. The metropolitan arts community reached outward to Lake Forest, where Ragdale, Howard Van Doren Shaw's own home, was turned into an artists' colony that awarded residential fellowships to writers, musicians, and painters from all over the country (an endeavor that recalled the pre–World War I estate patronage associated with the Chicago Literary Renaissance).

Meanwhile, members of the College's science faculty commenced to make regular visits to the nuclear research center of Argonne National Laboratory, twenty-seven miles southwest of the city. The lifestyles of the inhabitants of town and campus alike were affected by the expansion of exurbia, a nationwide phenomenon that has been described both as the gradual conversion of big cities into megalopolises and as the creation of a sprawl that has turned erstwhile farmland into totally new communities gathered around shopping malls accessible only by automobiles. The impact of this trend on Lake Forest, which began as a controlled town reachable by rail but otherwise

organizations, the better to learn how such groups conducted themselves at the practical level, emphasized off-campus involvement. The faculty, perhaps most notably Professor Michael Ebner of the Department of History, led students on tours of the city, which was transformed into a laboratory of sorts through which the theoretical lessons of textbooks took on new life. Art students were directed to write papers specifically based on visits to the Art Institute of Chicago. But especially valuable among the programs conceived with a direct urban slant were those, organized by the Associated Colleges of the Midwest, which enabled students to pursue studies utilizing the Newberry Library, the Chicago Historical Society, and the city itself, while living temporarily in officially sponsored residence halls.[98] The faculty too were eager to move beyond the confines of Lake Forest as they devoted more and more of their research to various aspects of the city's life.

1979

**The Business major, banished in 1959, is reinstated. When its enrollment swells out of proportion in the 1980s, requirements are tightened to limit its scale.**

with no entry or exit thoroughfares, has been greater than that felt by nearby towns, but there is little doubt that the demo-graphic changes will affect the totality of Chicagoland for decades to come.

The upgrading of Chicago's self-image and the burgeoning of its surrounding spaces occurred at approximately the same time the College had begun to enjoy greater financial stability and the gradual restoration of its own reputation. Gifts and benefactions targeted for various ends commenced to follow. One grant that had a long-lasting impact on the College came from the Lilly Foundation. Sponsored by the Department of English but deliberately developed separately from it, the grant encouraged writing across the curriculum and facilitated the organization of a Writing Center, where students could gain assistance from peer tutors in developing their skills in English composition.[99] A later, second Lilly grant,[100] supervised by Professor W. Rand Smith, provided faculty development programs that were exclusively related to teaching and eventually institutionalized in 1998 in the form of the Learning and Teaching Center, supported by a million-dollar endowment from a trustee and spouse.

Of comparable consequence were the monies that provided for upgrading the College's physical facilities, and the policy governing their outlay, which emphasized the restoration of old buildings rather than the construction of new. Although Hotchkiss himself remarked wryly in 1988, "They'll put on my tombstone, 'He never built a building'"[101] (ironically enough, the remark was made shortly before the drive began to add the Dixon Science Research Wing to the Johnson Science Center),[102] his approach proved doubly advantageous: Needed space was supplied or added more economically by renovation than by building from the ground up, and, at least as important, the sense of tradition and architectural variety associated with the school's older edifices was preserved. Thus, a number of

buildings were granted new life: Durand Institute,[103] which in interior restoration gained the Sonnenschein and Albright art galleries; Young Hall (old College Hall, renamed for its principal donor);[104] the Lily Reid Holt Chapel;[105] Reid Hall;[106] the Allan Carr Theater in Hixon Hall;[107] Glen Rowan (refurbished);[108] Donnelley Library (refurbished);[109] and the old North Gymnasium, its interior totally refashioned two decades after the 1969 fire that had gutted it.[110] The spruced-up campus was further enhanced by tree planting and the addition of two public sculptures to a site in front of Durand Institute. One was *Meander,* an abstraction in Cor-Ten steel by Chicago artist Richard Hunt,[111] brother of Marian E. Hunt '59, the other a figurative piece in bronze, *Wounded Angel*, by Michael Croydon,[112] to commemorate a beloved College figure, Ellen Mosey of the Department of Public Information.[113]

As the College's overall condition recovered, faculty morale improved proportionately. With efforts taken to appoint women and minorities to the instructional staff,[114] the 1980s, and into the 1990s, brought to campus another gifted group of appointees with solid academic backgrounds: in Art, Ann Roberts and Christopher Reed; in Biology, David W. Towle, William E. Zamer, and Anne E. Houde; in Business, Les R. Dlabay and Cynthia Lucking; in Chemistry, Elizabeth W. Fischer '72 (later appointed dean of the college); in Economics, Richard F. Dye, Carolyn Tuttle, Nader Nazmi, and Jeffrey O. Sundberg; in Education, Sandra M. Fox and Dawn M. Apt-Perkins; in English, Diane M. Ross, Benjamin Goluboff, Judith E. B. Harmon (whose untimely death was a major loss to the College), Philip E. Simmons, and Richard Mallette; in French, Cynthia T. Hahn; in German, C. Richard Fisher; in History, Pericles B. Georges; in Japanese, Pack Carnes; in the Library, Vanaja S. Menon (later to the University of Wisconsin at Milwaukee) and David E. Levinson; in Mathematics, Lowell A. Carmony, Robert L. Holliday, DeJuran Richardson, and Jill Van Newenhizen '81; in Music,

1982

1983

1987

**Into a fully-renovated College Hall – now Young Hall – move the departments of Economics and Business, History, Mathematics and Computer Science, and Politics.**

**Public-access personal computers for students are installed around campus, and faculty begin to integrate word-processing and electronic-format submissions into their classes.**

**The Richter Scholar Program offers promising freshmen, among other challenges, increased opportunities for summer research with faculty.**

**A**fourth

**international
exhibition of
HOLOGRAPHY**
july 20    august 18 1991

The Perfumed
Garden
INDIAN MINIATURES 1480-1850

Sonnenschein Gallery ● Durand Art Institute ● Lake Forest College
November 1 — December 14, 1985

Japanese Woodblock Prints

and Miniature Sculpture:

*Ukiyo-e and Netsuke*

Lake Forest College

Rami Levin; in Philosophy, Louis E. Lombardi and Janet McCracken; in Physical Education, Jacqueline A. Slaats; in Physics, Michael M. Kash '77; in Politics, Ghada H. Talhami and Siobhan M. Maroney; in Psychology, Naomi Wentworth, Nancy C. Brekke, and R. Sergio Guglielmi; in Sociology and Anthropology, Ahmad Sadri; in Spanish, David George; in Theater, Louise C. Mason; in Writing Programs and English, Bernice E. Gallagher.[115]

With increased resources, the faculty profited from the extension of health benefits, provisions for maternity leave,[116] and a further sabbatical option.[117] Some of the scholarly fruits of the improved atmosphere were apparent in an impressive record of publications,[118] among the strongest in the Associated Colleges of the Midwest. Lake Forest professors picked up many major grants and fellowships,[119] and several served as visiting faculty in distinguished institutions (LeMahieu at Michigan and later Harvard, Packel at Columbia, Ebner at Chicago, Zilversmit as a member of the Davis Center of Princeton, and for Richardson there were fellowships at Wisconsin and Harvard). Jeong's heralded work in holography carried him all over the world and brought numerous foreign authorities to campus for summer institutes,[120] while Donnally's photography garnered numerous honors both here and abroad.[121]

Of equal consequence to the faculty on home ground was a pair of teaching prizes: the Inland Steel/Ryerson Foundation award,[122] first given to Roger Faber, and the William L. Dunn award,[123] named in honor of the earlier dean of the faculty, who died in 1974, and meant for a junior faculty member. To the three long-established chairs (the William Bross in Religion, held earlier by Bartlett, in the 1980s by D. Cole, and later by R. Miller; the D. K. Pearsons, earlier by Steamer, in the 1980s by Galloway, and later by Moskoff, C. Miller, and Talhami; and the Jacob Beidler, earlier by Jensen and later by Faber) had been added new ones:

the Ernest A. Johnson (held first by Herlihy and later by Moskoff and Dye); the James D. Vail (first by Hale and later by Baade); the Betty Jane Schultz Hollender '42 (first by Schulze and later by Moskoff); the Ernest H. Volwiler (first by Coutts and later by Packel); the A. B. Dick, a rotating chair (by Jeong, A. Miller, and Ebner); the Hotchkiss Presidential, a million-dollar chair (first by Cowler and later by LeMahieu); the Foster G. McGaw (by Towle); the Irvin L. '26 and Fern Young Presidential (by Galloway), and the Distinguished Service (first by Donnally, then by Zilversmit, and later by Mallette).[124]

Important and valuable as these scholarly achievements were, they once again reflected a nationwide emphasis, in this instance one whose effects were less than welcome. In the tighter job market of the 1970s and 1980s, American college teaching became a pressured occupation, as the number of tenured faculty throughout the country was subjected to stricter limits in order to allow institutions future flexibility. As standards for achieving tenure grew more and more demanding, a greater focus was placed on scholarship.[125] Tensions developed at Lake Forest in the late 1980s over the issue of teaching versus research, and although they never took on the heat of the publish-or-perish atmosphere affecting the larger universities, evaluations for all faculty and third-year reviews of new faculty became normal.[126] Whatever the merits or necessities of these procedures, they created a measure of alienation among some of the younger instructors by forcing criteria upon them, as they saw it, that even when fulfilled might not, given staffing needs, earn them the security of a permanent position.[127]

**For all of that, the dawning of the 1990s found matters** at the College well in place—indeed, it could be argued, so fixed in patterns of established priorities that few if any new plans were put forward. President Hotchkiss, supported by his North Hall staff (including such senior figures as Theodore R. Carlus,[128] vice president for business affairs,

Opposite. The College's gallery was incubated in Donnelley Library in the 1970s, with Susan Morris '75 as its first director, and moved into permanent quarters in the renovated Durand Art Institute after 1980. Since then the Sonnenschein and Albright galleries on the second floor have been the settings for many outstanding exhibits, including those represented by the catalogs pictured here, the work, respectively of directors Robin Glauber and Kim Coventry and Professor Jeong.

Continuity and Consolidation

1990

1993

Yale administrator David Spadafora is appointed dean of the faculty, the first new outside dean in four decades.

Eugene Hotchkiss concludes his twenty-three-year presidency with a successful fund drive which significantly increases the endowment.

and George Speros,[129] associate dean of faculty), pressed ahead with his intention of creating a financial cushion for his successor, a goal he met in large part. Under his watch, the endowment, which was half the annual budget in 1970, had grown to twice the budget by the end of his tenure.[130] The position of second in command remained in the respected hands of one very much a faculty's dean, Bailey Donnally, until late in the decade.[131]

As for the majority of the faculty, they had settled into a life dominated by teaching duties (still the prime measure in the evaluative process), scholarly expectations, and the demands of community service. Actions taken in the 1970s had already placed the principal responsibility for governance on a faculty committee system which had gradually grown into the instrumentality through which most campus business was transacted. To curricular matters and housekeeping details were added increasingly important decisions affecting hiring policies and faculty allocations. Most trying of all these responsibilities was one, shared with the president and the dean, that called for judgments on promotion and tenure. The teaching staff participated even in budget discussions, which more and more involved questions pertaining to student recruitment and financial aid. Ironically, then, although the faculty as a body had felt insufficiently appreciated by Hotchkiss in the early years of his tenure, they now found themselves playing a greater part than ever in the task of running the institution in its day-to-day activities. Little time was left to them to ponder educational philosophy.

Nevertheless, and despite the concern that grew out of these conditions, the mood of the campus at the turn of the 1990s is most simply described as salubrious. The return of Bailey Donnally to the Department of Physics, leaving M. L. Thompson as acting dean,[132] led to a national search that produced an impressive successor, David C. Spadafora,[133] destined to become the College's next president. A graduate of Williams College with a doctorate in History from Yale, where he had served as associate dean of the graduate school

prior to his appointment at Lake Forest, Spadafora brought to his new position a combination of sound administrative experience and the dedication of a research scholar, who had just seen published his study *The Idea of Progress in Eighteenth-Century Britain*.

**Eugene Hotchkiss's retirement in 1993 was greeted** with expressions of goodwill as the campus bade farewell to a president the College family had learned to respect and appreciate.[134] While the trustees provided for a program of Hotchkiss Fellows, rewarding selected untenured instructors with one-semester sabbatical leaves,[135] it was the faculty and staff who petitioned the Board for renaming the refurbished North Gymnasium as Hotchkiss Hall, in honor of both Hotchkisses.[136]

# A New *Idea of Progress* for the Twenty-First Century

chapter

The national search for a president to guide the College into the next century produced no candidate so attractive as the school's new dean. Evidence of his academic leadership was already apparent. A significant and long-overdue curricular change consisting of a return to general education requirements, with a better balance in the academic program, occurred during his deanship,[1] while his desire to teach at least one class per year won him the collegial confidence of the faculty and, with the scholarly recognition of his recently published work,[2] their respect. (And it is from *The Idea of Progress in Eighteenth-Century Britain* that this chapter's title is derived.) Although he had declined at first to make himself available for the top position, he was eventually drafted, and in 1993 David Spadafora was installed as the twelfth permanent president of Lake Forest College.

1993–94

The 1993–94 MACW championship trophy, the first such win for the women's basketball team.

His elevation left the post of dean of the faculty open. With Professor Robert Troyer recalled from retirement to serve in acting capacity,[3] another national search led to the appointment (with the added title of provost) of Steven P. Galovich, a mathematician with a doctorate from Brown University and administrative experience as an associate dean of the faculty at Carleton College,[4] one of the nation's benchmark liberal arts institutions. The College now had at its helm two figures with fresh external perspectives, joined, moreover, by an essentially new administrative staff that included three alumni: Elizabeth W. Fischer '72,[5] dean of the College, Leslie T. Chapman '79,[6] vice president for business affairs, and Frederick M. Van Sickle '83,[7] vice president for alumni and development. These changes have effectively ushered in a recognizably new phase whose current early years are better noted only briefly in this concluding chapter of the College's history, leaving fuller, extended examination more appropriately for the future.

**However much the changes of the early 1990s affected** the composition and conduct of the administrative staff, major problems continued to confront the College, as acute as they were familiar, and most of them shared with the majority of liberal arts schools. Competition to attract students and retain them was fiercer than ever, and it was accompanied by rising costs, most manifest in the need for increased financial aid budgets[8] and for the kinds of computer and telecommunications technology essential for a modern campus.[9] While still the dean, Spadafora had strongly encouraged putting together the systems that would enable faculty and students to utilize such external networking devices as voice mail, electronic mail, and the Internet as well as internal academic computing.[10] If deficits had once more been mounting and balancing the budget was taking on highest priority,[11] the College's endowment had grown enough during the Hotchkiss years to provide some margin for action on issues, not merely *ad hoc* reaction. In 1995 Spadafora appointed a Strategic Planning Task Force, which a year later produced a report called "Toward a New Community." Appropriate to the title was the range of backgrounds and interests among the group's twenty-three members, who were composed of students, alumni, administrators, faculty both junior and senior, nonteaching staff, and trustees. Such involvement of all the College's constituencies as well as the breadth of the self-study undertaken has been characteristic of Spadafora's managerial approach.

David Spadafora, dean of the faculty from 1990 to 1993, was inaugurated Lake Forest's twelfth president in 1993.

The report began by identifying the College community in terms of three "environments": social and academic, financial, and physical. It went on to outline in detail the ends of each and in greater detail the means, short-, intermediate-, and long-term, by which they could best be achieved.

Virtually everything of consequence to the direction the school has followed since the publication of this exhaustive overview has derived from it. The falling enrollments of the early 1990s were reversed by aggressive recruiting, with greater emphasis on the Middle West, by Director of Admissions William Motzer, and on the international level, by Dean Speros. In fact the student body increased by twenty-five percent in a four-year stretch, with forty-three countries represented.[12] The implementation of a merit scholarship program, spearheaded by several faculty and trustees, has brought prospective Presidential Scholars to campus for an intensive weekend of academic competition, resulting in the matriculation of students who have done much to raise the scholastic tone of the school.[13] That boon is nowhere more evident than in the exceptional success of what has become an annual symposium showcasing the research and creative efforts of an increasingly diversified student body.[14] A Communications major has been added to the curriculum,[15] for several purposes: to help fulfill the College's belief that every graduate should write, speak, and use technology adeptly; to broaden the Chicago Outreach Program (funded in the early 1990s

SIR BARTIMEUS, BART., F. R. S.
'VARSITY MASCOT

PHOTOGRAPHED BY BRUBAKER          ENGRAVED BY

"FORESTERS"
Nickname
Selected

"Chop 'em Down!"

**Above.** This photo of Sir Bartimeus Bart., F. R. S., early varsity mascot, is taken from a poster accompanying the November 1894 issue of the *Stentor*.

**Center.** In the 1930s Lake Forest varsity teams were known as the Jaybirds, perhaps a play on the first letter of the name of the high-profile coach, Ralph Jones. By 1948, shortly before Jones's retirement, the students voted to change to the Foresters, connoting this time the fabled Paul Bunyan, and seen here depicted in life and "art."

**Below.** In 1995, following a student election much like that of 1948, the bear was selected as the new mascot – again perhaps a reflection of campus ties, this time to the Chicago Bears, "in residence" in Halas Hall from 1979 to 1997.

through the Christian A. Johnson Endeavor Foundation and then by the Kemper Foundation)[16] by active collaboration with appropriate institutions in the city; and, not least, to address student demand. An Academic Innovations Group set up to explore further options in the improvement of student learning has been assembled,[17] along with the Learning and Teaching Center, meant to benefit faculty and students alike.[18] In a move of major consequence to the College's daily operations, the Office of Library and Information Technology was established in 1996 under its director, James Cubit.[19] A decision with equally substantial implications for the future has been the College's choice of the Pennsylvania architectural firm of Spillman & Farmer to design and proceed with a campus master plan, the most encompassing effort of its kind in several decades.[20] Consisting of a review of the College's entire physical facility, with special attention paid to Donnelley Library, the Sports Center, Commons, and the residence halls, the initiative reached the construction stage in 1999, with a full-scale renovation of and addition to Deerpath Hall. Independent of the master plan but comparable in its effect on the physical character of the College has been the acquisition of a spacious new residence for the president, south on Sheridan Road. It is the Brown House, a gift of William and Malcolm Brown, sons of the late Gardner Brown, a trustee of the school, with William Brown a current trustee.[21]

These numerous recent developments are principal among the efforts to give substance to a passage of the report of the Strategic Planning Task Force that reads like a manifesto:

*Our reaffirmation of the traditional liberal arts stems from the firm belief that Lake Forest College provides its students with the most valuable education available, valuable both for personal development and for economic opportunity. Indeed, although it is increasingly difficult to be a small liberal arts college today, we believe that by contributing broadly educated, liberal intellects to the public weal, small liberal arts colleges in general and Lake Forest College in particular provide distinctive and meaningful benefits to society at large.*[22]

It bears adding that these remarks have come at a timely moment, framed as they were in 1996, almost exactly a century after Lake Forest's shift in identity from a university to a liberal arts college. Yet an inference of equal significance may be drawn from the statement, since the value of educated graduates to the common weal applies by extension to their role in the destiny of the College and its new community. President Spadafora has made a point of giving energetic attention to the generations of living alumni, seeking to reinforce and deepen their connection with the College. The importance of a stronger alumni association is reflected in the anticipated election in 2000 of David B. Mathis '60 as the first alumnus chair of the Board of Trustees in over a half century,[23] and on a Board now made up of fifty percent alumni. These developments certify that the College's foundation is sufficiently solid and its mission sure enough to warrant an administrative policy in which the future is assumed to build upon a creative past. Fittingly, the Strategic Planning Task Force in its 1996 report affirmed that it "believes that the College's most important strategic goal is to bring its members into a new community, a community we can all be proud to attend, happy to support, and eager to visit."[24]

**Above.** Urban historian Michael Ebner leading a group of students on a 1997 visit to Chicago's Newberry Library, a rich repository of historical source material. Professor Ebner's ties to the Chicago Historical Society and other organizations such as the Newberry have been a key link with the central city for Lake Forest.

**Below.** The internship program, launched in the 1970s and embodying ideas laid out as early as 1920 by Washington consultant Samuel Paul Capen, is a key focus of the 1990s College emphasis on Chicago. Here Scott W. (Sandy) Turner '76, vice president of the Chicago Corporation investment firm, counsels intern David E. Burt '92.

# Afterword

The present volume, tracing the record of the college from its earliest years to the present, suggests a convenient division of its history into three forty-year periods since its permanent founding in 1876. The initial phase, from 1880 (the year of the first graduating class) to 1920, was marked by steady, vigorous growth during which the school established itself as a strong small liberal arts college, with a record of institutional achievement, in close contact with a wealthy, supportive community. Local founders not only created a campus planned and designed by professionals of merit; they also provided an endowment to sustain their program. The next forty years saw a deflection from that course to a vocational orientation with diminished academic strength. No major benefactors stepped forward to fund major physical improvements, though late in the period events added the former Academy property to the campus. Even with the seeds of change so significantly sown in the 1950s, the reputation of the College remained that of a local school, closely interactive within its walls but effectively removed from the outer, larger academic world.

It is during the last four decades that the College's earlier vision has been restored, and its objective of becoming a school of distinction with a more nearly national character is demonstrably headed toward fulfillment. Despite varying financial fortunes, a steady increase in the quality of its faculty has been accompanied by a creatively flexible curricular program available to an able and diversified student body in campus facilities brought handsomely up-to-date. Again, as in the founding era, generous contributions of friends, parents, and now alumni are adding substance to the endowment in order to meet present and future needs.

An illuminating exemplar of developments in this most recent period is the record of one of the College's academic departments, for it bears out the progressive accomplish-

ments that have unfolded steadily across the span of three presidencies. A scrupulously detailed portrait of the Department of Chemistry was begun in 1959 by John W. Coutts, the chair for over two decades, whose effort to keep notes on graduates' careers was prompted by the anticipation of the new science center, then in the planning stage. Once completed, the building functioned in the 1960s as a proper laboratory for the new faculty appointments basic to any developing program to be undertaken there.[25] By 1973 a Research Corporation grant enabled two instructors to engage student assistants for summer projects in what was evolving as an important departmental objective, the involvement of students in faculty research, a prototype for the later Richter program. (In fact, it was to extend this activity that the Dixon Wing was built in 1990.) The energized department added further to its students' encounters with the professional world by creating an active chapter of the nationally recognized Student Affiliates of the American Chemical Society, which sponsored speakers, field trips, and social events. In turn, in 1977 and 1978, the Society's leadership singled out the Lake Forest chapter as one of 58 (out of 710 nationwide) for special commendation.[26]

**Opposite.** Students gathered in Durand Commons before Homecoming in the fall of 1995 to learn the results of the student poll on the new mascot.

**Above.** At the beginning of each winter term in January a community supper is held in Glen Rowan to commemorate Dr. Martin Luther King Jr.'s birthday and contributions. It is an appropriate setting, for in this, her family home (the only site in Lake County visited by Dr. King), trustee Lilace Barnes entertained him at the time of his 1966–67 open-housing efforts in Chicago. Here lighting a candle of remembrance is Stacy Jones '96. Also participating in this observance were (from the left) La Joyce Collins '95, Josh Farlow '97, Kurt Rogers '95, Corey Honore '98, and Hunter Piermont '98.

1994

**SPECTRUM**
*Lake Forest College Alumni Magazine*

*Spring 1994*

*Spectrum* unveils its new magazine format in 1994 under Editor Michelle L. Holleman.

1994

The *Chicago Tribune*, in reviewing the college faculties of the region, singles out Lake Forest as a smaller version of the University of Chicago.

# It's Not All Academic for Faculty Inventors

Irvin Young '26 invented many gadgets related to labeling technology, and it would be the fruits of his patents which in large part enabled the College in 1980 to undertake its renovation of the venerable College Hall. Perhaps Young gained some of his drive from professor of physics R. E. Harris, who, joining the faculty in 1925, was an early experimenter in television. Harris, though, has been just one of a series of Lake Forest physics professors whose inventions have been of national and international significance. Among these, from a range of periods in the College's history, are:

Elisha Gray, lecturer in Physics, 1882–92, a Presbyterian resident of Highland Park and founder in 1872 of Western Electric (today Lucent Technologies). He is famous for just missing the patent on the telephone, registered hours earlier by Alexander Graham Bell on February 14, 1876. Indeed Bell employed a metal-diaphragm receiver built and publicly used by Gray months earlier, and Bell's device depended on microphone elements credited to Gray. A court struggle ensued, which Gray failed to win.

R. E. Harris, mentioned earlier, professor of Physics, 1925–46 (after war service), who contributed to the evolution of television technology: scanning without the need of glaring lights after the introduction of a photocell in the camera, and developing a metallic rotating prism which allowed an 8"x10" picture rather than a postage-stamp-sized one. His leadership was acknowledged in 1927 when at the New York Radio World's Fair he presented a series of lectures on television that were presented by television. This was repeated in Chicago a few weeks later and again in 1929. Good scientist that he was, Dr. Harris missed the mark as a seer when he noted in a *Stentor* interview of January 17, 1936, "[television] will probably never take the place of radio in the home, but will be used more in business to view sample goods in distant cities.... " But, then again, was this a most early prediction of e-commerce, which in the era of the personal computer has linked television to Gray's telecommunications invention?

Tung Hon Jeong, professor of Physics, 1963–97, with the most international of reputations. From his arrival on campus Jeong has been one of the pioneers of holography – the creation of three-dimensional reproduction with laser beams. In 1965, with the help of two students he achieved the world's first image that could be viewed from all sides. For activity extending far beyond the laboratory, he has been acclaimed (by *Omni* magazine) "the guru of holography for the masses." If his efforts have carried him literally all over the globe, his series of summer symposia on Display Holography have brought to campus artists and scientists from equally distant lands.

Professor Jeong working on a hologram.

By the time Professor Coutts retired in 1986, his meticulously charted files took note of 37 alumni with the Ph.D. in Chemistry, 30 alumni with the M.D., and 26 alumni with other graduate degrees. In short, 93 advanced degrees had been won by graduates from one small liberal arts department,[27] whose loyalty led to a reunion in 1995 that honored the departmental faculty, headed by Coutts, Laura Kateley (Klingbeil), William Martin and M. L. Thompson. And while the carefully kept record of Chemistry is especially worthy of citation, other departments of the College can point with pride to achievements of a kindred kind.

This history of the College has also traced a record, however truncated and circumstantially focused, of the village of Lake Forest, as the relationship of town and gown has played its own part in the fortunes of the school. The patterns of continuity and change, closeness and separation, also reflect a three-part historical division. That parallel is discernible in yet another example (one that touches on a rather different but pertinent constituency): the history of Coterie, a Lake Forest organization founded in 1890 as part of the late-19th-century nationwide establishment of women's clubs and literary circles. While in its earliest days it included village matrons with locally celebrated names like Barnes, Durand, Farwell, and Holt (familiar also as university founders, parents, and alumni), it was made up predominantly of a campus group of faculty wives whose husbands were often invited to lecture on topics of intellectual interest. As decades passed, Coterie became almost exclusively (in all senses of the word) a town club, though membership was usually extended to the College president's wife and to the wives of the Presbyterian and Episcopal ministers. With the turn of the twenty-first century, conditions have once again changed, in ways reflecting another kind of social framework. There are still Farwells on the roster, as well as fourth gen

eration descendants of the Reverend McClure, and two Beidlers, one the great granddaughter of President Coulter, but the members are increasingly newcomers, often professional women, and Lake Forest College is represented again, not by faculty wives but by professors themselves.[28]

As for the Lake Forest community they share, it too has continued to undergo substantial material and immaterial changes. Thus the present stands in sharp contrast with the early years, when a university and its satellite secondary schools were the geographical and spiritual focus of a new, controlled and closely unified village. More of the town than ever now lies south and west of the original center, with three four-lane highways running through its outer edges, and its inhabitants are more varied than ever in their backgrounds and ambitions. To be sure, Market Square, nationally recognized as a work of architectural distinction, the

**Left.** Pictured here is Menominee/Potawatomi dancer Art Shegonee with Megan Cisne '95 and Christopher Bland '95, participating in a celebration of Native American Week.

**Right.** The breadth of campus religious expression quietly speaks for itself in this glimpse of a regularly scheduled meditation session in the Lilace Barnes Interfaith Center, Ravine Lodge, led by Jason A. Neal '98, left, and Christopher Bland '95, center.

1995

1996

**In 1995 the College adopts this one-oak-leaf design as its new seal.**

**The burgeoning computer and network operations are combined with the library to form one unit, Library and Information Technology (LIT).**

more so following a much-needed facelift in the late 1990s,[29] remains the aesthetic heart of what is still a palpably beautiful American suburb. Nonetheless, the locality's most expensive new houses are often taken largely from patternbooks and sited on uncomfortably small parcels of land, thus reflecting little of the estate grandeur of the mansions of the past. Condominiums and apartment buildings make up an ever more recognizable part of the contemporary real estate landscape. With the newly constructed Lake Forest Place,[30] a retirement community that has attracted many members of the town's long-established families, old Lake Forest is changing again, confronted now with the challenge of a new generation of citizens who define the village as "a special place" in their own, notably different terms.[31]

Viewed from a broader perspective than the bonding of town and gown in Coterie is the interaction between a "new" Lake Forest and a "new" College, the latter now reaching outward to play a more active role in the life of the total locality. In fact, since the early 1990s, a College prize established in honor of trustee Charlotte Simmons, has been awarded to individual campus figures specifically recognized for their activities in community service. Among the winners have been Eugene Hotchkiss, founding chair of the Committee Representing Our Young Adults (CROYA); Rosemary Cowler, for many years the president of the Lake Forest Library Board; Arthur Miller, president of the Lake Forest/Lake Bluff Historical Society and the Ragdale Foundation; Ronald Miller, a champion of volunteer services among College students in the community and one of the creators of Common Ground, a center for ecumenical religious studies; and Jonathan Galloway, the first College professor to serve on the Lake Forest city council since John J. Halsey.

At the same time, the energy lately directed by the school to its alumni is a sign of the College's commitment to develop and increase its institutional independence, a purpose that has brought it into the closest contact of recent history with its other original geographic neighbor, Chicago itself. Quite evidently, much of the historical interrelationship of College, town, and city is again being reassembled, nonetheless with some new twists.

In the concluding section of the Strategic Planning Task Force's report, "Toward a New Community," high among

1998

Jeff Bezos, CEO of Amazon.com and later *Time*'s "Person of the Year" for 1999, speaks on campus in the fall.

1998

The first annual all-day Student Symposium in April provides students a forum modeled after professional association conferences, where students present the results of their work – senior theses, independent studies, and group projects, offered through, papers, slide lectures, poster sessions, exhibits, and discussions.

**Above.** 1991 championship soccer teammates Daniel Bracken '92, Gregory Selby '93, Anthony Leraris '93, and Gregory Boltz '93.

**Center and below.** Staples of "school spirit" since the 1920s, cheerleaders and floats here, in the mid-90s, liven up the annual fall Homecoming parade and festivities. The International Students' organization float colorfully displays the flags of some of the nations represented in Lake Forest's student body.

**Above.** Asian Cultural Night dancers Jeena Alex '99, Julia Haskell '01, and Fakhia Rashid '01 in 1999.

**Lower right.** Joe Zemaitis '02, who participated in (and completed) the October 1998 Ironman Triathalon in Hawaii is interviewed by Chicago television reporter Harry Porterfield as part of his series "Someone You Should Know."

**Lower left.** Professor Donald Meyer's Music class in Reid rehearsal hall.

the goals expressed is the desire to "exploit the College's proximity to Chicago."[32] Little wonder there, since in the very period of the school's recent revivification, the city has grown culturally at a pace that has generated an overall quality greater than that of any period since the glory years of the 1890s and the Literary Renaissance. In the past forty years, several noteworthy art museums, led by the Museum of Contemporary Art, have been added to Chicago's offerings in the visual arts, and they in turn have been joined by university galleries and a small army of commercial showcases no longer confined to a tight district along Michigan Avenue, but threaded throughout the North, South, and West Sides. Music too has profited immeasurably during the last several decades, most notably in the spectacular success of the Lyric Opera and the unsurpassed international reputation of the Chicago Symphony Orchestra. Meanwhile, the current younger generation of drama buffs, many of them unaware of the time when the city was widely regarded as a theatrical graveyard,[33] has joined critical voices across the country in virtually unanimous praise of the ongoing excellence of the city's stage productions.

**Established institutions outside the realm of the arts** partake similarly in this prosperous condition, chief among them Argonne Laboratory, the Chicago Mercantile Exchange, the Field Museum of Natural History, the Shedd Aquarium, the Museum of Science and Industry, and the Chicago Historical Society.

And hardly least, the city's architecture, an international cynosure for more than a century, can boast of recent important designs by Chicagoans Helmut Jahn (O'Hare's United Airlines Terminal), Ralph Johnson (O'Hare's International Terminal), and Thomas Beeby (the Harold Washington Library), and by non-Chicagoans like Tokyo's Kenzo Tange and William Pedersen of the New York firm of Kohn, Pedersen & Fox.

But for the College, Chicago functions as more than an extended classroom for its students. Of major relevance to the fortunes and the repute of the school have been the contributions its faculty have made to the city's cultural and social progress. Probably the earliest to take advantage of Chicago and to participate actively in its affairs, Professor Franz Schulze was the senior art critic of the *Chicago Daily News* from the early 1960s to the late 1970s and thereafter of the *Chicago Sun-Times*. In 1983 Professor Michael Ebner was a central player in the development of the Urban History Seminars at the Chicago Historical Society, in time

**Above.** In the first annual Academic Symposium, held in 1998, George Anagnost '98 observes an exhibit.

**Below.** A dynasty of outstanding athletes is the Maiman family, honored at the 1997 dedication of the Athletic Hall of Fame. Elmer Maiman '39 (seated with his late wife, Ann) won seven varsity letters under Coach Ralph Jones. Among his children and grandchildren pictured here are sons Dennis '72, Richard '67, and Michael '70, himself inducted in 1983.

1999

**Marina Petcherskaia '00 (right) participating in the "Measure Our Success" program sponsored by Student Affiliates of the American Chemical Society (SAACS).**

becoming a trustee of that institution. Somewhat later, in the 1990s, when Solange Brown, a long-time member of the College's Women's Board and the wife of a College trustee, sought to reestablish the venerable library of the Alliance Française de Chicago (which in some degree owed its existence to Chatfield-Taylor), she called upon College Archivist Arthur H. Miller to jump-start the program. And subsequently Miller helped to plan a new library space and saw to the recruitment of a Lake Forest alumnus to the library staff. Brown has also involved Professor Jean-Luc Garneau in presentations at the Alliance that have high-lighted the library program.

The faculty's connections with the international scene have been profitably evident in the media. For well over a decade, Palestinian-born Professor Ghada Talhami has regularly provided Chicago public television commentary on Middle Eastern affairs, while Professor Ahmad Sadri, with his knowledge of the social and political character of his native Iran, recently has been a boon to local public radio audiences.[34]

Active too have been other of their social science colleagues. Beginning in the mid-1980s Professor Robert Baade became recognized as one of the nation's leading authorities on the high-profile topic of sports stadia, for Chicago chairing the Cost-Benefits Committee of the Metropolitan Planning Council when it studied the issue of a domed stadium. Professor Richard Dye, who collaborated with him on a major study on the impact of stadia on cities, in his own primary field of public finance served alongside elected state officials on the Research Committee of the Civic Federation of Chicago, the nation's oldest municipal reform body. Dye's expertise in property tax limitation in the collar-counties is paralleled by Professor Paul Fischer's significant work on suburban public housing, which, issued as a report in 1993, elicited the comment of the *Chicago Tribune* on its editorial page.

The *Tribune*'s attention was a signal of the increasing recognition of the College's new regional role. Indeed, early in 1994 a major feature story in that newspaper, following upon an earlier survey of local university faculties, singled out Lake Forest among all colleges in the area for the caliber of its teaching staff. In a sidebar titled "Smarter near the lake," seven of the College's faculty were profiled: Baade, Ebner, Fischer and Talhami, as well as Nancy Brekke, William Moskoff, and William Zamer, all of them cited varyingly for their visibility and scholarly endeavors. (Brekke, a psychologist, was recognized for her research on public perception of child abuse; Moskoff, an economist, for publications on the Soviet Union—and its splintered parts; and Zamer, a biologist, for his grant by the National Science Foundation, as a "top young investigator for bio-sciences," to study how genetic differences in individuals affect psychological performance.) The *Tribune* went on to characterize Lake Forest as "a sort of University of Chicago in microcosm."[35]

1999

**Pulitzer Prize–winning (1997) poet Lisel Mueller (Honorary Doctor of Fine Arts, 1985) donates her extensive holdings of poetry and literary books to Donnelley Library's Special Collections.**

**Above.** Pictured here in 1998, is a group of dedicated "res staff" members, Classes of '99 to '01.

Front row sitting, from left: Beth Kohr, (behind Beth) Hattim Razik, (next to Beth) Julia O'Connor, (behind Julia) Tori Jones, (next to Julia) Sara Zelonis, Julia Haskell, Kevin Fogelson, Tony Donovan, (behind Tony) Rob Holland, Melanie Macchio, Shenel Altinay, and Mitch King.

Second row standing: Josh Price, T. J. Hardaway, Marcus Collins, Shiraz Mushtaq, Van Stone, Scott Richardson, Matt Sena, Tomislav Milanovic, Reni Towns, Tarah Raymond, Eileen Young, and Lindsay Hall.

Third row sitting on wall: Ranetta Hardin, Laurie David, Masimba Rusununguko, Arnetta Johnson, Haley McIntosh, unidentified, and Laura Hilstrom.

Fourth row standing behind pillars: Tom Balazs (an associate dean of the college), Marita Labedz-Poll (an associate dean of the college), Pamela McCann, Laura Panko (resident academic fellow), Elizabeth Fischer '72 (dean of the college), Jenny von Helms, Matt Edwards, Abe Nelson, Chris Michelstetter, Melanie Rose, and Jack Macy (director of campus activities).

**Below.** In their new master's hoods the four M/LS graduates pose with Professor Rosemary Cowler, director of the program, at the 1999 Commencement. Left to right are Anita Cukier, Raelene Bowman, Jeffrey Gusfield, and Virginia Fiester Frederick.

In these evolving relationships, a most recent development acts almost like a coda: even as Lake Forest College is redirecting its attention thirty miles south, academic Chicago is moving thirty miles north, with several of its educational institutions establishing programs within the town's boundaries.[36] In fact, in a wondrously ironic centenary development, the University of Chicago, with its long, unmistakably urban tradition, has begun to offer some noncredit classes on the campus of Lake Forest College, the very school with which it proposed unification—just over a hundred years ago.[37]

Thus, as the College, its town, and its city together enter a new millennium, that very movement symbolizes change. Yet, paradoxically, it is change itself that is the most distinguishing element of permanence in the academic and communal relationships that have marked the past and will continue to mark the future of their individual and collective histories.

1999

1999–2000

BUILDING A NEW COMMUNITY

At Homecoming 1999 the College launches its largest fundraising campaign.

As the College moves into the new millennium, sample listings from the latest annually distributed "Facts & Figures":

1,210 students enrolled; 110 minority and 153 international – from 44 states and 43 countries.

Of 91 faculty, more than 30% have written books and more than 94% hold the Ph.D. or equivalent.

12,000 alumni of record.

Bagpiper Will Norman has been a much-beloved part of Commencement.

## KEY TO ABBREVIATED REFERENCES FOR FREQUENTLY CITED SOURCES

### PUBLISHED SOURCES

#### BY AUTHORS

**Arpee**
Edward Arpee, *Lake Forest, Illinois: History and Reminiscences, 1862–1962* [with] Susan Dart, Supplement (Lake Forest: Lake Forest/Lake Bluff Historical Society, 1991).

**De Koven**
Mrs. Reginald De Koven, *A Musician and His Wife* (New York: Charles Scribner's Sons, 1926).

**Ebner**
Michael H. Ebner, *Creating Chicago's North Shore: A Suburban History* (Chicago: University of Chicago Press, 1988).

**Halsey**
John J. Halsey, *History of Lake County, Illinois* (n.p.: Roy S. Bates, 1912).

**Rudolph**
Frederick Rudolph, *The American College and University: A History* (New York: Alfred A. Knopf, 1965).

**Schmidt**
George P. Schmidt, *The Liberal Arts College: A Chapter in American Cultural History* (New Brunswick, NJ: Rutgers University Press, 1957).

#### BY ACRONYMS

**ANB**
*American National Biography*

**BC**
*Book of Chicagoans*

**BDAA**
*Biographical Dictionary of American Architects*, comp. Henry F. Withey and Elsie Rathburn Withey (Los Angeles: Hennessey & Ingalls, 1970).

**BDABL**
*Biographical Dictionary of American Business Leaders*

**BSLMC**
*Biographical Sketches of the Leading Men of Chicago* (Chicago: Knight, Leonard & Company, 1868, and Wilson, Peirce & Company, 1876; 1868 unless noted as 1876).

**CB**
*Current Biography* (H.W. Wilson Co.), annual volumes.

**CT**
*Chicago Tribune*

**DAB**
*Dictionary of American Biography* (Roman numerals denote volumes of the original thirty-three volumes published in 1933; Arabic numerals represent supplementary volumes issued after 1933).

**DAH**
Henry Steele Commager, *Documents of American History*, fourth ed. (New York: Appleton-Century-Crofts, 1948), 3 v.

**F**
*Forester* (yearbook, since 1892, with gaps in the 1890s, 1910s, and 1990s).

**GRLFC**
*General Register of Lake Forest College, 1865–1931* (unless noted as 1914 volume).

**LFAQ**
*Lake Forest Alumni Quarterly*

**LFCAB**
*Lake Forest College Alumni Bulletin* or various titles between 1920 and 1950s.

**LFCBB**
*Lake Forest Cemetery Burial Book* (Lake Forest: Lake Forest/Lake Bluff Historical Society, 1995).

**LFCC/UC**
*Lake Forest College/University Catalog[ue], Annual Register, Bulletin*, etc., under various titles.

**LFCN**
*Lake Forest College News*

**LFJ**
*Lake Forest Journal* or *The Journal: Lake Forest* (periodical issued mostly monthly, 1992–99).

**LFUR**
*Lake Forest University Review*

**NCAB**
*National Cyclopedia of American Biography*

**NFLFC**
*News from Lake Forest College*

**NUC**
*National Union Catalog of Pre-1956 Imprints*

**NYT**
*New York Times*

**RB**
*Red and Black*

**RP**
*Report of the President*

**S**
*The Stentor* or *The University Stentor*, etc.

**Sp**
*Spectrum*

**TNC**
*Toward a New Community: Task Force Report* (Lake Forest College, 1996).

**WWA**
*Who's Who in America*

**WWAW**
*Who's Who of American Women*

**WWC**
*Who's Who in Chicago and Vicinity*

**WWCI**
*Who's Who in Commerce and Industry*

**WWM**
*Who's Who in the Midwest*

**WWP**
*The Papers of Woodrow Wilson*, ed. Arthur S. Link *et al.* (Princeton, NJ: Princeton University Press).

**WWWA**
*Who Was Who in America*

### MANUSCRIPT AND UNPUBLISHED SOURCES FROM THE LAKE FOREST COLLEGE ARCHIVES BY ACRONYMS

**AMC**
Alexander M. Candee Scrapbook Collection

**CHMP**
Cyrus H. McCormick Jr. Papers

**FM**
Faculty Minutes

**HFCD**
History file, Chemistry Department

**LFCA**
Lake Forest College Archives

**TM**
Trustee Minutes

# Notes

1   In a 1937 celebration of Lake Forest's history, students posed for a photograph on the steps of Durand Institute in period costumes – including stovepipe and bowler hats. ("College Looks Back 80 Years in Lake Forest," *CT* [14 Mar 1937], III, 1.)

2   Ebner, 21, 270–71*n*; Halsey, 371.

3   Ebner, 16.

4   Halsey, 483.

5   E[lijah] M. Haines, "History of Lake County" in *The Past and Present of Lake County, Illinois* ... (Chicago: Wm. Le Baron & Co., 1877), 304; James G. K. McClure, *Lake Forest Presbyterian Church Historical Discourse, Delivered on the 25th Anniversary, 27th July 1884* (Lake Forest: First Presbyterian Church, 1884), 15–16; Arpee, 30–31.

6   McClure (1884), 9; James G. K. McClure, *History of The Presbyterian Church, Lake Forest, Illinois, by the Pastor* ... (n.p.: April 1905), 10.

7   Envy of the more successful Chicago pioneers by the less prosperous was an issue discussed by Frederick Francis Cook in his 1910 memoir, *Bygone Days in Chicago: Recollections of the Garden City in the Sixties* (Chicago: A. C. McClurg, 1910), 541–42. See also the anecdote in Edwin O. Gale's *Reminiscences of Early Chicago and Vicinity* (Chicago: Fleming H. Revell, 1902), 137–38.

8   While many of the Chicago Presbyterian settlers had come from New York State, their origins were largely in New England. (Whitney R. Cross, *The Burned-Over District: The Social and Intellectual History of Enthusiastic Religion in Western New York, 1800–1850* [Ithaca, NY: Cornell University Press], 6.) That the site's wooded irregularity might have recalled not only the terrain of old New England but also the hilly character of eastern Tennessee, the childhood home of the Rev. Patterson, the central personage among the group by the lake, has some interesting associations. Raymond Patterson in his biographical outline on his father, noting the sheltering nature of those Tennessee mountains, observed that for the hill-country Scotch-Irish, it was a matter of living "surrounded by slavery, yet protected by ancestral traditions" (Raymond A. Patterson, *Dr. R. W. Patterson: Suggestions for Chapters* [typescript, 10 pp.], 1 [LFCA]). Patterson could well have envisioned in this setting such a protective environment for his flock.

9   Arpee, 26–27.

10   All five would serve on the first Board of Trustees of the University. (McClure [1884], 12.)

11   A focal figure in this narrative, the Rev. Robert W. Patterson (1814–94), as pastor of the Second Presbyterian Church of Chicago, was a founding father of Lake Forest, and, later, the first president of its university. For published accounts of his long and distinguished career, see *Biographical Sketches of the Leading Men of Chicago, Written by the Best Talents of the Northwest* (Chicago: Wilson & St. Clair, 1868), 559–61; *The Second Presbyterian Church of Chicago. June 1st, 1842, to June 1st, 1892* (Chicago: Knight, Leonard, 1892), 48–53 *et passim*; and J[ohn] J. Halsey," Robert W. Patterson. Lake Forest's First President," *S* (6 Mar 1894), 1.

12   The Rev. Harvey Curtis was pastor of the First Presbyterian Church of Chicago from 1850 to 1858 and president of Knox College from 1858 to his death in 1862. (Ruth C. Volpe [Sproat] '52, *Lake Forest College & Founders* [History Department graduate seminar paper, Northwestern University, 1962], 46.)

13   The Rev. Ira Weed's career with the Presbyterian Home Missionary Society is detailed in a memorial pamphlet tucked away in a 1926 scrapbook of Lake Forest College's fiftieth anniversary celebration that year: G. P. Tyndal, *In Memoriam. A Discourse on the Life and Character of the Late Ira J. Weed, December 10, 1871* (Ypsilanti, MI: Pattison's Steam Printing House, 1872, 30 pp). The pamphlet includes a tribute from the Rev. R. W. Patterson (15–16).

14   According to the Rev. McClure's early historical account [1884], "the Rev. J. J. Slocum, who had been successful in starting several educational institutions in other places, appeared in Chicago and stated to those who had been thoughtful concerning this educational project, that he had an acquaintance in Cincinnati who stood ready ... to endow a college near Chicago" (9); it was Slocum, again in McClure, who was given charge of soliciting subscriptions for the undertaking and "who in two weeks secured between $15,000 and $20,000 and in a very short time $59,000" (10). Research by Shirley M. Paddock has located biographical information on Slocum. The Rev. John Jay Slocum (1803–1860), a writer of well-known anti-Catholic books, after his work in organizing Lind University, went on to contribute to the organization of the Michigan Female Seminary at Kalamazoo, Michigan, and also to the founding of the *New York World* newspaper as a religious daily, which soon became a political daily after Slocum was forced to retire because of ill health. (Charles Elihu Slocum, *History of the Slocums, Slocumbs and Slocombs of America* ... [Defiance, Ohio: the author, 1882], 231 and 383–84.) See also McClure (1884), 16–17.

15   Devillo R. Holt, who as a businessman had made the first shipment of freight on the new Illinois-Michigan Canal, stands as a leader in the history of Lake Forest and its university, becoming a pioneer settler, helping to organize the First Presbyterian Church of Lake Forest, and serving on the first Board of Trustees of the newly chartered university. For his biography see Ellen Holt, *Holt, Hubbard and Allied Families: Genealogical and Biographical* (New York: American Historical Society, Inc., 1929), 23.

16   The Presbyterians involved in founding Lake Forest cherished their ties – genealogical and spiritual – to the conservative factions represented earlier by the Mathers, Timothy Dwight, and Lyman Beecher. In this context Patterson's Second Presbyterian Church reflected the more moderate position on abolition of its congregation and also the membership's general social conservatism, according to Cook (96). In his fiftieth-anniversary comments on Second Presbyterian, Patterson had this to say about the First Church: "during that time [1840–41] there was a further development in the Church of extreme abolitionism and of sympathy with what was then styled Oberlin Perfectionism, which led to a ... visible growth of aggressive and conservative parties." Patterson spoke further, about the origins of his congregation, at the same celebration, commenting, "I have said that the Church was at first conservative in regard to the slavery question and Christian doctrine, always decidedly anti-slavery, averse to revolutionary action on that subject, and moderately Calvinistic, while in sympathy with what was called New School theology." (See *Second Presbyterian* [1892], 68–69 and 270; see also the Mather connection, ch. 1, n. 34.)

To help with this and subsequent notes, very brief definitions are offered for three Presbyterian terms: New Light, New School, and Old School. New Light refers to a movement of emotional revivals and camp meetings. In 1836–38 New School Presbyterians separated from Old School Presbyterians most obviously over antislavery. In addition, denominational politics over accommodation of more radical Congregationalists on this issue played a role, derived from the Plan of Union of 1801, which had provided for reciprocity in church attendance in the West.

Interesting is a note in the minutes of Coterie (a Lake Forest ladies' paper-writing club [see p. 187]), describing in the late '20s a Lake Forest home's "air of aloofness and purity which belongs to the fine flower of Puritanism."

17   "He was then known as a student ... whom Dr. Beecher so honored as a thinker that when he questioned any of his statements of fact or doctrine, he always shoved his spectacles up his forehead and said: 'We will listen to you subjudice,' which was the highest compliment the dear old man could pay to his favorite disciple; one he seldom ever paid to anyone on the bench before him." (Quoted from Dr. Joseph F. Tuttle, "late President, Wabash College," in *From Those Who Knew Him*, a typescript [11 pp.] following Raymond A. Patterson's biographical outline on his father [in the same type, 1], Patterson file, Mosey Collection, LFCA.)

The Rev. Lyman Beecher (1775–1863) was a graduate of Yale in 1797 – from his sophomore year under the tutelage of new president Timothy Dwight, who brought Puritan orthodoxy and lifestyle back to Yale.

"The only serious call ever considered at length [by Patterson] was when urged to succeed Dr. [Lyman] Beecher as President of Lane Seminary in 1850, a negative reply being given." (*Memoranda*, a typescript [2 pp. single-spaced] following *From Those Who Knew Him*, cited above, in the same file.)

18  Schmidt, 56.

19  For the positions on slavery of Beecher, Lane, and Oberlin, see Lyman Beecher, *The Autobiography of Lyman Beecher*, ed. by Barbara Cross (Cambridge, MA: Harvard University Press, 1961), especially II, Chapter XXXIV: "Anti-Slavery Imbroglio," 240–49; and also Milton Rugoff, *The Beechers: An American Family in the Nineteenth Century* (New York: Harper & Row, 1981), 144–50. The Beecher quotation is cited by Rugoff, 109.

20  Over his career Beecher carved out a unique, Puritan-based position that was at once Edwardsian New Light faithful (see n. 22 below), anti-enthusiast, and anti-Unitarian: "although Lyman Beecher had tried to soften some of the harsher doctrines of his faith and even seemed a heretic to the orthodox, he never abandoned certain oppressive Puritan dogmas." (Rugoff, 295–97). Rugoff also quotes the highly critical Robert Ingersoll, who, writing about Lyman's son Henry Ward Beecher, asserted that Henry grew up in the Puritan "'prison'" of his father's beliefs.

21  Schmidt, 54.

22  Timothy Dwight (1752–1817), born in Massachusetts, entered Yale at thirteen and tutored there from 1771–77. Theologically Dwight's position reflected the New Light perspective of his grandfather Jonathan Edwards, but was relatively conservative or Trinitarian compared to the swelling Deist or Unitarian position gaining ground at the end of the eighteenth century in intellectual circles. He is credited with bringing the old faith back to Yale by building up once again the membership in the campus church, which had dwindled to almost nothing. For Dwight's biography, see Charles E. Cunningham, *Timothy Dwight, 1752–1817, A Biography* (New York: Macmillan, 1942). See also the Mather connection, n. 34 below.

23  In style and theme Dwight echoed Oliver Goldsmith's 1770 poem, "The Deserted Village." In his "Flourishing Village" – a significant section, Part II, of his long poem – Dwight described a thriving, virtuous social order in the Connecticut town like the one Goldsmith recalls in Britain, by 1770 lost there to enclosure. On the New England village's destiny in the West Dwight wrote:

All hail, thou western world! by heaven
                                    design'd
Th' example bright, to renovate mankind.
Soon shall thy sons across the mainland
                                    roam;
And claim, on far Pacific shores, their
                                    home;
Their rule, religion, manners, arts, convey,
And spread their freedom to the Asian sea.
. . . . . . . . . . . . . . . . . . . . . . . . .

Then nobler thoughts shall savage trains
                            [*sic*] inform;
Then barbarous passions cease the heart to
                            storm:
. . . . . . . . . . . . . . . . . . . . . . . . .
But peace, and truth, illume the twilight
                            mind,
The gospel's sunshine, and the purpose
                            kind
. . . . . . . . . . . . . . . . . . . . . . . . .
Where slept perennial night, shall science
                            rise,
And new-born Oxfords cheer the evening
                            skies....

This passage comes from near the close of Part II of *Greenfield Hill: A Poem ...* (New York: Childs and Swaine, 1794 [fascimile, New York: AMS Press, 1970], 52).

24  Daniel J. Boorstin, *The Americans: The Colonial Experience* (New York: Random House, 1958), 4.

25  Chicago's population in 1840 was 4,417 and in 1843, 7,580. (Bessie Pierce, *A History of Chicago, Vol. I: The Beginnings of a City 1673–1848* [New York: Alfred A. Knopf, 1937], 414–15.)

26  See n. 16 above.

27  These in that era included William Blair, the *Chicago Tribune's* William Bross, T. B. Carter, Mrs. John V. (Emeret Cooley) Farwell, and sometime mayor "Long" John Wentworth. (See both *Manual of the Second Presbyterian Church: Chicago, Ill./R. W. Patterson, Pastor/Compiled April 1, 1856* [Chicago: Charles Scott, 1856], 31 pp. and Henry M. Ralston, "A List of the Members of the Church/1842–1892" in *Second Presbyterian* [1892], 153–206.)

28  "In the old [Second] church, previous to the war, Abraham Lincoln always attended when he came to Chicago and frequently remained after the service to speak to the pastor. Stephen A. Douglas was almost a regular attendant, especially during the summer, with his wife and children. R.W.P. knew Douglas intimately in Jacksonville [where he attended Illinois College]. David Douglas was an attendant of the church always when he was in the City. George B. McClellan, then engineer of the Illinois Central Railroad, was a very constant and faithful member of the congregation and especially devoted to the pastor and his sermons." (Raymond A. Patterson, *Memoranda*, [1] and Raymond A. Patterson, outline for ch. 6, "The Slavery Question," in his *Dr. R. W. Patterson: Suggestions for Chapters* [typescript, 10 pp.], 5.) Raymond A. Patterson, son of R. W. Patterson, was chief of the *Chicago Tribune*'s Washington Bureau; R. W. Patterson Jr. was the *CT's* publisher after Joseph Medill's death, having married Medill's daughter Elinor. The statement from the transcribed *Memoranda*, listed internally as "probably" by Raymond Patterson, is noted as being copied from yellowed *Tribune* scrap newsprint.

29  See Ray Allen Billington, *Westward Expansion: A History of the American Frontier* (New York: Macmillan, 1949),

301, 334–35, and Stewart H. Holbrook, *The Yankee Exodus: An Account of Migration from New England* (Seattle: University of Washington Press, 1950).

30  "[F]or many of [Cotton Mather's] *Magnalia's* heroes, Puritanism opened the way to material as well as spiritual prosperity" (Sacvan Bercowitz, *The Puritan Origins of the American Self* [New Haven, CT: Yale University Press, 1975], 3).

31  Ebner, 6.

32  Cook's 1910 memoir (see n. 7 above), 99–100, sorts out some of these complex ethnic issues:

*The native American element derived from an English-speaking ancestry, and inheriting the Protestant faith, was sufficiently dominant to entitle it to be spoken of as the arbiter of the social order. Yet more than a third of the city's population was Catholic, chiefly Irish; while probably a fifth was rationalistic German. But these different classes hardly affected each other socially, in terms of interacting modes of thought. So long as the beliefs of the community did not infringe on his Sunday amusements, the agnostic German did not in the least concern himself about them; and what to a casual observer might have seemed like a native indifference about German doings was equally marked. Indeed, considering the serious attitude of American evangelism toward Sabbath observance, few of the paradoxes of the times are more remarkable than the tolerance of German violations of strict Sabbatarian notions.*

*However, one need not go far to find the cause. The uncompromising Sabbatarian in the pulpit, and to a less degree in the pew, was pretty certain to be anti-slavery if not an out-and-out Abolitionist; and the free-thinking, Sabbath-breaking German was invariably of the same political brand. This coincidence brought the Sabbatarian face to face with a serious dilemma. Everything was conceived intensely in those days, and here was a battle royal to be fought between two sets of convictions that seemingly admitted of no compromise. But the abolition issue was too urgent to take a second place; and so the German was left unmolested in the enjoyment of his diversions, lest he be pushed where he would not hesitate, on local issues, to make common cause with pro-slavery Catholicism. This was regarded as even less American than the Teutonic ideas, and was generally spoken of as an adjunct to Rome....*

(For the tougher Irish youths, see, for example, Ernest Poole, *The Bridge: My Own Story* [New York: Macmillan, 1940], 38.)

33  The Articles of Association provided for three institutions of learning (College, Academy, and Female Seminary) with Article 9 stating that these educational institutions shall "at all times be subject to the ratification and approval of the Synod of Peoria or its legal successor." (*The Articles of the Lake Forest*

*Association: Adopted February 28th, 1856* [Chicago: Democratic Press Job Office, 1856], 16 pp.)

34   Perhaps it was "Deacon" William Bross, a trustee of Lake Forest University, who covered extensively for the *Chicago Tribune* on July 13, 1868, the funeral sermon for Hiram Foote Mather (1796–1868) delivered by Dr. Patterson. Mather had been preparing for the ministry at Andover Seminary but left to study law because of family obligations after his father's death. (See also Horace E. Mather, *Lineage of Richard Mather* [Hartford, CT: Press of the Case, Lockwood & Brainard Company, 1890], 254–55.)

35   "The land purchased for the purposes of the Association comprises about Thirteen Hundred Acres." (*Articles of the Lake Forest Association*, 16.) More land gradually was acquired: a total of 2,000 acres, according to Halsey (483) or 2,300 ("instead of the contemplated twelve hundred") according to Arpee (37).

   Early on, a meeting of subscribers (recruited by the Rev. J. J. Slocum) was convened at the Second Presbyterian Church to form the "Lake Forest Association" and "to purchase the land," which was already virtually in the control of the proposed association. "Though an effort was made to conduct negotiations as quietly as possible," the Association was forced to buy more land than was originally projected. But McClure suggests how attractive the enterprise proved to be: "The cholera troubles of 1854 which had caused several families to leave Chicago and seek out temporary homes in suburban places, prepared many to look favorably on this scheme which offered the double inducement of doing good through an Educational Institution and of securing admirable locations for suburban homes" (McClure [1884], 10–14).

   While much of the founding of communities and colleges in the Midwest came as a result of real estate speculation, a combination of piety and boosterism, Lake Forest stands singularly apart from this kind of development. However, a history of the University (apparently by Patterson), appended to the first (1876–77) Lake Forest University catalog, ruefully reports, "it was thought by many that the whole enterprise was commenced in the interests of public speculation, and it seemed impossible to remove this impression, although not a stockholder among the original purchasers ever made a cent by his investment, or, so far as we are aware, ever expected to realize more than the principal and lawful interest of his money" (42).

   And indeed there is very much the sense of a controlled, exclusive undertaking. The landscaping that immediately followed on registration of the town clearly established Lake Forest as a restricted, "no-growth" community of like-minded citizens – in the spirit of the History cited above, which also refers to "the thorough education of our own sons and daughters in an institution planted and sustained by ourselves and in

the midst of our own people" (43).

36   Haines, 303; McClure (1884), 16; Arpee, 31.

37   "First trustee" of the newly chartered Lind University, "Pappy" Lind was heralded by Arpee as the village's "number one citizen" (45), four times its mayor (55). For a biographical sketch, see Halsey, 514. See also the biographical summary in Volpe, 7–9, with the accompanying references to directories and earlier histories. His offer is outlined in Halsey, 620.

38   Halsey, 514. But McClure (1884, 9) notes that the Rev. Ira Weed, based in Waukegan, urged the committee looking for a "suitable location for the college … to examine this lakeshore."

39   Halsey, 620.

40   "An Act to incorporate the Lind University," *Laws of the State of Illinois Passed by the Twentieth General Assembly, Convened January 5, 1857* (Springfield: Lamphier & Walker, 1857), 514–19. "The charter named a board of Trustees, limited to twenty names, with Sylvester Lind designated the *first trustee* …" (Arpee, 34).

41   The University's theological position was essentially that of its Second Presbyterian Church parent; see n. 16 above.

42   Since the Congregationalists, more radical on the slavery issue than the "New School" Presbyterians, were already represented by Illinois College, Knox College, and Beloit College, it appeared fitting to the Lake Forest group to found their own school on a Presbyterian platform. (John J. Halsey, "The Beginnings of the University," *S* [May 1890], 192.) (For example, Edward Beecher, first president of Illinois College, had tried to make it an antislavery outpost [Schmidt, 38].) See also John Frederick Lyons, *Centennial Sketch of the Presbytery of Chicago* (Chicago: privately printed, 1947), 7–15.

43   *LFUC*, 1878–79, 20.

44   Haines, 303–06, 309–11.

45   Schmidt, 54.

46   Ebner, 28 and 273, 273n.21 and Halsey, 489.

47   "On motion of H. F. Mather the Secretary was instructed to invite A. Hotchkiss Esq. to visit Chicago to consider the subject of laying out our grounds." (*Records of the doings of the Trustees of the Lake Forest Association* [bound manuscript book, 171 pp.], Feb 29, 1856–Apr 4, 1862, 31.) For more on this issue and on Almerin Hotchkiss (1816–1903) see "Appendix Two: Who Did, and Didn't, Design Lake Forest" in Ebner, 243–46 and 315–17nn. According to S. D. Ward in a letter to President Harlan of March 19, 1902, "The original plot was by the Landscape gardener who laid out Greenwood and Mount Auburn cemeteries" (original holograph letter in the Ashton historical file, LFCA). Early Lake County historian E. M. Haines observed that "the town plat of Lake Forest was laid out … under the direction of Mr. Hotchkiss, of St. Louis,

which is a marvel of landscape design work" (304).

48   Blanche Linden-Ward, "Cemeteries," *American Landscape Architecture: Designers and Places* (Washington, D.C.: Preservation Press, 1989), 121.

49   McClure (1884), 14.

50   The author of a 1993 book, *The Landscape Architecture Heritage of Illinois*, landscape architectural historian Malcolm B. Cairns observed on a visit to Lake Forest in August of 1997 that Rock Island's Chippiannock Cemetery, 1855, probably was the first designed landscape in Illinois. (See Arthur Miller, "Lake Forest's 1857 Plan by Almerin Hotchkiss and the Woodland Garden at 1030 East Illinois Road," *LFJ* [Sept 1997], 2–3.)

   The Lake Forest group's awareness of the importance of their design is reflected in the Rev. R. W. Patterson's 1876 description: "Lake Forest is finely located on the bluffs of Lake Michigan…. Its sylvan features, system of ravines, and lake front, give it great natural beauty, which has been so far developed by landscape gardening as to make the place one of the most charming suburban towns of the Northwest." ("Location, Buildings, and Grounds," *LFUC*, 1876–77. See also Halsey, 483–84.) Though there were a few farms east of the railroad, mostly the land was heavily wooded, and the minutes of the trustees of the Association reflect this in their struggles to clear stumps from the new roads as designed.

51   Michael Ebner has pointed out Richard Guy Wilson's 1979 article, "Idealism and the Origin of the First American Suburb: Llewellyn Park, New Jersey," *American Art Journal* (XI, Oct 1979), 79–90, and also the discussion of Llewellyn Park in John Reps's *The Making of Urban America: A History of City Planning in the United States* (Princeton, NJ: Princeton University Press, 1965), 339–41. Llewellyn Park, also with a curvilinear street plan in a parklike community, not only was one-third the size of the Lake Forest plan and a dependent subdivision of Orange, New Jersey, but lacked a town center, which the Academy and University Parks provided for Lake Forest.

52   Reps, 342, 344–45, and 348.

53   An article, "Notes on the First College Year," in the January 1932 *LFCAB* (8), quotes from a memorandum by Professor Walter Bridgman on information he received from Dr. Ralph Starkweather, Class of 1865 [also cited p. 20]: "[Devillo R.] Holt said he didn't want to live in Lake Forest if there were to be any shops east of the tracks."

54   "Fifty acres were set aside by the [Association] Trustees for three institutions of learning; thirty acres for College grounds, ten for an Academy, and ten for a Female Seminary." (Arpee, 32.) The Seminary, Ferry Hall, didn't materialize until 1869 – on a parcel between the lake and the thirty-acre "University" plot, now the College's Middle Campus.

55 The few roads across the tracks on the west were grouped near the center of town, and only a service road to Half Day led beyond. (Trustees, Lake Forest Association, *Records*, 31.)

56 The *Records* of the Trustees of the Lake Forest Association report approval of plans by Mr. Carter on August 31, 1857; arrangement for improvements around the hotel on May 15, 1858; and removal of the hotel manager on September 30, 1858 (32, 35, and 36).

57 Arpee, 42.

58 Arpee, 43.

59 McClure (1884), 21.

60 The Rev. Baxter Dickinson (1795–1876) was educated at Deerfield Academy, Yale College (Class of 1817), and Andover Seminary. Thus, like Lake Forest Association president Hiram F. Mather (Yale, Class of 1813) and the Rev. Patterson's mentor Lyman Beecher (Yale, Class of 1797), Dickinson had studied under Timothy Dwight. He was the only instructor in Lake Forest personally to have experienced Dwight's own teaching. (Arthur Miller, "The Dickinsons and Their Seminary for Young Ladies, 1859–69," *LFJ* [Jul 1998], 2–5.)

61 William B. Hunt, "Brief History of Ferry Hall," *S* (Mar 20, 1894), 3–4. See also McClure (1884), 24; Halsey, 621; and Arpee, 48.

62 Arpee, 61.

63 Though Arpee (61) indicates Roxana's father was Edward Beecher of Jacksonville, research undertaken by Lake Forest resident Shirley M. Paddock into Roxana Beecher's background establishes that William was Roxana's father; see Rugoff, xvi. Also, when William died in Chicago in 1889 Roxana Preuzner, a daughter, is listed as residing with him there. See "The Rev. William H. Beecher Dead," *CT* (24 Jun 1889) and *NCAB* III, 128. William's extreme abolitionist position is discussed by Rugoff, 233 and 418.

64 "Aroused to a pitch of excitement by [brother] Henry [Ward Beecher]'s bold schemes for awakening the nation to the evil of the Fugitive Slave Act, [Harriet Beecher Stowe] finally disclosed her own plan of contributing to the cause." (Rugoff, 319–21, 615–16.)

65 College trustee Geoffrey Shields and his wife, Eugenie Bird Shields '68, contributed this anecdote concerning the Polk place, just west of the Skokie River, on the north side of the road.

66 According to Ruth C. Sproat '52 and Rosemary Cowler, professor emerita, the house at 583 East Spruce was reported by a previous owner, Ellen Mosey (Lake Forest College's director of public relations, now deceased), to have been an Underground Railroad stop. The house has been remodeled, but the stable behind may date from the period.

67 For Dyer's visit to Lake Forest see Arpee, 47–48. For Dyer's Underground Railroad

role see both Arpee (66–67) and *Biographical Sketches* (1868), 76–77.

68 See sidebar and see also Arthur Miller's article on Sylvester Lind in *LFJ* (Mar 1997), 2–3.

69 See [Arthur Miller and Charles A. Miller], *African American History in Lake Forest: A Walking Tour* (Christopher C. Mojekwu Memorial Fund for Intercultural Understanding, Lake Forest College, 1997), 10 pp.

70 Arpee, 76.

71 Arpee, 61, 79.

72 Arpee, 78.

73 An inset 1861 map of Lake Forest on a wall-size *Map of Lake County, Illinois* (St. Louis: L. Gast Bros. and Co., 1861) shows the houses of the Rossiters, Quinlans, Benedicts, Holts, Thompsons, and Linds. In 1872, according to a list of thirty-one business commuters to Chicago, Devillo Holt of Holt, Balcum & Co. was in the wholesale lumber business and Sylvester Lind was in real estate ("Lake Forest Residents, Who Do Business in Chicago," *Lake Forest Reporter*, 1:1 [Aug 1872], 7). Harvey Thompson owned the Brevoort House hotel in Chicago (Arpee, 86); Gilbert Rossiter was in groceries (Halsey, 523–24); Quinlan, a doctor and dentist, had real estate interests (Halsey, 522).

74 Arpee, 61.

75 The stable at 100 North Sheridan Road (for the Harvey Thompson house, beyond flies' reach at 560 North Sheridan Road), according to a data sheet in the Lake Forest Library's "Community Cornerstones" collection, was originally constructed in 1860 – on Illinois Road just east of the historic local African American community – and therefore may have employed blacks before the Civil War.

76 This early sympathy for the African American may have been part of the attraction for succeeding liberal generations of the town. (Arthur Miller, *LFJ* [Mar 1997].)

77 As discussed in the text, much does suggest the presence of such African Americans. An additional argument is the unusually closed and labyrinthine 1857 street plan, which would have provided for atypical secrecy.

78 This *Daily Commencement Bulletin* is reported by Arpee (143) to be the first campus daily in the nation, beginning in 1893. From then to 1906 (LFCA), it was issued each day during Commencement week only and covered the graduation exercises and related news of the various branches of the University.

79 Stewart H. Holbrook, *The Story of American Railroads* (New York: Crown, 1947), 5.

80 Carl Sandburg, *Abraham Lincoln: The Prairie Years* (New York: Harcourt, Brace; 1926) 2 vol. in 1, II, 114 *et passim* and Billington (n. 29 above), 643: "So long as sectionalism plagued the nation, no road could be built."

81 "Probably no bill ever introduced to

Congress was fraught with graver consequences" (*DAH* I, 321).

82 Sandburg, *The Prairie Years*, II, 108.

83 "Chicago ... stands alone as the champion railroad junction of the country ..." (Holbrook, *Railroads*, 132). See also Sandburg, II, 336.

84 "16. That a Railroad to the Pacific Ocean is imperatively demanded by the interests of the whole country; that the Federal Government ought to render immediate and efficient aid to its construction." ("Republican Party Platform; Chicago, Illinois, May 16, 1860," *DAH*, I, 365.)

85 LFCA holds a holograph letter from Mary Todd Lincoln to Adeline Rossiter Judd, wife of Norman B. Judd, an important figure in Lincoln's political career. Hitherto unnoted, this letter of September 28, 1860, is brief but significant. It not only offers a glimpse of a much discussed personality during a crucial period of her life, but, indirectly, reaffirms the strong political ties, railroad related, between Lake Forest and Lincoln.

It was Norman Judd, railroad lawyer (as was Lincoln) and political strategist – "an intimate friend of several Lake Forest residents and promoters" (Arpee, 67) – who had nominated Lincoln for president in 1860.

Judd's wife, Adeline, was a sister of Gilbert Rossiter, who in his Lake Forest home, built in 1859, "entertained," according to the *Tribune*, Lincoln and a party en route to Chicago after a Waukegan speech on April 2, 1860 (Arpee, 61). Later Judd resided in Lake Forest, where after his death in 1878 Mrs. Judd made her home with the Rossiters. After the turn of the century Mrs. Judd presented some of her husband's and her papers, including the letter to her from Mrs. Lincoln, to the College's then-new Reid Library. (LFCA.)

86 See n. 73 above.

87 See n. 15 above.

88 "[T]he superior use which the North was able to make of its own railroads and those of the Southern and Border states which came into its possession did 'as much, certainly, as any one thing to settle the issue of the struggle.'" (Historian Robert S. Henry, quoted in Holbrook, *Railroads*, 132.) See also the "Preface" to George Edgar Turner's *Victory Rode the Rails: The Strategic Place of the Railroads in the Civil War* (Indianapolis: Bobbs-Merrill, 1953), ix–x.

Overscaled for the day, John V. Farwell's 1856 warehouse would have been uniquely positioned to support the rail-based Union effort in supplying the troops; certainly the Farwells came out of the Civil War era with vast financial resources, as is evidenced by the scale of their Lake Forest mansions and estates of 1869–70. (*Biographical Sketches* ... [1868], 101.)

89 Arpee, 48–49.

90 William C. Dickinson (born Longmeadow, Massachusetts, January 26, 1826; died

Evanston, Illinois, March 12, 1899) was the son of the Rev. Baxter O. Dickinson (see n. 60 above), who organized the first school for girls in Lake Forest. As a child in Cincinnati William also may have known the Rev. Patterson when he was a student at Lane Seminary (1837–39), where William's father was a professor (1835–39). William, graduated from Amherst College in 1848, was "teacher of the college class in Lake Forest University, 1859–63," when at the same time he was the first pastor of the Lake Forest Presbyterian Church. (Halsey, 499.) For his relationship to the Amherst Dickinsons and mentions in Emily Dickinson's correspondence, see Arthur Miller's article on the family in *LFJ* (Jul 1998); for more on his pastorate at the First Presbyterian Church, see a biographical sketch by Donald Spooner in W. C. Dickinson's faculty file, LFCA.

91   See sidebar.

92   See n. 90 above.

93   Samuel F. Miller (Amherst, Class of 1848 with William Dickinson), an engineer, built both the first bridge over the north branch of the Chicago River (Arpee, 27) and also the tracks of the Chicago & Milwaukee Railroad from Chicago to Waukegan. In 1858 he became the first principal of Lake Forest Academy (teaching all subjects, including his favorite mathematics) and in 1864 he became Lake Forest's first postmaster and also its first superintendent of schools. He helped organize the first Sunday School and later the Church (Arpee, 43). From 1859 to 1860 Miller and his family lived in an apartment in the 1859 Academy building; after that he lived in his house on the north side of Deerpath farther east, roughly where 808 E. Deerpath is today. In 1868 Miller returned to Amherst as a professor of mathematics and engineering. (See also Arthur Miller's article on the Dickinsons, *LFJ* [Jul 1998].)

94   Miller, *LFJ* (Jul 1998).

95   See accompanying sidebar from *F*, 1911, which suggests that because of transferring students the class may have broken up as early as 1862. But Arpee (59) observes that the Rev. William Dickinson, the instructor for the College class, became pastor full-time of the Presbyterian Church in July 1863, the small college class having been "suddenly ... absorbed by the Union army."

96   The medical school became independent, later joining Northwestern University. 1863 war pressures drew workers away from Lake Forest; public school attendance dropped from 48 in 1862 to 36 by 1864. (Arpee, 79.)

97   See sidebar on Anna Farwell, p. 33.

98   Charles B. Farwell served in the U.S. Senate from 1887 to 1891. He also served in the House of Representatives from 1870 to 1876 and from 1880 to 1882. (*DAB*, III, 294–95.)

99   *Biographical Sketches of the Leading Men of Chicago. Photographically Illustrated*

(Chicago: Wilson, Peirce & Co., 1876), 66.

100  Arpee (78) reports that Frederic Law Olmsted was the architect of Charles B. Farwell's house across Deerpath and east of his brother's. These houses were in a new, less-austere vein than the New England or Downingesque norms of the pre–Civil War houses.

101  The scale of John V. Farwell's greenhouse, designed by prominent Chicago architect George Edbrooke, was very substantial, as is documented in photographs on lantern slides in a collection transferred to the LFCA from the Lake Forest Library. (Courtesy of Harold T. Wolff, a reference to Farwell's "Gothic green-house" in "Building Architectural Progress in Chicago Since January 1, 1870," *CT* [7 Oct 1870, 2] [Wolff file, LFCA].) Simon Schama in *Landscape and Memory* (New York: Alfred A. Knopf, 1995) puts into perspective these innovative greenhouses (560–70).

102  Arpee, 56. In his Preface Arpee acknowledges assistance from Miss Ellen Holt, who "wrote extended reminiscences ... at my request, which I have used freely ..." (xii).

103  John Gloag in his 1977 book, *The Architectural Interpretation of History* (New York: St. Martin's), argues that "Buildings cannot lie; they tell the truth directly or by implication about those who made and used them and provide veracious records of the character and quality of past and present civilizations" (1). Gloag continues by observing "that architecture should be considered a supplementary subject for the student of history, because the character of architecture may readjust some of the emotional and intellectual loyalties that we all hold, secretly or openly, and may also implant healthy doubts that modify the compulsive authority of the written or spoken word."

104  William B. Hunt, "A Brief History of Ferry Hall," *S* (20 Mar 1894), 3–4.

105  Harold T. Wolff called attention to the reference to a "Lake Forest Presbyterian Female Seminary" by O. L. Wheelock in "Building: Architectural Progress of Chicago During the Season of 1869," *CT* (20 Jul 1869), 4. (Wolff file, LFCA.)

106  Grace Farwell McGann [Class of 1888], "Early Lake Forest," *Chicago Yesterdays: A Sheaf of Reminiscences*, ed. Caroline Kirkland (Chicago: Daughady & Co., 1919), 244–45.

107  Reid (1824–89), a Scot who came to Chicago in 1865, led the substantial railroad-era wholesale grocery firm of Reid, Murdock & Co. He and his family moved to Lake Forest in the late 1860s, and in 1872, on what would become the southwest corner of College and Sheridan roads, built their commodious home, The Lilacs (demolished in 1971), which was designed by prominent Chicago architect Rufus Rose (with Harold T. Wolff drawing attention to Rose's Reid commission in "Building Projects: What the Architects and Builders Have in Hand for 1871," *CT* [20 Mar 1871], 4). Reid and the family he

founded became important benefactors of the College: Reid Hall and Lily Reid Holt Chapel, especially. (Halsey, 522.)

108  Durand (1827–1901) also was a major benefactor of the College, presenting the institution with the Durand Art Institute (1891), Lois Hall (1898), and the Alice Home Hospital (1898; since demolished). (*Biographical Sketches* [1876], 242 and Halsey, 500.)

109  "[Lake Forest] is one of the oldest and altogether the *par excellence* of Chicago's suburbs.... The village at present numbers about 1,200 inhabitants, representing more millions than probably any other equal number of people similarly situated, in the West." ("Lake Forest," *Our Suburbs. A Resume of the Origin, Progress and Present Status of Chicago's Environs, reprint from "The Chicago Times"* [Chicago: L. Hodges, 1873], 20–21.)

110  Raymond A. Patterson, 6. This title is a proposed chapter heading, following "The Slavery Question" and preceding "Influence in the Denomination."

111  Raymond A. Patterson, 5.

112  When the Lind University charter was granted in 1857, Knox was firmly in the hands of Congregationalists more abolitionist than Chicago's Second and even First Presbyterians.

In 1858 the Rev. Harvey Curtis of Chicago's First Presbyterian Church – one of the four clergymen to select the site of Lake Forest – became president of Knox College (until his death in 1862), reversing what to that point had been a more liberal course for the institution. In the early 1850s Curtis already had brought a more conservative perspective to Chicago's First Church, more in line doctrinally and socially with the views of Second Church members ("Dr. Patterson's Address" [at the Fellowship Meeting, Monday evening, June 20, 1892] in *Second Presbyterian* [1892], 268–78). Knox in 1866 – with the conclusion of the war having made the issue of slavery moot – adopted a governance compromise to avoid domination either by Presbyterians (more orthodox doctrinally) or by Congregationalists (more flexible on theological questions); technically nonsectarian, it was functionally bisectarian. (Hermann R. Muelder, *Missionaries and Muckrakers: The First Hundred Years of Knox College* [Urbana and Chicago: University of Illinois Press, 1984],41–44.) This change in the denominational winds at Knox could have contributed to the delay in initiating college-level work at Lind University until 1859 or 1860, informally, and 1861, formally. The 1866 compromise at Knox also may have contributed to the eclipse of college-level ambitions in this period.

113  A new charter was approved by the state on February 16, 1865. (*Charter of Lake Forest University with the Rules and Duties of the Board of Trustees* [Chicago: Geo. E. Cole & Co., 1883], 2.) A catalog was issued for Lake Forest Academy in 1866, but it mentions only once, in small

print on p. 16, Lake Forest University. (*Catalogue of Lake Forest Academy, Lake Forest, Ill.* [Chicago: Horton & Leonard, 1866], 22 pp.)

114 This "sister institution to Lake Forest Academy" opened September 2, 1869, on Mayflower Park, east of University Park, on Mayflower Road south of Deerpath. The first catalog "envisioned a four year college course for women in addition to the preparatory school" (Arpee, 82–83), a program that would develop later.

115 From Sunday night, October 8, 1871, to Tuesday, October 10, "[t]hree and one-half square miles of [Chicago's] area had been blackened; 98,500 people had been burned out of their homes; 17,450 buildings had been destroyed.... In the business section everything was gone between lake and river north of a line from Congress Street to Wells and Polk" (Lloyd Lewis and Henry Justin Smith, *Chicago: The History of Its Reputation* [New York: Harcourt Brace, 1929], 130). According to Lewis (133), "Chicago's fire was one of the great events of the nineteenth century."

116 William Bross and Joseph Medill of the *Chicago Tribune*, both with Lake Forest ties, promoted the public relations effort in New York and in the Midwest that argued it would be a bargain to invest in Chicago as it rebuilt from the fire. ( Lewis, 135–38.) Bross was University trustee after 1865; the donor of a chair, house, and prize fund; and the subject of a biography published by Lake Forest on the fiftieth anniversary of his death: Charles A. Yount, *William Bross 1813–1890* (1940), 30 pp. Medill (see n. 28 above) visited the new Lake Forest Hotel around 1871 (McGann, "Early Lake Forest," 244).

117 Since 1861 when Lincoln went to Washington to assume the presidency, Illinois had been in or loomed over the White House. In 1865–69, Grant's shadow as heir apparent shrouded Andrew Johnson's administration, much of which was taken up by impeachment proceedings; in 1869–77, Grant served two terms as president, though after the Credit Mobilier scandal of 1872–73 his prestige and power were circumscribed. But the brief period of political hegemony from the early 1860s to the late 1870s brought Chicago its unassailable position as rail capital and therefore economic capital of the West, the vast empire William Cronon discusses in his 1991 book, *Nature's Metropolis: Chicago and the Great West* (New York: W. W. Norton). By the mid 1870s, when Grant's power was waning, Chicago's position was secure.

118 Arpee, 99.

119 For C.B. Farwell's assumption of management of J.V. Farwell & Co., see A.T. Andreas, *History of Chicago* (Chicago: A.T. Andreas, 1885), II, 694. For Mary E. Farwell see sidebar and portrait. The main sources for Mrs. Farwell's life (she died September 26, 1905) are the personal reminiscences and biographical details provided by Mrs. Reginald (Anna Farwell, Class of 1880) De Koven in *A Musician and*

*His Wife* (New York: Scribner's, 1926), 15–20 *et passim.*

120 John J. Halsey, "Our Founder," *S* (3 Oct 1905), 11.

121 Her enrollment in Maplewood Seminary's predecessor, the Pittsfield Young Ladies' Institute, in Pittsfield, Massachusetts, was first documented in a paper for Professor Ebner by Anna Youngerman '98 (Mary Farwell file, LFCA) and later by copies from annual catalogs supplied by the Berkshire Atheneum, Pittsfield (Arthur Miller, *LFJ* [Jul 1998] and Mary Farwell file, LFCA). The Chicago Fire (1871) and a fire at the Farwell's Lake Forest home (1920) make other verification, including of her Chicago teaching, difficult. (See Andreas, *History of Chicago*, I, 219–20.)

Mary Eveline's image appears in College publications, in old age in the *GRLFC* (1914) and in middle age in the semicentennial issue of the *Stentor* (1 Nov 1926). Two oil portraits of her from 1865 and 1866 are owned by the College, gifts in the 1950s of Farwell Winston, son of Grace Farwell Winston McGann, Class of 1888, and grandson of Mary. Material on the artist of the portrait illustrated in this chapter, Charles Highwood, and on his background is from Esther Sparks, *A Biographical Dictionary of Painters and Sculptors in Illinois 1818-1945* (Ph.D. diss., Northwestern University, 1971), II, 432, and John Steegman, *Victorian Taste: A Study of the Arts and Architecture from 1830 to 1870* (Cambridge, MA: M.I.T. Press, 1971), *passim.*

122 Arpee, 98–99.

123 Coeducation was a topic of interest in the early 1870s when there appeared both a major survey of women in colleges (survey reported in Thomas Woody, *History of Women's Education in the U.S.*, 2 vols. [Science Press, 1929], II, 251) and a collection of essays on the subject, *The Liberal Education of Women: The Demand and the Method. Current Thoughts in America and England*, ed. James Orton (New York and Chicago: A. S. Barnes & Co., 1873). Though Schmidt reports (134) that by the 1870s coeducation was common in the Midwest (Knox offering a range of options for women's education, for example, while Beloit still was male only), satisfying the Farwell's requirements of a coeducational institution not too distant that was denominationally *and* socially acceptable was another matter; the answer was the Collegiate Department of Lake Forest University. See also Mary Farwell, n. 121 above, the final reference for n. 35 above, and ch. 2.

124 Arpee, 99.

125 While Academy and Ferry Hall faculty appear to have augmented the collegiate department staff, most teaching undertaken in the first year was by three persons: Patterson, John H. Hewitt (Latin and Greek languages), and E. P. Morris (mathematics). (*LFUC* [1876] and Haines, 311.)

126 Arpee, 50–51.

127 Arpee, 99.

128 Halsey (1894), 1; see also n. 11 above.

129 John Haskell Hewitt was an 1859 graduate of Yale, where he also received his M.A. in 1867 and completed theological studies in 1863. Subsequently he received an M.A. from Williams in 1888 and an L.L.D. from Union Theological Seminary in 1895. He taught Latin at Olivet College, 1865–75; Greek and Latin at Lake Forest, 1875–81; and Ancient Languages at Williams, 1882–1909. He served as acting president at Olivet, 1872–75; at Lake Forest, 1878; and at Williams, 1901–02. (*GRLFC* [1914], 17). Hewitt, then, was – if only for a half a decade – Lake Forest's first "senior" faculty member, also serving as the first librarian. According to a monograph by E. Herbert Botsford (*Fifty Years at Williams College Under the Administrations of Presidents Chadburne, Carter, Hewitt, Hopkins, and Garfield* [Pittsfield, 1932], III, 14), at Lake Forest Hewitt "became a leader in building up the institution, first applying his energies to development of the college library and then drawing up plans for a new college building, now the oldest on campus."

130 Recent investigation establishes the identity of the 1878 architect of the present Young Hall as Leon C. Welch (1843?–1926), who was associated with early Chicago architects O. L. Wheelock and W. W. Boyington. There are entries in the Lake Forest University record-of-payments book of the time (LFCA) for payment to "L. Welch" for plans. The detailed 1926 *Chicago Tribune* obituary for Welch (29 Jan 1926, 18) and a further article, "The Plans" (*CT*, 20 Apr 1873, 70), provide much about his career. (References courtesy of Harold T. Wolff.)

131 Arpee, 99.

## CHAPTER 2

1 See ch. 1, n. 109.

2 Arpee, 103. Reid (1837–1912), born in Ohio and during the Civil War a war correspondent for the *Cincinnati Gazette*, succeeded Horace Greeley as editor and publisher (1872–1905) of the *New York Tribune*, among the nation's most influential newspapers during much of this era. From 1905 to 1912 he was ambassador to Great Britain, having been the unsuccessful candidate for vice president on Benjamin Harrison's Republican ticket in 1892. Reid had close ties to the Chicago-elite Republican group that had put Abraham Lincoln in the White House in 1861 and 1864.

3 Arpee, 103. General John A[lexander] Logan (1826–86) became an important post–Civil War Illinois Republican member of Congress and senator. He was a political rival of College founder Senator Charles B. Farwell, who, upon Logan's death, succeeded him in the Senate in 1886. In the Civil War Logan served under Grant in the west, part of the dynamic Illinois team that tipped the scale in that great struggle.

(See the article on Charles B. Farwell in *DAB*, III, 294–95 for the Logan-Farwell political differences of 1880 and 1885.)

4   Arpee, 103. During the Grant administration Sherman, who had served under General Grant and executed a major part of the president's Civil War strategy, refused to be drafted for political office but served as head of the Army.

5   Arpee, 103. After success in the Civil War, General Philip H[enry] Sheridan (1831–88) during the late 1860s and 1870s ran the western campaigns against the Native Americans. In 1871 and 1877 he returned east with his command to restore order in Chicago, first after the disastrous fire and then in 1877 to put down the Chicago railroad strike–related violence.

6   Arpee, 101. President Hayes (1822–93), a prewar Cincinnati antislavery lawyer, as a Republican squeaked into the White House in 1877 after the scandalous debacle of the Grant administration (1869–77). In the railroad strikes around the country in 1877, including those in Chicago, he employed federal troops against the strikers. His 1878 Lake Forest visit was to William Henry Smith, head of the Associated Press in Chicago.

7   The presence of sometime Congressmen Norman B. Judd (also Lincoln's ambassador to Bismarck's Berlin, 1861–65) and Charles B. Farwell in the 1870s and 1880s along with John V. Farwell, who served in the Bureau of Indian Affairs, would alone have warranted such visits by national figures on government matters.

8   Arpee, 102. Devillo Holt's sons were Arthur, George, Charles, and Alfred.

9   See ch. 1, n. 53.

10  See ch. 1, n. 129.

11  The Rev. Daniel Seelye Gregory (1832–1915) was born in Carmel, New York. He was the great-grandson of "prominent divine" Elnathan Gregory, a graduate of Princeton – where Daniel also took a degree, in 1857. He graduated as well from Princeton Theological Seminary in 1860 and was ordained in the ministry in 1861. He received a D.D. degree from Princeton in 1873 and an L.L.D. degree from Wooster in 1895. His career included teaching, higher education and denominational administration, the ministry, and scholarly editing. Beginning with teaching rhetoric at Princeton, 1858–60, he later taught at Wooster, as professor of Metaphysics and English Literature, 1871–78, before becoming president of Lake Forest from 1878 to 1886; in 1884–85 he lectured at Princeton Theological Seminary. His pastorates were at Galena, Illinois, 1860–63 (where U.S. Grant and Congressman Elihu Washburne lived prior to the Civil War); Troy, New York, 1863–66; New Haven, Connecticut, 1866–69; South Salem, New York, 1869–71; and Morgan, Minnesota, 1886–89. His later career saw him as managing editor of the *Standard Dictionary*, 1890–94, and editor, *Homiletic Review*,

1895–1904. After 1904 he was secretary of the Bible League of North America and managing editor of its *The Bible Student and Teacher*.

The *Standard Dictionary* (1893) was a pragmatic (putting, for example, meanings in front of etymologies) response to the two ambitious English and American dictionaries of the day: the scholarly *Oxford English Dictionary* (1858–1928) and the genteel *Century Dictionary* (1889–91, 1894). (See M. M. Mathews, "The Largest English Dictionaries" in *Words: How to Know Them* [New York: Holt Rinehardt and Winston, 1956], 1–9, reprinted in *Dictionaries and That Dictionary: A Casebook on the Aims of Lexicographers and the Targets of Reviewers* [Chicago: Scott, Foresman, 1962], 21–27.)

The Rev. Gregory published several books: *Christian Ethics* (1875), *Why Four Gospels?* (1877), *Practical Logic* (1881), *Christ's Trumpet Call to the Ministry* (1896), *The Crime of Christendom* (1900), *Bible League Primer, No. 1* (1904), and *Constructive Studies in John, the Gospel for the Christian* (1909). (*GRLFC* [1914], 11–12, *DAB* VII, 602, and *NCAB* 19 [1926], 252–53.)

12  Helen Lefkowitz Horowitz, *Campus Life: Undergraduate Cultures from the End of the Eighteenth Century to the Present* (New York: Alfred A. Knopf, 1987), 45–47, 89–92; Schmidt, 149–58 *et passim*.

13  Quoted by Rudolph, 241.

14  Schmidt, 158–61 *et passim*.

15  See *English in American Universities*, ed. William Morton Payne (Boston: D. C. Heath, 1895), including Hiram M. Stanley, "Education and Literature," 179–82, and also Julian Hawthorne and Leonard Lemmon, *American Literature: A Text-Book for the Use of Schools and Colleges* (Boston: D. C. Heath, 1891).

16  *S* (6 Nov 1894), 6 and Francis G. Peabody, "The Proportion of College-Trained Preachers," *Forum* XVIII (Sep 1894), 30–41.

17  Quoted by Schmidt, 132.

18  Harold F. Williamson and Payson S. Wild, *Northwestern University. A History, 1850–1975* (Evanston, IL: Northwestern University, 1976), 23.

19  Schmidt, 133.

20  While in 1876, when the collegiate department of Lake Forest University resumed, there was only the coeducational postsecondary program at the institution, by 1879, when apparently the first catalog under Gregory was issued, Ferry Hall also offered a single-sex collegiate-level program for women (*LFUC*, 34). But this still differed from the norm, where typically there were two parallel single-sex programs. The 1879–80 *LFUC* on p. 24 lists the Collegiate Department of the University with sixty-six enrolled, the Seminary's Collegiate "course" with fifty-three enrolled. The listings of names, pp. 8–10 (Collegiate Dept.) and pp. 18–20

(Seminary Collegiate course), make clear that these are two nonoverlapping lists. The curriculum listed for the Ferry Hall Seminary Collegiate course is distinctly less rigorous in traditional liberal-arts disciplines, with lower-level mathematics and language work at each grade; also the Ferry Hall course includes what today is referred to as "studio" work in art and music. The academic programs, then, differed not only on gender but also on curriculum.

21  By the mid-1890s Josephine White Bates (Mrs. Lindon W.) ranked among the leading literary figures of Chicago, one of just two women pictured in an 1894 article, "Literary Chicago," by Moses P. Handy in *Munsey's Magazine*, V. 12 (Oct 1894), 77–88, along with Mary Hartwell Catherwood. Men discussed and pictured in Handy's article included Eugene Field, Henry Blake Fuller, Hobart Chatfield-Taylor (spouse of Rose Farwell, Class of 1890, sister of Anna), and Harry B. Smith, librettist for "Robin Hood," Reginald De Koven's 1890 comic opera. Living for a while in the West with her engineer husband, Mrs. Bates developed a series of stories and novels based on her experiences in Montana and elsewhere. Her early books include *A Blind Lead: The Story of a Mine* (Philadelphia: Lippincott, 1888), *A Nameless Wrestler* (Philadelphia: Lippincott, 1889), *Armais and Others* (Chicago: F. J. Schulte, 1892), and *Bunchgrass Stories* (Philadelphia: Lippincott, 1895).

Years later and in a totally different vein Mrs. Bates wrote some reform and political documents: *Mercurial Poisoning in the Industries of Great Britain* (London: Crowther & Goodman, 1909), *Mercurial Poisoning in the Industries of New York* (New York: National Civic Federation..., n.d.), and *Make America Safe* (New York: National Security League, 1916). This work appears to parallel interests of her Yale-educated husband, Lindon W. Bates, and later her son, Lindon Bates Jr., as seen in their publications. (See *NUC* 39, 72.) Mrs. Bates's activities and visits were reported in *Stentor* issues of Mar 1888 (174), 24 Oct 1893 (10), 5 May 1894 (7), and 21 May 1895 (9).

22  The Rev. L. J. Halsey, "Lake Forest University," *Interior* (1 Jul 1880), reprinted in *LFUR* (Jun 1880), 69. ("We combine in this issue of the *REVIEW* the June and July numbers," 70.)

23  After his light opera or musical "Robin Hood" was produced and became a major hit in 1890, De Koven was a well-known figure. His piece "Oh, Promise Me," included in the show, was a staple wedding solo into the mid-twentieth century. He went on to write other comic or light operas and "regular" ones, but never with the success of his "Robin Hood," which today sounds in the vein of Gilbert and Sullivan. (See George P. Upton, *The Standard Operas: Their Plots, Their Music, and Their Composers*, new ed. enl. and rev. [Chicago: A. C. McClurg, 1908], 64–68.)

24  Unlike Josephine White Bates, Anna

Farwell De Koven (1860–1953) was not mentioned in Handy's 1894 article on the Chicago literary scene because – though summering in Lake Forest each year while her parents were alive – after 1890 the De Kovens lived in Washington, New York, and abroad, architect John Russell Pope having designed for them a notable Park Avenue townhouse, built in 1912. In addition to her writings mentioned in the text and in the sidebar, her books were: *Les Comtes de Gruyere* (in French, 1914; in English, 1916), *A Cloud of Witnesses* (1920), *A Primer for Citizenship* (1923), *Horace Walpole and Madame du Deffand, an Eighteenth Century Friendship* (1929), and *Women in Cycles of Culture* (1941). For a listing of her articles, reviews, and reviews of her works, see *Literary Writings in America: A Bibliography* (Millwood, NY: kto press, 1977), II, 2732–34. See also *WWWA*, 3, 218–19; *NCAB* XVI, 290; *NYT* (13 Jan 1953), 27; and the Anna Farwell De Koven file, LFCA.

25  Arpee, 103–04.

26  An LFU expenditures book (see also ch. 1, n.130), begun in 1878, after the New Hotel fire of December 1877, notes (32) payment of $100.00 (plus $28.00 train fare to "Pon'c" [Pontiac?] – compared to $300.00 for the University Hall plans (LFCA).

27  The style of the 1879–80 Academy building, now North Hall, recalls the floor plan of the original 1858–59 design by Carter & Drake for the Academy, with two entries at the two stairways at the ends of the building. This same floor plan would be repeated in the 1892–93 East House (now Moore Hall) when the Academy moved to South Campus.

28  There appears to be no separate record of payment for architectural plans for the president's home, though that might have been included in the Academy payment to Welch.

29  The LFU expenditures record (32) shows a payment on July 24, 1879, of $10.00 to "W. H. Castner" for the "DH," or dining hall, later known as Academia. According to Haines (424), W. H. Castner was listed in 1877 as an "architect" living in Lake Forest.

30  A sequence of references in monthly issues of the *LFUR* suggests the presence of Gordon as developer of the campus landscape in the spring of 1880. First, an advertisement reading "William Gordon, Landscape Gardener, is prepared to improve and lay out gentlemen's grounds and gardens, in Lake Forest and its vicinity, on moderate terms" appeared in the March 1880 issue (36). It was repeated in the April issue (48). In May it was no longer there, but there does appear (60) for the first time the engraving of the campus of 1880: from the left showing the president's house, the Academy, Academia, and University Hall – all set in a designed landscape with a circular drive serving the buildings. In that issue included is an obituary of Gordon, age 77, sexton of the church and formerly a gardener at

Kensington Palace, where he used to carry the daughter of the Duke of Kent, a young future Queen Victoria (b. 1819), around the grounds "in his arms." (Kensington Palace is in the eighteenth-century English landscape style, by Charles Bridgeman and "Capability" Brown. [George Plumptre, *The Garden Makers: The Great Tradition of Garden Design from 1600 to the Present Day* (New York: Random House, 1993), 361.)

31  "Hildegard," *LFUR* (Mar 1881), 44–45. The article is unsigned and there is no masthead listing staff for this issue, so the author perhaps was Gregory.

32  *LFUR* (May 1881), 71.

33  *LFUR* appeared from January of 1880 to May/June of 1883. (N. K. Burdick, "A History of Journalism in Lake Forest," *S* [20 Dec 1892], 5–7.) Anna Farwell was the editor of the first six numbers, through June of 1880, which constituted the first volume.

This appears to be the first of a series of Chicago-area periodical ventures of Anna's, funded by Farwell largesse over the next decade. In her 1926 memoir (98) she notes *The Rambler*, on which she and her husband and also De Koven's future librettist Harry B. Smith lavished much energy in 1884–85 (there is a run of *The Rambler* at the Chicago Historical Society); the format resembled that of the old, nineteenth-century *Life* with Anna largely contributing poetry. Also, in the autobiography she reports that in the late 1880s she was the first (unpaid) literary editor of the new Chicago *Evening Post*, the journal that by 1912 would have a Friday literary page supervised by Floyd Dell and later by Burton Rascoe. Anna mentions that she was succeeded at the *Evening Post* by Mary Abbott, the wife of Peter Dunne, who would become well-known for the series of columns, with his character Mr. Dooley, that later were collected into popular books. The Farwells appeared to be behind *America* (1887–91), an odd mixture of post-Haymarket Riot vitriolic nativism and high literary ambition, especially at the outset. Early on the young Hobart Chatfield-Taylor shared editorial responsibility with career journalist (and later Lake Forest resident) Slason Thompson, future biographer of Eugene Field (Bernard Duffey, *The Chicago Renaissance in American Letters: A Critical History* [East Lansing: Michigan State College Press, 1954], 57–62). Finally, Anna contributed to Chicago's *Chapbook* of the mid-1890s, in many ways a successor of these earlier vehicles – catering to an elite audience of about 10,000 and centered on Chicago – this time published by Stone & Kimball, who also published novels by Anna De Koven and Chatfield-Taylor. While the *Chapbook* clearly was a new type of magazine (expensively produced, experimental, insouciant of circulation [See Richard H. Brodhead, "Literature and Culture," *Columbia Literary History of the United States*, ed. Emory Elliott (New York: Columbia University Press, 1988), 479]), it appears to have developed out of a

decade-spanning context of Farwell family-supported Chicago literary magazines commencing with the *LFUR* in January of 1880. This links the *LFUR* to the origins of the Chicago Literary Renaissance, the first phase of which is recognized by Duffey as beginning a decade later. (See also De Koven, *Musician, passim*.)

34  "Lake Forest University" in Halsey, 623. John J. Halsey (1848–1919) received his bachelor's and master's degrees from the old Baptist-supported Chicago University in 1870 and 1873. From 1871 to 1878 he was in Chicago in business and newspaper work (the *Tribune* and the *Inter-Ocean*), but in 1878 he joined the Lake Forest faculty, becoming in time its first distinguished career faculty member. In this capacity he wore many hats, including those of professor of Political Science and English (1878–89), librarian (1881–87), professor of Political and Social Science (1889–1919), acting president (1896–97, 1905–06), and dean of the faculty (1899–1900). In 1897 he was awarded an honorary Doctor of Laws degree by Centre College, Kentucky, where Dr. William Roberts, Lake Forest's president from 1886 to 1892, was president. Halsey wrote a final chapter on "Reconstruction" for William Henry Smith's posthumous *Political History of Slavery* (1903), which he also edited; and his 1912 *History of Lake County* was recognized as "the best Illinois county history" by bibliographer Wright Howes in *U.S. iana (1650–1950): A Selective Bibliography in which are Described 11,620 Uncommon and Significant Books Relating to the Continental Portion of the United States*, rev. and enlarged ed. (New York: R. R. Bowker for the Newberry Library, 1962), 247. Halsey also reviewed social science books for the Chicago genteel literary periodical *The Dial*. (Halsey's thumbnail autobiography in his 1912 Lake County history, 509–10, and *GRLFC*; see also Halsey file, LFCA.)

35  The Rev. William Charles Roberts (1832–1903), born in Wales, came to this country with his family in 1849. Arriving in New York, the parents and two children died of cholera within a week of disembarking – leaving William the oldest of the six remaining children. By 1855 he had graduated with honors from Princeton, and from the Princeton Theological Seminary in 1858. Later he received honorary degrees from Union College in 1871 and from Princeton in 1886 and 1889. He served pastorates in Wilmington, Delaware, 1858–61; Columbus, Ohio, 1861–64; and Elizabeth, New Jersey, 1864–82. From 1882 to 1886 he was corresponding secretary of the Presbyterian Board of Home Missions. From this important administrative post (Halsey, 623) he came to Lake Forest University, serving from 1886 to 1892, and during that time served a year (1889–90) as moderator of the church's General Assembly. After his years at Lake Forest, he returned to his previous organization from 1892 to 1898, this time as senior secretary, before returning to higher education as president of Centre College in

Kentucky, 1897–1901, and then president of a merged Central University of Kentucky from 1901 to 1903. He served as founding trustee of Wooster College and as a trustee also of Lafayette College (1859–63), and of his alma mater, Princeton (1866–86).

The Rev. Roberts's publications included *A Translation of the Shorter Catechism into Welsh* (1864), *Letters on Eminent Welsh Clergymen* (1868), *Letters on Travels in Egypt and Palestine* (1891), and *New Testament Conversions* (1896). *(GRLFC, DAB* XVI, 17, and *NCAB* II, 387.)

36   "Anarchism was not a labour movement and was no more than one element in the general upheaval of the lower class. But anarchists saw in the struggles of labour the hot coals of revolution and hoped to blow them into flame." (Barbara Tuchman, *The Proud Tower, A Portrait of the World Before the War: 1890–1914* [New York: Macmillan, 1966], 77. Tuchman saw the riot and the subsequent high-profile trial of the Anarchists as a major public relations boost for the anarchist movement [76].)

37   Lloyd Lewis blames an excitable police inspector for precipitating the riot after mayor Carter Harrison had quieted everyone down and gone home. (Lloyd Lewis and Henry Justin Smith, *Chicago: The History of Its Reputation* [New York: Harcourt Brace, 1929], 160. See also Donald L. Miller, *City of the Century: The Epic of Chicago and the Making of America* [New York: Simon & Schuster, 1996], 467–81.)

38   Cyrus Hall McCormick (1809–84) manu-factured and marketed the reaper and key farm implements that opened the prairies and plains to cost-effective agriculture. Though his claim to inventing the reaper was never secure, he held onto the business through his effective business methods: selling and efficient production. This drive for ultimate productivity was inherited by his son, Cyrus Jr. (1859–1936), who, after graduating from Princeton in 1879, suc-ceeded his father in business in 1884. By 1886, still under thirty, McCormick Jr. was at the center of the Haymarket Affair. The effort by the strikers to implement an eight-hour day met determined resistance at the McCormick plant. When shootings at the plant ended a demonstration with six fatalities, the meeting was called at the Haymarket. (Lewis, 159–66; Halsey, 515; and *GRLFC*.)

39   Quoted by Ebner, 140–41 and 298, n. 21.

40   According to Arpee, 121, the purchase price from the Commercial Club was $10.00.

41   The affiliated professional programs were the Northwestern College of Dental Surgery, 1887–89; the College of Dental Surgery, after 1890; Rush Medical College, 1889–98; and the Chicago College of Law, after 1889. The second dental and the law school relationships were terminated between 1901 and 1903. (Halsey, 625; Jim Bowman, *Good Medicine: The First 150 Years of Rush-Presbyterian-St. Luke's Medical Center* [Chicago: Chicago Review Press, 1987], 36–37, 66.)

42   "The Medical School of Lind University had opened in 1859 with thirty-three students, in the Lind Block in Chicago" (Arpee, 66). A medical diploma from this school, which later became Northwestern's medical school, listing Lind University has been reported as late as 1865, though the rela-tionship ceased after 1863. The loss of the University Trustee minutes in the 1871 fire has made this date difficult to determine with certainty.

43   "Among the more striking changes ... are, the designation of the college as *Lake Forest College*...." ("The Reorganization of the University," *S* [1887], 66–68.) For "Topical Statements of Work," see for example *LFUC* (1888–89).

44   Accounts of English curricula in the leading colleges and universities in 1895 (*English in American Universities* [Boston: D. C. Heath, 1895]) make clear how limited offerings in American literature were even a decade later – usually a matter only of one course (at Wellesley, for example, "one-hour lecture courses, alternating, year by year in American literature and in poetics [147]," while among the twenty-nine courses in the University of Chicago's "condensed list" of classes, only one is in American literature). See also "W. W. Johnson '88" [William Wycoff Johnstone, Class of 1888], "American Literature," *S* (Dec 1887), 153–54.

45   Schmidt, 166.

46   Schmidt, 163.

47   (Baldwin's anecdote about Lake Forest – and his role in pioneering modern psychology – was noted for the authors by Psychology Professor David Krantz.) *ANB* 2, 51–53; *DAB* 1, 49–50; *GRLFC*, 20; and see also J. M. B., "James McCosh," *S* (Dec 1887), 85–86, in which Princeton doctoral candi-date Baldwin discusses Princeton president McCosh's key position in American philosophy ("If in the future the American philosophy be a realistic philosophy, it will be in large measure his work...." [96]).

48   James Mark Baldwin, *Between Two Wars, 1861–1921, being Memories, Opinions and Letters Received* (Boston: Stratford, 1926), I, 40–41.

49   *By the turn of the century, the Harvard his-torian Ephraim Emerton observed sadly that "the qualities of gentility and schol-arship were no longer regarded as necessar-ily combined or as forming two essential parts of a single complete and beautiful whole." Neither ideal had been abandoned, but they seemed to have become separated from each other. The traditional education of a gentleman had been liberal rather than professional. It had provided a certain body of knowledge, a kind of power of thought and expression, and a sense of the largeness and beauty of intellectual life. In America, the gentle life had implied a devotion to intellectual culture rather than the pursuit of a practical calling. German scholarship and the rapid growth of inter-est in science had dealt a fatal blow to the genteel tradition.... [I]n England gen-tility had been largely confined to a social class, to which the universities were merely appendages. In America, where no such confines were recognized, the col-leges and universities themselves came to bear an increasing share of the burden of maintaining gentility. By the First World War, Henry Holt would note that "cul-ture" was largely restricted to the teach-ing class, a sufficient indication of its anemic condition.* (Stow Persons, *The Decline of American Gentility* [New York: Columbia University Press, 1973], 200–01.)

50   "Lecturer in Theoretical and Applied Electricity, 1887–92," *GRLFC* 25, and *LFUC*s. See also "Elisha Gray: Inventor as Churchman" in Bruce L. Felknor, *The Highland Park Presbyterian Church: A History, 1871–1996* (Highland Park Presbyterian Church, 1996), 18–22; see sidebar on inventors (p. 186), *ANB* 9, 441–42, and *DAB* IV, 514.

51   George T. Hayes, *Presbyterians: A Popular Narrative of the Origins, Progress, Direction and Achievement ...* (New York: J. A. Hill, 1892), 266–67.

52   Memorandum of W. C. Larned, CHMP, Box I.

53   *NCAB* XVI, 387.

54   *WWC* [1931], 644, and *James Gore King McClure/ November 24, 1848 /January 18, 1932* (Chicago: printed for private cir-culation, 1932), 74 pp. See also McClure file, LFCA.

55   Indeed, McClure represented the Eastern social establishment to the newly well-to-do grocers and merchants of Lake Forest. Compared to McClure's father, who had made his money in the wholesale paint and hardware business at Albany, the eastern terminus of the Erie Canal, during an ear-lier wave of westward expansion in the mid-dle of the century, the new Lake Forest crowd of the 1860s and 1870s, represented by the Reids and the Durands, were relative latecomers to wealth. In fact, the Simon Reids in Buffalo around 1850 had been a bookbinder and the daughter of a shoe-maker, according to the city directories of the day (formerly in the Chicago Historical Society library, these were transferred to Lake Forest in the 1980s). Moreover, McClure's mother's family could trace its ancestry back to five separate Mayflower lines, and McClure, much interested in his-tory, later was a leader in the national Society of Mayflower Descendants. Throughout the nineteenth century, the Dixons, Mrs. McClure's family, also old New England stock, were leaders of the business and social community in Westerly, Rhode Island. Three generations of Nathan Fellows Dixons attended Brown University and sat in Congress for Westerly. In all this the McClures, whose financial security and position were of East Coast origins, dra-matically outpaced socially the Farwell brothers, whose parents had been Yankee pioneer farmers at Morris, Illinois, and even the Scotch-Irish Virginian McCormicks, Cyrus Sr. having come from the family farm to Chicago in the 1840s.

56 There is some likelihood that Asher Carter of Carter & Drake, the architect(s) for the original hotel (1857–58) and Academy (1858–59) buildings, was/were the architect(s), too, for the 1862 First Presbyterian Church. This would have been a wooden version of the Renwick – inspired Gothic style brought west from New York in 1848 for Chicago's Second Presbyterian Church, a project guided after mid-1849 by superintendent Asher Carter, of Morristown, New Jersey, who had consulted with Renwick before leaving the East. (*Second Presbyterian* [1892], 32–33.)

57 These stones came from a Chicago quarry that yielded a unique limestone impregnated with tar. The story of these stones and their arrival in Lake Forest ultimately for the 1886–87 First Presbyterian Church is recounted in Russell Kohr's documented study, "The Saga of the Stones of the First Presbyterian Church of Lake Forest, Illinois," published in *History of First Presbyterian Church, Lake Forest, Illinois, 1859–1984*, 16–23.

58 The firm of Cobb and Frost designed the First Presbyterian Church, according to multiple listings in the Church's trustee minutes as reported in an historical survey for the church by Barbara Buchbinder-Green and in a letter to Arthur Miller from Jeanette Mattoon, dated December 2, 1997.

Henry Ives Cobb (1859–1931), born in Brookline, Massachusetts, graduated from Harvard in engineering (1880) and M.I.T. in architecture prior to joining Peabody & Stearns in Boston. Cobb had traveled and studied in Europe when he joined this firm led by Robert Peabody, who had studied at the Ecole des Beaux-Arts in Paris with Charles McKim. In 1881 Cobb came to Chicago to design the Union Club; calling on fellow Peabody & Stearns colleague Charles S. Frost to join him as a partner, they went into practice in 1882.

Charles S. Frost (1856–1931) was born in Lewiston, Maine, and joined Peabody & Stearns in 1876 after graduating from M. I. T. He and Cobb brought to Chicago the new wave of Beaux Arts–inspired historicism that was becoming the polite standard with the Eastern establishment. Their first high-profile commission was the trend-setting Potter Palmer mansion on Lake Shore Drive in 1882–85 (David Lowe, *Lost Chicago* [Boston: Macmillan, 1975], 35), the "castle" that established that neighborhood and set the trend for historically based residential and genteel institutional architecture in Chicago. This eclipse of the functional, commercially based, innovative "Chicago School" would be secured by the 1893 World's Columbian Exposition a decade later, but by that time Cobb's activity had somewhat diminished. He left a solid fabric of institutional building (done in partnership with Frost to 1889): the University of Chicago campus (1891–1900) and Yerkes Observatory at Lake Geneva (1895), the Chicago Historical Society, the Newberry Library (1893), Lake Forest College's Durand Art

Institute and Gymnasium (1891), and many important Chicago and Lake Forest residences. The First Presbyterian Church of Lake Forest (1886–87) is a key link in this development, after the Palmer commission and prior to the major institutional work of the 1890s. Also for Lake Forest College the firm designed two substantial brick faculty residences, Bross and Beidler houses, around 1890; both were demolished after the College's Johnson Science Center was built, 1961–62. LFCA has blueprints and drawings for some of this work and files on both architects. (*BDAA*, 128–29, 224, and *NCAB* XI, 128–29, 224 and XXVI, 144. See also Julius Lewis, *Henry Ives Cobb and the Chicago School* [A.M. thesis (Art), University of Chicago, 1954], Arthur Miller's articles on Cobb and on Frost in *LFJ*, respectively Mar 1998 and Nov 1997, and Mary Ruth Yoe, "Cobb's Other Buildings," *University of Chicago Magazine* [Oct 1999], 28–33.)

59 Arpee, 117.

60 Arpee, 115, 149.

61 In an experience not unlike that of the original Lind University Collegiate Department of 1859–63, Chicago University (founded in 1856 under Baptist denominational auspices) foundered, though after three decades. The Baptist Morgan Park Seminary's Thomas W. Goodspeed approached the Baptist Rockefeller in the 1880s to keep Chicago University afloat, but without success – though a connection was made that led to a refounding as the University of Chicago in the early 1890s. (Ron Chernow, *Titan: The Life of John D. Rockefeller* [New York: Random House, 1998], 307.)

62 The firm of Cobb and Frost "dealt in all manner of revival styles, including the Romanesque wherin it achieved several stunning successes such as the Gymnasium (1890) and Durand Art Institute (1891) on the campus of Lake Forest College." (Thomas J. Schlereth, "H. H. Richardson's Influences in Chicago's Midwest, 1872–1914," *The Spirit of H. H. Richardson on the Midland Prairies: Regional Transformations of an Architectural Style*, ed. by Paul Clifford Larson with Susan M. Brown [Ames, IA: Iowa State University Press, 1988], 57, 143*n*.)

63 The Gymnasium opened in April 1891. (*S* [1 May 1891], 153–4, and Arpee, 132, who reports that "it erected in 1890.")

64 Arpee, 134.

65 Irving K. Pond (1857–1939) and Allen B. Pond (1858–1929), brothers, practiced architecture in Chicago, most notably designing the Hull House complex on the West Side. Irving, who studied in Europe in 1880–82 and worked in the offices of Jenney and Beman, went into practice with his brother in 1886. He was president of the A.I.A. in 1908. The brothers later planned a school and at least two substantial country houses in Lake Forest, for Helen Culver (patron of Jane Addams) in 1900 and for Arthur Wheeler (Class of 1881) in 1909. (*BDAA*, 478–79; Pond and

Pond file, LFCA; articles by Arthur Miller in *LFJ* for Nov 1995 and Apr 1998.) Actually, of the four structures, Remsen Cottage (dormitory) was designed by Cobb in harmony with the other three. See ch. 7, n. 26.

66 Plan, LFCA. Simonds (1855–1931), graduate of the University of Michigan, worked for Jenney in Chicago and then briefly, around 1880, formed the firm Holabird & Simonds. Though he quickly moved into landscape design and left the firm, he continued to work with Holabird & Roche on, among other undertakings, the Fort Sheridan project in the late 1880s and early 1890s. He may have done Lake Forest estates at the same time which were Holabird & Roche commissions: for Henry N. Tuttle (941 E. Westminster), for Carter Fitzhugh (360 N. Mayflower), and for Byron Laflin Smith (c. 1200 N. Lake, demol.); actual plans for two Lake Forest estates are known – one for the Misses Colvin on Lake Road (original at the Morton Arboretum, copy LFCA) and one for Franklin P. Smith (on earlier property of Henry C. Durand, father of Mrs. Smith, on East Deerpath; blueprint at the Lake Forest/Lake Bluff Historical Society). (For more information on Simonds and the Prairie Style of which he was an early practitioner, see Robert E. Grese, *Jens Jensen, Maker of Natural Parks and Gardens* [Baltimore, MD: Johns Hopkins University Press, 1992], 249–50, and the Simonds file, LFCA.)

## CHAPTER 3

1 Philip Pregill and Nancy Volkman, *Landscapes in History: Design and Planning in the Western Tradition* (New York: Van Nostrand Reinhold, 1993), 521.

2 Quoted by Spiro Kostof, *A History of Architecture: Settings and Rituals* (New York: Oxford University Press, 1985), 671.

3 According to Robert Bruegmann, *The Architects and the City: Holabird & Roche of Chicago, 1880–1918* (Chicago: University of Chicago Press, 1997), 69.

4 The Durand Art Institute opened on February 12, 1892, when George Kennan, of the family of future president Eugene Hotchkiss, lectured on Russia's Caucasus Mountains. (*S* [15 Feb 1892], 109.)

5 For these references to the De Kovens, see De Koven, *Musician*, 98, 133, and 142. See also Ch. 2, nn. 23, 24, and 33.

6 De Koven, *Musician*, 142.

7 For Reginald De Koven's advocacy of an orchestra for Chicago, see particularly "Orchestras – Past, Present, and Future," *America* I, 40 (3 Jan 1889), 13–14; "Wanted – An Orchestra," *America* II, 58 (9 May 1889), 186, 188; "A New Art Temple," *America* III, 11 (Dec 12, 1889), 348, 350 [referring to the Auditorium Theater]; and "Orchestral Music in America," *America* III, 17 (23 Jan 1890), 538, 540.

8 Hobart Chatfield-Taylor, "A Brief History

of the Onwentsia Club," *Onwentsia Club: 1895–1995: A Centennial History* (1995), 16.

9  "Dancing in that era was looked upon as the last form of wickedness, – Mr. Holt said he would rather see all his children in their coffins than see them dancing." (Mrs. Robert Greaves [Grace Farwell] McGann, "Early Lake Forest," *Chicago Yesterdays: a Sheaf of Reminiscences*, ed. Caroline Kirkland [Chicago: Daughady and Company, 1919], 243, and Ebner, 72–73.)

10  Polo began at Onwentsia in 1896, played on Ferry Field, east of Sheridan Road, just north of Spruce. (*Onwentsia Club*, 62.) See also Jean Rumsey, *Walking Tour of Lake Forest* (Lake Forest/Lake Bluff Historical Society, ca. 1977) and Arpee, 144.

11  The sequence of events, 1895–96, leading up to the organization of Onwentsia and the occupation of the current grounds is detailed in *Onwentsia Club*, 1–8. (For fox-hunting, see 74–75.)

12  McGann, "Early Lake Forest," *Chicago Yesterdays*, 256.

13  Arthur Meeker, *Chicago with Love: A Polite and Personal History* (New York: Alfred A. Knopf, 1955), 85.

14  *WWA* (1926–27), 445.

15  Meeker, 107.

16  The "proud mansion" of Chatfield–Taylor's Chicago West Side boyhood previously had been the home of Joseph Medill, when it was visited by a Russian grand duke and by General Sheridan. (Chatfield-Taylor, *Cities of Many Men: A Wanderer's Memories of London, Paris, New York, and Chicago During a Half-Century* [Boston: Houghton Mifflin, 1928], 232.)

17  Novels: *With Edge Tools* (McClurg, 1891), *An American Peeress* (McClurg, 1894), *Two Women and a Fool* (Stone & Kimball, 1895), *The Vice of Fools* (H. S. Stone, 1897), *The Idle Born* (H. S. Stone, 1900), *The Crimson Wing* (1902), *Fame's Pathway* (Duffield, 1909). Nonfiction: *Land of the Castanet* (H. S. Stone, 1896), *Moliere* (Duffield, 1906), *Goldoni* (Duffield, 1913), *Chicago* (Houghton Mifflin, 1917), *Tawny Spain* (Houghton Mifflin, 1927), *Cities of Many Men...* (see n.16 above), and *Charmed Circles...* (Houghton Mifflin, 1935). (See *NUC* 104, 540–41.)

18  Chatfield-Taylor, *Cities*, 267.

19  John Merle Coulter (1851–1928) was born in Ningpo, China, of missionary parents and received his B.A. from Hanover College (Indiana) in 1870. As assistant geologist of the Hayden Survey of the West, 1872, he began collecting plants and was made the expedition's botanist by Hayden. After becoming Asa Gray's "most distinguished pupil," he received his M.A. from Hanover in 1873 and was appointed professor of biology there, 1874–79, and also at Wabash, 1879–91, having taken his Ph.D. at Indiana University in 1884. In 1891 he became president of Indiana, prior to coming to Lake Forest in 1893. After 1896 he

spent the next three decades at the University of Chicago building its botany department, retiring from teaching in 1925. While at Hanover in 1875 he founded the *Botanical Gazette* and over the years published a number of important manuals, text books, and other writings. (*DAB* IV, 467–8; H. C. Cowles, "John Merle Coulter," *Botanical Gazette*, LXXXVII, 2 [Mar 1929], 211–17; and Andrew Denny Rodgers III, *John Merle Coulter: Missionary of Science* [Princeton: Princeton University Press, 1944].)

20  Rodgers, 43–47, 149–50 *et passim*.

21  Rodgers, 126.

22  For example, November 3, 1893, and October 16, 1894. (*Records of Lake Forest University Club Organized Feb. 4, 1890* [to 1914], 43 and 53, LFCA.)

23  *LFUC* (Summer 1896).

24  After Harriet McCormick's death in 1921, Cyrus published her 1899 talk to the Fortnightly Club on landscape architecture, accompanied by historical plates and photographs of the "Walden" estate illustrating points in her talk. One of these showed the dramatic change in the condition of the bluff under her stewardship. Harriet Hammond McCormick, *Landscape Art: Past and Present* (New York: Scribner's, 1923), plate XXVI, "Bluff: 1895–1922."

25  John M. Coulter, *The Work of a University: Inaugural Address at Lake Forest, Ill., June 15, 1893* (Madison, WI: Tracy, Gibbs & Co., Printers, 1894), 7. (Coulter folder, Presidents' Speeches and Pamphlets Collection, LFCA.)

26  Rodgers, 183.

27  Laurence R. Vesey, *The Emergence of the American University* (Chicago: University of Chicago Press, 1965), 137 (citing Rodgers, 107, 147, and 183–84); Rodgers, 183.

28  John M. Coulter, *Proposed Policy of Development Submitted to the Trustees Jan. 2, 1894...* (n.p., n.d.), 2. (Coulter folder, Presidents' Speeches and Pamphlets Collection, LFCA.)

29  Coulter, *Proposed Policy*, 4–5. Coulter calls here for a new recitation hall, departmental buildings, and "cottage" dormitories with a common refectory. He recognized the role of suitable rooms and dining facilities in recruiting beyond "needy students who must be helped" (5).

30  *LFUC* (1895–96), 9–10.

31  Enrollment for the University as a whole in 1895–96, for example, was 2,225. This included 116 for the College, 127 for Ferry Hall Seminary, 102 for Lake Forest Academy, 33 for summer school, 839 for Rush Medical College, 436 for the Chicago College of Dental Surgery, and 572 for the Chicago College of Law; the three professional programs totaled 1847. (*LFUC* [1895–96], 193.)

32  Hiram Miner Stanley (1857–1903), Class of 1881 and M.A. 1882, studied further at Andover Seminary (1882–83) and was a

fellow at Harvard, 1883–85. He was an instructor at Lake Forest from 1887 to 1892 in Philosophy and Art, and part-time librarian until 1892, when he assumed full-time duties, producing in 1893 the first catalog, in book form, of the library's holdings. Stanley also was a scholar, contributing articles to American and English periodicals in Philosophy and English and publishing several books: *An Outline Sketch, Psychology for Beginners* (Chicago: Open Court Publishing Co.,1899), *Evolutionary Psychology of Feeling* (New York: Macmillan, 1895), and *Essays in Literary Art* (London, 1897). (*F* [1903], 17 [illus.] and "Hiram M. Stanley," *S* [15 Apr 1903], 2–3.) (See also p. 75.)

33  The Rev. Hannibal Lowe Stanley (1824–83) and his wife, Cornelia Caroline (Miner) Stanley (1832–1911), with their family came to Lake Forest in 1878, the Rev. Stanley arriving to help raise funds for Lake Forest University at the time of the building of the three yellow brick buildings on Middle Campus, 1878–80. Mrs. Stanley was from a well-to-do family of Freedonia, New York, where they were married, and the couple was able to buy the commodious house still located on the southwest corner of College and Washington roads, a block just west of the entrance to Middle Campus. From this house in 1895 the Stanleys' daughter Grace, Class of 1890, married by-then Professor Albert Jack, Class of 1884, and they would become the parents of Grace Jack Smith (b. 1909). The Stanleys were friends of the Charles B. Farwells and Grace Stanley accompanied classmate Rose Farwell and her father on a trip to Alaska in 1888. (From an interview with Grace Jack Smith in Lake Forest, January 7, 1996; see Stanley/Jack family file, LFCA.) (See also p. 75.)

34  Stanley, "Education and Literature," reprinted in *English in American Universities*, ed. William Morton Payne (Boston: D. C. Heath, 1895), 181.

35  This high-profile collision between labor and capitalists occurred in the summer of 1894, in the midst of the economic downturn, when sleeping-car magnate George Pullman's model town on the south side of the city erupted into a strike. Earlier hailed as a visionary for his enlightened workers' suburb adjacent to his sleeping-car works, Pullman squeezed his workers/tenants when he lowered wages, as orders dropped off, but maintained rent levels. Angry workers under labor union leader Eugene Debs struck, bringing in American railroad workers for solidarity. Federal troops were called in by President Cleveland to break the strike, which ended in deadly violence. Pullman won, but at the cost of "his reputation, his town, and, some said, his life" since he died soon after in 1897. (Donald Miller, *City of the Century*, 541–47 *et passim*.)

36  *ANB* 10, 131–34; *DAB* VIII, 287–92.

37  Consolidation, the elimination of competition, was very much a Rockefeller principle,

which he applied to education at the University of Chicago. (Ron Chernow, *Titan: The Life of John D. Rockefeller, Sr.* (New York: Random House, 1998), 309, 314.

38 The Sub-Committee met January 6, 1893. See n. 41 below for the formal report of that conference and n. 40 for an unofficial, earlier version.

39 Rodgers, 124–25.

40 [To Cyrus McCormick Jr., trustee] from George H. Holt, Chicago, January 9, 1893. (CHMP, Series I, Box I, folder 5 [LF Univ. Bd. of Trustees, 1893], 4 pp. [legal-pages, typed], LFCA.) George Hubbard Holt (1852–1924) was the second child and oldest son of Devillo Holt (1823–99), founding trustee, and after 1888 vice president of the Holt Lumber Company under his father. On the Board from 1892 to 1895, he served as its secretary, 1892–94. (*GRLFC* and Ellen Holt, *Holt, Hubbard and Allied Families: Genealogical and Biographical* [New York: American Historical Society, Inc., 1929], 28–33.)

41 See particularly the two-legal page typed document beginning "The Sub-Committee on the Union of the Universities... ," dated in ink January 11, 1893, in the the same folder as cited in n. 40 above.

42 See particularly the Herodotus sidebar: "A surprising Scheme! The Napoleon of Education. A Handle to the Telescope Offer," *RB* (21 Dec 1892), 1; and a note on the subject, *RB* (18 Jan 1893), 120. See also "The Proposed Union with Chicago University," *S* (10 Jan 1893), 3.

43 "Views of an Alumnus," *RB* (18 Jan 1893), 121. For material on Albert Jack see *GRLFC*, 21, and the Stanley/Jack family file, LFCA. Class of 1884, brother-in-law of Hiram Stanley, and professor of English, 1893–1906, apparently Jack was not yet on the faculty when this was written. (See also pp. 75 and 86.)

44 "A Surprising Scheme.... ," *RB* (21 Dec 1892), [105].

45 [William C. Roberts], "From Our Ex-President," *RB* (13 Jan 1893), 121.

46 *S* (21 Feb 1896 [extra] and 23 Feb 1896). The sequence of Coulter's new appointment and resignation may have been affected by the appointment of a nontrustee consultant committee, suggested by Cyrus McCormick, on January 7, 1896 (TM) and receipt of the report on February 19, 1896 (TM). The committee – proposed by McCormick and to include William H. Swift, A. C. Zenos, John P. Hale, Hugh McBirney, and Henry V. Freeman – was charged "to investigate thoroughly the present conditions and needs of the University...." Their report found an unencumbered endowment of $270,725.75 yielding annually $14,047.77. Current year expenses were $90,602.50 against estimated income of $68,007.99. See also Rodgers (151–52), for reproduction of the February 21, 1896, *Chicago Evening Post* article breaking the story – the occasion for the *Stentor* extra of the day.

McCormick, just at this time building his substantial country place, Walden, and Board chairman Henry C. Durand, living across the ravine northeast of the campus, might particularly have reacted to the prospect of comparable expansion in their pastoral community.

47 Jean F. Block, *The Uses of Gothic: Planning and Building the Campus of the University of Chicago, 1892–1932* (Chicago: University of Chicago Library, 1983), 12.

48 Five "major" buildings designed by Cobb were completed in 1892 and five more in 1893. (Chernow, 323.)

49 For example, in 1918–19 Coulter was engaged as a consultant, as discussed in ch. 6.

50 *LFUCs* (1890s).

51 Refer to ch. 2, n. 49.

## CHAPTER 4

1 Rudolph, 156, 288–90, 446–49.

2 *LFUC* (1893–94), 22.

3 Rudolph, 290–93, 305.

4 Rudolph, 289.

5 Rudolph, 154–55. For an illustration of the new evolving traditions see *F* (1909), 78–79.

6 See p. 60. A dimension of college spirit was "class spirit," heralded in *F* (1909), 48: [but] "over and above this absorbing class spirit reigns an undying and filial love for that gentle and most lovable of Alma Maters, Lake Forest College."

7 *F* (1896), 53–55.

8 AMC for this specific (from a musical program on the scrapbook leaf numbered 10) and for other campus entertainments.

9 Rudolph, 137.

10 For the Society's history see *F* (1896), 21–22, and for the references from its constitution see *Constitution of the Athenean Literary Society of Lake Forest University. Organized November 1876, revised 1887.* (Luther Rossiter, personal scrapbook collection, 8. LFCA.)

11 See *LFUC* (1876–77), 27 and (1885–86), 20.

12 *F* (1896), 19–20.

13 *F* (1896), 16.

14 One leaf, unattached sheet in box: "1887–98 Lake Forest University College Commencements, Society Programs, etc. Collected and bound by donation of Dr. J. G. K. McClure." (LFCA.)

15 AMC.

16 *F* (1903), 25, 33. And like the 1880 class, its own song, such as that of the freshman Class of 1893, with this characteristic stanza:

Oh! The Freshies met the Semies [lady seminarians]
Coming home from tea,

Said the Semies to the Freshies,
Oh! how you tire me,
CHORUS: ——
Tweedle dinctum, tweedle dinctum,
Tweedle dinctum, tweedle dee. (AMC, 2.)

17 AMC.

18 *F* (1916), 108.

19 See *LFUC* (1884–85), 1, and (1887–88), 2.

20 *LFUR* (May 1882), 58.

21 Rudolph, 373–74.

22 G. W. Axelson, "Heroes of Gridiron: Lake Forest College's Greatest Football Player," *Chicago Record–Herald* (21 Oct 1913) (copy in Athletics file, LFCA).

23 *S* (12 Dec 1893).

24 "A Statistical History of Lake Forest Athletics," *F* (1916), 108. For Lake Forest football history, see also *S* (22 Oct 1895) and Richard Topp, *Lake Forest Football History, 1886–1991* (Niles, IL: typescripts, [1991] and rev. 1996). (LFCA.)

25 *S* (1891–93), *passim*.

26 *S* (23 Feb 1896).

27 *F* (1909), 18.

28 *F* (1909), 82.

29 *Onwentsia Club 1895–1995: A Centennial History* (Lake Forest: Onwentsia Club, 1995), 6.

30 *F* (1909), 84.

31 Rudolph, 146–49.

32 Cited by Rudolph, 148.

33 Helen Lefkowitz Horowitz, *Campus Life: Undergraduate Cultures from the End of the Eighteenth Century to the Present* (New York: Alfred A. Knopf, 1987), 45–47; Rudolph, 149; and Schmidt, 192–93.

34 Schmidt, 196.

35 *F* (1896), 27, 29.

36 Rudolph, 97–98; Schmidt, 193.

37 AMC and Rossiter scrapbook; *F* (1903), 4–5.

38 For general reference to the following faculty, see *GRLFC*; see also the series of articles detailing the history of departments in *S* (1935–36) by Harlan McClung and Faculty files, LFCA. For Kelsey see also *ANB* 12, 539–40; *DAB* V, 313.

39 *S* (11 Oct 1935).

40 Refer to p. 39.

41 *DAB* 1, 49–50.

42 Besides Baldwin, the following Lake Forest College professors are included in volumes of *Who Was Who in America*: Robert Almer Harper, John Haskell Hewitt, Francis Kelsey, William Albert Locy, James Needham, and Fernando Sanford.

43 In the *DAB* Lake Forest's faculty is represented by Baldwin, Kelsey, and Locy; in the *ANB*, Baldwin and Kelsey.

44 For general reference to these faculty, see *GRLFC*. For Malcolm MacNeill see the

historical article on the Mathematics Department, *S* (6 Mar 1936).

45 Refer to ch. 3, n. 43.

46 Refer to ch. 3, n. 32.

47 Refer to ch. 2, n. 34; see also Arpee, 197–98 *et passim*.

48 Arpee, 124.

49 "Early College Enrollment, 1876–1911: Totals, Gender, and Geographic Distribution," tables "compiled from annual catalogs and records, Registrar's Office files, LFCA" by Arthur Miller and Brian Galbreath '00, November 1998.

50 Schmidt, 274.

51 Northwestern: Harold F. Williams and Payson S. Wild, *Northwestern University: A History, 1850–1975* (Evanston, IL: Northwestern University, 1976), 64, 78; University of Illinois: *Northwestern*, 64*n*; Lawrence: Charles Breunig, *"A Great and Good Work": A History of Lawrence University 1847–1964* (Appleton, WI: Lawrence University Press, 1994), 69; Illinois College: Charles Henry Rammelkamp, *Illinois College: A Centennial History, 1829–1929* (New Haven, CT: Published for Illinois College by Yale University Press, 1928), 571.

52 "Early College Enrollment."

53 "The Misses Adams, Lake Forest" in "They Take Honors. Bright Young Students Who Lead Their Classes....," *CT* (2 Jul 1883), 33. (Reference provided by Bernice Gallagher, M/LS '85, director of Writing Programs and instructor in English.)

54 "Early College Enrollment."

55 Rudolph, 288–89, and *F* (1910), 16–22.

56 For example, seven out of ten graduating women in the Class of 1909 intended to become teachers. (*F* [1910], 37–44; *GRLFC*.)

57 *ANB* 10, 818–19; *DAB V*, 56–57; and *F* (1907), 23–24.

58 *GRLFC*, 26 and 50; *WWWA 2*, 322.

59 See p. 76. (Anna Davies file, LFCA.)

60 See p. 57. (*DAB* 3, 457–58.)

61 See p. 57. (*WWWA* 3, 848, and Thom file, LFCA.)

62 See p. 37. (See for Theodore, Class of 1884, *WWWA* 1, brother Paul's autobiography, *Changing the Skyline* [1938], and *F* [1907], 24–25; for Paul, Class of 1887, see *ANB* 20, 578–80; *DAB* 6, 592–93, and his autobiography.)

63 See p. 78. (*ANB* 9, 369–70; *DAB* 7, 294–95; and *Catalogue of the Everett D. Graff Collection of Western Americana*, compiled by Colton Storm [Chicago: Published for the Newberry Library by the University of Chicago Press, 1968].)

64 *ANB* 24, 169–70.

65 Linebarger file, Office of Alumni and Development.

66 *GRLFC*, 60, and Izumi file, Office of Alumni and Development.

67 *ANB* 11, 466–67; *DAB V*, 367.

## CHAPTER 5

1 Halsey, 625.

2 Halsey, 625; see also *S* (15 Oct 1902).

3 *S* (24 Mar 1896).

4 CHMP 1:9; for general references to him, see *ANB* 7, 928–29, and *DAB* 2, 185–87.

5 CHMP 1:11.

6 *S* (16 Nov 1897).

7 *S* (24 Sep 1899), 7–8; for Lois Barnes Durand see Frances Bailey Hewitt, *Genealogy of the Durand, Whalley, Barnes and Yale Families...* (Chicago, 1912) and Miller, *LFJ* (Aug 1998), 4.

8 For Frost, see ch. 2, n. 58; for Granger see *BDAA*, 247; *NCAB* E, 452 and XL, 45; and Miller, *LFJ* (Jun 1997). Granger (1867–1939), from Ohio and a Kenyon graduate, studied architecture at M.I.T., completing his studies in 1887, and worked for the firm of H. H. Richardson (d. 1886), when it was working on expansion plans for the library at the University of Vermont, designed by Richardson in the early 1880s. The floor plan of the Reid Library closely resembled that of the University of Vermont Library, a plan Richardson had employed similarly in the Crane Library (Quincy, Massachusetts), 1880–82. The inclusion of stacks in the Reid Library's east room rather than alcoves of library shelves appears derived from critiques of Richardson's plans by William F. Poole, librarian at Chicago's Newberry Library in the early 1890s. (Miller, *LFJ* [Jun 1997] and Kenneth A. Breisch, "William Frederick Poole and Modern Library Architecture," *Modern Architecture in America: Visions and Revisions*, ed. Richard Guy Wilson and Sidney K. Robinson [Ames, IA: Iowa State University Press, 1991], 53–72.) Frost and Granger worked together from 1898 to 1909; Granger practiced briefly in Philadelphia before returning to Chicago, chairing there the committee to judge the Tribune Tower competition in the early 1920s and designing several houses in Lake Forest. In 1913 he wrote his biography, still in print, of Charles Follen McKim and in 1933 he wrote a Century of Progress guidebook to Chicago and suburbs, *Chicago Welcomes You*, which remains a useful reference for the Beaux-Arts period architecture of the city.

9 *GRLFC* and *LFCBB* (A); *F* (1909), 18–19.

10 *F* (1909), 18–19.

11 *S* (9 Mar 1899). A women's residence hall after the early 1940s, it was demolished in the 1960s.

12 Still standing: Young Hall, North Hall, Patterson Lodge, Hotchkiss Hall, Durand Art Institute, Lily Reid Holt Chapel, Reid Hall, and Lois Hall. No longer standing: Bross House, Beidler House, Alice Home, and Academia.

13 *F* (1909), 18, and *230 North Mayflower Road* (Lake Forest: Lake Forest/Lake Bluff Historical Society, 1997).

14 The two consistent groups were these two, their houses pictured in *F* 1896, 1901, and 1907.

15 Arpee, 132.

16 Richard Davenport Harlan (1859–1931) served as president of Lake Forest, 1901–06. Born in Evansville, Indiana, he took his education mostly at Princeton: B.A. (valedictorian) 1881, M.A. 1884, D.D. (Seminary) 1885, with study at the University of Berlin in 1890–91. Prior to coming to Lake Forest the Rev. Harlan held two major pastorates: First Presbyterian Church of New York City (1886–90) and Third Presbyterian Church of Rochester, New York (1894–1901). After his resignation, during 1907–10 he was a special representative, George Washington University Movement in Washington, D.C. (*WWWA* 1, 520; *GRLFC*, 10; *After Twenty Years: The Record of The Class of 1881, Princeton* [1901], 116–19; *Bulletin of Class News: Class of 1881 Princeton University* [Apr 1908], 29–30; *After Fifty Years: The Record of the Class of 1881, Princeton*, 194–96; and Harlan file, LFCA. The Princeton sources were supplied by Professor of Politics Emeritus Charles A. Miller.)

17 *RB* (16 Nov 1892).

18 *ANB* 10: 95–98; *DAB* IX; 363–65.

19 *Plessy v. Ferguson*, 163 U.S. 210 (1896).

20 Harlan file, LFCA.

21 *F* (1909), 31–32, and *LFCC*s to 1915; *S* (14 Jan 1904).

22 *LFCC* (1903), 75.

23 *S* (19 May 1903).

24 Patton had just yielded in 1902 Princeton University's presidency to Woodrow Wilson; in 1901 at Harlan's inaugural he had been lobbied to do so by Lake Forest and Princeton trustees Cyrus McCormick and David B. Jones (*PWW* 12, esp. 313, n.1, and 371–402).

25 *LFCC* (1903), 73.

26 The farm implement trust's internal discord required Cyrus McCormick's full attention at the time he relinquished the chair of the Lake Forest Board and it was at that time Rockefeller became involved in the trust. (Ron Chernow, *Titan: The Life of John D. Rockefeller, Sr.* [New York: Random House, 1998], 148–49, and see also Jean Strouse, *Morgan: American Financier* [New York: Random House, 1999], 469–70.)

27 David Benton Jones (d. August 22, 1923) was a graduate of Princeton, Class of 1876 (and A.M. 1879), and a trustee there, 1901–08. He was a trustee of Lake Forest, 1896–1915: secretary, 1896–98; and president, 1903–04. He was chairman of the board, Mineral Point Zinc Company. A member of Onwentsia, he lived in Pembroke Lodge (Henry Ives Cobb, 1895) on the west side of Green Bay Road, south of Deerpath. He is the grandfather of Barbara

Wood-Prince '87, the great-grandfather of Edward H. Bennett III '71, and the great-great grandfather of Christopher E. Bennett '92. (Arpee, 324; *BC* [1917], 369, and [1926], 466; and *GRLFC*, 10.)

28 Dixon Wector, *The Saga of American Society: A Record of Social Aspiration, 1607–1937*, intro. L. Auchincloss (New York: Scribner's, 1970), 282–85.

29 Wector, 284.

30 But see n. 24 above.

31 Wector, 285.

32 Delavan Smith, Class of 1884, was a trustee, 1897–1905, and trustee president 1904–05. He was the son of William Henry Smith, a Lake Forest resident and builder of Lost Rock (Henry Ives Cobb, 1894) just south of David B. Jones's Pembroke Lodge and immediately north of the Onwentsia Club grounds. To Cyrus McCormick, Delavan Smith wrote on March 22, 1905, that the faculty "state that the institution educationally, with Dr. Harlan as President, is a hopeless problem, that it has drifted aimlessly for four years...." (Halsey, 525–26; *GRLFC*; and CHMP, Box I. )

33 Massachusetts-born lawyer and stockbroker Alfred L. Baker (b. 1859) was a trustee from 1904 to 1921; he was vice president 1904–05 and president 1905–08. His home was Little Orchard (Howard Shaw, 1898), 255 North Mayflower Road, near other lakefront homes of sisters of his spouse, Mary Corwith Baker. (*WWA* [1926–27], 204; Halsey, 493; *Prominent Citizens and Industries of Chicago* [Chicago: German Press Club of Chicago, 1901], 65; and *GRLFC*.)

34 Louis Swift (1861–1937), son of Gustavus F. Swift, was president of Swift & Co., founded by his father, from 1903 to 1931 and a trustee from 1898 to 1937. His Westleigh Farms was just south of the Onwentsia Club. "Mr. Swift was quite generous in assisting various causes in and about Lake Forest, but he never wished to have his name connected with his gifts. In 1917 he built on the College campus a heating plant for Ferry Hall, Lake Forest Academy and the College, and was a large contributor to the development of Farwell Field." ("Mr. Louis F. Swift, Trustee, Dies," *LFCAB* [Jun 1937]; see also *WWA* [1926–27], 1852, Halsey, 527, and *GRLFC*.)

35 Nathan Butler Swift, son of Louis and Ida (Butler) Swift, died in a polo accident in September 1903, aged twenty-two. An Academy student, he also belonged to Phi Pi Epsilon and was listed (and pictured) as a freshman member in the 1902 *Forester*. (*S* [10 Nov 1900]; *F* [1901], 46–47; *F* [1902], 34–35; and *S* [24 Sep 1903], 7. Not listed in *GRLFC*.)

36 Refer to ch. 4, n. 58.

37 See n. 32 above.

38 For Jack, Harlan file and see also ch. 3, n. 43. For possible defections, see the letter cited in n. 32 above.

39 Mark Alan Hewitt, *The Architect and the American Country House, 1890–1940* (New Haven, CT: Yale University Press, 1990), 279, and Lawrence Wodehouse, *American Architects from the First World War to the Present: A Guide to Information Resources* (Detroit: Gale Research, 1977), 158.

40 The 1906 plan is mounted in the main stairway of Donnelley Library, restored in the early 1990s through a grant from the Lake Forest Foundation for Historic Preservation. Originally it hung in the then–administration building, Durand Institute, as late as 1933, when it is pictured there (LFCA). For information on Manning and his work on campus and in Lake Forest beginning in 1897, see William Grundman, "Warren H. Manning," *American Landscape Architecture: Designers and Places*, ed. William T. Tischler (Washington, D.C.: Preservation Press, 1989), 56–59 and 224; Hewitt, *Architect*, 279, and the Manning file, LFCA.

41 *S* (1907), 175; *F* (1909), 19.

42 Harlan file, LFCA. "A Record of Gifts to Lake Forest University," [p.4] in folder 8, shows Mrs. Blackstone's gift of $81,500 and Andrew Carnegie's of $34,000.

43 *F* (1909), 19.

44 Alfred Granger's understanding of Beaux-Arts hierarchy of form is reflected in his discussion of Columbia University's campus in his 1913 biography of Columbia architect Charles Follen McKim. See n. 8 above and Alfred Granger, *Charles Follen McKim: A Study of His Life and Work* (New York: AMS Press, 1972), 39–40.

45 *ANB* 19, 740–41 and Virginia Greene, *The Architecture of Howard Van Doren Shaw* (Chicago: Chicago Review Press, 1999), 76.

46 *S* (22 Nov 1906) and Harlan files, LFCA.

47 Linn, listed in 1914 as a teacher at Trinity School in New York City, was killed in battle in World War I in France, October 8, 1918. (*GRLFC* [1914], 46; *GRLFC*, 41; *S* [1 Nov 1918]; and Linn file, LFCA.)

48 *S* (15 Jan 1895); for Addams, see *ANB* 1, 139–40, and *DAB* IX, 10–13.

49 Arpee, 137.

50 *S* (6 Dec 1906); *LFCC* (1907–08); and *GRLFC*, 11.

51 *S* (25 Apr 1907); *S* (9 May 1907); *S* (3 Oct 1907); *GRLFC*, 11; *AB* (Apr 1952); *WWA* (1926–27), 1442–43; and transcriptions of letters of recommendation for Nollen addressed to Prof. John M. Clapp, 1907, in a journal labeled "John M. Clapp, Lake Forest, Illinois," Nollen file, LFCA.

52 Schmidt, 182–83.

53 [Program for] *Bross Lectures for 1911*, November 13–19, 1911: Josiah Royce on "The Sources of Religious Insight" (Irma Bockhoff '15 scrapbook collection [24]) and *LFCC* (1911), 92. The lectures were published in 1912 under that title for the College by Scribner's in the Bross Foundation Series. For Royce, see *ANB* 19, 16–18, and *DAB* VIII, 205–211 (esp. 210

for the context of the Bross Lectures).

54 For general background see Bernard Duffey, *The Chicago Renaissance in American Letters: A Critical History* (East Lansing, MI: Michigan State College Press, 1954).

55 *Newspaper Days*, quoted in *The Literary History of the United States*, 4th ed., ed. Robert Spiller (New York: Macmillan, 1974), 1200.

56 McClurg was the mid-continental genteel trade publisher, with *The Dial* its house periodical. (Jack Cassius Morris, *The Publishing Activities of S. C. Griggs and Company, 1848–1896; Jansen McClurg and Company, 1872–1996; and A. C. McClurg and Company, 1886–1900; With a List of Publications*, [Ph.D. diss., University of Illinois, 1941].)

57 Stone & Kimball in the mid-1890s was a small-press alternative to larger-circulation genteel publications, and was more advanced in its content; the *Chap-book* was its house periodical. (Sidney Kramer, *A History of Stone & Kimball and Herbert S. Stone & Co.: With a Bibliography of Their Publications, 1893–1905* [Chicago: N. W. Forgue, 1940].)

58 Way & Williams, like Stone & Kimball, was a small experimental publisher, with the distinction of issuing under its name one of the books printed by William Morris's Kelmscott Press in Britain. (Joe Walker Kraus, *A History of Way & Williams: With a Bibliography of Their Publications, 1895–1898* [Philadelphia: George S. MacManus Co., 1984].)

59 Reprinted in the Wednesday Book Page, *CT* (12 May 1920) and in pamphlet form (LFCA).

60 James S. Ackerman, *The Villa: Form and Ideology of Country Houses* (Princeton, NJ: Princeton University Press, 1990), 261–62, and Leonard K. Eaton, *Two Chicago Architects and Their Clients: Frank Lloyd Wright and Howard Van Doren Shaw* (Cambridge, MA: M.I.T. Press, 1969).

61 Halsey, 491; Duffey, *passim*; Maurice Browne, *Too Late to Lament, An Autobiography* (London: 1955); Arpee, *passim*.; and Dawn K. Kimbrell, *The Aldis Compound* (Lake Forest: Lake Forest/Lake Bluff Historical Society, 1994), 8–9.

62 Kimbrell, *Aldis*, 8–9.

63 Browne, *Too Late*.

64 Arpee, 155.

65 Playbill, Aldis papers, LFCA.

66 Also note Mary Aldis papers, LFCA.

67 Greene, *Shaw*, 18 and 60–61; Alice Hayes and Susan Moon, *Ragdale: A History and Guide* (Berkeley, CA: Open Books; Lake Forest: The Ragdale Foundation, 1990), 67–73; Ragdale scrapbook, 78–90 (Shaw collections, LFCA).

68 *A Sawdust Doll* (Chicago: Stone & Kimball, 1894) and *By the Waters of Babylon* (Chicago: H. S. Stone & Co., 1901); see also Ch. 2 on Anna Farwell and

n. 24 there.

69 Ellen Williams, *Harriet Monroe and the Poetry Renaissance: the First Ten Years of Poetry, 1912–22* (Urbana, IL: University of Illinois Press, 1977), 15–16.

70 For the list of subscribers, see *Poetry: A Magazine of Verse* (Chicago: Ralph Fletcher Seymour Company, 1912–13), I, 29.

71 *F* (1909), 106.

72 *F* (1905), 64. Also see *F* (1907) where listed as playing the title role in *David Garrick*, the first play of the club, was Clarence Diver '05, much later to become president of the trustee Board (trustee, 1925–62; president, 1927–45). (Office of Development Services, Department of Development and Public Affairs, Lake Forest College, *Lake Forest College Trustees* [1994], 2 and 8.)

73 *F* (1909), 106; *F* (1917), 94; and *GRLFC*.

74 Clapp attended Amherst (B.A. 1890; M.A. 1893) with Calvin Durand's son, Harry, and trustee Charles Dyer Norton. (Halsey, 518.)

75 Clapp's transcriptions of letters about Nollen; see n. 51 above.

76 "Chairman, Drama League Amateur Department and Director Chicago Drama League." (*F* [1915], 13.)

77 Halsey, 518, and *F* (1910), 24.

78 Halsey, 518–19, and Miller, *LFJ* (Mar 1997); Granger, *McKim*; and *F* (1910), 24.

79 *GRLFC*, 31; *S* (8 May 1936); and *LFCAB* (Jan 1952).

80 *Moliere: A Biography* (New York: Duffield, 1906). Duffield was the successor to H. S. Stone & Co. (see n. 57 above).

81 *Goldoni: A Biography* (New York: Duffield, 1913).

82 His plays became popular enough during this time that in 1924 the University of Michigan presented and printed one of his plays, *A Curious Mishap*, adapted by Richard D. T. Hollister.

83 Appendices – including a "Catalogue of Goldoni's Works," 601–37; a "Biographical Chronology," 638–45; and a "Bibliography of Sources," 646–68 – were "prepared by" van Steenderen [595].

84 See sidebar.

85 See ch. 6, n. 57, second paragraph.

86 In connection with the campaign, the College was the first in Illinois to receive a grant from John D. Rockefeller's General Education Board in New York City, of $50,000, on condition that a total amount of $400,000 be pledged. (*F* [1914], 61.)

Wesleyan presents a useful analogy, as developed in David B. Potts, *Wesleyan University, 1831–1910* (New Haven, CT: Yale University Press, 1994), 228–32. Wesleyan alumnus and trustee Stephen Olin sought to reposition Wesleyan as a distinguished (male only) liberal arts college and

saw that he needed the recognition of two foundations, Carnegie's and Rockefeller's. The latter by 1914 gave about one hundred colleges and universities over $10 million in grants, with $100,000 going to Wesleyan in 1910. Carnegie recognition came soon after. By 1913 Lake Forest as well had both Carnegie and Rockefeller gifts to its credit.

Concerning Rockefeller, "[a]s the General Education Board bolstered college and university endowments, it applied the rules that Rockefeller had insisted upon, often futilely, with William Rainey Harper: that gifts should stimulate matching gifts; that local communities should help take up the financial burden of their schools; that universities should be founded in population centers with thriving economic bases; and that endowment income should not cover more than half the operating expenses" (Chernow, *Titan*, 486). Lake Forest's location thirty miles north of Chicago would have given it an edge with Rockefeller's foundation.

87 Faculty Circle folder, Buildings, LFCA.

88 According to architectural historian Richard Longstreth, "Market Square was perhaps the first business district laid out specifically to accommodate motor vehicles." (Richard Longstreth, *City Center to Regional Mall: Architecture, the Automobile, and Retailing in Los Angeles, 1920–1950* [Cambridge, MA: M.I.T. Press, 1997], 150–52 and 404–5*n*.) See also Susan Dart, *Market Square* (Lake Forest, IL: Lake Forest/Lake Bluff Historical Society, [1984]); Ebner, 203–9 and 308–9*n*; and Laurie Grano, "Hunt Uncovers Artifacts of Architecture: Van Doren Shaw Design a Prototype," *CT* (23 Feb 1999), II, 1ff.

89 A list of "Programs" printed after November 1917 in the Lake Forest Garden Club archives, Box I (LFCA), lists the first club program as August 27, 1912.

90 *GRLFC*, 22, and Root folder, local landscape architects file, LFCA; Landscape box, Nollen and Moore presidents' papers, LFCA.

91 School of Music catalog, 1917–18.

92 "Athletics have now given place to military drill.... Twelve of the men have already taken and passed the preliminary examinations for entry to the Officer's Training Camp...." ("Military Drill," *S* [27 Apr 1917], 194–95.) See also "The Students' Army Training Corps at Lake Forest," *S* (1 Nov 1918), 1; "Professor van Steenderen Teaching French at Ft. Sheridan," *S* (19 Jun 1917), 253; and Arpee, 191–96. The *Stentor* included frequent reports from France – for example: "Lake Forest at the Front: L. G. Smith Chased by Aeroplanes," *S* (9 Nov 1917), 1, and "Men (and Women) in National Service," *S* (12 Dec 1917), 19–20.

**CHAPTER 6**

1 James S. Olson, *Historical Dictionary of the 1920s. From World War I to the New Deal, 1919–1933* (New York: Greenwood Press, 1988), 93.

2 To appreciate how prevalent this fear was, one needs note only that *The Reader's Guide to Periodical Literature* (1919–1921) lists three pages (five columns) of articles on "Bolshevism" (162–64) and two pages (more than two columns) on "Radicals and Radicalism" (1352–53). (See also Stanley Coben, "A Study in Nativism: the American Red Scare of 1919–1920," *Twentieth Century America: Recent Interpretations*, ed. Barton J. Bernstein and Allen J. Matusow [New York: Harcourt Brace, 1969], 88–109). That the economic and social elite, including Lake Forest's first families, specifically saw this as an acute concern is strongly suggested by the editorial coverage in 1919 in a New York publication *The Spur*, which, modeled on England's *Country Life*, would well have been in North Shore hands since the April 1, 1919, issue had had a "Chicago Supplement," heralding socially prominent Midwesterners of the area. A week before Wright's chapel talk with its criticism of big business and reference to Bolshevism (see nn. 3 and 5 below), the April 15, 1919, issue of *The Spur* (XXXII, no. 8) had carried an editorial "The Enemy Within Our Gates: What Does the Government Propose to Do with Dangerous Aliens and Others?" noting that "Many men and women who ought to know better are playing with the fire of Bolshevism" (24). And as early as July 1, 1918, an editorial had opposed antibusiness governmental bias: "The Problem of Taxing Luxuries: Views of the business man versus those of the professor" (18). While the reference was to an academic witness testifying in Congress, it would no doubt have been more widely applied by anti-intellectual, conservative readers.

3 Henry Wilkes Wright (b. 1878) was educated at Cornell University (Ph.B. 1899, Ph.D. 1904), where he was an instructor until coming to Lake Forest in 1907 as professor of Philosophy, the same year Nollen became president. After 1920 he was professor of Philosophy at the University of Manitoba in Winnipeg. (*GRLFC*, 11, 21; *WWA* [1926–27], 3090; and *WWWA* 6, 449.)

4 *S* (30 Jan 1918), 4–6.

5 *President Wright has returned from Iowa City where he has been attending a meeting of the Western Philosophical Association. On last Tuesday morning he gave a brief account of the meeting in chapel. Two things especially impressed Dr. Wright. One was the fact that the interest of the Association was concentrated particularly on the relations of the individual to the state. The other was that the attitude of the last year has decidedly changed. A year ago the college professors in the Association were unanimous in emphasizing the good points of our government. Now they are criticizing these institutions where it is felt such criticism is needed. "This does not mean," said Dr. Wright, "that the majority of college professors are Bolshevists, but it does mean*

*that they felt that the criticism of big business which was begun before the war should continue.*" Another interesting fact noted by Dr. Wright was the number of college professors there present who are connected with great industrial and governmental enterprises. ( *S* [25 Apr 1919], 1.)

6   *It [democracy] is the ideal of a society which provides for the free personal development of all its members. But it is also a method. Material necessities and comforts it proposes to produce and distribute through the co-operative industry of its citizens; no privileged class is to be permitted to live in idleness, supported by the labor of the remainder. For no class is to be exempted from toil and given leisure and enjoyment; hence, if spiritual values are to be realized, they must be found in the performance of the common task* (274–75).

   *One who labors for the spiritual advancement of humanity cannot allow his own taste and talents, in science or in art, to interfere with his social responsibility; nay, more he must be prepared to suffer misunderstanding and even opprobrium on account of his devotion to social progress and reform* (277). *Here, then, is the new need created by democracy, which religion can alone fulfill – the need of faith in the superior reality of the social community, the community of persons united through mutual understanding, service, and sympathy, over that of natural individuality, with its narrow interests and exclusive ambitions* (279). (Henry Wilkes Wright, *Faith Justified by Progress. Lectures Delivered Before Lake Forest College on the Foundation of the Late William Bross* [New York: Charles Scribner's Sons, 1916].)

7   According to the title page of the ninety-seven-page follow-up analysis by Swift & Company, noted below, the original FTC report was issued on November 25, 1918, two weeks after the armistice. The charge to the FTC had been issued February 7, 1917, according to the transmittal letter to President Wilson by William Colver, FTC chair, on July 3, 1918. The "Foreward" to the Swift rebuttal makes clear the company's sense of injury: "The investigation of the packing industry by the Federal Trade Commission was one-sided. The charge that the packers have a monopoly is not founded upon fact. In its report, the Federal Trade Commission has presented only such information as could be used, by means of wrongful interpretation and insinuation, to make out a case against the packers. The Trade Commission had free access to Swift & Company's files, and in publishing letters and telegrams taken therefrom, the Commission has actually failed to reproduce in its report letters and telegrams – and even parts of telegrams – which controvert some of the very contentions that it tries to establish." (Federal Trade Commission. *Report on the Meat Packing Industry, Food Investigation.* [Washington: Governmental Printing Office, 1919], 3 vols.; *Swift & Company's*

*Analysis and Criticism of Part II of the Report of the Federal Trade Commission on the Meat Packing Industry of November 25, 1918, Issued April 5, 1919* [n.p.]). Louis Swift, president of the company 1903–31, served on the College Board of Trustees and on both its finance and executive committees at the time. (*WWWA* 1, 1211; *LFCC* [1918–19], 14–15.)

8   The Supreme Court ruling of March 11, 1912, on the A. B. Dick case, that the company stipulation to customers of its mimeograph that they must use only company supplies (tied sales) was within its right under federal statute and that only Congress could amend the right, sparked considerable opposition: "A Mischievous Decision," *Independent* 72 [Jan–Jun 1912], 633–34; "Enforcing Monopoly by Law," *Outlook* (23 Mar 1912), 599–600; "A Startling Patent Decision," *The Literary Digest* 44, 12 (21 Mar 1912), 373–74; *The American Economic Review* 2 (1912), 720–22; "The Rotary Mimeograph Case," *Scientific American* (23 Mar 1912), 202. In fact *The Reader's Guide to Periodical Literature* from 1910–14 lists eight articles under "Restraint of Trade," twelve under "Monopolies," and twelve under the "Mimeograph Case" – with the concentrated coverage of the A. B. Dick issue. This further intensified when on October 5, 1912, presidential candidate Woodrow Wilson, spurred on by Supreme Court Associate Justice Louis Brandeis (*PWW*, 25, 289–94), took up the crusade against trusts, a crusade that would lead after Wilson's victory to the October 15, 1914, Clayton Anti-Trust Act. Though the Clayton Act addressed the concerns raised by the A. B. Dick case only in Section 3 (*DAH*, II, 279–81), the catalyst for bringing to a head two decades of post–Sherman Act "experience" was the "startling" and "mischievous" A. B. Dick decision. (For a fuller history on the A. B. Dick episode see a paper by Andrew H. Miller '98, "Monopoly and the A. B. Dick Company," 1998, in the file on trustee A. B. Dick, LFCA).

9   Olson, "Depression of 1920–1921," *Historical Dictionary of the 1920s*, 93–94.

10  With automobiles, rural residents were traveling farther to larger towns and patronizing bigger stores with their own buying organizations (such as Sears, Roebuck) that did not rely on the Chicago wholesale houses as had the small, country-town general stores. (Melvin T. Copeland, "The Present State of Wholesale Trade," *Harvard Business Review* 6, no. 3 [Apr 1928], 258.)

11  Schmidt, 247–53.

12  *ANB* 17, 137–38; *DAB* 4, 645–46; and Joseph Medill Patterson, *Confessions of a Drone: Marshall Field's Will and the Socialist Machine* (Chicago: C. H. Kerr), also published in *The Independent* (Aug 30, 1906), 493–95.

13  *ANB* 17, 667–69, and *DAB* 4, 671–74. (For Poole's involvement with Sinclair, see Ernest Poole, *The Bridge. My Own Story*

[New York: The Macmillan Company, 1940], 95–96.)

14  Maurice Browne, quoting from The Little Theatre's announcement for its sixth and last season: "After meeting the costs of those two productions [*Candide* and *Medea*] we had no money to pay Shaw's royalties or our storage bill, let alone Murray and the painter; we never saw the *Trojan Women* shield and those other treasures again. We had only just enough left to make pro-rate repayments to those comparatively few endowment fund subscribers who had honoured their pledges. Sixty per cent of them, including members of the committee itself, had failed to keep their written promise." In ruminating on this demise of one of the Chicago Literary Renaissance's most notable achievements, Browne echoes sentiments of Wright's (n. 6): "Life, always insecure, is today perilous; right conduct, always difficult, is today almost impossible; independent thinking, the basis of right conduct, never generally practiced, is today generally condemned; and those values which mankind has slowly and painfully built for itself, the eternal verities as they are sometimes called, today are themselves shaken. In such a time service is not lightly to be given, not to a light cause, not for profit." (Maurice Browne, *Too Late To Lament. An Autobiography.* [London: Victor Gollancz, 1955], 211.)

15  Two outspoken literary figures who both had left the city by 1920 were Margaret Anderson and Sherwood Anderson. Margaret Anderson, publisher of Chicago's *Little Review* in the teens, printed the first appearance of James Joyce's *Ulysses* (censored by the Post Office) and writings by anarchist Emma Goldman. (Margaret Anderson, *My Thirty Years' War: An Autobiography* [New York: Covici, Friede, 1930], 35–102; for withdrawal of patronage see p. 101.)

   Sherwood Anderson had been encouraged by "the literary and artistic excitement of the ... Chicago Renaissance" to continue writing. His first two novels, of 1916 and 1917, were *Windy McPherson's Son*, "the autobiographical story of a man's rise and rejection of business," and *Marching Men,* a "labor novel" – both in the same social justice vein as Wright's Bross volume, also of 1916. (*ANB* 1, 483–85, and *DAB* 4:12–15.)

16  *CT* (6 Apr 1918); Rose had died in California early in 1918 and Chatfield-Taylor's permanent departure from Lake Forest for his Santa Barbara home later that year is evidenced by his donation to the College library of his collection of rare sixteenth-century to eighteenth-century volumes and literary books. (Library accession records, October 30, 1918, to November 7, 1918, LFCA.)

17  *It was an awful world three years ago with its strife and its misery. But somehow it had something fine about it that we miss in these sordid days. Then a challenge of a great cause rang out, and nations and classes forgot their differences, their*

*legal rights and their material advantage. They were moved with a world vision, and they gave without stint and without measure. Those were terrible days, but glorious days, days when the world lived in the spirit of the second mile. But with peace we settled down to the 'economic basis of society,' nations and men jockeying for their own advantage, the whole world doing no more than it has to do, and fumbling for some adjustment to make this permanently possible.*

*That is what is wrong with these days.*

*The real solution must be more inclusive, less artificial. It can be nothing less than creating a new heart in humanity – the cultivating in men and women the spirit of the second mile – the sending of an ever-increasing host of young people like you out into life motivated by ideals rather than by compulsion. This is not a new heart; it is an old heart, as old as the heart of Him who said: "Whosoever shall compel thee to go one mile, go with him two."* (15)

If this sounds rather innocuous, there is an earlier illustrative example (actually not so critical in context) that could well have seemed inflammatory:

*We find men of this type [some businessmen] hiring lawyers to measure off their mile for them, and stake off their legal boundaries. "Our proposition is strictly legal," the promoter tells us; but just the same, widows lose their life insurance money on their investments. "Our shop conditions meet the requirements in every particular," the mill owner asserts. Yes; but women still get consumption in your factory and little children lose their fingers in your machinery.*

*Not only do they measure off their mile according to state law, but by economic laws. "I see by the paper that you cut a fine melon the other day, Mr. Capitalist."*

*"Yes," he chuckles and rubs his hands. "Good year! Good management!"*

*"But why didn't you share that dividend with your employees in the form of wages or with the public in the form of reduced prices?"*

*"Don't you know anything about economics?" he demands in amazement. "The law of supply and demand regulates wages and prices."* (11)

(John C. McCoy, "Senior Chapel Address," *Baccalaureate Sermon by Henry Wilkes Wright, Ph.D., Acting President June 6, 1920, and Senior Chapel Address by John C. McCoy, '20 June 4, 1920* [Lake Forest College, 1920], 9–15; Wright folder, Presidents' Speeches, etc., file, LFCA.)

18  One might note a somewhat similar situation, referred to by Schmidt (150) and Chernow, *Titan* (327), in which Edward W. Bemis of the University of Chicago (after earlier having received a written warning, which he disregarded, for a speech made attacking the railroad companies during the Pullman strike) was summarily dismissed in 1895 over criticism of a Rockefeller-owned gas company. In the Bemis affair, President Harper in both instances acted without even waiting to hear from his patron; Wright, as acting president, had no administrative buffer between himself and the trustees.

19  Throughout the wartime and postwar years of 1918 and 1919 discussions were underway at the Board level to take action to resolve the institution's chronic financial distress. Many consultants were sought out, including Rockefeller's General Education Board, Coulter, and S. P. Capen (for the last two, see nn. 20 and 28 below). Leading the call for definite action was Cyrus McCormick, who in the mid-1890s had spearheaded proposals for changes. (TM [21 Feb 1918], [13 Nov 1918], [12 Dec 1918], [7 Jan 1919], [30 Jan 1919], and [9 Jun 1919].) Also the severity of the deficit problem was underscored by the two-year rental of the President's House (now Patterson Lodge) to a local resident, starting March 1919. (TM [20 Mar 1919].)

20  Typed report identified as from Coulter and dated 1919, President Herbert Moore papers (received 1988), folder 4, LFCA.

21  Paul Elmer More, "Religion and Social Discontent," *Christianity and Problems of To-day, Lectures Delivered Before Lake Forest College on the Foundation of the Late William Bross* (New York: Charles Scribner's Sons, 1922), 106.

22  The proposal for conversion to a women's college, along with the possibility of merging with Dubuque College (with the president of that institution a Board visitor that day), was discussed at the first Trustee meeting in early January 1919. The Dubuque notion was rejected at a meeting later that month. (TM [7 Jan 1919] and [30 Jan 1919].)

23  TM (7 Jun 1919).

24  *S* (1 May 1920), 1.

25  Board chairs from 1921 to 1945 were John H. S. Lee, Class of 1895 (1921–23); Frank Fitt '12 (1923–27); and Clarence Diver '05 (1927–45). (Office of Development Services, Department of Development and Public Affairs, Lake Forest College, *Lake Forest College Trustees* [1994], 8, and *GRLFC*, 163.)

26  Henry Wilkes Wright, "American College Under Fire," *F* (1911), 17–18.

27  Editors' introductory note to, and text of, Edward E. Purinton, "Business as the Savior of the Community," *Annals of America*, ed. Mortimer J. Adler *et al.* (Chicago: Encyclopedia Britannica, 1976), XIV, 298.

28  Samuel Ford Capen (1878–1956) was perhaps the foremost authority on higher education administration and strategic planning in 1919–20. A Clark University German professor, 1902–14 (trained at the University of Pennsylvania [Ph.D.] and Leipzig), from 1914 to 1919 he was the higher education specialist for the U.S. Bureau of Education in Washington, D.C. "Because his [U.S. Office of Education] work entailed preparing annual reports on educational movements and conditions throughout the country, … Capen quickly gained a reputation as a systematic observer and advisor." Capen recommended sweeping changes and innovative approaches. Between 1915 and 1919 he consulted with eight state higher education authorities, though it's not mentioned how many small private institutions he advised. From 1919 to 1922 he was the director of the American Council on Education and he went on to be chancellor at the University of Buffalo (later SUNY-Buffalo) from 1922 to 1950. (*ANB* 4, 353–54.)

29  S. P. Capen, two-page typed letter (on American Council of Education letterhead) to the Board of Trustees, Lake Forest University, June 1, 1920. (Herbert Moore papers, LFCA.)

30  Herbert McComb Moore, Class of 1896, was acting president 1920–21 and president 1921–42. Born in Macomb, Illinois, in 1876, he died in 1942, a few months after retiring, in Lake Forest. (*GRLFC*, 11; *LFCAB* [Apr, Jul 1942]; *CT* [8 May 1942], *WWA* [1926–27], 1383; and *WWWA* 2, 380.)

31  The Cripple Creek gold mining country of central Colorado (towns of Cripple Creek [seat of Teller County], Victor, Altman, Elkton, Goldfield, etc.) was a flashpoint of labor-management conflict after an 1894 strike. In 1902–03 problems heated up, with a strike again by September of 1903 and troops being called in and establishing a notorious prison camp at Camp Goldfield, a federal post. (Emma F. Langdon, *The Cripple Creek Strike, A History of Industrial Wars in Colorado, 1903–04, Being a Complete and Concise History of the Efforts of Organized Capital to Crush Unionism* (Denver: Great Western Publishing, 1904–05), 15–24, 152, 173 *et passim*.)

32  Rudolph, 170.

33  Moore, letter of acceptance, February 1, 1921. (Moore papers, Box 1, folder 1, LFCA.)

34  James G. K. McClure, *Historical Address Delivered at the Inauguration of Herbert McComb Moore as President of Lake Forest University, November 4, 1921* (Lake Forest: Lake Forest University, 1921), 8pp.

35  Received with Moore administration documents given by president Moore's son, Charles, 1988. (LFCA.)

36  See p. 117.

37  Majors of graduates were mostly in liberal arts disciplines in the 1920s, but from 1930s through the 1950s there were increasing numbers in applied areas, 20% to 25% in the 1930s and 1940s: business administration (1920s, 8; 1930s, 224; 1940s, 367; and 1950s, 1,079), speech (1920s, 3; 1930s, 82; 1940s, 148; and 1950s, 346), and education (1920s, 1; 1930s, 79; 1940s, 64; and 1950s, 2). Aviation-related subjects were taught within the Physics Department. ("Majors

Distribution, 1900–1989; Tables Compiled from Registrar's Office Records, Commencement Programs, and Yearbooks" by Arthur Miller and Brian Galbreath '00 [Spr 1999], Enrollment Data File, LFCA, and "Digest of Administrative and Academic Material Gathered from Lake Forest University/College Catalogs, 1910–1940," compiled by Paul Wierzbicki '00 [Sum 1998], College History Data File, 1998, LFCA.)

38  Wright, "American College Under Fire."

39  For general background, see Schmidt, ch. 10, and Rudolph, chs. 21 and 22.

40  Philosopher and educator John Dewey (1859–1952), with early ties to the University of Chicago and later to Columbia University, sought a middle ground between curriculum-centered and child-centered educational theories, integrating "subject ideas" with "the test of concrete experience." (*ANB* 6, 514–18.)

41  Irving Babbitt (1865–1933) promoted a "new humanism" that favored classical traditions over romanticism. He sought an ideal new aristocracy as a counterweight to unenlightened, utilitarian plutocracy. (*ANB* 1, 804–6; *DAB* 1, 36–37.)

42  Alexander Meiklejohn (1872–1964) was president of Amherst from 1912 to 1923, deemphasizing athletics and introducing, with Robert Frost, a high-profile writer-in-residence program. At Wisconsin, in 1928, he created a two-year experimental college that put into practice some of the progressive theories of education. (*ANB* 15, 260–61; *DAB* 7, 523–24.)

43  Nicholas Murray Butler (1862–1947), long-time president of Columbia University, found his ideal in the liberal arts, believing "that overspecialization and overly technical knowledge was rooted in, and perpetuated by, materialism and greed." (*ANB* 4, 101–3; *DAB* 4, 133–38.)

44  Robert Maynard Hutchins (1899–1977) in 1929 became the reform president of the University of Chicago, looking for a core liberal arts curriculum in "the great books" and countering adolescent frivolity of the flapper era by lowering the college-entrance age of freshmen. (*ANB* 11, 580–93; *DAB* 10, 363–66.)

45  Virginia Gildersleeve (1877–1965) led Columbia University's affiliated Barnard College for women (1910–47), pioneering liberal education for women at a women's college within a university framework.

46  Frank Aydelotte (1880–1956) was an accomplished literary scholar and author who had studied at Oxford and taught English at Indiana University and M.I.T. before assuming the presidency of Swarthmore, where he established a model honors program (reflecting Oxford's attention to "more talented and ambitious students"). (*DAB* 6, 29–30; *ANB* 1, 788–89.)

47  As dean at Grinnell, Nollen followed the model of president John Main, 1906–31, who had been Grinnell's first dean (1903–06) before becoming president. Of Main's administration, Nollen (in his

*Grinnell College* [Iowa City, IA: State Historical Society of Iowa, 1953], 110) observed that "he [Main] raised the College to a new height of importance and influence." Perhaps especially in his later years Main, according to Nollen, was aloof, autocratic, and unsympathetic to criticism (120), but Nollen, by his own description, was a complementary sort, perhaps with just the pragmatic type of approach for the difficult 1930s, when he took over the presidency (1931–40) at age 62. Through the interwar period Nollen was a key architect of Grinnell's strong position among twentieth-century liberal arts colleges. (See also *WWWA* 3, 643.)

48  See n. 37 above.

49  Helen Lefkowitz Horowitz, *Campus Life: Undergraduate Cultures From the End of the Eighteenth Century to the Present* (New York: Alfred A. Knopf, 1987), 118–19, 130–31.

50  For Lake Forest College: "Percentage of Students in Fraternities and Sororities," table and statistics, 1900–1960s, compiled from yearbooks by Scott Richardson, '00. (Student Organizations file, LFCA.)

51  "Enrolment [*sic*] of Lake Forest College, 1900–01 to 1946–47," Otto Mayer, *Fund Raising Survey of Lake Forest College* (Church Progress Institute, Inc., April 1947), 20.

52  Interviews with Dorothy ('34) and Elmer ('39) Maiman, July 22, 1997. There is also a very telling account by Frank L. Spreyer '35 of his casual matriculation at the college in the Depression year of 1931: "When I graduated [from Crystal Lake High School] in 1931, the Depression was beginning to blossom. I had no plans for work. One of my classmates, Lloyd Roberts who I believe is still living in Hendersonville NC, received a scholarship at Lake Forest and asked me what I was going to do, and I told him I had no immediate plans. He said 'Why don't you come over to the college?' I said that I didn't have enough money to go, and he replied 'Well, come on over anyhow.' … So I said 'Why don't I see if I can get a scholarship too?' Lloyd received a half-tuition scholarship, so I applied for a scholarship and lo and behold I was granted a half tuition scholarship. " (Transcript, interview with Frank Spreyer '35 by Michael E. Dau '58, 23 May 1996.)

53  See n. 52 above; also interviews with Joseph B. Ogrin '41, February 2, 1995, and Ruth Jackson (spouse of the late Lee W. Jackson '24), November 11, 1995. Shirley MacDonald Paddock has noted the estate-era practice of owners sending the sons of their service employees to Lake Forest College, even when the patron had no close tie to the College, as with the case of Edward Larrabee Baker of 1110 North Sheridan Road – where Mrs. Paddock grew up in the 1930s and 1940s.

54  See n. 50 above.

55  Iron Key (pictured in *Forester* yearbooks from 1922 to 1968) was an honorary fraternity whose members were chosen at the

close of their sophomore year, "but not announced until the end of their Junior year." Membership was determined "*by scholarship and activities*" of the student during his early years at Lake Forest. The purpose was to promote "*better college spirit*" and to foster cooperation and fellowship among campus fraternal organizations. ("Organizations in 1920s," *Organizations, 1880–1990s*, compiled by Natsuko Hamai '98 and Scott Richardson '00, Sum 1998. Student Organizations file, LFCA.)

56  Faculty apartments in academic and dormitory buildings continued until the 1960s when faculty houses were built on South Campus. See ch. 8.

57  While the previous aspirations and achievements of the College are well noted (especially p. 94) and may, in part, be inferred from the stature of the earlier faculty, the evidence for a decline in academic rigor is largely anecdotal, but tellingly so. Oral accounts of professors Richard Hantke, Rosemary Hale, and Arthur Voss characterize an institution intellectually undemanding, where the dean could approach a faculty member to change a grade because the student was "so nice." These faculty were unanimously critical of the administration and the general academic tone. A review of the faculty also suggests much less professional distinction than was true in prior decades.

Significantly, the thick presidents' office file on "Phi Beta Kappa, 1912–1948" (LFCA) shows the loss of interest in the College's applications for membership by that organization after early 1919, when Wright was in touch with Phi Beta Kappa leaders, such as Barnard's Virginia Gildersleeve (February 21 letter from her office to Wright; also see n. 45 above). Although passed up in 1916, Lake Forest had been encouraged to apply again in three years, when more growth would justify admission (letter of 16 September 1916 to Nollen from Phi Beta Kappa Secretary Oscar W. Voorhees), but by that time the College was in the disruption of the Wright affair. After that, consistently over the course of the 1920s to the 1940s, Phi Beta Kappa rebuffed Lake Forest overtures. In 1937 the secretary of the organization visited Lake Forest on Sunday, May 16, apparently to an indifferently small audience of students and faculty, and made reference to a visit earlier, in 1920, that resulted in a similar negative impression, with President Moore left hoping Secretary William Shimer could "come again to see us." (Letter of 18 May 1937.) (By 1937 Grinnell, Beloit, Lawrence, and Carleton all had chapters.)

58  J. Howard Wood '22 (1901–88) was publisher of the *Chicago Tribune* from 1960 to 1968, CEO of the Tribune Co. from 1960 to 1971, and a trustee of the Robert R. McCormick Charitable Trust from 1955 to 1976. (*WWWA* 9, 386.)

59  Arnold W. Carlson '28 (born in Lake Forest in 1906) after graduation was on the staff of local trustee Lawrence Scudder's public

accounting firm 1928–30 and received his M.B.A. from Harvard in 1932. From 1936 he was associated with Time, Inc., rising to a senior post. (*WWCI* [1964–65], 195.)

60   Mary Longbrake '35, having achieved the rank of Lt. Commander of the Navy WAVES in World War II, after 1946 rose from secretary to vice president of the Northern Trust Company. In addition, she has had an outstanding career as a volunteer for the Lyric Opera, the Chicago Symphony, and Lake Forest College. (*WWAW* [1975–76], 535.)

61   See p. 110. (*CB* [1954], 95–97; *WWA* [1998], 394.)

62   See p. 114. (*International Dictionary of Films and Filmmakers*, III, *Actors and Actresses*, 3d ed., ed. Amy L. Unterburger [Detroit, MI: St. James Press, 1997], 1280–81; *CB* [1963], 462–65; and *WWA* [1998], 4617.)

63   Roscoe Harris (1896–1949) was head of the Physics Department from 1925 to 1946; subsequently he was head of Physics at the University of Illinois' Chicago campus. ("Authority in Field of Television found in Professor Harris," *S* [17 Jan 1936], 8; Harris file, LFCA; see also sidebar on *Lake Forest inventors*, p. 186.)

64   Jones's 1938 and 1940 Lake Forest College football teams were undefeated. From 1933 to 1948 his football record included "52 wins, 30 losses and 10 ties." (Robert D. Suess, "Jones Retirement" [press release], Department of Publicity, Lake Forest College, April 24, 1949, Ralph Jones file, Athletic Department historical collection; Jay Pridmore, *Many Hearts and Many Hands: The History of Ferry Hall and Lake Forest Academy* [Lake Forest Academy, 1994], 111, 113–14; article on George Halas, *ANB* 9, 805; and Jones files, LFCA.)

65   This was a national phenomenon, but as late as 1941 the top of the full-professor salary scale, as reported in a Phi Beta Kappa chapter application, was $4,000. (Phi Beta Kappa file, LFCA; Schmidt, 201.)

66   Arpee, 215.

67   For the Armour family see *BDABL*, 22–24; "Salvaging the Armour Fortune," *Fortune* (April 1931), 49–57, 158; and Arpee, *passim*.

68   For Louis F. Swift see ch. 4, n. 34. For the family, see *BDABL*, 1415–19.

69   The children of John G. Shedd, chairman of the board of Marshall Field & Company, were Laura Abbie (Mrs. Charles Schweppe) and Helen May (Mrs. Kersey Coates Reed). (*WWA* [1926–27], 1724–25.)

70   Thomas E. Donnelley, son of the founder of the printing firm and an 1889 graduate of Yale, in 1911 was president of the family concern when he and his family moved to Lake Forest, residing at Clinola on Green Bay Road, designed by Howard Shaw, Yale, Class of 1890. (Halsey, 500; *WWC* [1931], 264; and Virginia A. Greene, *The*

*Architecture of Howard Van Doren Shaw* [Chicago, IL: Chicago Review Press, 1998], 79–80.)

71   The estate of electricity and light rail baron Samuel Insull was just west of the Des Plaines River at the western extent of the Onwentsia Hunt; his town home was 1100 North Lake Shore. (*ANB* 11, 670–73; *WWA* [1926–27], 1033; and *BDABL*, 658–62.)

72   Second-generation wholesale iron and steel merchant Edward L. Ryerson listed his main residence as Havenwood in Lake Forest, designed by Howard Shaw. (*WWA* [1926–27], 1667–68.)

73   Goldman, Sachs investment banking partner Alfred E. Hamill (1883–1952) was president of the Lake Forest Library from its completion in 1931 until his death; 6,500 of the books from his own famous library, designed by David Adler for his home The Centaurs at Mayflower and Illinois roads, were given to the College library by Mrs. Hamill in 1953. (*WWWA* 3, 362.)

74   Innovative advertising entrepreneur Albert Lasker (1880–1952) built his David Adler-designed Old Mill Farm in west Lake Forest in the 1920s. (*ANB* 13, 221–22; *BDABL*, 760–62; see also John Gunther, *Taken at the Flood: The Story of Alfred D. Lasker* [Harper & Brothers, 1960].)

75   Montgomery Ward's chief executive, Robert J. Thorne (1875–1955), had his estate immediately south of Middle Campus on Sheridan Road. (*WWWA* 3, 853.)

76   *The History of Onwentsia, 1895–1945*, 122, and Arpee, 213; Arpee, 204–5.

77   Persons listing in *Who's Who in America* their main place of residence as Lake Forest included, for example, Alfred L. Baker, Clifford Barnes, Edward L. Ryerson, and Louis Swift.

78   Shaw died in 1926 but was ill with pernicious anemia much of the 1920s. (Greene, *Shaw*, 73–76, and Edwin Roseman interview, Dart series, Shaw collections, LFCA.)

79   *ANB* 1, 157–58.

80   *ANB* 13, 687–88.

81   Yale-educated (Class of 1900) architect Edwin Hill Clark (April 11, 1878–January 20, 1967) was the Beaux-Arts designer of the Lake Forest Library (1931) and several Lake Forest estate homes. His drawings and papers recently were donated by his grandson to the Chicago Historical Society. (*WWC* [1931], 180; Clark file, thanks to Clark researcher Charles W. Askins, LFCA.)

82   Beaux-Arts-trained architect Walter Stephen Frazier (October 29, 1895–April 20, 1976) designed a number of significant Lake Forest estate houses in the 1920s and 1930s. (Barbara Buchbinder-Green, Application to the National Register of Historic Places for the Green Bay Road Historic District [1995], 42.)

83   Robert E. Grese, *Jens Jensen: Maker of*

*Natural Parks and Gardens* (Baltimore, MD: The Johns Hopkins University Press, 1992).

84   William Grundman, "Warren H. Manning," *American Landscape Architecture: Designers and Places*, ed. William Tischler (Washington, D.C.: Preservation Press, 1989), 56–59, 224; Manning file, LFCA.

85   *Woman's Who's Who of America 1914–15*, ed. John William Leonard (New York: American Commonwealth Company, 1914), 598; Arthur Miller, "Rose Standish Nichols (1872–1960), Garden Architect: Her Work in and Association with Lake Forest, Illinois," unpublished essay, 1997, in LFCA; and Nichols file, LFCA.

86   Judith Tankard, *The Gardens of Ellen Biddle Shipman* (Sagaponack, NY: Sagapress, 1996).

87   Arleyn A. Levee, "John Charles Olmsted" and Shary Page Berg, "Frederick Law Olmsted, Jr.," *American Landscape Architecture*, 48–52, 60–66, and 224–25.

88   Arpee, 208–9.

89   Ebner, 195–96 and 307, n. 4.

90   Frederick Mercer Van Sickle '83, "A Special Place: Lake Forest and the Great Depression, 1929–40," *Illinois Historical Journal* (Sum 1986), 213–26. See also Van Sickle's 1983 senior thesis of the same title and the back-up files of oral history interviews, LFCA.

91   [Martha Briggs], "Chronology," in Pridmore, *Many Hearts*, 238; see also Pridmore, *Many Hearts*, 124–25, and Arpee, 211.

92   Arpee, 211.

93   Among those expressing regrets for the November 13 occasion were owners of larger estates in Lake Forest, the J. V. Farwell Jrs., the Ernest Hamills, the Louis E. Laflins, and the Donald McLennans; also locals such as the Alfred Grangers and Miss Ellen Holt. Accepting were alumni Clarence Diver '05 and Marion Woolsey, Class of 1896, the Cornelius Trowbridges (a local Durand family), and such local community supporters as Dr. Alfred Haven and banker Frank Read. (*1876–1926: Fiftieth Anniversary Lake Forest College, Lake Forest, Illinois, November 13 and 14, 1926* [scrapbook].)

94   The foundation ran from 1926 to 1935, after a pilot program in the summer of 1925. (Ferruccio Vitale, "An Interesting Experiment in Architectural Education," *Western Architect* [Jun 1926], 67–68; Kate L. Brewster, "Foundation for Architecture and Landscape Architecture," *American Architect* [20 Aug 1928], 241–50; and [Minutes book], Foundation for Architecture and Landscape Architecture, 1926–35 [photocopy of original in the Lake County Forest Preserve District's Ryerson Woods collection], LFCA.)

95   "Treasurer's Report for Paid Period from December 1, 1927, to September 11, 1928," following the minutes for the annual meeting of September 11, 1928. (Foundation minutes book [chronologically

arranged].)

96   Minutes, 20 Feb 1930, Foundation minutes book.

97   Herbert Moore, *RP,* 1929. (LFCA.)

98   Francis Willard Puckey (June 2, 1874–January 7, 1954) received his architecture degree from M.I.T. in 1901 and after a year of postgraduate study there was enrolled in the ateliers of Duquesne and Chifflot at the Ecole des Beaux-Arts, 1905–06. He married Eleanor M. Rutan in 1906 and was in the Chicago office of Shepley, Rutan, and Coolidge [Richardson's associates], 1910–15, when following Cobb they were engaged in the development of the University of Chicago. After 1916 he practiced with Austin Dickinson Jenkins (January 19, 1879–April 29, 1954), a graduate with master's level study at M.I.T., 1903 and 1904, with whom he designed the house at 1300 North Green Bay Road in Lake Forest as well as nos. 14–17 of Campus Circle. (Buchbinder-Green, [Green Bay Road application], 81, and *BC* [1931], 503, 792; and Arthur Miller, *Lake Forest Classic and Prairie School Architects: A Revised Bibliographical Checklist.* [unpublished document, LFCA, 1997], 19, 22.)

## CHAPTER 7

*With this chapter personal recollections and conversations of the authors begin to provide material for the narrative, sometimes available only from their accounts. These are not necessarily referenced in the text or identified in notes.*

1   In the fall of 1940, President Moore, in his concern over decreasing enrollments, appointed a faculty committee to study the issue (FM [8 Oct 1940]). For enrollments, see *LFCC,* (1940–41), 116; (1941–42), 117; (1942–43), 98; and (1943–44), 96).

2   FM (12 Dec 1941): "It is important that the College maintain its enrollments if it is to continue to function as a strong liberal arts college." Credit was given, for example, for courses in beginning shorthand, advanced typing, and dictation. (*LFCC* [1941–42], 78–80.)

3   *LFCAB* (Apr 1942); *LFCAB* (Jul 1942); see also ch. 6, n. 30.

4   Ernest Amos Johnson (1895–1959) received his A.B. degree in Business Administration from Colorado College (Phi Beta Kappa), his A.M. degree from the University of Denver in 1924 (after wartime service), and his Ph.D. from Northwestern University in 1933. He came as an instructor in Economics in 1924, and was made an assistant professor in 1926, an associate professor in 1929, and a full professor in 1933. After 1929 he was head of the Economics Department (publishing a series of articles on real estate securities) until he was appointed acting president on February 6, 1942 (FM, 10 Feb 1942) and then president on October 1, 1943 (FM, 12 Oct 1943) – the only Lake Forest faculty member made permanent president of the College. Johnson quickly grabbed hold of

the difficult situation and then after the war, in February of 1946, he distributed a plan for development (new residence additions, etc.), noting that "Lake Forest now has a very good faculty" (3), with strategies for further improvement ("wise selection," "higher salaries," and "encouragement of faculty members to study... new educational advances... ") ("A Proposed Program for the Future Development of the College" [25 Feb 1946], 16 pp., LFCA). Until his death in 1959 he continued to strive to build and improve Lake Forest College, always living in his teaching-era house on Faculty Circle. An active Presbyterian lay leader, in the 1950s he was elected president of the Presbyterian College Union (forty-three church-related and approved colleges), served as a trustee of the McCormick Theological Seminary, and was a member of the General Council of the United Presbyterian Church, an executive committee for the General Assembly. (*WWWA* 3, 451; and Johnson Papers, LFCA; *LFCAB* [Jan 1954, May 1959].)

5   *LFCC* (1942). The day after assuming the acting presidency, Johnson called Amaden to appoint him. Amaden had interviewed over the holidays, when Moore was in the hospital. He reported for work on February 18, 1942. (Phone interview with Amaden by Arthur Miller, 18 November 1999.)

6   FM (13 Oct 1942).

7   FM (11 Sep 1943) and *LFCAB* (Oct 1943); for an earlier – apparently precursor – non-credit training program for Johns-Manville clerical workers, see FM (2 Mar 1943).

8   Capen's 1920 recommendations are discussed in ch. 6, pp. 101, 103.

9   The term "Johns Manville Girls," known from reminiscences of faculty of the era, is used in the yearbook (*F* [1944], 33).

10   The Armed Services Training Program participants arrived in August of 1943 (*F* [1944], 39) and left in March 1944 (FM [14 Mar and 11 Apr 1944]). For a history of Lake Forest College's participation in World War II, see the 199-page *Lake Forest College World War II Military Records,* ed. Francis Beidler II (n.p., n.d.).

11   FM (10 Mar 1942).

12   FM (12 Sep 1942 and 16 Feb 1943); *LFCAB* (Feb 1943); and [Louis J. Keller], "Report of First Semester of Evening School, 1942–43," 8 pp. ("Enrollment, Evening Session [1942/43–60/61]" folder, Office of the Registrar, Box 8, LFCA).

13   Two male students, Nobby Arata '49 and John Tachihara '47, whose names suggest their Japanese ancestry, are pictured in the 1944 *Forester,* with the Economics Club (67) and with the International or Skyline Club (81); and Toshiko Komatsu, female, is shown with the Class of 1947 (14–15). This would suggest Lake Forest participation in the substantial public-private partnership to relocate Japanese young people from internment camps to colleges, as described in Robert W. O'Brien's *The*

*College Nisei* (Palo Alto, CA: Pacific Books, 1949). But for the 1943–44 academic year no distribution to Lake Forest is listed in that text, apparently in error, since typically two students were sent that year to many Illinois colleges (139). One is listed for 1945–46 (144). (Amy Abe '74 pointed out the O'Brien reference.)

14   Arpee, 259–60; Arthur Meeker, *Chicago With Love: A Polite and Personal History* (New York: Alfred A. Knopf, 1955), 277–78.

15   *LFCAB* (Oct 1946), 2 and (Dec 1947), 3, 6.

16   *LFCAB* (Jun 1956), 9; Kemper Foundation and Mathis files, Office of Alumni and Development.

17   *LFCC* (Jun 1944).

18   FM (10 Oct 1944).

19   FM (30 Apr 1957, 15 Oct 1957, 19 Nov 1957, and 22 Apr 1958); see also FM (22 Nov 1955).

20   A telephone conversation with Professor Emeritus Arthur Voss by Rosemary Cowler and a letter from Mrs. Arthur (Isabel) Voss, January 1999.

21   *LFCC* (Apr 1947), 110.

22   FM (9 Apr 1946).

23   *LFCAB* (Jun, Aug 1946); Blackstone and Harlan file, LFCA.

24   [Martha Briggs], "Chronology," in Jay Pridmore, *Many Hearts and Many Hands: The History of Ferry Hall and Lake Forest Academy* (Lake Forest Academy, 1994), 244.

25   According to key Johnson faculty ally Richard W. Hantke (professor of History, 1942–73), Ernest Johnson at first did not want the Academy grounds, later South Campus; he thought it would be a burden, a "white elephant." Hantke also recalled a proposal to build faculty houses on the Academy property, to be sold to the faculty. But the Marshall Johnson campus plan does not seem to include a new field house, identified as a need, on North or Middle Campus, so at least some of the land adjacent to Farwell Field may have been intended for athletics in any case. Marshall Johnson (no relation to Ernest) was the assistant, 1915–35, of Jens Jensen, the Highland Park-based Prairie Style landscape architect, and was also Jensen's successor. (Notes, interview with Hantke by Arthur Miller, 22 Aug 1995, LFCA; Marshall Johnson, "A Preliminary General Plan for the North [and Middle] Campus[es] of Lake Forest College... December 1948," copy [of an original at the Morton Arboretum library], LFCA; notes of Arthur Miller, conversation with Bruce Johnson, son of Marshall Johnson, 15 Feb 1997.)

26   Of these three original Academy residence halls, only East House (Moore Hall) is extant in February 2000. Annie Durand Cottage, given to Lake Forest Academy by Henry C. Durand and named for his wife, and East House were designed by Chicago

Beaux-Arts architects Pond and Pond and built in 1892–93. Eliza Remsen Memorial Cottage, designed by Henry Ives Cobb in 1894 (*S* [2 Oct 1894]) and built in 1895, was given by Ezra J. Warner in memory of a sister of Mrs. Warner. The two cottages represented a superior level of comfort, for those able to pay, while the East House was more spartan. East House burned in the early 1920s and was refitted with a third floor added, presumably under the guidance of Pond and Pond. The cottages were demolished in the mid-1960s to make way for Roberts and McClure halls. (*LFCAB* [Aug 1948]; Edward Arpee, *The History of Lake Forest Academy* [Chicago: Alderbrink Press, 1944], 89–90; Arpee, 134; and *BDAA*, 478–79. See also ch. 2, n. 62.)

27  *LFCAB* [Aug 1948].

28  Hixon Hall, an Academy dining hall after 1940, was built as the garage for the Finley Barrell estate (1909, 1912) at 855 East Rosemary Road; the architect was Howard Van Doren Shaw. An early twentieth-century site plan of the South Campus area (Facilities Management) identifies this structure as the Barrell garage. (Virginia A. Greene, *The Architecture of Howard Van Doren Shaw* [Chicago: Chicago Review Press, 1999], 77; Arpee, 340; *LFCAB* [Aug 1948].)

29  TM (13 Mar 1950 and 5 Oct 1950). The Alumni Memorial Fieldhouse was dedicated December 6, 1950, with a representative of the Naess & Murphy firm present. (*LFCAB* [Jan 1951].) This replaced the 1906 Lake Forest Academy gymnasium, now demolished and the site of the parking lot serving the Sports Center and Hockey Rink.

30  FM (12 Sep 1942 and 15 Sep 1945).

31  Elizabeth Teter Smith (Lunn) was originally on the staff 1930–35; Arthur Voss's original appointment had been in 1941–42.

32  See *LFCC*s for the period.

33  William Lewis Dunn (1914–77) served as dean of the faculty from 1949 to 1974, also with the titles of vice president under Ernest Johnson (after 1953) and later provost. Dunn was a graduate of the University of Illinois (Phi Beta Kappa) with a Ph.D. in Chemistry from the University of Wisconsin (1941). He came to Lake Forest after teaching at Cornell College (Iowa; 1941–45) and Colorado State (1945–49). The year of his arrival a publicity office compilation prefaced a list of "Outstanding Faculty" with this *caveat*: "Because Lake Forest College is a small school, its faculty is primarily a teaching faculty, for it does not have the time or facilities at hand to do large scale research." He was to contribute much to changing this. (*WWM* [1954]; "Historical Sketches" file, Physical Plant Collection, LFCA.)

34  AAUP files, LFCA. AAUP pressure helped introduce in the era faculty tenure guidelines following AAUP national recommendations; see FM (8 May 1951 and 19 Mar 1957).

35  See AAUP meeting minutes for 1957–58. ("Minutes, 1946–69" folder, AAUP files, Box 5, LFCA.)

36  FM (13 Dec 1949, 16 Feb 1954, 16 Mar 1954 and [grants] 24 Apr 1959).

37  FM (22 Nov 1955).

38  FM (20 Jan and 19 May 1953).

39  FM (27 Apr 1954).

40  For example, a cooperative program with the Presbyterian Hospital School of Nursing (FM [17 Jun 1949 and 9 May 1950]) and a joint program with Illinois Institute of Technology (FM [8 Jun 1951]).

41  *LFCAB* (Oct 1956). A report to the Board of Trustees (7 May 1956) noted that some 150 community members and 15 faculty members had participated in the seminars.

42  "Art, June 1953–72" folder, Box 1, College Community Programs [Ruth Winter files], LFCA.

43  Ruth Elting (Mrs. Edwin) Winter, a Lake Forest resident with old Chicago roots, began to accumulate her files on the College-Community program in June 1953. Her interest in the College had been stimulated when she had taken, with Jane Warner (Mrs. Edison) Dick, an American History course with Richard Hantke about 1950. (Hantke interview, 1995, LFCA.)

44  FM (14 Oct 1957).

45  Conversations with Coach Michael Dau '58 by Franz Schulze, Spring 1999.

46  *LFCAB* (Jan 1952).

47  See *Foresters* and *Stentors* for the period.

48  By 1950 some fraternities on campus, increasingly popular again in the late 1940s, had gone national ("Greeks," *F* [1948], 79–83; *LFCAB* [Oct 1955], 17; see also ch. 9, n. 76.)

49  Though the "Tony Banks Incident" was not officially reported to the faculty until 17 May 1955, the issue of racial discrimination by campus social organizations had arisen earlier (FM [17 Jan 1950]), and the episode itself, in the fall of 1953–54, had sparked much concern and action by the College: the appointment of a committee to study the issue (FM [16 Nov 1954]), a subsequent detailed report from the General Policies Committee (FM [18 Jan and 15 Feb 1955]), with faculty recommendations to the Board of Trustees, who in turn named a Committee to Eliminate Discriminatory Practices (TM [7 Mar 1955] and FM [22 Mar 1955]), which ultimately became a committee of trustees, alumni, faculty, administration and students (FM [19 Apr 1955]); see also FM (10 Jun 1955, 15 Oct 1957, 21 Jan 1958, 25 Mar 1958, 26 May 1958, and 18 Nov 1958) and TM (6 May 1957). At the 16 May 1958 faculty meeting there was presented the "Proposed Statement by the Board of Trustees on Discrimination in Social Organizations," which reiterated required compliance with the principle of nondiscrimination, or progress toward such compliance, with annual status reports to be made. (The 15 Oct 1957 FM had reported that most of the fraternities and sororities "were doing nothing about the problem of discrimination.")

50  FM (16 Feb 1954 and 20 Mar 1956).

51  FM (24 Apr 1959).

52  Voss: FM (22 May 1956); Milne and Coutts: FM (22 Apr 1958); Phillips: FM (15 May 1952).

53  Files, Office of Alumni and Development.

54  An outgrowth of a three-college conference with Beloit and Kalamazoo that summer on this issue, held at Beaver Dam, Wisconsin, and funded by the Danforth Foundation (TM [3 Oct 1955]).

55  The conference on the liberal arts college, part of the centennial festivities, was held on March 1 and 2, 1957 (*LFCAB* [Jan 1957]). The Centennial Development Commission focused the observance on fundraising and public relations (TM [12 Oct 1953] and FM [27 Oct 1953]). Special events included also an address on "The God of Our Fathers" by Time, Inc. founder Henry R. Luce on March 26, a visit by theologian Paul Tillich (three Bross lectures) on May 5–7, and an exhibit of American art from the Art Institute in June. Not materializing was a history of the College (for which a committee chaired by History professor Richard Hantke had been appointed in 1955) perhaps due to a conflict between professional standards and amateur ambitions. (For in November 2, 1955, committee minutes of the group [including also James R. Getz, librarian Martha Biggs '28, Ruth Winter, and Carroll Sudler] there is mention of a 20,000-word narrative, even with Professor Hantke indicating he would need a leave from teaching to accomplish this. ["Centennial Program 1857–1957" file, Presidents' Papers, LFCA].)

56  *LFCAB* (Feb 1948), 2.

57  TM (7 Dec 1953).

58  TM (9 Mar and 12 Oct 1953), FM (17 Mar and 16 Sep 1953), and Booz, Allen & Hamilton, "General Survey, Lake Forest College, Lake Forest, Illinois, June 1953," Planning Box, Hotchkiss Papers, LFCA.

59  TM (12 Oct 1953) and *LFCAB* (Jan 1954). For Donnelley, see n. 73 below and p. 145.

60  The landscape plan by Hill, included in the Booz, Allen report, still projects a new field house, either on Middle or South Campus, indicating it was drawn up before plans to build this structure, now the Hockey Rink, were firmly elaborated. This may date it from about the same time (1948) as the Marshall Johnson plan (see n. 25 above). (Planning Box, Hotchkiss Papers, LFCA.) Chance S. Hill had been a visitor to the campus in 1931, to the summer program of the Lake Forest Foundation for Architecture and Landscape Architecture (Stanley White, "Sixth Annual Report of the Director," Foundation for Architecture and Landscape Architecture [1931], 9, in Minutes book,

Foundation..., LFCA).

61 Though bids had been sought early in 1956 both for a women's residence hall and a group of faculty houses, the trustees authorized only the former – Deerpath Hall (TM [15 Feb 1956]). The building was dedicated, with a Naess & Murphy representative on hand, at Homecoming that year (TM [3 Dec 1956]). For the first time the trustees authorized borrowing to underwrite construction, an action in contrast to the slow and tedious "grassroots" fundraising for the field house a few years earlier (TM [7 May 1956]).

62 LFCAB (June 1959), campus plan file and file on the Fall 1995 exhibit on the history of Lake Forest campus plans, LFCA.

63 In early 1959, before Johnson's death, gifts for the Science building had been received from the Robert R. McCormick Trust for $150,000 and from Thomas Galt for $125,000, bringing the total on hand to about $500,000 – about one-third of the projected $1.3 to $1.5 million anticipated in expense. (LFCAB [Jan and Apr 1959].)

64 LFCAB (May 1959).

65 LFCAB (May 1959). See also n. 4 above.

66 Howard (University of Pennsylvania, B.A. 1947, M.A. 1948) was new to the campus as the business manager when, in the spring of 1959, he was appointed acting president after Johnson's death; in previous weeks he had been serving in an acting capacity while Johnson was ill. (FM [24 Mar and 21 Apr 1959]; LFCAB [May 1959], 3; F [1959], 15; see also n. 81 below.) Subsequently he served as president of Lewis and Clark College (Oregon), 1960–80.

67 Clarence W. Diver '05 (Michigan L.L.B., 1908), Waukegan, was president of the Board of Trustees, 1928–45. President of the Illinois State Bar Association in 1942–43, he also was president of the Waukegan Township High School Board, 1927–40 (WWM [1958], 266.)

68 Joseph B. Fleming, a prominent Chicago attorney and associate of Col. Robert R. McCormick of the Chicago Tribune, was president of the Board of Trustees from 1945 to 1957. Born in Scotland in 1881, he received his L.L.B. from John Marshall Law School in 1905. Fleming lived in Lake Forest and belonged to the Onwentsia Club, sending his gardener's son to Lake Forest College (Shirley MacDonald Paddock Spr 1999). He also served as president of the board of the Chicago Public Library. (WWM [1958], 330; TM [16 June 1957].)

69 Lilace Reid Barnes (1899–1989) was the daughter of Clifford and Alice Reid Barnes (Class of 1886) and the granddaughter of Simon and Martha Reid, Mrs. Reid the donor of Lily Reid Holt Chapel and of the Arthur Somerville Reid Memorial Library in 1899. Miss Barnes, after her father's death in 1944, carried on his reform tradition, serving as president of the world YWCA in the 1940s (LFCAB [Feb 1948]; LFCBB).

70 George R. Beach Jr. (1903–90), an executive with du Pont in Chicago after 1946 and married first to Jane Grant Schuttler (1907–72) of an old Chicago German family, was a trustee beginning in 1955. He was board chair 1971–74. (WWM [1958], 67; "Lake Forest College Trustees" [1994], 1, 8; George R. Beach, Remembrances of Walter Schuttler [Lake Forest, 1979], [60] et passim.) His second spouse, Mary Beach, donated many of his books to the Donnelley Library.

71 Francis Beidler II, also of an old Chicago German family, was a trustee from 1933 to 1984. His grandfather, lumber baron Jacob Beidler, had given the Beidler House and a science professorship when he was a trustee from 1880 to 1897 (see ch. 2).

72 Phoebe Norcross (Mrs. Richard) Bentley was a granddaughter of Chicago book collector John Wrenn and daughter of collector F.F. Norcross. A political liberal, she was a trustee, 1950–62 and 1968–87. Many of her books were donated to the Donnelley Library. Hantke interview, 1995; Frank J. Piehl, The Caxton Club 1895–1995: Celebrating A Century of the Book in Chicago (Chicago: Caxton Club, 1995), 178–79; The Caxton Club [yearbook] [Chicago: Caxton Club, 1965], 17, 20, 108.)

73 Elliott Donnelley (1903–75), grandson of the founder of the Chicago printing concern, was active in civic affairs and a trustee of Lake Forest from 1942 until his death, serving as Board chair from 1967 to 1971. (WWM [1954], 212.) See sidebar, p. 145.

74 Francis C. Farwell II, Yale '44 and a descendant of John V. Farwell, in investment banking, has been a trustee since 1958.

75 Although not appointed a trustee until 1962, the service of Lake Forest area resident and local historian James R. Getz (1910–86) began in the mid 1950s with the Centennial activities and then, beginning in 1958, chairing the Friends of the Library promoting the new college library of the 1960s. After his death his collections came to the Donnelley Library. (LFCAB [Nov 1958]; Piehl, The Caxton Club, 158.)

76 C[harles] Daggett Harvey, an attorney and officer of Fred Harvey, Inc. [restaurants], served on the Board from 1958 to 1976. He was a member of Onwentsia and Shoreacres. (WWM [1954], 338.)

77 Frances (Mrs. William) Odell, an artist residing on Lake Road in Lake Forest, was a trustee beginning in 1950. As cochair with Elliott Donnelley of the Property and Operations Committee, she would bring her artist's eye to bear on matters relating to new buildings. (NFLFC [Jan 1962].)

78 Two Frank Reads, father and son, played important trustee roles during much of the twentieth century. Frank W. Read, founder of the First National Bank of Lake Forest (now Northern Trust, Lake Forest) served 1921–58 and was followed by his son Frank S. Read (also heading up the bank) serving 1971–96. (WWM [1972–73], 603.)

79 Carroll Sudler, Yale '17 (Phi Beta Kappa), a cofounding partner in 1927 of the Chicago real estate firm Sudler & Co., who lived in Lake Forest and was a member of Onwentsia and Shoreacres, served on the Board beginning in 1954. He was president of the Board in the crucial years of 1958 to 1962. (WWM [1958], 975; "Trustees," [1994], 7–8.)

80 Ernest Volwiler, B. A. Miami University (Phi Beta Kappa) and Ph.D. in Chemistry from the University of Illinois, was a well-known scientist and executive vice president of Abbott Laboratories when he became a trustee in 1950 (WWA [1978]; LFCAB [Jan 1951], 6.)

81 FM (21 Oct 1958, 17 Feb 1959, 24 Mar 1959, 15 Dec 1959).

82 FM (21 Oct 1958 and 17 Feb 1959). Efforts had been made over the recent years to raise faculty salaries, especially with the impetus of a Ford grant in 1956 (TM [5 Mar 1956]) in recognition of the progress the College had made in that direction.

83 Sudler and fellow trustee Daggett Harvey called a meeting of the faculty members of Phi Beta Kappa – Lindley Burton, Rosemary Cowler, Harold Curtis (emeritus), William Dunn, Ann Hentz, Harold Hutcheson, and Gordon Milne – to discuss the College's application for membership and its plan for addressing the earlier-cited weaknesses (FM [24 Mar 1959]). When the issue of vocationally oriented majors, with a degree in Business Administration, arose, the trustee observation was that they be eliminated, despite the opposition of Mr. Howard, representing President Johnson.

84 FM (5 Jun, 10 Sep, 20 Oct, 22 Nov, 30 Nov, and 15 Dec 1959). (The major in Speech was replaced by a major in Dramatic Art, and changes in departmental offerings were introduced, with courses in Secretarial Training and Physical Education Theory no longer normally carrying credit.)

85 Business Administration majors totaled 145, Economics majors 47, and Speech majors 51, leading to a sum of 243. ("Majors Distribution" tables compiled [Spr 1999], 11.) For comparable statistics for the Moore years, see ch. 6, n. 37.

86 In the half-century between 1907 and 1959, after Nollen's departure for wartime service, Henry W. Wright had served as acting president, 1918–20, and Herbert Moore, 1920–21, which led to alumnus Moore's appointment as president. Johnson, like Wright as a senior faculty member, became acting president when Moore fell ill in 1942, in 1943 being appointed president. Since Johnson had been on the faculty in a key role since 1924, essentially the entire Moore administration, the resulting continuity of administration was significant.

87 Cole's appointment was announced

December 1, 1959, effective September 1, 1960. At that time he was Cluett Professor of Religion and chair of the department as well as dean of freshmen at Williams College. Cole had served also as administrator of the Summer Institute in American Studies for Executives at Williams, and in 1956 had been a delegate to the international Conference on Student Mental Health at Princeton University. Cole had written two books that would not be without relevance in the 1960s, *Sex in Christianity and Psychoanalysis* (Oxford, 1954) and *Sex and Love in the Bible* (Association Press, 1959). His education included Mount Hermon School, Columbia University (B.A. 1940; Ph.D. 1954), and Union Theological Seminary (B.D. 1943). From 1948 to 1952 he was chaplain and assistant professor of Religion at Smith College, after which he joined the Williams faculty in 1952 as chaplain and associate professor of Religion. (*WWA* [1978]; *LFCAB* [Dec 1959]; *Leaders in Education*, 4th ed. [1971], 211; and Cole file, LFCA.)

## CHAPTER 8

*In this chapter again personal recollections and conversations of the authors provide material for the narrative, sometimes available only from their accounts. These are not necessarily referenced in the text or identified in notes.*

1   FM (19 Jan 1960).

2   *LFCC* (Oct 1960).

3   The new director of admissions was John C. Hoy (b. 1933), B.A. Wesleyan (1955), who had been assistant director of admissions at Swarthmore, 1956–59. In 1962 he left the College to become dean of admissions at Wesleyan and later, in 1978, president of the New England Board of Higher Education, headquartered in Boston (*LFCAB* [Sep 1960], *WWA* [1990–91], 573).

4   Conversations with William Graham Cole, 1997–99.

5   Events of 1960: groundbreaking for the science center and annual giving (*LFCAB* [Nov 1960]), largest-ever class of 1964 (*LFCAB* [Oct 1960]), new calendar (*NFLFC* [Jan 1961]), reduced teaching load (FM [18 Oct 1960]), faculty sabbatical leave program (FM [13 Dec 1960]), tenure rules (TM [2 May 1960]), new president's house (FM [3 May 1960]), Perkins and Will (FM [Nov 1960]), student union (FM [13 Dec 1960]), and faculty housing on South Campus (FM [13 Dec 1960]).

6   Events of 1961: enrollment statistics (*NFLFC* [Oct 1961]; "Commencement Notes," Commencement Program, 1961), new coed dormitories (*NFLFC* [Oct 1961]), new grading system (FM [16 May 1961]; *NFLFC* [Oct 1963]), revised curriculum (*NFLFC* [Jan 1961]), faculty tuition benefit (FM [21 Feb 1961]), fraternity charter suspension and faculty resolution (*NFLFC* [Mar 1961]), faculty salaries (*NFLFC* [May 1961]), United Christian Fellowship (FM [21 Mar 1961]), soccer team (FM [16 May 1961]), comprehensive examinations

proposed (FM [16 May 1961]) and approved (FM [16 Jan 1962]), student union groundbreaking (*NFLFC* [Nov 1961]), Community Government Association (FM [17 Jan 1961]), record budget (*NFLFC* [Apr 1961]), graduate school statistics ("Commencement Notes," Commencement Program, 1961), and new seal adopted (*NFLFC* [Jul 1961]).

7   Events of 1962: 30% increase in applications (*NFLFC* [Jan 1962]), Phi Beta Kappa charter granted (FM [22 Sept 1961]) and installed (*NFLFC* [Feb 1962]), Ford Foundation grant (*NFLFC* [Jul 1962]), site for library (*NFLFC* [Oct 1962]), counseling center established (*NFLFC* [Sep 1962]; FM [20 Oct 1962]), withdrawal from College Conference of Illinois (*NFLFC* [May 1962]), P. E. requirement lowered (FM [15 Jun 1962]), scholarship program for students from Africa (*NFLFC* [Feb 1962]), and "Understanding the New Africa" and Stevenson (*NFLFC* [Mar 1962]).

8   Events of 1963: ground broken for new library (*NFLFC* [Jul 1963]), South Campus dormitories (*NFLFC* [Jan 1963]), College Board Achievement Tests (FM [19 Feb 1963]), faculty salary increase (*NFLFC* [Apr 1963]), enrollment at 1,172 (*NFLFC* [Oct 1963]), size of the faculty (*NFLFC* [Jul 1963]), Latin America conference (*NFLFC* [Mar 1963]), conference on race relations (*NFLFC* [Sep 1963]), student tutoring program (*NFLFC* [Nov 1963]), Jewish Activities Group (FM [21 May 1963]), and Commencement symposium on the creative arts (FM [14 Jun 1963]).

9   Events of 1964: fine arts center planned (*NFLFC* [Aug 1964]), retirement supplements for emeriti (FM [19 May 1964]), focus on India (*NFLFC* [Mar 1964]), Operation Opportunity (*NFLFC* [Nov 1964]), house system (FM [21 Apr 1964]), radio station (*NFLFC* [Jun 1964]), "Next Steps" conference on race relations (*NFLFC* [Sep 1964]), study abroad in Spain (FM [18 Feb 1964]), Dijon (FM [10 May 1966]), Berlin (FM [28 Nov 1967]), and Athens (FM [4 Mar 1969]), Catholic Guild constitution approved (FM [19 May 1964]), International Relations major added (FM [19 May 1964]), and evening school disbanded (Enrollment files, Office of the Registrar, LFCA.)

10   Events of 1965: new library opened ("Commencement Notes," Commencement Program, 1965), Holt and Reid Houses (*NFLFC* [Aug 1965 and Nov 1965]), Glen Rowan (the Barnes place fitting a larger strategy to acquire the continuous land west of Sheridan Road from Middle Campus, with the College by 1970 leasing Glen Rowan to the First National Bank of Chicago [*Lake Forester* (9 Mar 1970 and 22 Oct 1970)]), Lutheran student group (FM [19 Jan 1965]), Quaker student group (FM [16 Feb 1965]), Reid Hall (FM [18 May 1965]), South Campus dorms and faculty housing completed (*NFLFC* [Aug, 1965]), faculty tenure and academic freedom (FM [12 Mar 1963 and 18 May 1965]), fundraising exceeds goal (FM [11 Jun 1965], *NFLFC* [Jul 1965]), and first-rate students and professors

("Commencement Notes," Commencement Program, 1965).

11   Cole's ubiquitousness as a speaker is perhaps unmatched in the history of this College. Like Dr. McClure, who annually traveled to speak to students at Harvard and Yale, Cole was widely sought after as a speaker, but still was highly visible, even inescapable, on the Lake Forest campus. His talks off campus included, for example, "Creating a Favorable Climate for Learning via Student Personnel Services" for the Pennsylvania State Education Association on October 28, 1960; "Between Two Extremes" (billed as "A College President Frankly Discusses The Radical Right") for a special North Shore meeting of the American Jewish Committee on May 2, 1962; "The Crisis in Education" to the Executive's Club of Chicago on October 25, 1963; a sermon on the existence of God at the Rockefeller Chapel of the University of Chicago on October 11, 1965; "The Muddle of Middle Class Morality or Confusion on the Campus" to an unidentified, apparently Chicago group on July 16, 1966; and "Private Morality and Public Law" for the Chicago Law Club on October 6, 1967. His tight off-campus schedule is discussed in a memo to Ellen Mosey from President Cole's secretary that refers to one Eastern school's efforts over three years to book Cole as a speaker and Cole's use of the same talk in different states (attached to press release 66/233, "Speeches and Lectures" folder 4, Box 1, Cole Personal Papers, LFCA). On and near campus he also spoke from prepared remarks for all manner of occasions, for example: "The Demand for Greatness," to launch a fundraising campaign on January 7, 1961; "The Mind and What Matters," preached at the First Presbyterian Church of Lake Forest, April 25, 1965; "The Student as Scholar," for the New Student Convocation of September 20, 1965; "Building and Destroying," for the Baccalaureate service of June 10, 1966; remarks for Parents' Day, May 6, 1967 ("Conflict, tension, disagreement, misunderstanding between adolescents and adults have been with us for centuries"); and "Welcome to the class of 1972," opening with Dickens's "It was the best of times; it was the worst of times" from *A Tale of Two Cities* on September 14, 1968. ("Speeches and Lectures," Folder 3, Box 1, Cole Personal Papers, LFCA.)

12   Conversations with William Cole, 1998–99.

13   Conversations with Doris Cole Yankee, 1998–99.

14   FM (15 Nov 1960).

15   Conversations with Rosemary Hale.

16   Notices of the appearances of the speakers mentioned are listed below, alphabetically by name rather than in the subject-group order in the text. In some cases citations to College publications are provided for discussion of the event; otherwise reference is made to the date of appearance only. This latter is derived from a card file database

for 1960s speakers and performers, prepared in 1998–99 by Doris Cole Yankee and based on publicity and cultural office files of the day (now deposited in the College Archives) along with her own recollections.

Adler (*S* [17 May 1968]); Albright (1965); Algren (*NFLFC* [Feb 1963]); Arendt (6 Dec 1963); Barth (3 Sep 1966); Barton (*NFLFC* [Oct 1966]); Baxter (19 Nov 1960); Beadle (*NFLFC* [Dec 1965]); Bennett (*NFLFC* [Jan 1968]); Bettelheim (*S* [22 May 1964]); Blanshard (*NFLFC* [Oct 1963]); Bond (25 Apr 1969); Bowen (*NFLFC* [Mar 1971]); Bree (*S* [24 Feb 1965]); Brooks (19 Jan 1962, 26 Oct 1965, and 7 May 1968); Buckley (Aug 1961); Commager (*S* [12 May 1967]); Creeley (25 Jan–5 Feb 1969); Crewe (*NFLFC* [Oct 1962]); e. e. cummings (*NFLFC* [Feb 1961]); Dickey (*NFLFC* [Jan 1964]); Donovan (*NFLFC* 9 Feb 1968]); Eibl-Eibesfeldt (*NFLFC* [Feb 1967]); Eisley (15 May 1963); Ellison (*S* [2 Oct 1964]); Feiffer (Nov 1969); Franklin (25 Oct 1966); Friedman (*NFLFC* [Oct 1966]); Fromm (7 Oct 1964); Gabriel (*NFLFC* [Oct 1963]); Golub (*NFLFC* [Jan 1968]); Hadas (*S* [13 Nov 1964]); Heller (*S* [3 May 1968]); Hutchins (18 Apr 1963); Huxley (18 Mar 1960); Jackson (5 Apr 1967); Kitto (*NFLFC* [Oct 1962]); Langer (*S* [13 Apr 1962]); Logan (*NFLFC* [Sep 1962]); Luening (*NFLFC* [Feb 1968]); Marty (19 Feb 1961); May (15–16 Oct 1965); Menninger (*NFLFC* [Feb 1969]); Mills (5 Feb 1964); Morgenthau (20 Nov 1966); Mosse (*S* [24 Feb 1965]); Nagy (*NFLFC* [Jan 1966]); Nemerov (2 Dec 1960 and 16–23 Jan 1968); Perry (15 Jun 1962 and 1 Nov 1966); Porter (*NFLFC* [Oct 1968]); Proxmire (16 Jan 1963); Rexroth (*NFLFC* [Sep 1965]); Rosenberg (*NFLFC* [May 1968]); Rumsfeld (*NFLFC* [Jan 1968]); Samuelson (*NFLFC* [Sep 1966]); Siegel (*NFLFC* [Feb 1966]); Singer (*S* [12 Apr 1968]); Skinner (4 May 1964); Spender (5 May 1965); Stigler (*NFLFC* [Jan 1964]); Stevenson (*NFLFC* [Jul 1965]); Thomas (2 Dec 1964); Tillich (*NFLFC* [Feb 1961, Sep 1962]); Viereck (*S* [15 Jan 1964]); Vonnegut (*NFLFC* [Oct 1968]); von Schuschnigg (7 Nov 1961); and Wicker (11 Nov 1969).

17 Anecdote from a conversation with Doris Cole Yankee, 1999.

18 The dates of appearance, from lists of campus performers maintained by the Office of Public Information (LFCA) except where noted, are arranged alphabetically by name of performer or performing group: Addison, 16 May 1960; Chicago City Players, 28 Apr 1967; Chicago Woodwinds, May 1962, July 1963, Apr 1964, and May 1964; Contemporary Jazz, 15 Oct 1967; Ossie Davis and Ruby Dee (*LFAQ* [Spr 1968], 8); Fine Arts Quartet, 22 Nov 1963; Ustad Ghulamhusain, 22 May 1968; Junior Wells Blues Band, 2 Dec 1966; Lane, 4 Nov 1962; Lorado, 15 Jan 1966; Luca, 8 Oct 1967; Montoya, 6 Apr 1968; National Theater of the Deaf, 24 Oct 1968; New York City Camarata, 8 Dec 1966; Odetta (*NFLFC* [Jan 1968]); Pomara Dance, 10 Oct 1969; Silver, 6 Oct 1957; Simone, 25

Oct 1968; Staples, 6 Apr 1966; Vronsky and Babin, 16 Jan 1965; Wallenborn, 3 May 1964; Wanderers Three, 19 Oct 1963; and White, 12 May 1962.

19 *LFCAB* (Nov 1960).

20 For dates of service, see directories in annual catalogs of the period or, more recently, listings under "Faculty Emeriti" also.

21 It was a College-wide focus, too: "Chicago Offers Culture: Off-Campus Activities Committee Promotes Cultural Events," *S* (28 Oct 1960).

22 The film "The Challenge of Change" is structured around a cinemagraphic visit to the campus by actor Richard Widmark '36. Because of his Hollywood contract, Widmark could not appear in the movie but his voice is heard as narrator and commentator, noting the many differences since his time on campus. Included in the visit are a walk around campus, a conversation with President Cole in Donnelley Library, students in a physics lab, English and history classes, a Homecoming celebration, and tutorial work with young children. The film was student produced, though supervised by Gunter Doetsch, who headed up the project as a campus workshop from December of 1963 through the spring of 1965. (*NFLFC* [Oct 1965].)

23 The near-completed yearbox project almost didn't happen, since the yearbook office was in North Gym when it burned on June 4, 1969. Though only a few photographs were totally lost, most had to be redone because of damage. (*LFCN* [Jun 1969].)

24 For students' involvement in planning of physical space see FM (7 Mar 1967); parietal rules and *in loco parentis* are discussed in a "Report of the Student Life Committee, Spring 1966," appendix B to the FM (5 Apr 1966); further faculty discussion and action appear in FM (3 May and 10 May 1966). For parietal rules see also *S* (21 May 1965, 9 Dec 1966, and 7 Apr 1967). For *in loco parentis* see also *S* (14 May 1965 and 9 Feb 1968) and *Between the Generations*, discussed below in n. 40.

25 Alumni information supplied by Office of Alumni and Development.

26 *S* (24 Feb 1967).

27 Iron Key last appears in yearbooks in 1968. ("Organizations of the 60s," Organizations' histories file, LFCA.)

28 FM (15 May 1962).

29 Recollections of William Graham Cole and Doris Cole Yankee, 1998–99.

30 See sidebar on photographers, p. 155. Joann H. Lee Schaeffer, assistant librarian emerita (1950–51, 1960–84), in October 1999 recounted her experience – accompanied by other Lake Forest participants – of being present at the Grant Park Democratic Convention confrontation with police.

31 FM (7 May 1968 and 4 Jun 1968).

32 FM (5 Nov 1968).

33 FM (1 Feb 1966).

34 In the Student Affairs office records for the period, the file for the "Provisional Revolutionary Government" covers only 1971–72. Minutes are somewhat fragmentary, but reflect the *zeitgeist*: from an early meeting, a report that the PRG "had little money this year and there was to be no 'bullshit' spending." At the second meeting, a constitutional convention was called for October 30. On October 19, 1971, the PRG formally took over, and Dean of Students Hoogesteger ("Hoogie," as he is reported in the minutes) endeavored to convey information about some of the responsibilities of the new government: managing collected fees, balanced representation, etc. The leader, designated in the minutes "El Presidente" (and replaced soon by another), saw the school becoming the "watchdog of society," and, according to the "Minister of Information," a committee was set up to work for the abolition of requirements, while later a review of the athletic department was launched.

35 *S* (10 May 1968).

36 For the trashing of Commons, see *S* (30 Jan 1970); for drugs, see FM (3 May 1966 and 6 Dec 1966).

37 *NFLFC* (Jun 1969).

38 *NFLFC* (May 1967).

39 *NFLFC* (Dec 1967).

40 See Cole's "Preface: Behind the Scenes" introducing the conference proceedings and reviewing them: "As the Convocation proceeded through the fifty or so hours of its life, everyone wondered whether it would widen the gap between the generations, weaken mutual confidence, and leave the campus torn apart, or heal the breach, bridge the gulf, and unify the College community. The outcome was anybody's guess" (ix). The topics, reflecting Cole's largely early-1960s grasp of the issues, included "Manners and Morals," "In Loco Parentis?" "Youth and the Law," and "Youth and the Nation." The students, countering with their own teach-in at the same time, focused on both larger social issues and also more earthy questions, which they distributed to the audience and with which Cole prefaced each section. (If James Simon Kunen's *Strawberry Statement* about the Columbia strike of 1968 documents the student side [as cited by Helen Lefkowitz Horowitz, *Campus Life, Undergraduate Cultures from the End of the Eighteenth Century to the Present* (New York: Alfred A. Knopf, 1987), 238–39], Cole's volume documents too the parent generation's effort to bridge the gap through dialogue.) (*Between the Generations: the Confidence Gap, A Convocation Held at Lake Forest College, Lake Forest, Illinois April 24–26, 1968*, ed. William Graham Cole [Lake Forest: Lake Forest College, 1968], 121 pp.) Two years previously Cole had published *The Restless Quest of Modern Man* (New York: Oxford University Press, 1966), which had made clear that "those who attack and revile call forth in me the desire not so

much to defend as to interpret and explain" (vi).

41   *LFCN* (Feb 1969).

42   *LFCN* (Jun 1968).

43   *NFLFC* (Sep 1965).

44   Elliott Donnelley, as cochair with Mrs. Odell of the Board's Property and Operations Committee, became the principal benefactor of this phase of the architectural history of the campus. His gifts made possible the new president's house and grounds (1961), the Donnelley Library (1965), and the Sports Center (1968), the last two being major structures comparable to the Reid Library/Chapel contributions of 1899–1900 (two-thirds of a century earlier), greater than Mrs. Blackstone's donations of the quadrangles in 1906–07, and the first such gifts since that era. Thus, Donnelley family generosity to Lake Forest College ranks with that of the Farwell, Durand, and Reid families, breaking the ice for further significant donations (Young, McGaw, Dixon, etc.) in the Hotchkiss era. (See also ch. 7, n. 73 and p. 145.)

45   *NFLFC* (Oct 1969).

46   *NFLFC* (Oct 1969).

47   From Lake Forest Cole went on to other administrative and academic posts, including the Chicago Council on Foreign Relations, Chicago State University, Nasson College, and, most recently, Loyola University.

48   See p. 128.

49   Conversations with Doris Cole Yankee, 1998–99, and with Marcia Gillespie '66 (by David Spadafora) on this point.

50   *LFCC* (Jan 1968).

51   FM (4 Feb 1968).

52   *LFCN* (Jan 1968); *S* (27 Oct 1967).

53   Rosemary Hale, in a conversation with Rosemary Cowler, September 26, 1999.

54   *NFLFC* (Apr 1969).

55   *S* (4 Mar 1969).


## CHAPTER 9

*In this chapter personal recollections and conversations of the authors continue to provide material for the narrative, sometimes available only from their accounts. These are not necessarily referenced in the text or identified in notes.*

1   Hugh Hawkins, "The Making of the Liberal Arts College Identity," *Daedalus* (Winter 1999), 19.

2   For example, concern about a possible decline in alumni donations arose immediately after the Cambodia bombing/Kent State incidents of May 1970. This concern turned out to be well founded, according to articles reported in *The Readers Guide to Periodical Literature*, 30 (Mar 1970–Feb 1971), 285: "College Budgets Fall on Violence," *Business Week* (16 May 1970), 23; R. A. Freeman, "Coming: A Financial Backlash Against Colleges? Excerpts from

an Address, June 19, 1970," *U.S. News* (29 Jun 1970), 72–73; "Businessmen Sour on College Support," *Nation's Business* (Sep 1970), 22; and "A Plea to Alumni Not to Forsake Their Colleges," *U.S. News* (11 Jan 1971), 84.

3   Hawkins, 21.

4   Hawkins, 19–21.

5   In marked contrast would be the strategy of the next decade, away from the "rocking chair" or campaign-and-then-rest theory of development (*LFAQ* [Fall–Winter 1971–72]).

6   *LFCN* (Oct 1969).

7   *LFCN* (May 1970).

8   "Alumni donors and dollars fell from the previous year." (Robert Amaden, "Among Us," *LFAQ* [Fall 1970], 13.) When the *U.S. News* editorial (11 Jan 1971, 84) "A Plea to Alumni Not to Forsake Their Colleges" was reprinted in *LFAQ* (Winter 1971), 21, a double message was sent to Lake Forest alumni: (1) we need your support and (2) your concerns with Lake Forest reflect those shared generally among alumni of American colleges.

9   Selected by a trustee-faculty-student-alumni Presidential Selection Committee (FM [11 Mar 1969]), Eugene Hotchkiss was appointed Lake Forest's eleventh president on January 5, 1970, to take up his duties on September 1, 1970. His appointment was announced on January 30, 1970, by Board chairman Elliott Donnelley. (*LFCN* [Feb 1970].)

10  Dunn and Bartlett (FM [7 Oct and 4 Nov 1969]; *LFCN* [Sep 1969]).

11  Hotchkiss had graduated Phi Beta Kappa from Dartmouth in 1950 and, after three years as a Korean-era naval officer, returned to his alma mater for two years as assistant dean of the college. At Cornell as assistant dean from 1955 to 1958, he undertook doctoral-level work on the history of education before returning once more to Dartmouth from 1958 to 1960 as associate dean of the college. From there, having completed his doctorate, he went to Harvey Mudd of the Claremont (California) Colleges as lecturer in History and dean of the college. From 1968 to 1970 he was executive dean of Chatham College in Pittsburgh. (*LFCN* [Feb 1970]; *WWA* [1990–91], 1561.)

12  *Sp* (Spr 1993), 8. Before Hotchkiss's arrival, the trustees had observed their "unusual predicament," as development chair Augustin Hart noted, concerning finances: "the Breakthrough Campaign [designates that] all monies raised go into plant and endowment, with very little being channeled into current support," a Camelot-era perspective that Hart suggested they "restructure" (TM [3 Nov 1969]). Also, endowment income for 1970–71 was $111,000 for expenditures of $5.5 million, from an endowment nominally valued at $2.9 million, with much in nonperforming or problematic real estate in Chicago and Lake Forest. The projected 1971–72 budget, after Hotchkiss's arrival,

included an increase in endowment income to $170,000. The restricted endowment, about half, was for the most part scholarship funds invested in securities. Virtually all of the unrestricted endowment income was in real estate, yielding under $50,000 per year. (Audited financial statement for 1970 [as of 31 May 1970], Business Office.) In this situation Hotchkiss immediately tore down the old Reid place across Sheridan from the Chapel/Reid Hall complex, no doubt in part because upkeep cost exceeded potential rental income, the circumstance that drove the sale of the Holt property later in the decade. See n. 130 below.

13  FM (2 Nov 1970).

14  FM (10 Feb 1970).

15  In 1969 Princeton, Vassar, Wesleyan, and Yale all became coeducational institutions. In 1970 Williams College followed suit, with Dartmouth holding out until 1972. ("Lake Forest Enrollment, 1957–75" Johnson/Cole/Hotchkiss Eras and Coeducation," comp. Arthur Miller [Spr 1999], "Enrollment Data [Aggregate]" folder, LFCA.)

16  FM (5 May 1970).

17  President Hotchkiss has provided examples of the loss of substantial promised gifts upon the appearance on campus of Angela Davis on one occasion and the Soviet ambassador on another.

18  FM (7 Nov 1972).

19  FM (7 Nov 1972).

20  FM (13 Mar, 4 Apr, 5 Dec 1972).

21  FM (6 Apr 1971 and 1 Feb 1972); *S* (4 Feb 1972).

22  FM (2 Mar 1971).

23  FM (2 Mar 1971).

24  FM (1 Feb 1972).

25  FM (3 Oct 1972).

26  *Sp* (Nov 1972).

27  FM (29 Feb 1972).

28  FM (1 Feb 1972).

29  FM (1 June 1971); *S* (29 Sep 1972).

30  The sudden development of the faculty in the late Johnson and Cole years was not matched, even with new library buildings in 1962 and 1965, with equivalent upgrades in the library holdings of retrospective and recent scholarly books and journals. Nor could the tighter 1970s budgets keep up with expanding information needed by a newly scholarly faculty. Resource sharing, via the statewide circulation system of the University of Illinois (*S* [12 Feb 1980]; *Sp* [Sum 1990], 4–5), was an alternative for meeting Lake Forest's strong faculty demand and faculty-inspired student demand. In 1976–77 a Council on Library Resources grant also had enabled Public Services librarian Joann Lee to establish Lake Forest as the first liberal arts college to offer students (and faculty) mediated online database searching across a range of disciplines (see *Online Searching: The*

*Basics, Settings, & Management*, ed. Joann H. Lee [Littleton, Colorado: Libraries Unlimited, 1984, rev. ed. 1988]).

31   FM (6 Feb 1973).

32   FM (6 Nov 1973). Appended to the Minutes is a seven-page proposal, "The Institute Plan for Lake Forest College" (1 Nov 1973).

33   *Sp* (Spr 1991 and Spr 1993).

34   Hawkins, 19.

35   *S* (24 Sep 1971).

36   FM (2 Apr 1974).

37   FM (11 May 1976); *Sp* (Jul 1977), 3.

38   FM (2 Mar 1971).

39   FM (1 Dec 1970); *S* (13 Nov 1970 and 26 Feb 1971).

40   *LFCN* (Jan 1972).

41   *Sp* (Jun 1972).

42   FM (7 Nov 1972 and 5 Dec 1978); *Sp* (Mar 1975).

43   FM (3 Oct 1972).

44   FM (1 Feb 1972).

45   FM (7 Nov 1972).

46   For periods of service, see catalogs of the time and current ones.

47   FM (1 Dec 1970); *LFCN* (Jan 1971).

48   The Women's Board was organized in 1971 (*Sp* [Apr–May 1981]).

49   James Donnelley, vice chairman of R. R. Donnelley & Sons Company, has served on the Board, except for a year off in 1984–85, since 1974. He is also the father of Niel Donnelley '84 and the uncle of Marshall Donnelley '92. He holds a B.A. from Dartmouth (1957), having started there when President Hotchkiss began his career at Dartmouth in student services. (*WWA* [1993], 1110.)

50   Wesley Dixon has been on the Board since 1966 and served as chair 1983–90. He and his wife, Suzanne, were profiled in *Spectrum* in 1989 when their challenge gift of $5 million (to raise an additional $10 million), the largest dollar-amount gift in the history of the College, launched the $40 million campaign, which was completed in 1992–93. Dixon attended Yale (1950) before joining the G. D. Searle organization, ultimately becoming president and vice chairman; after 1964 he was engaged in venture capital operations while serving many organizations in addition to the College, including Lake Forest Hospital and the Art Institute. (*WWA* [1990–91], 842; TM (12 May 1989), Appendix A-2, 3; *Sp* [Win 1989]).

51   Arthur G. Hailand Jr. has been a trustee since 1968 and was Board chair 1974–76. His son, Arthur G. Hailand III '74, also is a trustee, since 1990. (*Sp* [Sum 1990]).

52   Listed here by last name are the "newer appointees" and their dates of service: Beidler, 1986–88 and since 1990;

Chandler, since 1983; Fisher, since 1979 and chair, 1994–97; Gorter, since 1971 and chair 1990–94; Augustin S. Hart, 1964–77; Margaret Hart, since 1979; Meyer, 1974–96 and chair 1976–83; Shields, since 1985 and chair 1997–2000; Simmons, since 1973; Sonnenschein '44, 1970–82; and Vail, 1977–85 and since 1986. ("Lake Forest College Trustees" [1994], LFCA, and current files, Office of Alumni and Development.)

53   *Sp* (Nov 1976 and Jan–Feb 1982).

54   *Sp* (Win 1989).

55   Jewel Rogers Lafontant served on the Board 1969–73 and 1975–82. Her son, John W. Rogers Jr., also served as a trustee, 1987–97 (*LFCN* [Mar 1969], and "Lake Forest College Trustees," 4, and *LFCC* [1997]).

56   *Sp* (Spr 1993), 16.

57   "Spike" (Francis) Gummere (A. B. Trinity [Connecticut], M.Ed. St. Lawrence) came as director of admissions in 1968. (*Sp* [Nov 1973 and Sep–Oct 1974]).

58   Gordon White (B.A., M.A. University of Colorado), arriving in 1965, was associate director of admissions before assuming the roles of assistant to the president and director of financial aid in the Hotchkiss administration.

59   FM (12 Oct 1976).

60   FM (4 Sep 1985); *Sp* (Sep 85).

61   FM (7 May 1974); *Sp* (Jan–Feb 1975).

62   *Sp* (Sep–Oct 1974).

63   Hawkins, 22–23.

64   FM (10 May 1977); tracing through the catalogs from 1975 to 1979 is to note the expansion of listings under "Pre-Professional and Career Preparation."

65   Computer Science: FM (6 Nov 1979); Business: FM (4 Dec 1979).

66   *Sp* (May 1984 and Oct 1988).

67   *Sp* (Sep 1986, Oct 1987, 3, and Oct 1988).

68   *Sp* (Oct 1988), 8.

69   *Sp* (Apr–May 1985).

70   Interview with Eugene Hotchkiss, July 1999.

71   *Sp* (Nov 1983).

72   *Sp* (Jul 1987 and Oct 1988). For Dean of Faculty Bailey Donnally, see n. 131 below.

73   *Sp* (Oct 1988).

74   *Sp* (Oct 1988).

75   *LFCN* (Oct 1971)

76   Helene Lewis, "An Historical Perspective on LFC's Greek Letter Societies," *Sp* (Spr 1991), 3–9.

77   *Sp* (Nov–Dec 1977).

78   3 May 1978 (List of Taped Programs, LFCA).

79   *Sp* (Jan 1980).

80   *Sp* (Feb 1984).

81   *Sp* (Feb 1985).

82   Marcus's appearance was on November 18, 1985 (A. B. Dick Fund Events files, Office of Alumni and Development).

83   Steven L. Mintz '75.

84   The skill of Wayne Doleski (long-time campus activities coordinator and associate dean of students) in bringing "hot" acts to campus "year in and year out" was heralded in a 1983 *Stentor* article: excellent Chicago-area bands cited that fall were Big Twist and the Mellow Fellows, Billy Price and the Keystone Rhythm Band, and the Mistakes; for comedy and performance, Locomotion Vaudeville and the Second City Theater. (*S* [25 Oct 1983].)

85   *Sp* (Jul 1977).

86   Drinking age lowered (FM [14 Jan 75]); pub closed (FM [2 Oct 1978]); and then – from work begun in the Hotchkiss administration – pool hall transformed into the Coffeehouse, October 1, 1993 (*Sp* [Winter 1994]).

87   *Sp* (Nov 1974).

88   *Sp* (Mar 1975 and Nov–Dec 1978).

89   FM (12 Oct 1976 and 15 May 1981).

90   *Sp* (Apr–May 1981) and conversations between Coach Dau and Franz Schulze, summer 1999.

91   *Sp* (Jan–Feb 1974).

92   Peter E. Guernsey Jr. '70 (All-American right wing, Lake Forest), "From the Ohio River to the Rocky Mountains: College and Club Hockey" (copy of an article, Hockey [Athletics] file, LFCA.)

93   FM (28 May and 12 Oct 1976).

94   Volleyball (*Sp* [Nov 1976]); basketball developed very successfully, especially after Coach Slaats arrived on campus in 1986 (*Sp* [Sum 1992], 6).

95   *Sp* (Sum 1992), 6.

96   *Sp* (Nov 1974), 11.

97   Information from Office of Alumni and Development.

98   ACM programs listed in the catalog for 1975–76 included the Argonne Semester, Newberry Library Program in the Humanities, Urban Teaching, and Urban Studies.

99   FM (1 Feb 1977); *Sp* (Jul 1977).

100   Original proposal, Dec 1987; implemented 1988–89 (Dean of Faculty files).

101   Informal comment made at the time to Arthur Miller.

102   Following their work on the conceptual stage for the science building annex, the architectural firm of Matthei & Colin was hired to design the project (TM [12 Dec 1988]).

103   *Sp* (Jan and Sep 1980 and Feb 1981).

104   FM (1 Oct 1980 and 6 Oct 1982); *Sp* (Jan–Feb, Sep, and Nov 1982).

105   Named The Lily Reid Holt Memorial Chapel in 1900, the chapel, following a request of

the family (in a letter of November 1921 to Herbert Moore), was designated the Reid Memorial Chapel. In the 1970s, the family request long forgotten, it was once again called the Lily Reid Holt Chapel. (Chapel building file, LFCA.) (*Sp* [Nov 1976 and Nov–Dec 1977].)

106    *Sp* (Oct 1988).

107    FM (4 Oct 1977); *Sp* (Sep 1982).

108    S (30 Oct 1979).

109    *Sp* (Jan–Feb 1983), 1.

110    *Sp* (Oct 1988).

111    Richard Hunt file (Campus Art), LFCA.

112    *Sp* (Aug–Sep 1981).

113    She was director from 1957 to 1973; see also sidebar on student photographers of the era, p. 155 (*Sp* [Sep–Oct 1974].)

114    FM (1 May 1979 and 1 Apr 1981).

115    For periods of service, consult catalogs of the period and current listings.

116    Interest in faculty maternity leaves came up as early as 1975 (FM [4 Feb 1975]), but a specific Newborn Child Leave Policy was first adopted by the trustees on May 6, 1988, with amendments of September 1988, May 12, 1989, and September 1992 (Lake Forest College, *Faculty Handbook* [Sep 1999 revision], 29).

117    After three years of countable service, a leave of one semester at three-fourths of salary. (FM [6 Mar 1979]).

118    See sidebar "Publish and Prosper," p. 168.

119    Examples of faculty grants and fellowships, as reported in various *Spectrums*, include: T. H. Jeong (Physics), $15,000 from the Museum of Science and Industry (Jul 1977); Arthur Zilversmit and Carol Gayle (History), $11,600 from the Illinois Humanities Council (Jul 1977); Robert Glassman (Psychology), $60,000 from the National Science Foundation (NSF) (Oct 1977); Dan L. LaMaheiu (History), Rockefeller Humanities Fellow (May–Jun 1978); M.L. Thompson (Chemistry), $24,500 from NSF (Feb 1981); Franz Schulze (Art), from the Graham Foundation (Feb 1981); Rand Smith (Politics), Fulbright Lectureship to Grenoble, France (Apr–May 1981); Edward Packel (Mathematics), $40,641 from NSF (Apr–May 1981); Lowell Carmony and Robert Holliday (Mathematics and Computer Science), $300,000 from NSF (Apr–May 1985).

120    *Sp* (Sep 1984; Jul 1985, 15; Mar 1988, 2).

121    The Photographic Society of America's *Who's Who* listed Donnally as one of the "Top 50 Monochrome (black and white) Print Exhibitors in the World" for seven years; Donnally also won four Eastman-Kodak Kinsley awards, in three areas: black and white, color, and photojournalism (*Sp* [Apr 1983], 7).

122    *Sp* (Sep–Oct 1978).

123    The Dunn Award, first presented in the spring of 1974, was created by an anonymous donor to honor the late Dean Dunn's role and example in nurturing young faculty. (William L. Dunn Award file, Box 9.4, President Hotchkiss Papers, LFCA.)

124    Files, Dean of the Faculty Office.

125    *Policy on Promotion and Tenure, Revised Statement*, approved and appended to FM (14 Jan 1975), 4 and 6, and also *Lake Forest College Faculty Handbook* (Sep 1999), 10 and 42.

126    Evaluation (FM [14 May 1974 and 20 May 1975]) and third-year reviews (*Policy on Promotion and Tenure, Revised*, 3 and 5; TM [22 Oct 1977]).

127    Hawkins, 20–21.

128    Carlus, commenting on the occasion of his 1992 retirement, observed that he arrived in 1963 (after a visit to the College as a public accountant) as controller, becoming business manager in 1972 as the Hotchkiss administration brought a heightened level of "financial awareness" to this key post. (*Sp* [Sum 1992], 16.)

129    Speros was named associate dean of the faculty in 1979–80, a new position to work closely with students on academic matters. Former chair of Foreign Languages, he had arrived in 1963 with his Ph.D. from the University of Madrid and his M.A. from Middlebury College. (*Sp* [Jul–Aug 1979].)

130    As detailed in n. 12 above, at the end of the fiscal year prior to Hotchkiss's arrival, there was a total endowment of $2.9 million, which in 1970–71 would yield only $111,000 – being heavily weighted (about half) with problematic, poorly performing, or nonperforming real estate. The 1970–71 budget was $5.5 million, almost double the hypothetical market value of the real estate–laden endowment. The 1992–93 budget model in February 1993 projected operating expenditures of $17,079,384 and an endowment market value of $44,818,915. Endowment income, at a 5.9% draw, was budgeted at $2.5 million for 1992–93; even with an over $.8 million deficit projected, the "rainy-day" fund (Hotchkiss in the 1970s would refer in staff meetings to putting away surplus for a rainy day) provided a cushion for his successor proportionally far greater than the one he had inherited. (TM [12-13 Feb 1993], append. H [dated 19 Feb 1993]). Also, while expenses tripled on Hothckiss's watch, endowment income rose by more than 200 times – to once again play a role in meeting expenses, as it had prior to World War II.

131    Donnally, Physics Department chair, was appointed acting dean of the faculty in 1977 following the resignation of associate professor of German and three-year dean Friedhelm Radandt, who left the College for a vice presidency. Donnally had joined the Physics Department in 1961, as the Johnson Science Center was about to open. His B.S. and M.S. degrees were from Auburn University in his native Alabama and his Ph.D. from the University of Minnesota. In 1977 he was cited by the American Association of Physics Teachers for "demonstrating that productive research and liberal arts college teaching are compatible enterprises" (*Sp* [Jul 1977]). The next year he was appointed dean and, in 1981, also provost (*Sp* [Spr 1989]), returning to teaching in 1989.

132    *Sp* (Sum 1989).

133    In addition to David Spadafora's administrative role for the Biological and Physical Sciences in Yale's Graduate School beginning in 1985, he previously had served as dean of Yale's Calhoun College and as acting dean of Morse College at the University. When he was about to arrive on campus in 1990, Spadafora commented for *Spectrum* as follows: "'It's been a long time since a dean came to Lake Forest from outside, therefore I've got to learn more before I can make recommendations on how a good place can get better.'" He went on to comment on Lake Forest's "'first-class reputation'" for liberal arts education and on its many-years' record of attracting quality faculty. "'I think we need to keep building in both of these areas.'" On a note characteristic of the tone of the campus at that time, he concluded by saying that "'This College is poised to make a great leap forward. We're in a strong position to go to the next plateau.'" *Sp* (Sum 1990), 19.

134    An exhibit in Donnelley Library on "The Hotchkiss Years" was created by Professor Ebner's History class on Museums, Archives, and Libraries (*Lake Forester* [14 Jan 1993], 37). The Spring 1993 issue of *Spectrum*, focusing on the Hotchkiss years and including an assessment of the early phase by Arthur Zilversmit (6, 27), concludes with an interview in which President Hotchkiss reflected on how his role changed over two decades and on what he saw for the future of Lake Forest (28–30).

135    TM (7 May 1993), 5.

136    This proposal, conceived and formally carried out by a joint faculty-staff committee, was realized at the dedication ceremony on Friday, May 7, 1993 – part of the Commencement weekend activities. (*Sp* [Sum 1993]).


### CHAPTER 10

*Once again personal recollections and conversations of the authors continue to provide material for the narrative, sometimes available only from their accounts. These are not necessarily referenced in the text or identified in notes.*

1    *Sp* (Win, Spr 1994).

2    Spadafora's book was reviewed in *Choice*, the American Library Association's standard review medium for college libraries, in February 1991 (986), and then in May of 1992 it was selected (1356) for *Choice*'s list of "Outstanding Academic Books" (from 6,500 reviewed in 1991, one of the 578 best in all fields in English and one of the 315 best university press books). See also *Spectrum* (Sum 1993, Spr 1994) and *Book Review Digest* (1991), 1750, which includes extensive quotations from four U.S. and British reviews, including the following from Roy Porter in the *New*

*Statesman* (27 Jul 1990), 39: "'Not the least virtue of David Spadafora's richly documented study is that it revises [the] pedigree of progress by stressing the seminal importance of the intellectual ferments of 18th century Britain. Spadafora meticulously unravels the practical experiences of Britons under the Georges, and their swelling sense of a manifest national destiny....'"

3   Troyer, Ph.D. Indiana University, had served on the faculty in the Mathematics Department from 1968 to 1992; for 1993–94 he was recalled to active duty as acting dean of the faculty. (*Sp* [Sum 1993].)

4   Dean Galovich became the first Lake Forest dean of the faculty (and provost) to bring to the College administrative experience at a closely comparable small liberal arts college. Galovich (Ph.D. Brown) is the author of two books, including *Doing Mathematics*, published in 1993. (*Sp* [Spr 1994].)

5   Fischer, a Phi Beta Kappa graduate in Chemistry, had earned her doctorate in Chemistry from Northwestern. Prior to joining the Lake Forest Chemistry faculty in 1992, she had been academic dean at Barat College. (*Sp* [Win 1995].)

6   Chapman, an American Studies major, had joined the Facilities Management (then Physical Plant) office staff in the early 1970s. After moving to the business office under Theodore Carlus, she completed her M.B.A. at the Lake Forest Graduate School of Management (formerly the Industrial Management Institute, but renamed after its organizational separation from the College in the mid 1960s). Her experience of growth as an employee utilizing staff tuition benefits exemplifies a pattern followed by others as well. Chapman is the mother of C. Robin Thomas '91. (*Sp* [Fall 1994].)

7   Van Sickle, "third-generation Forester" (see photos of his grandfather in ch. 5), after Lake Forest joined the development staff at Wesleyan. He received his Ed.M. from Harvard and served there in the development office, going on, in 1989, to Princeton as director of principal gifts. In 1994 he returned to his alma mater as secretary of the College and executive assistant to the president and in 1995 became vice president for alumni and development (*Sp* [Spr 1994 and Sum 1995]). In 1996 he was awarded an Ed.D. from the University of Pennsylvania.

8   *S* (21 Sep 1994).

9   *S* (26 Jan 1994 and 11 Sep 1996).

10   Spadafora's work was mostly behind the scenes, but the summer of 1991 saw the appointment of a head of a new information technology unit, with progress on the new infrastructure for phone and data lines and systems by the fall of 1992. The new president's interest in this area was evidenced by his attention to it in his inaugural address on October 1, 1993. (*S* [25 Sep 1991 and 5 Feb 1992]; FM [2 Sep 1992]; *Sp* [Win 1994].)

11   *RP* (1998–99).

12   *RP* (1998–99).

13   *S* (18 Nov 1992); *LFCC* (Feb 1993).

14   *S* (23 Apr 1998); programs for Symposia, 1998 and 1999, LFCA.

15   *LFCC* (Feb 1997); *Sp* (Sum 1997).

16   *Sp* (Win 1994).

17   *RP* (1998–99).

18   *RP* (1998–99).

19   Cubit, formerly associate librarian at Williams College (M.L.S. University of Iowa), joined the administration in early 1996 and within weeks was appointed to a newly created role of director of a combined library and information technology office, following a trend among national liberal arts colleges (as found in the Oberlin Group of college libraries, of which Lake Forest had been a founding member in the 1980s). Like Galovich, Cubit came to the College from a benchmark similar institution. (*S* [11 Sep 1996]; *Sp* [Win 1996].)

20   "Executive Summary of Toward a New Community" (1999), LFCA.

21   *Sp* (Win 1997).

22   *TNC*, 1.

23   The Board leadership of Clarence Diver '05 ended in 1945; see chs. 6 and 7.

24   *TNC*, 1.

25   The other three of a permanent quartet of Chemistry faculty with Coutts (1955–86; B.Sc., M.Sc. University of Manitoba, Ph.D. Purdue) were (by order of seniority): (1) since 1961, William Martin (B.S. Franklin & Marshall, Ph.D. Northwestern; prior to Lake Forest with Abbott Laboratories); (2) 1962–97, M. L. Thompson (B.A. Concordia College, Ph.D. Indiana); and (3) since 1965, Laura Kately (Klingbeil) (B.S. University of Detroit, M.S. Michigan State).

26   HFCD.

27   For advanced degree material, HFCD, and also current records, Chemistry Department; up to 1990 Registrar's Office listings of alumni advanced degrees are available.

28   *The Coterie: The First One Hundred Years, 1890–1990* (Lake Forest, [1991]), 86 pp., and minutes, yearbooks, and papers of the Coterie, on deposit, LFCA.

29   *Market Square 2000. Overview of Market Square 2000 Project* (one leaf), distrib. 27 Jan 1998, City Hall (Market Square File, Lake Forest Architecture vertical file, LFCA).

30   Lake Forest Place opened in 1998 and was developed adjacent to the grounds of Lake Forest hospital under the sponsorship of Evanston's Presbyterian Homes, with a variety of living options – bungalows, apartments, and assisted care facilities.

31   *Coterie*, 85. This has become a rallying point in political opposition to the long-established Caucus system of identifying candidates for village posts.

32   *TNC*, 1–3.

33   For the contrast with the early days of Chicago's theater rebirth, see the master's thesis of Bobbie R. Glick, M/LS '98, "Spirited Stages: Focus on Four Off-Loop Theatres, 1970–1980," LFCA.

34   Talhami has appeared often on "Chicago Tonight" on WTTW, Chicago's public television station. Sadri has been interviewed live on numerous occasions by WBEZ, Chicago's public radio station.

35   Paul Galloway, "All-Professor Team II," *CT* (28 Jan 1994), Sect. 5, 1–2; "Smarter near the lake," with the seven Lake Forest faculty pictured individually, is on 2. For the earlier story on faculty at larger area universities, see *CT* (5 Feb 1993), Sect. 5, 1.

36   DePaul University is establishing a site for advanced technical education at Conway Park in west Lake Forest. St. Xavier University has offered nursing education courses at Lake Forest Hospital. National-Louis University also has offered remote-site learning for education in Lake Forest, in connection with Lake Forest District 67 (K–8).

37   The University of Chicago's Graham School began offering noncredit courses on the Lake Forest campus in the late 1990s.

The authors' role in this, the first substantial record of Lake Forest College and its relationship with its surrounding community, was greatly dependent on knowledge imparted and assistance provided by a wide variety of appropriately well-informed people. The concept originated with the College's president, David Spadafora, who appointed a committee drawn from the faculty and staff to launch the endeavor: Michael E. Dau '58, Handball Coach and Assistant Football Coach, unsurpassed in his knowledge of the College's athletic history; Michael Ebner, A. B. Dick Professor of History, widely respected for his scholarly work on Chicago and that city's North Shore; Arthur Miller, College Archivist and Librarian of Special Collections, who has written authoritatively on the townscape of Lake Forest; Frederick M. Van Sickle '83, Vice President for Alumni and Development, whose own research in the College's history is sufficient to confirm his importance to the project; and two faculty emeriti with records of long experience at the College, Rosemary Cowler, Hotchkiss Presidential Professor of English, Emerita, who served as the committee chair, and Franz Schulze, Hollender Professor of Art, Emeritus.

In the early stages the committee relied on oral history interviews with people whose memories were as instructive as they were comprehensive. These included such retired faculty and staff as William Graham Cole, former president of the College; Rosemary Hale and Miller Upton (one-time instructor and later president of Beloit College) from the Department of Economics; the late Richard Hantke of the Department of History; Ralph Shively of the Department of Mathematics; Arthur Voss of the Department of English and his wife, Isabel Voss; Robert Amaden, former Senior Advisor in the Department of Development; and Theodore Carlus, former Vice President for Business. Trustees were

likewise notable for their personal recollections: Clarissa Chandler, Francis Farwell, Arthur Hailand, Margaret Hart (granddaughter of President James McClure), Frank Spreyer '35, and the late Harris Wilder, while a number of alumni offered comparably valuable individual perspectives: Marion Phipps Dobbins '37, Hollis Thorpe Edwards '45, Thomas Hawkins '40, Dorothy Maiman '34, Elmer Maiman '39, and Harry Meadows '44. Carolyn and Thomas Goetz, formerly of Lake Bluff, now of Inverness, California, friends of the College, were also consulted. The interviews were conducted by the late John Coutts, Volwiler Professor of Chemistry, Emeritus; Coach Dau; Eugene Hotchkiss, President, Emeritus; Robert Troyer, Professor of Mathematics, Emeritus; and the three authors.

The estimable service of all the above mentioned was joined by that of a number of people who amplified the research necessary to the final product: William Becker, Research Officer in the Office of Development; Ruthane Bopp '60, Registrar; Ann Bowen, Professor of Music, Emerita; Joseph Burman, Director of Alumni and Development Research; Valerie Carlson, Glen Rowan Conference Director; Presidents Cole and Hotchkiss; Bailey Donnally, Professor of Physics, Emeritus and former Dean of the Faculty; Bernice Gallagher, Director of Writing Programs; Marcia Gibbs, Executive Secretary to the Vice President for Alumni and Development; Benjamin Goluboff of the Department of English; Professor David Krantz of the Department of Psychology; Jacqueline Slaats, Director of Athletics; Ruth Christensen Sproat '52, former Registrar; M. L. Thompson, Professor of Chemistry, Emeritus; and Carol Dunn Brown, daughter of the late Dean of the Faculty William Dunn. Alumni Barbara Ickes Hewey '55, Frederick Krehbiel '63, Ralph Mills '54, and Roger and Margaret Wilhelm '58, warrant mention, as do

# Acknowledgments

members of the College Library's staff – especially James Cubit, Director of Library and Information Technology, as well as Susan Cloud, Sarah Drehobl, Rita Koller '95, David Levinson, Karen Ludlow, and Ruth Sharvy. The College Archives' student assistants also served: Eric Anderson '02, Rachel Corey '00, Brian Galbreath '00, Natsuko Hamai '98, Jan Kordylewski '02, Tim Lunn '03, Kate Murphy '01, Jessica Ibarra '01, Joanna Ortynska '01, Scott Richardson '00, Jennifer Woodruff '00, and Paul Wierzbicki '99. And Joyce Fox, Secretary for English and Foreign Languages, offered helpful technical assistance.

More than a few citizens of the community deserve acknowledgment for their voluntary efforts. Doris Cole Yankee and Shirley Paddock were especially noteworthy in this regard, and they were joined by members of the Lake Forest Garden Club, whose archival efforts merit recognition. In addition, worthy information was forthcoming from Kent Chandler, Nora Chandler, and Lucia Heyworth.

Included among library and archive personnel at a number of other academic institutions, all of them generous in providing essential data and illustrative material, are Daria D'Arienzo of Amherst College, Sylvia Kennick Brown of Williams College, Leslie Czechowski of Grinnell College, Doug Erickson of Lewis and Clark College, Debra Levine and Daniel Meyer of the University of Chicago, John Straw of the University of Illinois at Champaign-Urbana, and Elaine Snyder of the College of Wooster. Similar archival facts were provided by Millicent Kreischer, Jeannette Mattoon, and Donald Spooner of the First Presbyterian Church of Lake Forest; Carol Doty, Scott Mehaffey, and Michael Stieber of the Morton Arboretum of Lisle, Illinois; and Kathleen Reilly of the Berkshire Atheneum of Pittsfield, Massachusetts.

Other figures independent of the College, researchers, dealers, collectors, and historians, provided significant assistance. Included among them are Carmen Adduci, who donated to the College archives heretofore unknown papers of Cyrus McCormick Jr.; Paul Bergmann, authority on the work of Lake Forest architect Stanley Anderson '16; Malcolm Cairns, Professor of Landscape Architecture at Ball State University; William Greene of the Panhandle-Plains Historical Museum of Canyon, Texas; William Grundman, Professor of Landscape Architecture at Iowa State University; Thomas Joyce, who found the editor's own run of the periodical *America*; Paul Myers of the Howard Van Doren Shaw Society; Tony Tanner of the book dealers Hamill & Barker; and Harold Wolff, historic property researcher who identified the architects of many early Lake Forest buildings.

With the completion of the first draft of the history, independent and in-house readers were called upon to examine and assess the text. This stage was crucial to the finished publication, since none of the authors holds degrees awarded specifically in the discipline of history. Thus they are deeply indebted, for expert commentary and advice, to Frederick Rudolph, Professor of History, Emeritus, of Williams College, a renowned authority on the higher learning in America; historian Francis Oakley, President, Emeritus, of Williams College, and a Trustee at Lake Forest; Steven Galovich, Lake Forest College's Provost and Dean of the Faculty; Professor Ebner; Mr. Van Sickle; the three living presidents of the College, William Graham Cole, Eugene Hotchkiss, and David Spadafora; and the College's own authority on education, Arthur Zilversmit, Professor of History, Emeritus.

The history could not have materialized without the commitment and expertise of the producer, Kim Coventry of Chicago, and several members of the College staff who assisted her, principally Michelle Holleman, Associate Director of Marketing and Communications, and Emily Holmes '99 and Elizabeth Thomson '96 of the same office.

On a personal note, Arthur Miller expresses his gratitude to his spouse, Janet Miller (also the College's Writing Programs Assistant and Special Programs Associate), for her encouragement, able assistance and support throughout this whole adventure.

It is essential to point out that all the efforts leading to the materialization of this book would have been in vain had it not been for the goodwill of the R.R. Donnelley & Sons Company. In this regard special thanks are due primarily to College trustee James R. Donnelley. Lastly, generous financial support of the writing, provided by the Northern Trust Bank and The Oakleigh L. Thorne Fund, is also most gratefully acknowledged.

# Index

**COLOPHON**

*30 Miles North* was typeset
in Filosofia and Monotype
Grotesque. It was printed
computer-to-plate on
Mead Signature Dull 100 lb.
text and notch-bound by
R.R. Donnelley & Sons, using
color separations made by
Professional Graphics,
Rockford, Illinois.